BETWEEN JUSTICE AND STABILITY

Southeast European Studies

Series Editor: Florian Bieber, Centre for Southeast European Studies, University of Graz, Austria

The Balkans are a region of Europe widely associated over the past decades with violence and war. Beyond this violence, the region has experienced rapid change in recent times, including democratization and economic and social transformation. New scholarship is emerging which seeks to move away from the focus on violence alone to an understanding of the region in a broader context drawing on new empirical research.

The Southeast European Studies Series seeks to provide a forum for this new scholarship. Publishing cutting-edge, original research and contributing to a more profound understanding of Southeastern Europe while focusing on contemporary perspectives the series aims to explain the past and seeks to examine how it shapes the present. Focusing on original empirical research and innovative theoretical perspectives on the region, the series includes original monographs and edited collections. It is interdisciplinary in scope, publishing high-level research in political science, history, anthropology, sociology, law and economics and accessible to readers interested in Southeast Europe and beyond.

Forthcoming titles in the series

Debating the End of Yugoslavia
Edited by Florian Bieber, Armina Galijaš and Rory Archer

After Ethnic Conflict
Policy-making in Post-conflict Bosnia and Herzegovina and Macedonia
Cvete Koneska

Cultures of Democracy in Serbia and Bulgaria
How Ideas Shape Publics
James Dawson

A Discourse Analysis of Corruption
Instituting Neoliberalism Against Corruption in Albania, 1998–2005
Blendi Kajsiu

State-Building and Democratization in Bosnia and Herzegovina
Edited by Soeren Keil and Valery Perry

Between Justice and Stability

The Politics of War Crimes Prosecutions in Post-Milošević Serbia

MLADEN OSTOJIĆ

ASHGATE

Published by

Ashgate Publishing Limited
Wey Court East
Union Road
Farnham
Surrey, GU9 7PT
England

Ashgate Publishing Company
110 Cherry Street
Suite 3-1
Burlington, VT 05401-3818
USA

www.ashgate.com

British Library Cataloguing in Publication Data
A catalogue record for this book is available from the British Library

The Library of Congress Data has been applied for.
Ostojić, Mladen.
Between justice and stability : the politics of war crimes prosecutions in post-Miloševic Serbia / by Mladen Ostojić.
pages cm. -- (Southeast European studies)
Includes bibliographical references and index.
ISBN 978-1-4094-6742-7 (hbk) -- ISBN 978-1-4094-6743-4 (ebook) -- ISBN 978-1-4094-6744-1 (epub) 1. War crime trials--Serbia. 2. War crimes--Political aspects--Serbia. 3. Criminal justice, Administration of--Serbia. 4. International criminal courts. 5. Miloševic, Slobodan, 1941-2006. I. Title.
KKS1003.9.O88 2014
341.6'90268--dc23

2014003368

ISBN 9781409467427 (hbk)
ISBN 9781409467434 (ebk – PDF)
ISBN 9781409467441 (ebk – ePUB)

MIX
Paper from responsible sources
FSC® C013985

Printed in the United Kingdom by Henry Ling Limited,
at the Dorset Press, Dorchester, DT1 1HD

To my grandparents

Contents

List of Tables

Preface

The wars that tore apart the former Yugoslavia in the nineties left a permanent scar in the lives of all those who lived in or identified themselves with that country. The brutality of those conflicts generated a deep rift among the people, communities and nations that once made up Yugoslavia. This was no conventional warfare fought by well-organised armies targeting each other. To a great extent, these were wars of annihilation in which the warring parties sought to permanently remove entire ethnic communities from territories over which they claimed ownership. On many occasions, the belligerents deliberately and systematically targeted civilians, on whom they inflicted terrible suffering. The war reporters and photojournalists who covered the conflict witnessed levels of hatred and cruelty unseen elsewhere. The practices of the warring parties were vicious, wicked, inhuman. To many, these wars amounted to a massive crime.

Sadly, this was not the first time that such wars had been waged in Yugoslavia's short history. Without falling into the trap of the 'ancient hatred' thesis, one ought to acknowledge the causal links between the genocidal conflicts that followed the fall of Yugoslavia in 1941 and in 1991. For many observers, the failure to address the crimes perpetrated during World War II amply contributed to the resurgence of ethnic antagonism and war 50 years later. The role of grievances and memories of World-War-II-era atrocities in nurturing discourses of victimisation and nationalist mobilisation has been well documented by social anthropologists working on the former Yugoslavia in the late 1980s and early 1990s. In view of this, seeking accountability for war crimes perpetrated during the wars of Yugoslav succession seemed to be a necessary step in order to avoid the repetition of the same scenario in the future.

It is against this backdrop that the International Criminal Tribunal for the former Yugoslavia (ICTY) was created to establish justice. The expectations associated with the ICTY ran high: it was thought that war crimes trials would contribute to durable peace by bringing perpetrators to justice and establishing a measure of truth about the Yugoslav conflicts. In principle, these lofty objectives seemed honourable and desirable for bringing about peace and reconciliation in the former Yugoslavia. In practice, the Tribunal's work has produced a complex set of processes whose outcomes are uncertain. Twenty years after the creation of the ICTY, the extent to which the Tribunal has genuinely pursued and achieved the above-stated objectives is a subject of much debate. This book seeks to contribute to this debate by exploring how the Serbian authorities handled the issue of the war crimes legacy in the post-Milošević era. I hope that this piece of research will allow for a better assessment of the ICTY's impact and a deeper understanding of public attitudes towards war crimes in Serbia.

I dedicate this book to my grandparents, to whom I owe my bonds to the former Yugoslavia. I am particularly indebted to my grandfather, Mladen Draškić, who keenly nurtured my interest in Yugoslav history and politics. His personal accounts and memories gave me an insight into 20th-century Yugoslav history that no history book could convey. My grandparents' generation was marked by World War II, when they endured several waves of bombings, state collapse, occupation and persecution. As if this were not enough, they had to go through all of this once again towards the end of their lives. To my own generation, the nineties will remain a trauma which, one hopes, will not be repeated.

This book has been in the making for over seven years. My interest in transitional justice in the former Yugoslavia developed through an MA course in historical anthropology of South-East Europe delivered by Ger Duijzings at the UCL School of Slavonic and East European Studies. I subsequently enrolled on a PhD programme at Queen Mary University of London, under the insightful supervision of Adam Fagan and with generous financial support from the AHRC and the School of Politics and International Relations. The last stage in this process, the conversion of my thesis into a book, was achieved during my stay at the CEU Institute for Advanced Study where I benefited from a fellowship funded by the Volkswagen Foundation.

During these many years, I benefited from the support, insights and feedback of many friends and colleagues. I am particularly indebted to Maja Draškić and Ilija Vojnović, who helped me arrange many interviews with high-profile political figures in Belgrade. I am thankful to all the politicians, NGO activists, lawyers, academics and journalists who consented to requests for interviews. The employees of the Politika media archives also deserve a mention here for helping me gain access to the right information in spite of their services being downsized. Among my academic colleagues, I would especially like to thank Jasna Dragović Soso who encouraged me to pursue a PhD on this topic and helped me formulate my ideas at critical junctures. Eric Gordy, Dejan Jović, Bojan Bilić and Branislav Radeljić also provided valuable feedback at various stages. Naturally, all omissions are mine.

Finally, I would like to thank Romy Danflous for having accompanied me during most of this journey. Her affection and support helped me overcome the emotional strain and solitude that this project entailed. I owe a particular debt to her mother, Katherine Danflous, who has invested so much time and effort in helping me with my English. Above all, I am grateful to my parents, Ranko and Jelica, for their continuous support throughout my studies and allowing me to realise my ambitions.

Mladen Ostojić
Bucharest, July 2014

List of Abbreviations

DOS	Democratic Opposition of Serbia
DPS	Democratic Party of Socialists
DS	Democratic Party
DSS	Democratic Party of Serbia
EULEX	European Union Rule of Law Mission in Kosovo
FRY	Federal Republic of Yugoslavia
GSS	Civic Alliance of Serbia
HLC	Humanitarian Law Centre
HRW	Human Rights Watch
ICC	International Criminal Court
ICJ	International Court of Justice
ICTR	International Criminal Tribunal for Rwanda
ICTY	International Criminal Tribunal for the former Yugoslavia
IMT	International Military Tribunal
JNA	Yugoslav People's Army
JSO	Special Operations Unit
JUL	Yugoslav United Left
KLA	Kosovo Liberation Army
LDP	Liberal Democratic Party
NATO	North Atlantic Treaty Organisation
NGO	Non-Governmental Organisation
NS	New Serbia
OSCE	Organisation for Security and Co-operation in Europe
OSF	Open Society Foundation
OTP	Office of the Prosecutor of the ICTY
OWCP	Office of the War Crimes Prosecutor of the Republic of Serbia
SAA	Stabilisation and Accession Agreement
SDC	Supreme Defence Council
SIA	Security Intelligence Agency
SNP	Socialist People's Party
SNS	Serbian Progressive Party
SPO	Serbian Renewal Movement
SPS	Socialist Party of Serbia
SPU	Special Police Units
SRS	Serbian Radical Party
TRC	Truth and Reconciliation Commission (South Africa)
UNMIK	United Nations Interim Administration Mission in Kosovo

WCC	War Crimes Chamber within the Belgrade District Court
WCIS	War Crimes Investigation Service within the Serbian Ministry of Interior
ZES	For a European Serbia

Chapter 1
Introduction: International Justice and Transitional Democracy

On 20 July 2011, the Serbian authorities arrested Goran Hadžić, the last remaining fugitive sought by the International Criminal Tribunal for the Former Yugoslavia (ICTY). Hadžić was indicted for war crimes and crimes against humanity allegedly committed during his tenure as President of the self-proclaimed Republic of Serbian Krajina between 1991 and 1993. He went into hiding in July 2004, hours after his sealed indictment was handed over by the ICTY to the Serbian authorities. This episode caused considerable embarrassment for the Serbian government at the time, as it reinforced the widespread belief among foreign diplomats and observers that Serbia was unwilling and unable to bring war crimes suspects to justice. The fact that it took seven years to find and capture Hadžić illustrates the extent to which ICTY cooperation was a sensitive and difficult issue for the Serbian authorities.

Less than two months earlier, the former Bosnian Serb general, Ratko Mladić, was arrested in a small village in northern Serbia after having escaped justice for 16 years. Mladić was one of the highest-profile individuals sought by the ICTY, which indicted him in 1995 for genocide, war crimes and crimes against humanity, committed during the Bosnian war. The former general is said to have enjoyed the protection of the Serbian authorities and freedom of movement at least until October 2002.[1] Foreign pressures for Mladić's arrest subsequently increased, and in early 2006 his extradition to The Hague became a precondition for Serbia's rapprochement with the European Union (EU).[2] Mladić's capture five years later was thus praised as a success of the EU's policy of conditionality and a sign of progress on Serbia's path to democracy.[3]

After the downfall of Milošević in October 2000, cooperation with the ICTY was set as a symbolic measure of Serbian society's willingness to come to terms with the war crimes legacy and its adherence to the principles of liberal democracy. Just as for Bosnia-Herzegovina and Croatia, Serbia's access to international financial assistance and European integration was conditioned upon cooperation

1 'Tadić: Srbija unapredila ugled' (Serbia Improves Its Image), *B92*, 3 June 2011.

2 In Serbia, the ICTY is colloquially referred to as 'the Hague tribunal' or 'The Hague'. I use these terms interchangeably throughout the book.

3 'Ešton: Kraj krvoprolića na Balkanu' (Ashton: End of Bloodshed in the Balkans), *B92*, 3 June 2011.

with the ICTY.[4] International pressure on these states to cooperate with the ICTY allowed the Tribunal to bring war crimes suspects to justice and thus partly fulfil its mission. But despite all the economic and political incentives and sanctions deployed by Western governments, Serbia's compliance with the ICTY was sporadic, protracted and, for over a decade following the overthrow of Milošević, incomplete. In the 2000s, the lack of cooperation with the ICTY was arguably the biggest obstacle to Serbia's process of European integration.[5]

What's more, in spite of its success in bringing perpetrators to justice, the ICTY largely failed to raise awareness about war crimes and advance the need for accountability in Serbian society. Public opinion polls carried out throughout the 2000s show that only 15 per cent of the Serbian population supported the handover of indicted war criminals to the ICTY for the sake of justice.[6] The majority of respondents supported ICTY cooperation only to the extent necessary to avoid international sanctions or advance Serbia's integration in the EU. This is not surprising bearing in mind that most people in Serbia were convinced that the Tribunal was biased against Serbs. In 2009, almost half of the respondents (49 per cent) believed that the proceedings against the former Serbian leadership for war crimes and crimes against humanity perpetrated in Kosovo had not established the truth because they were based on false evidence.[7] Furthermore, the majority of the population believed that the former Bosnian Serb leaders Radovan Karadžić (55 per cent) and Ratko Mladić (56 per cent) were not responsible for the crimes they were charged with. A survey carried out in 2011 showed that only 34 per cent of the population supported the handing-over of Ratko Mladić to the ICTY.[8]

This state of affairs may seem paradoxical and confusing at first sight. Why would a country shelter war crimes suspects at the cost of international isolation and economic deprivation? If the handover of a few dozen indictees to the ICTY was the price for Serbia's full reintegration into the international community, why did it take the Serbian democratic authorities over a decade to complete this task?

---

4 For an analysis of the impact of ICTY conditionality on politics in Croatia, see Dejan Jović, 'Croatia after Tudjman: The ICTY and Issues of Transitional Justice', *Chaillot Paper* 116, (2009): 13–28; for an assessment of the Tribunal's contribution to democratisation in Bosnia, see Lara J. Nettelfield, *Courting Democracy in Bosnia and Herzegovina* (New York: Cambridge University Press, 2010).

5 I use 'ICTY cooperation' to refer to broader adherence to the norms and principles on which the ICTY was founded, in addition to the handover of indictees and documentation to the Tribunal, which constitute 'ICTY compliance'.

6 Public opinion polls were regularly carried out by the Belgrade Centre for Human Rights in cooperation with Strategic Marketing and the OSCE Mission to Serbia. See www.bgcentar.org.rs.

7 Belgrade Centre for Human Rights, OSCE Mission to Serbia, and Strategic Marketing Research, 'Views on War Crimes, the ICTY, and the National War Crimes Judiciary', April 2009. Retrieved from www.bgcentar.org.rs on 7 March 2010.

8 'Serbia Loses Faith in European Future', *Guardian*, 22 July 2011.

If the ICTY prosecuted war crimes committed in the wars of Yugoslav succession, and established facts about them, why were these facts largely ignored or denied in post-Milošević Serbia? These are the questions I address in this book by exploring the attitudes of the Serbian authorities towards the ICTY in the decade following the overthrow of Milošević in October 2000.[9] Whereas the Milošević regime had obvious reasons to oppose a Tribunal that targeted its most prominent representatives, it is less clear why the Serbian democratic authorities struggled to cooperate with the ICTY. After all, most of Serbia's democratic leaders had vehemently opposed Milošević in the nineties and were in principle supportive of the Tribunal's aim of prosecuting war crimes. Furthermore, all the Serbian governments in the period 2000–2011 were genuinely committed to European integration, which was conditioned upon cooperation with the ICTY.

By exploring official thinking and policy-making on transitional justice among Serbian political elites, this book aims to elucidate the politics of war crimes prosecutions and ICTY cooperation in post-Milošević Serbia.[10] It thereby seeks to contribute both to an understanding of Serbia's contemporary history and to the broader literature on international criminal tribunals and transitional justice. Serbia constitutes an ideal case study for exploring the relationship between externalised justice and democratisation in target countries, an issue that remains under-scrutinised in existing publications. While there is a considerable body of research on the role of international tribunals in promoting peace and reconciliation, relatively few attempts have been made at assessing the implications of international war crimes trials on transitions to democracy. This book seeks to partly fill this gap by offering an in-depth account of the ICTY's repercussions on political dynamics in post-Milošević Serbia.

The ICTY and the Rise of Transitional Justice

More than any other institution, the ICTY embodied the international community's commitment to tackling violations of international humanitarian law in the last decade of the twentieth century. The creation and functioning of this ad hoc tribunal required the international community to mobilise substantial financial and diplomatic efforts. The ICTY was established by UN Security Council Resolutions 808 and 827, adopted on 22 February and 25 May 1993 respectively. This decision was the culmination of a series of incremental measures taken by the Security Council in response to the bloody break-up of the Socialist Federal Republic of

9 For practical reasons, I use 'Serbian authorities' here to refer to both the governments of the Republic of Serbia and those of the Federal Republic of Yugoslavia (FRY) and the State Union of Serbia and Montenegro. Where relevant, a distinction is made between these various levels of government in the remainder of the book.

10 Throughout the book, I use the notion of 'political elites' to refer to a group of individuals who are, or were, in a position to shape or substantially influence policy-making.

Yugoslavia.[11] Prior to establishing the ICTY, the UN had set up a commission of experts to investigate violations of international humanitarian law in the former Yugoslavia, which compiled substantial evidence of breaches of international law and recommended the establishment of an ad hoc international criminal tribunal.

From a legal standpoint, the establishment of the ICTY heralded the reawakening of international criminal law. The ICTY was the first international tribunal since the International Military Tribunals (IMT) established in Nuremberg and Tokyo in the aftermath of World War II.[12] Although the IMTs laid the foundation of international criminal justice, the subsequent development of institutions for the enforcement of international law was paralysed by the Cold War. The competition among Great Powers and the establishment of the principle of state sovereignty as the cornerstone of the international order allowed perpetrators of mass atrocities to go unpunished. Nevertheless, the 'Nuremberg ethos', which posited that political and military leaders should be held internationally accountable for violations of international law, remained high on the agenda of human rights activists.[13] This legal and ethical tradition provided grounds for the resurgence of international criminal justice in the 1990s, as the end of the Cold War and the concomitant erosion of the principle of state sovereignty removed a structural obstacle to the development of international mechanisms for the enforcement of international humanitarian law.

In political terms, the creation of the ICTY represented a major novelty in the international community's approach to tackling armed conflict. The Tribunal was created under Chapter VII of the UN charter as a mandatory mechanism for the restoration and maintenance of international peace and security. The UN Security Council thus established a direct link between the administration of criminal justice and peacebuilding.[14] At the conceptual level, the link between justice and peace was articulated by human rights activists and international lawyers who provided a strong moral and political impetus for the creation of the ICTY. Theodor Meron, who later became the President of the ICTY, thus advanced the idea that, besides being a moral imperative, prosecutions would deter future offenders and 'educate the general public not to accept egregious violations of human rights and

11 These measures included the imposition of an arms embargo on Yugoslavia, the sending of peacekeeping forces to Croatia and Bosnia, the imposition of sanctions on Serbia and Montenegro, the imposition of a no-fly zone and the creation of 'safe areas' in six Bosnian towns [Rachel Kerr, *The International Criminal Tribunal for the Former Yugoslavia* (Oxford: Oxford University Press, 2004), 32–4].

12 Note that the ICTY was the first international tribunal established in the name of the international community, whereas Nuremberg and Tokyo were military tribunals established by the victorious powers in World War II.

13 Richard Falk, 'Accountability for War Crimes and the Legacy of Nuremberg', in *War Crimes and Collective Wrongdoing: A Reader*, edited by Aleksandar Jokić (Oxford: Blackwell Pub., 2001), 113–17.

14 Rachel Kerr, 'International Judicial Intervention: The International Criminal Tribunal for the Former Yugoslavia', *International Relations* 15:2 (2000): 20–21.

humanitarian norms'.[15] He further suggested that, in the long run, war crimes trials would open the way for reconciliation by establishing individual responsibility and thus removing blame from entire ethnic groups.

This belief in the capacity of international justice to promote peace and reconciliation in the former Yugoslavia was premised upon a specific understanding of the Yugoslav wars, attributing responsibility for the conflict and war crimes to local political elites rather than historical legacies and structural factors. This interpretation constituted a radical break from the 'ancient hatred' thesis which informed early Western approaches to the conflict.[16] The proponents of the ICTY strongly believed that the Yugoslav wars were engineered by nationalist politicians who manipulated their constituents in order to cling on to power. As a result, the architects of the Tribunal considered that the ICTY ought to remove threatening leaders from local politics and individualise responsibility for war crimes in order to defuse ethnic tensions on the ground. Furthermore, the ICTY was deemed to promote reconciliation by establishing the truth and building an authoritative account that would form the basis of a shared history of the Yugoslav wars. Payam Akhavan, the former advisor to the Prosecutor's Office of the ICTY, thus argued that the ICTY should seek to construct an overall picture of the conflict that would provide optimal cathartic and reconciliatory potential 'by telling the truth about the underlying causes and consequences of the Yugoslav tragedy'.[17]

The idea that international tribunals can defuse ethnic tensions in war-torn countries provided a strong rationale for the establishment of the ICTY, at least at the rhetorical level. While making a case for the Tribunal, the former US ambassador to the UN, Madeleine Albright, declared:

> Truth is the cornerstone of the rule of law, and it will point towards individuals, not peoples, as perpetrators of war crimes. And it is only the truth that can cleanse the ethnic and religious hatreds and begin the healing process.[18]

The extent to which the goals of promoting peace and reconciliation actually informed the creation and the working of the Tribunal is nonetheless debatable. Some critics have denounced the creation of the Tribunal as a fig-leaf for inaction

15 Theodor Meron, 'The Case for War Crimes Trials in Yugoslavia', *Foreign Affairs* 72:3 (1993): 123.

16 For an overview of the various approaches to the disintegration of Yugoslavia, see Dejan Jović, *Yugoslavia: A State that Withered Away* (Indiana: Purdue University Press, 2009), 13–33 and Jasna Dragović-Soso, 'Why Did Yugoslavia Disintegrate? An Overview of Contending Explanations', in *State Collapse in South-Eastern Europe: New Perspectives on Yugoslavia's Disintegration*, edited by L. Cohen and J. Dragović-Soso (West Lafayette: Purdue University Press, 2007).

17 Payam Akhavan, 'Justice in The Hague', Peace in the Former Yugoslavia? A Commentary on the United Nations War Crimes Tribunal', *Human Rights Quarterly* 20:4 (1998): 741–2.

18 Akhavan, 'Justice in The Hague', 765.

by the international community which would thus 'prosecute the crimes that it would not prevent'.[19] Others saw it as a bargaining chip in the peace negotiations.[20] The indictments of the ICTY were indeed used to delegitimise and isolate political actors on the ground. Radovan Karadžić and Ratko Mladić were excluded from the peace negotiations in Dayton on the basis of their indictment by the Tribunal. Likewise, the indictment of Slobodan Milošević during the Kosovo war effectively turned him into an international pariah. This concurrence between ICTY indictments and Western political interests has at times raised serious doubts about the Tribunal's independence and integrity.[21] Suspicions were particularly heightened following the controversial acquittals of several Croatian and Serbian wartime commanders in the latter stages of the ICTY's work.[22] These decisions were imputed to external pressures by critics from within and outside the Court, which seriously undermined the ICTY's credibility.[23] Whether or not these allegations were founded, the acquittals called into question the Tribunal's commitment to establishing responsibility at the highest level and to promoting reconciliation. Judge Meron, who presided over the Appeals Chambers that acquitted the Croatian generals Gotovina and Markač and the Yugoslav general Perišić, seemed to have retracted his earlier views remarking 'facilitating reconciliation is not a classical function of courts, much less in the context of the Tribunal'.[24]

Beyond the former Yugoslavia, the establishment of the ICTY epitomised the advent of transitional justice as a strategy of post-conflict reconstruction that was endorsed by Western governments, inter-governmental bodies and non-governmental organisations. The United Nations have defined transitional justice as 'the full range of processes and mechanisms associated with a society's attempts to come to terms with a legacy of large-scale past abuses, in order to ensure accountability, serve justice and achieve reconciliation'.[25] While the compatibility

19 Gary J. Bass, *Stay the Hand of Vengeance: The Politics of War Crimes Tribunals* (Princeton and Oxford: Princeton University Press, 2000), 209.

20 Rachel Kerr, *The International Criminal Tribunal for the Former Yugoslavia*, 38.

21 These doubts were notably raised by the fact that Milošević was indicted for Bosnia and Croatia only in 2001, six years after the end of the Bosnian war and two years after his fall-out with the West over Kosovo.

22 This refers to the acquittals of the Croatian generals Ante Gotovina and Mladen Markač in November 2012, the former Yugoslav Army Chief of Staff Momčilo Perišić in February 2013, and the former Serbian State Security officials Jovica Stanišić and Franko Simatović in May 2013.

23 'Hague Judge Faults Acquittals of Serb and Croat Commanders', *New York Times*,14 June 2013.

24 'Hague Tribunal President: "Convictions Shouldn't Be Automatic"', *Balkan Insight*, 1 July 2013.

25 *Report of the Secretary-General on the Rule of Law and Transitional Justice in Conflict and Post-Conflict Societies*, UN Doc. S/2004/616 (3 August 2004), cited in Christine Bell, 'Transitional Justice, Interdisciplinarity and the State of the "Field" or "Non-Field"', *International Journal of Transitional Justice* 3:1 (2009): 9.

between these goals is subject to debate among academics, policy-makers have principally adhered to a legalist notion of transitional justice which assumes that accountability is critical for a lasting peace.[26] As a result, war crimes prosecutions have become the norm for addressing the legacy of mass violence in (post-)conflict states. Following the ICTY, the international community established the ad hoc tribunal for Rwanda (ICTR) in 1994 and the permanent International Criminal Court (ICC) which became operational in 2002. In addition, the UN took part in the creation of several internationalised ('hybrid') tribunals which incorporate both international and national features.[27] In this context, the former Yugoslavia has become a laboratory for testing the impact of international criminal tribunals on target states.

Assessing ICTY Cooperation and Impact in Serbia: A Contested Issue

The ICTY has received considerable attention in academic literature. Whereas the early scholarship essentially focused on the Tribunal's contribution to international criminal law, recent studies have increasingly sought to explore the ICTY's interaction with, and impact on, target states. This body of literature can be divided into two broad strands. The first strand consists of comparative studies examining state compliance with international tribunals from an international relations or international law perspective. These studies have primarily sought to explore the drivers of state compliance with the ICTY (and ICTR) in order to generate theories of state cooperation with international criminal tribunals. The second strand of this literature consists of studies that seek to assess the broader repercussions of the ICTY in target states. These studies draw on a transitional justice perspective to examine the Tribunal's legacy in terms of promoting accountability and reconciliation in the region.

The establishment of the ICTY and ICTR soon led to the realisation that, in the absence of international police forces capable of apprehending indictees, international tribunals depend on the goodwill of target states to bring perpetrators to justice. During the nineties, the nationalist authoritarian regimes in Serbia and Croatia were generally reluctant to cooperate with the ICTY.[28] The situation changed

---

26 Legalism refers to the belief in the importance of promoting universal standards of justice through the systematic enforcement of international humanitarian and human rights law (Leslie Vinjamuri and Jack Snyder, 'Advocacy and Scholarship in the Study of International War Crimes Tribunals and Transitional Justice', *Annual Review of Political Science* 7 (2004): 346–52).

27 These internationalised courts were established in Sierra Leone, East Timor, Kosovo and Cambodia.

28 The Dayton Agreement required the signing parties to cooperate with the ICTY. During the 1990s, the authorities of the Federal Republic of Yugoslavia handed over only 2 indictees, both of whom chose to surrender to the ICTY. The Croatian authorities

in the 2000s insofar as the Serbian and Croatian democratic governments were much more responsive to foreign pressure for cooperation than their predecessors. As a result, several authors have sought to determine the mechanisms of state cooperation with international tribunals by exploring the relationship between tribunals, target states and the international community. Victor Peskin thus draws on the experiences of the ICTY and ICTR to demonstrate how international tribunals rely on powerful states and international organisations to enforce cooperation on target states.[29] He argues that state cooperation is determined by the tribunals' capacity to induce powerful international actors to enforce cooperation on states and by the balance of power between moderate and nationalist groups within these states. This rationalist account is complemented by the work of those authors who emphasise ideational factors in state cooperation with the ICTY. Christopher Lamont thus argues that the internalisation of the norm of state sovereignty during the nineties restricted the scope for compliance with the ICTY in post-Milošević Serbia.[30] Nikolas Rajković shows how normative shifts in the framing of ICTY compliance by Serbian and Croatian authorities altered policy choices in terms of state cooperation with the Tribunal.[31]

These analyses have contributed to a solid understanding of state compliance with international tribunals. Nevertheless, they offer only a partial account of ICTY cooperation insofar as they regard it as an international relations issue that transcends domestic politics. By detaching ICTY cooperation from local political dynamics, these studies fail to fully grasp the motives for (non-)cooperation within state authorities. They tend to overlook the way in which the domestic transitional political context characterised by instability and uncertainty influenced decision-making on ICTY cooperation.[32] Also, by disregarding the impact of the ICTY on target states, these studies fail to notice how perceptions of the Tribunal's performance and effect among political elites shaped official attitudes towards the ICTY. For example, Peskin and Boduszynski examined how the EU balanced the goals of justice and stability in pressuring Serbia to cooperate, without

---

handed over 13 Bosnian Croat indictees to the Tribunal, but they fiercely obstructed the ICTY's investigations into crimes perpetrated by Croatian forces against ethnic Serbs in Croatia.

29 Victor Peskin, *International Justice in Rwanda and the Balkans* (New York: Cambridge University Press, 2008).

30 Christopher K. Lamont, *International Criminal Justice and the Politics of Compliance* (Farnham: Ashgate, 2010).

31 Nikolas M. Rajković, *The Politics of International Law and Compliance: Serbia, Croatia and the Hague Tribunal* (London: Routledge, 2012).

32 Peskin's and Boduszynksi's analysis of the ICTY's impact on political dynamics in post-Tudjman Croatia is a notable exception to this. See Victor Peskin and Mieczyslaw P. Boduszynski, 'International Justice and Domestic Politics: Post-Tudjman Croatia and the International Criminal Tribunal for the Former Yugoslavia', *Europe–Asia Studies* 55:7 (2003): 1117–42.

looking at how this trade-off informed the approach of the Serbian authorities to ICTY cooperation.[33]

The impact of the ICTY in Serbia has been assessed by a number of authors who have offered divergent views on the Tribunal's legacy. These studies have generally sought to examine how the ICTY contributed to broader political and social change beyond mere prosecution. Several authors have an overly positive opinion of the ICTY's record in promoting transitional justice in Serbia and other Yugoslav successor states. As an early proponent of international tribunals, the legal scholar Diane Orentlicher has credited the ICTY with dispelling impunity, removing perpetrators from Serbian politics and contributing to the establishment of the rule of law at the domestic level.[34] The ICTY's impact has also been positively assessed by Patrice McMahon who, although initially critical of the ICTY's lack of effect in Serbia,[35] subsequently praised the Tribunal for promoting liberalising political change in the Balkans by informing the policies of powerful international actors such as the EU.[36]

Although some of the developments highlighted by these authors are irrefutable, their overall positive assessment of the ICTY's impact is debatable. For the most part, these studies are based on anecdotal evidence which does not indicate a causal link between the ICTY and political or societal developments on the ground. Public opinion polls carried out throughout the past decade in Serbia and other Yugoslav successor states show that there is a wide discrepancy between the ICTY's achievements in terms of bringing perpetrators to justice and public support for accountability in target societies. According to Mirko Klarin, 'the popularity of the ICTY in the former Yugoslavia is inversely proportional to the number of accused that come from these countries, entities and ethnic communities'.[37] In Serbia, only between 8 and 14 per cent of the population had a positive view of the ICTY during the 2000s.[38] Mirko Klarin notes that, as for other Balkan ethnic groups, the majority of Serbs were either uninformed or suspicious

---

33 Victor Peskin and Mieczyslaw P. Boduszynski, 'Balancing International Justice in the Balkans: Surrogate Enforcers, Uncertain Transitions and the Road to Europe', *International Journal of Transitional Justice* 5:1 (2011): 1–23.

34 Diane F. Orentlicher, 'Shrinking the Space for Denial: The Impact of the ICTY in Serbia', *Open Society Justice Initiative Report*, May 2008.

35 Patrice C. McMahon and David P. Forsythe, 'The ICTY's Impact on Serbia: Judicial Romanticism Meets Network Politics', *Human Rights Quarterly* 30:2 (2008): 412–35.

36 Patrice C. McMahon and Jennifer L. Miller, 'From Adjudication to Aftermath: Assessing the ICTY's Goals Beyond Prosecution', *Human Rights Review* 13:4 (2012): 421–42.

37 Mirko Klarin, 'The Impact of the ICTY Trials on Public Opinion in the Former Yugoslavia', *Journal of International Criminal Justice* 7:1 (2009): 92.

38 Belgrade Centre for Human Rights 'Public Opinion in Serbia: Attitudes Towards the ICTY', July 2003 and Belgrade Centre for Human Rights, OSCE Mission to Serbia, and Strategic Marketing Research, 'Views on War Crimes, the ICTY, and the National War Crimes Judiciary', April 2009. Retrieved from www.bgcentar.org.rs on 30 January 2013.

about the crimes imputed to members of their community, while they were well aware of the suffering of Serbs in Croatia, Bosnia and Kosovo.[39]

The apparent failure of the ICTY to promote accountability and raise awareness in Serbia about the war crimes imputed to the Milošević regime has been interpreted in various ways. Some authors have attributed this outcome to the behaviour of the Serbian authorities, whom they perceive as damaging to transitional justice. Nenad Dimitrijević thus argues that the Serbian authorities chose to condone the war crimes legacy by endorsing a strategy of opportunistic pacification of the past and continuity with nationalism.[40] Jelena Subotić claims that international justice was 'hijacked' by domestic elites who used ICTY cooperation to attain their own political goals, such as getting rid of political opponents, obtaining financial aid or gaining membership of international clubs while keeping the domestic normative and ideological structures intact.[41] Others have imputed the ICTY's failure to advance transitional justice in Serbia to the nature of Serbian political culture. Drawing on psychological concepts, Sabrina Ramet argues that Serbian society is plagued by the 'denial syndrome' characterised by victimisation, revisionism and defensive nationalism.[42] In a similar vein, Iavor Rangelov claims that the ICTY's goal of individualising responsibility is incompatible with the collective nature of Serbian nationalism, defined in terms of group ethnicity and collective victimisation.[43]

While it is important to take into account the specificities of the Serbian case, societal resistance to addressing past human rights abuses is by no means particular to Serbia. Those authors emphasising the exceptional nature of Serbian political culture or nationalism overlook the fact that denial and forgetting of past atrocities has been the norm rather than the exception in countries undergoing transition from a criminal regime. Memories of the Holocaust were repressed all over Europe in the post-war years as every former occupied country developed its own 'Vichy syndrome'.[44] Even Germany, which is often considered a success

39 Klarin, 'The Impact of the ICTY Trials', 93. A closer analysis of public opinion polls carried out between 2001 and 2010 reveals that there was general amnesia about war crimes, regardless of the nationality of the victims, and that there was a wide discrepancy between what people 'heard of' and what they 'believed in', which shows a lack of trust in the ICTY and other institutions that have documented war crimes. I owe this observation to Jasna Dragović Soso.

40 Nenad Dimitrijević, 'Serbia After the Criminal Past: What Went Wrong and What Should Be Done', *International Journal of Transitional Justice* 2:1 (2008): 5–22.

41 Jelena Subotić, *Hijacked Justice: Dealing with the Past in the Balkans* (Ithaca: Cornell University Press, 2009).

42 Sabrina P. Ramet, 'The Denial Syndrome and Its Consequences: Serbian Political Culture since 2000', *Communist and Post-Communist Studies* 40:1 (2007): 41–58.

43 Iavor Rangelov, 'International Law and Local Ideology in Serbia', *Peace Review* 16:3 (2004): 331–7.

44 Tony Judt, *Postwar: A History of Europe since 1945* (New York: Penguin, 2005), 804–8.

in terms of societal reckoning with past wrongs, confirms this pattern. While the Allies prosecuted Nazi officials at Nuremberg and carried out a vast campaign of political purging in the second half of the 1940s, the West German administration subsequently revoked those measures by pursuing a policy of amnesty and integration of former Nazi Party members in the 1950s.[45] Societal resistance to confronting war crimes in post-Milošević Serbia cannot therefore be reduced to some (im)moral or ideological characteristics peculiar to Serbian political elites or society. Serbia's uneasy relationship with the ICTY is rather emblematic of the difficulties associated with attempts to seek accountability for, and acknowledgment of, past atrocities in post-conflict and post-authoritarian countries.

Finally, a last group of authors has adopted an overtly critical stance towards the ICTY. These authors argue that the Tribunal has not only failed to promote transitional justice on the ground, but that it has actually exerted a negative impact on post-conflict reconstruction and democratisation processes. Robert Hayden thus claims that, instead of advancing reconciliation, the ICTY has contributed to protracted instability in the Balkans by keeping the region in isolation and nurturing nationalist tensions.[46] Likewise, Marlene Spoerri and Annette Freyberg-Inan argue that the threat of international isolation associated with ICTY conditionality has destabilised Serbia's democratic transition by bolstering support for anti-reform forces and undermining the strength of the liberal democratic movement.[47] A similar argument was advanced by Peskin and Boduszynski in the case of Croatia, where the ICTY indictments stirred nationalist mobilisation and political turmoil in the post-Tudjman era.[48]

I concur with these authors insofar as my research also shows that the international judicial intervention had an adverse effect on political stability and, to a certain extent, transitional justice in Serbia.[49] However, I contend that the

45 Norbert Frei, *Adenauer's Germany and the Nazi Past* (New York: Columbia University Press, 2002); German society only started to confront the Nazi crimes in the 1960s and 1970s.

46 Robert M. Hayden, 'Justice Presumed and Assistance Denied: The Yugoslav Tribunal as Obstruction to Economic Recovery', *International Journal for the Semiotics of Law* 19:4 (2006): 389–408; Robert M. Hayden, 'What's Reconciliation Got to Do with It? The International Criminal Tribunal for the Former Yugoslavia (ICTY) as Anti-War Profiteer', *Journal of Intervention and Statebuilding* 5:3 (2011): 313–30.

47 Marlene Spoerri and Annette Freyberg-Inan, 'From Prosecution to Persecution: Perceptions of the International Criminal Tribunal for the Former Yugoslavia (ICTY) in Serbian Domestic Politics', *Journal of International Relations and Development* 11:4 (2008): 350–84.

48 Peskin and Boduszynski, 'International Justice and Domestic Politics'.

49 I have borrowed the concept of international judicial intervention from David Scheffer and Rachel Kerr. David J. Scheffer, 'International Judicial Intervention', *Foreign Policy* 102, (1996): 34–51; Rachel Kerr, 'International Judicial Intervention: The International Criminal Tribunal for the Former Yugoslavia', *International Relations* 15:2 (2000): 17–26.

ICTY's impact cannot be reduced to a shift in the power balance between reformist and nationalist forces. While the ICTY was indeed used as a catalyst for nationalist mobilisation, there is no evidence that it actually generated an increase in public support for nationalist parties in Serbia. The success of the right-wing Serbian Radical Party (SRS) in the 2000s derived primarily from a populist rhetoric which drew on the difficult socio-economic conditions of a large section of the Serbian population.[50] At the same time, public support for Milošević's Socialist Party of Serbia (SPS) declined sharply until 2008. It is thus difficult to establish causality between the work of the ICTY and public support for anti-reform forces. The mechanisms at play are more complex.

Building on the existing literature, this book examines the domestic political dynamics that informed ICTY cooperation and transitional justice policies in Serbia in the period 2000–2011. My analysis specifically focuses on the Serbian political elites' perceptions of the Tribunal, and attitudes towards it, in order to elucidate the motives behind (non-)cooperation with the ICTY. As such, this book complements those studies that have explored state compliance with international tribunals by offering a new perspective on ICTY cooperation that focuses on the recipients of international judicial intervention. It also contributes to the work of those authors who have probed the impact of the ICTY in Serbia by shedding light to an unprecedented degree on official thinking and policy-making on transitional justice in Serbia during the first decade after the overthrow of Milošević. My analysis challenges the view that Serbia's reluctance to cooperate with the ICTY was brought about, as existing accounts suggest, by a nationalist backlash or instrumentalisation of international justice by domestic elites. While political opportunism and power dynamics played an important role, I contend that Serbia's policy of cooperation with the ICTY was essentially informed by frustration and disapproval of the Tribunal among those political actors who were in principle supportive of transitional justice.

I argue that the ICTY alienated the Serbian transitional authorities for two reasons. First, in the context of Serbia's precarious transition to democracy, foreign pressures for the arrest and transfer of ICTY indictees stirred political and institutional turmoil, thus jeopardising the stability of the new democratic regime. As a result, the Serbian transitional authorities sought to implement non-confrontational policies of cooperation with the ICTY that involved inciting indictees to surrender instead of carrying out arrests. In addition to dragging out ICTY cooperation for over a decade, these policies significantly undermined the transitional justice agenda by detaching the transfer of indicted war criminals to The Hague from any notion of justice and truth. Second, the prosecution of former high-ranking Serbian officials at the ICTY and the concomitant genocide lawsuits brought by Bosnia and Croatia against Serbia before the International Court of Justice (ICJ) blurred the distinction between individual and collective responsibility in the eyes of the Serbian ruling elite. The fear of seeing the Serbian

50 Jovo Bakić, 'Extreme-Right Ideology, Practice and Supporters: Case Study of the Serbian Radical Party', *Journal of Contemporary European Studies* 17:2 (2009): 193–207.

state being held responsible for genocide substantially diminished the commitment of the Serbian authorities to cooperation with the ICTY and reduced the room for truth-telling and acknowledgment of war crimes in Serbia.

My research thus shows that the Serbian authorities were reluctant to cooperate with the ICTY and publicly denounce war crimes because they perceived the Tribunal as a potential threat to regime stability and state interests.[51] While there were deep divergences regarding the war crimes legacy among the political parties that assumed power after the overthrow of Milošević, these divergences were overshadowed by apprehension for political stability and state interests, which were major concerns for Serbian political elites across the board. These concerns largely informed both the way and the extent to which the Serbian authorities cooperated with the ICTY and endorsed the work of the Tribunal. The Serbian case therefore suggests that international war crimes trials are potentially at odds with political stability in democratising countries and that externalised justice is conditioned by democratic consolidation on the ground.

Justice and Stability in Transitions to Democracy

The nexus between justice and political stability in transition countries was at the centre of academic debates on transitional justice in the 1980s and early 1990s. These debates were substantially informed by the experience of Argentina, the only Latin American country to have put high-ranking officials of a former dictatorial government on trial in the immediate aftermath of regime change. Under the pressure of local human rights groups, the Argentinian transitional authorities sought to extend the prosecutions to middle and lower-ranking army officers; this provoked a series of military rebellions that forced the government to put an end to human rights trials altogether.[52]

This aborted attempt at administering justice in the wake of a transition from authoritarian rule generated a significant debate regarding the trade-offs between the pursuit of justice and the consolidation of democratic stability in transition countries.[53] Prominent human rights activists considered that democratising

---

51 I deliberately refer to 'state interests' and not 'national interests', which in the Serbian context encompass the interests of Serbian communities outside Serbia.

52 Alexandra Barahona de Brito, 'Truth, Justice, Memory and Democratisation in the Southern Cone', in *The Politics of Memory*, edited by Alexandra Barahona de Brito, Carmen Gonzales-Enriquez and Paloma Aguilar (New York: Oxford University Press, 2001), 120–24.

53 In contemporary transitional justice literature, this is often referred to as the 'peace versus justice' debate. I deliberately use 'stability' instead of 'peace' in order to distinguish between the menace of reversal of democratisation in a post-authoritarian setting and the risk of prolongation or resumption of hostilities in a post-conflict setting, although I acknowledge that the two may be related.

countries have an overriding moral duty to redress past human rights violations and that accountability should therefore not be a matter of political judgment.[54] They advocated the establishment of an international duty to prosecute human rights violations of a prior regime in order to rule out amnesties and pardons. Diane Orentlicher thus made the case for the further development and enforcement of international law so that governments 'do not forego trials simply because it seems politically expedient to do so'.[55] This initiative was opposed by a group of scholars and practitioners who had taken part in the design and implementation of transitional justice policies in Argentina and Chile. They argued that, in practice, transitional governments must counter-balance the goal of prosecuting perpetrators with the aim of building a stable democratic system. Accordingly, the pursuit of justice in transitions to democracy is as much a question of political feasibility as it is one of moral desirability.[56] In the light of this, Carlos Nino asserted that an international duty to prosecute past human rights violations would undermine efforts to secure democracy and, hence, human rights for the future.[57]

Along these lines, the scholarship on transitional justice has been characterised by a divide between idealist and pragmatist orientations.[58] Idealists see the prosecution of human rights violations as a necessary step for redressing victims and assuaging desires for revenge that fuel cycles of violence. They generally dismiss the trade-offs between justice and stability as 'false dichotomies', arguing instead that the goals of justice, peace and democracy are complementary and mutually reinforcing. Sikkink and Walling thus contend that 'the pessimistic claims of 'sceptics' that human rights trials threaten democracy, increase human rights violations, and exacerbate conflict are not supported by empirical evidence from Latin America'.[59] They point to the fact that Latin American countries, including Argentina, have undergone successful democratisation despite having made extensive use of human rights trials. The idealist view that justice is a prerequisite for a durable peace and democracy has permeated academic, activist and policy circles. In this spirit, Ellen Lutz argues that decision-makers today understand that

---

54 Aryeh Neier, 'What Should Be Done About the Guilty?' *The New York Review of Books*, 1 February 1990.

55 Diane F. Orentlicher, 'Settling Accounts: The Duty to Prosecute Human Rights Violations of a Prior Regime', *The Yale Law Journal* 100:8 (1991): 2537–615.

56 Jose Zalaquett, 'Truth, Justice, and Reconciliation: Lessons for the International Community', in *Comparative Peace Processes in Latin America*, edited by Cynthia J. Arnson (Stanford: Stanford University Press, 1999), 341–62.

57 Carlos S. Nino, 'The Duty to Punish Past Abuses of Human Rights Put into Context: The Case of Argentina', *The Yale Law Journal* 100:8 (1991): 2619–40.

58 Vinjamuri and Snyder, 'Advocacy and Scholarship'.

59 Kathryn Sikkink and Carrie Booth Walling, 'The Impact of Human Rights Trials in Latin America', *Journal of Peace Research* 44:4 (2007): 427.

'all of the accountability goals must be met', since 'ignoring any of them risks destabilising both governments and the sustainability of peace'.[60]

On the other hand, pragmatists believe that the systematic prosecution of human rights violations can potentially undermine peace processes and democratic transitions, thus causing additional rounds of violence and atrocities. Rather than being driven by normative or principled beliefs, pragmatists consider that policy-makers should take into account political considerations when administering justice. In this spirit, Vinjamuri and Snyder argue that 'choices about punishment of past abuses must be made through the application of resolutely forward-looking criteria designed to avert atrocities and secure human rights, not backward-looking strategies based on rigid rule-following or on what "feels right"'.[61] Accordingly, amnesties and pardons are legitimate when they allow for removing spoilers from power and building a stable political order capable of enforcing justice. Pragmatists are generally dismissive of the idealist claims that justice and truth-telling contribute to consolidating peace and democracy in the short term. In their view, justice is a consequence rather than a cause of democratisation.[62] In point of fact, with the exception of Argentina, all Latin American countries held their human rights trials at a later stage of their democratisation processes, when their political systems and institutions were to a large degree consolidated.[63]

Empirical studies focusing on the relationship between justice, peace and democratisation have highlighted the importance of timing and sequencing in the implementation of transitional justice policies. Chandra Lekha Sriram thus demonstrated that, while the goals of peace or stability and justice are at odds with each other in the early stages of the transition, this does not preclude the pursuit of justice once the new regime has been consolidated. Furthermore, transitional governments can draw on a range of alternative accountability mechanisms, such as purges or commissions of inquiry, in order to mitigate the tensions between justice and peace. Therefore, Sriram argues that 'the question is not whether or not accountability can be achieved, but what point on the accountability continuum can be achieved by a given state at a given

---

60 Ellen Lutz, 'Transitional Justice: Lessons Learned and the Road Ahead', in *Transitional Justice in the Twenty-First Century: Beyond Truth Versus Justice*, edited by Naomi Roht-Arriaza and Javier Mariezcurrena (Cambridge: Cambridge University Press, 2006), 325–41.

61 Jack Snyder and Leslie Vinjamuri 'Trials and Errors: Principles and Pragmatism in Strategies of International Justice', *International Security* 28:3 (2003/04): 44.

62 Ibid.; David Mendeloff, 'Truth-Seeking, Truth-Telling, and Post-Conflict Peacebuilding: Curb the Enthusiasm?', *International Studies Review* 6:3 (2004): 355–80.

63 Even Sikkink and Walling concede that 'while trials were considered impossible in many transitional countries immediately after transitions, with the passage of time conditions changed and trials became not just possible but likely' (Sikkink and Walling, 'Human Rights Trials in Latin America', 435).

point in time'.[64] Fletcher and Weinstein came to a similar conclusion on the basis of a comparative analysis of seven countries affected by mass violence and repression. They consider that justice delayed is not justice denied and suggest that transitional justice should await the development of a judicial and policing system that is transparent and legitimate.[65]

My research comes out in support of the view that the relationship between justice and democratic stability is dynamic and variable. I argue that, owing to the compromises made with elements of the former regime to overthrow Milošević, the Serbian transitional authorities had to balance the pursuit of justice with the safeguarding of political stability in the wake of regime change. However, unlike their Latin American counterparts, the Serbian authorities could not opt for alternative accountability mechanisms or grant amnesties and pardons without being subject to international sanctions and isolation. Indeed, Serbia lost its sovereignty over transitional justice matters with the creation of the ICTY. In this context, the Serbian authorities mitigated the destabilising effects of international justice by delaying arrests and promoting or staging 'voluntary surrenders' of indicted war criminals. Ultimately, the completion of ICTY cooperation through the arrest of the last remaining indictees, including Karadžić and Mladić, was premised upon democratic consolidation and the establishment of government control over the security apparatus.

Furthermore, this book brings to light the tensions that can arise between individual and state responsibility in the current international justice system. The unprecedented degree of international involvement in the prosecution of war crimes in the former Yugoslavia and Serbia's perceived role as an aggressor in the wars of Yugoslav succession gave a peculiar dimension to transitional justice in Serbia. Whereas the ICTY sought to individualise responsibility for war crimes, the above-mentioned genocide lawsuits brought by Bosnia and Croatia against Serbia before the ICJ linked the fate of the Serbian state with that of former high-ranking officials indicted for genocide by the ICTY.[66] In those circumstances, disclosure of evidence incriminating former Serbian officials by the authorities in Belgrade was informed by concerns for state interests. Instead of promoting a break with the past, international war crimes trials have restricted the scope for truth-telling and acknowledgment of past atrocities in Serbia by raising the spectre of collective responsibility. The Serbian case thus illustrates the inherent contradictions of international justice and their negative repercussions in target states, which have so far received little attention in the academic literature.

64 Chandra Lekha Sriram, *Confronting Past Human Rights Violations: Justice v. Peace in Times of Transition* (New York: Frank Cass, 2004), 212.

65 Laurel E. Fletcher and Harvey Weinstein with Jamie Rowen, 'Context, Timing and the Dynamics of Transitional Justice: A Historical Perspective', *Human Rights Quarterly* 31:1 (2009): 218.

66 In practice, this only applied to the Bosnian genocide lawsuit since none of the Serbian defendants brought before the ICTY was indicted for genocide in Croatia.

Sources, Scope and Structure of the Book

This book examines the challenges and dilemmas associated with official attempts to address the war crimes legacy in post-Milošević Serbia. This endeavour required a close inspection of the perceptions, attitudes and experiences of those people who were in positions of power following the overthrow of Milošević. For this purpose, I have carried out extensive field research which involved over 40 interviews conducted in 2009, 2010 and 2012. Most of the politicians I have interviewed were in positions of power during the first two democratic governments that were in place from 2001 to 2007. My informants included high-ranking officials such as the former Prime Minister Zoran Živković; former Minister of Foreign Affairs Goran Svilanović; former Ministers of Justice Momčilo Grubač and Zoran Stojković; former Deputy Prime Ministers Miroljub Labus and Žarko Korać; former advisor to President Koštunica and Minister for Kosovo Slobodan Samardžić; former President of the Parliament Dragoljub Mićunović; former representatives of the Serbian state before the ICTY and ICJ Vladimir Djerić and Tibor Varady; and former head of the Serbian State Security Service Goran Petrović.

Since ICTY cooperation was in the remit of the Ministry of Foreign Affairs during this period, this research particularly draws on interviews with former Foreign Minister Goran Svilanović and representatives of his legal team.[67] These elite interviews were used both to examine official thinking on transitional justice and to obtain or corroborate information on events that took place behind closed doors. I have also carried out a number of interviews with legal experts, representatives of international and non-governmental organisations, and journalists with specialised knowledge on war crimes prosecutions. Besides data collection, these expert interviews were used to provide alternative interpretations of specific events or issues.[68] In order to diversify my sources and broaden the scope of my research, I have complemented these interviews with an extensive review of the Serbian press as well as an analysis of parliamentary debates and conference proceedings at which political elites expressed their views on ICTY cooperation and war crimes. This allowed me to trace the sequence of events, double-check the information obtained in the interviews and analyse the evolution of public discourses on ICTY cooperation and war crimes during the period 2000–2011.

67 Goran Svilanović was Foreign Minister from 2001 to 2004, which corresponds to the most critical period in terms of ICTY cooperation. The fact that his legal team remained in place at the Ministry of Foreign Affairs reflects a degree of continuity in state policy towards the ICTY.

68 I am aware that experts are not a source of objective information and that the distinction between 'elite' and 'expert' is not clear-cut. In line with Beatte Littig, I believe that elites and experts are distinguished by different positions of power [Beatte Littig, 'Interviewing the Elite – Interviewing Experts: Is there a Difference', in *Interviewing Experts*, edited by A. Bogner et al. (Basingstoke: Palgrave Macmillan, 2009)].

A number of issues are deliberately omitted from this study. First, while I am aware of the potential benefits of comparative research, I believe that stretching the geographical scope of this study would have cast a shadow on the singularity of the Serbian case. Besides having the highest number of citizens indicted by the ICTY, Serbia is the only state to have been requested to deliver its top political and military leadership to an international criminal tribunal while at the same time being sued for genocide before the ICJ. Focusing on Serbia alone has allowed me to illuminate the deep contradictions and dilemmas of transitional justice in Serbia, which have thus far been overlooked in the literature. Second, this book does not deal with the controversies associated with the actual work of the ICTY, such as whether the Tribunal was fair or biased towards one ethnic group or individual. The ICTY's performance is only considered to the extent that it has influenced public opinion or elite perceptions of, or attitudes towards, the Tribunal. Third, questions of societal reckoning with war crimes are limited to discussions on the repercussions of transitional justice measures on public opinion. A deeper assessment of these questions requires different approaches and methodologies which have been applied to the study of the Serbian case elsewhere.[69] Finally, this study does not encompass aspects of transitional justice that are not related to violations of international humanitarian law, such as the failed attempt to enact lustration or the prosecution of former regime officials for political murders or corruption in local courts.

Investigating the attitudes of the Serbian political elites towards the ICTY requires understanding of the context in which international judicial intervention took place. Therefore, Chapter 2 provides an overview of Serbian politics since Milošević's rise to power, with a particular focus on the events surrounding 5 October 2000 and political developments in the following decade. I argue that Serbia has gone through a protracted transition and that the consolidation of democracy in the post-Milošević period was hampered by political polarisation and precarious stateness. This set of circumstances substantially informed the attitudes of the Serbian authorities towards ICTY cooperation and the war crimes legacy, as shown in the subsequent analysis.

The remainder of the book consists of in-depth empirical analyses of policy-making and official thinking and on ICTY cooperation and transitional justice in Serbia in the period 2000–2011. By exploring the politics of cooperation with the ICTY, Chapter 3 highlights the tensions between externalised justice and stability in post-Milošević Serbia. I argue that these tensions led the Serbian authorities to increasingly promote surrenders instead of carrying out arrests, which in turn undermined the transitional justice agenda of the ICTY. I also demonstrate how cooperation with the ICTY was shaped by shifts in the domestic power balance and how the arrest of the last indictees was ultimately made possible by democratic

---

69 See Eric Gordy, *Guilt, Responsibility and Denial: The Past at Stake in Post-Milošević Serbia* (Philadelphia: University of Pennsylvania Press, 2013) and Jelena Obradović-Wochnik, *Ethnic Conflict and War Crimes in the Balkans* (London: IB Tauris, 2013).

consolidation. Chapter 4 draws on interviews carried out with representatives of the Serbian state to show that the transitional authorities were reluctant to come out with the truth about war crimes out of fear for democratic stability and state interests. By focusing on elite perceptions of Milošević's trial, this analysis demonstrates that externalised justice paradoxically inhibited truth-telling in Serbia. This chapter also looks at public debates and discourses on Srebrenica in order to shed light on the mechanisms behind official acknowledgment of past atrocities. Chapter 5 explores how the establishment and functioning of the special institutions for prosecuting war crimes in Serbia have been shaped by international judicial intervention and regime change. By gauging the achievements and limitations of domestic war crimes trials, this chapter also scrutinises the extent to which these institutions have endorsed the transitional justice agenda. I argue that the scope and potential of these prosecutions are conditioned by changing political and institutional circumstances and ponder on the potential of domestic trials to contribute to reconciliation in the region. Finally, the conclusion offers a retrospective on my findings and a reflection on the ICTY's legacy and on possible avenues for future research.

Chapter 2
Setting the Context: Serbia's Protracted Transition

Introduction

The Serbian trajectory of democratisation is in many ways unusual. It does not fit into the classic 'transition paradigm', which assumes that elite-pacting generates a departure from authoritarianism that opens the way for the establishment and consolidation of democracy. In Serbia, the breakdown of communism did not lead to fully-fledged democratisation. Instead, the socialist system was replaced by a hybrid regime which maintained authoritarian practices behind the façade of democracy. Under Milošević's rule, Serbia experienced pluralist elections and proto-democratic institutions without any genuine alteration of power. It is only with the overthrow of Milošević in October 2000 and the rise to power of parties emanating from the democratic opposition that the conditions were created for the substantial democratisation of the Serbian political system. However, the preservation of existing institutions and the difficulty in evaluating democratic practices renders the distinction between authoritarianism and democracy rather ambiguous.[1]

The specificity of the Serbian case partly stems from the fact that the process of democratisation took place in the context of state disintegration and ethnic conflict. The process of Yugoslavia's disintegration culminated with the outbreak of war in Croatia and Bosnia and Herzegovina in 1991 and 1992 respectively. Serbia and Montenegro established the Federal Republic of Yugoslavia (FRY) in April 1992 after the four other republics were recognised as independent states by the international community.[2] While the Serbian authorities continually claimed that Serbia and the FRY were not involved in the wars in Croatia and Bosnia, they provided vital support in manpower and material to the Serb belligerents.[3]

---

1 As a matter of fact, there is no consensus among Serbian scholars on when the transition away from authoritarianism occurred. See the debates on this topic in Dušan Pavlović, ed., *Konsolidacija demokratskih ustanova u Srbiji: Godinu dana posle* (Consolidation of Democratic Institutions in Serbia: A Year Later) (Belgrade: Službeni Glasnik, 2008).

2 Slovenia, Croatia and Macedonia declared independence during 1991, while Bosnia and Herzegovina did so in March 1992.

3 The degree of involvement of the Serbian state in the wars in Croatia and Bosnia is a matter of controversy among observers and a subject of enquiry at the ICTY. In any

In view of his authority over the Bosnian Serb leadership, Milošević played a key role in the brokering of the Dayton peace agreement that put an end to the war in 1995. The Serbian army and police subsequently waged a war against the ethnic-Albanian separatist Kosovo Liberation Army (KLA) in 1998, which culminated with the NATO bombing campaign and the withdrawal of the Serbian forces and administration from Kosovo in 1999. State disintegration continued after the removal of Milošević, as Montenegro and Kosovo declared independence in 2006 and 2008 respectively.

This chapter seeks to set out the context in which international judicial intervention took place in Serbia. Before analysing the incidence of the ICTY on domestic politics, we need to develop an understanding of contemporary Serbian politics. This is a prerequisite for grasping the impact of international judicial intervention on regime change, and domestic responses to such intervention, in the remainder of this book. Therefore, I first proceed with a brief account of Milošević's rule over Serbia in the nineties. Secondly, I examine the factors that brought about regime change and scrutinise the transitional compromises made in the wake of Milošević's overthrow. Finally, I give a detailed analysis of Serbian politics in the post-October 2000 period by focusing on two major challenges to the consolidation of democracy: political polarisation and precarious stateness.

1. Serbia Under Milošević: From Socialism to Nationalist Authoritarianism

The difficulty in assessing the regime of Milošević rests upon the fact that it was not an outright totalitarian dictatorship, but rather a scrupulous subversion of democracy orchestrated by segments of the old communist elite that endorsed nationalism. Observers have commonly qualified this regime as 'nationalist authoritarianism' or 'electoral/competitive authoritarianism'. Nationalist authoritarianism denotes a regime that 'seeks to justify its continuation in power by means of nationalist rhetoric or to secure its future by appealing to nationalist movements'.[4] While drawing on nationalist discourses to secure power, the Milošević regime derived its legitimacy from elections that were just competitive enough to allow the opposition some room for manoeuvre, and thus provide the political system with a semblance of democracy.[5] In this respect, Milošević's rule

event, this involvement varied periodically. While Serbia initially took part in the hostilities directly, at least until the retreat of the JNA from Croatia and Bosnia in 1992, its support for the belligerents subsequently declined, especially after Milošević introduced an embargo on the Bosnian Serbs for rejecting the Vance–Owen peace plan in 1994.

4 Eric D. Gordy, *The Culture of Power in Serbia: Nationalism and the Destruction of Alternatives* (Pennsylvania: Penn State Press, 1999), 8.

5 Mark R. Thompson and Philipp Kuntz, 'Stolen Elections: the Case of the Serbian October', *Journal of Democracy* 15:4 (2004): 159–60.

bore a strong resemblance to the authoritarian regimes that emerged at the same period in Slovakia and Croatia.[6]

A. Serbia's Distorted Transition

In the second half of the eighties and beginning of the nineties, Serbia experienced a 'transition' away from communism to nationalist authoritarianism carried out 'from above' under the leadership of Slobodan Milošević.[7] Milošević rose to power in 1987 by taking control over the Serbian Communist Party. Although he was initially an inveterate communist adhering to the Yugoslav ideal of 'brotherhood and unity', Milošević increasingly drew on Serbian national grievances to boost his popularity. These grievances were prompted by reports of discrimination and repression against Serbs and Montenegrins by the predominantly ethnic-Albanian authorities in Kosovo.

The Serbian provinces of Vojvodina and Kosovo were granted substantial autonomy by the constitutional reform of 1974.[8] This reform produced considerable resentment among Serbs, who perceive Kosovo as the 'cradle' of their civilisation. Following the death of Tito in 1980, nationalist tendencies progressively resurfaced in the public sphere throughout Yugoslavia, and especially in Serbia.[9] This trend was supported by the intellectual elites, which openly promoted the nationalist rhetoric through the workings of the Serbian Academy of Sciences (SANU) and the Serbian Writers' Union (UKS).[10] Hence, Milošević appropriated a nationalist discourse that was already established amongst intellectual circles and the wider population.[11] By portraying himself as a socialist leader working for the defence of Serbian national interests, he managed to gather the support of both regime

---

6 The difference is that, while the Slovakian and Croatian regimes were led by communist dissidents or former anti-communists, the Serbian regime consisted in an extension of the incumbent elite's rule. See Sharon Fisher, *Political Change in Post-Communist Slovakia and Croatia: From Nationalist to Europeanist* (New York: Palgrave Macmillan, 2006).

7 Gordy, *The Culture of Power in Serbia*, 25.

8 The province of Vojvodina included a substantial proportion of ethnic Hungarians, while Kosovo was overwhelmingly populated by ethnic Albanians. These two groups were recognised as 'nationalities', that is national minorities, as opposed to the constituent South Slav nations of Socialist Yugoslavia and were therefore not entitled to have their own republics. For an overview of political developments in Kosovo, see Lenard J. Cohen, *Serpent in the Bosom: The Rise and Fall of Slobodan Milošević* (Oxford: Westview Press, 2002), 47–86.

9 Robert Thomas, *Serbia under Milošević: Politics in the 1990s* (London: Hurst & Co, 1999), 35–42.

10 See Jasna Dragović-Soso, *Saviours of the Nation: Serbia's Intellectual Opposition and the Revival of Nationalism* (London: Hurst and Montreal: McGill-Queen's University Press, 2002).

11 Gordy, *The Culture of Power in Serbia*, 11.

followers and its nationalist opponents. As he abolished the autonomy of both Serbian provinces and gained control over the communist party in Montenegro, Milošević shifted the focus of his nationalist rhetoric onto the Serb communities in Croatia and Bosnia by promoting their right to self-determination.[12]

By the time of the first pluralist parliamentary elections in December 1990, Milošević already held all the cards in his hands. A new Serbian constitution had previously been adopted by the one-party parliament, along with an electoral law that was largely favourable to the ruling party, which was renamed Socialist Party of Serbia (SPS).[13] In addition, the regime controlled the state media – the only source of information available across the whole country. While independent newspapers, radio stations and television made their appearance in 1990, they were almost exclusively available to urban dwellers, essentially in Belgrade. Although the SPS did not win an absolute majority of votes (46.1 per cent) in these first elections, it did get an overwhelming majority of seats (194 out of 250), which allowed Milošević to consolidate his rule. From then on, support for the ruling SPS declined continuously. Nevertheless, Milošević was able to perpetuate his rule by co-opting segments of a deeply divided and increasingly discredited opposition.[14]

As Gordy argues, Milošević's regime constituted both a continuation of, and departure from, the old communist regime.[15] It relied on a similar structure of power by maintaining absolute control over executive and judiciary positions, distributive mechanisms and the state security apparatus. Maintaining control over sources of information was a key element in the regime's strategy for remaining in power. Not only did it allow Milošević to sideline political opponents, but it also constituted an essential tool for shaping public opinion through nationalist propaganda. Hence, Milošević secured power through 'the destruction of alternatives', by 'closing off avenues of information, expression and sociability' in order to produce political

12 Milošević ousted the communist leaderships in Vojvodina and Montenegro through a wave of mass protests dubbed 'anti-bureaucratic' revolution in the summer and autumn of 1988. He subsequently purged the key leaders in the Kosovo League of Communists and suspended the autonomy of Kosovo and of Vojvodina in March 1989 (Cohen, *Serpent in the Bosom*, 118–23).

13 The Serbian Communist Party had two successor parties: the Socialist Party of Serbia (SPS) led by Milošević, and the League of Communists – Movement for Yugoslavia (SK–PJ) presided over by Milošević's wife, Mirjana Marković. The latter subsequently formed the Yugoslav United Left (JUL), which participated in government 'despite having no parliamentary seats and in fact never having participated in an election' (Gordy, *The Culture of Power in Serbia*, 25).

14 Although the SPS held a majority of seats in the Serbian parliament throughout the nineties, it lost the absolute majority following the 1992 elections. Milošević's party subsequently formed governments through alliances with the right-wing SRS or by breaking off renegade elements from the parties that constituted the democratic opposition (Gordy, *The Culture of Power in Serbia*, 43–51).

15 Gordy, *The Culture of Power in Serbia*, 14.

inertia and apathy.[16] The most serious attempts by the opposition at challenging the regime were suppressed through the use of force. The most dramatic events took place on 9 March 1991, when a mass protest organised by opposition parties calling for the liberalisation of the media was crushed through the intervention of the army.[17] For many commentators and participants, this tragic event marks the beginning of the war(s) in the former Yugoslavia.[18] Indeed, this episode showed that the federal army was under Milošević's control, and that he did not hesitate to use it in order to hold onto power.

The war constituted another crucial element in the regime's strategy.[19] The conflicts in Croatia and Bosnia effectively allowed Milošević to thwart domestic opposition by associating any challenge to the regime with treason towards Serbian national interests. The nationalist propaganda organised by the state media gave prominence to the right-wing paramilitary leaders, who thus rapidly became politically influential.[20] The most important of them, Vojislav Šešelj, was the leader of the Serbian Radical Party (SRS), which emerged as the second biggest single party in 1992. Throughout the nineties, the SRS played a major role on the political scene, either by supporting SPS-led governments, or by acting as a 'counter-opposition' to the 'pro-democratic' parties.[21] The pro-democratic parties were themselves nationalist to different degrees and, while some of them campaigned against the war, most supported the Serb belligerents in Bosnia and Croatia. This partly explains the reluctance of the West to actively support the democratic opposition in Serbia. The pro-nationalist tendencies of most opposition leaders initially played into Milošević's strategy of presenting himself to the outside world as the only moderate choice.[22] Moreover, in view of the deep fragmentation and constant infighting among pro-democratic parties, Milošević appeared to Western diplomats as the only legitimate and authoritative interlocutor.[23]

---

16 Ibid., 2.

17 These protests were organised by the Serbian Renewal Movement (SPO), which was the most influential party of the democratic opposition throughout the nineties.

18 Thomas, *Serbia under Milošević*, 87.

19 See Diane Masson, *L'utilisation de la guerre dans la construction des systèmes politiques en Serbie et en Croatie, 1989 –1995* (How War Was Used in the Construction of the Political Systems in Serbia and Croatia, 1989–95) (Paris : L'Harmattan, 2002).

20 Gordy, *The Culture of Power in Serbia*, 45–6. Note that most of these paramilitary groups had links with the Serbian State Security Service and that some of these nationalist leaders, such as Vojislav Šešelj, were actively promoted by the regime.

21 The SRS was in government coalition with the SPS from 1992 to 1993 and 1997 to 2000.

22 Obrad Kesić, 'An Airplane with Eighteen Pilots: Serbia after Milošević', in *Serbia since 1989: Politics and Society under Milošević and After*, edited by Sabrina P. Ramet and Vjeran Pavlaković (Seattle and London: University of Washington Press, 2005), 98–9.

23 Florian Bieber, 'The Serbian Opposition and Civil Society: Roots of the Delayed Transition in Serbia', *International Journal of Politics, Culture, and Society* 17:1 (2003): 73–82.

B. Foreign Intervention and Domestic Politics

During the first half of the nineties, international isolation widely contributed to upholding and consolidating Milošević's rule. The economic embargo introduced by the UN Security Council in May 1992 drove the country into deep impoverishment and chaos. As a result of the sanctions, the supply and distribution of goods were entirely performed through illicit smuggling channels that were controlled by the regime, which thus benefited from an important source of revenue.[24] The regime extracted additional resources from the population by conducting a drastically expansionist monetary policy that produced one of the highest hyper-inflations in history.[25] Having lost their savings through financial bankruptcies, the impoverished citizens were forced to use up their very last resources to ensure mere survival. During this period, the regime proceeded with the partial privatisation of state-owned companies, thus allowing the ruling elites to take hold over vast segments of the economy. In view of this, the nineties have been widely interpreted by Serbian scholars as a period of 'blocked transformation' during which the former communist elites converted their political resources into private capital.[26]

Besides economically reinforcing the regime, the international sanctions increased the effectiveness of its propaganda machine by reducing the population's opportunities to travel and access alternative channels of information. Paradoxically, instead of diminishing domestic support for the regime, the embargo generated an increase in Milošević's popularity by reinforcing the view fed by the state-run media that there was a 'conspiracy of foreign powers' against Serbia.[27] In addition, the withdrawal of international organisations from Serbia precluded external monitoring of the elections, which allowed the regime to manipulate the ballots in favour of the ruling party. This was extensively practised in Kosovo, where the ethnic Albanians continually boycotted the elections, which made it easy for the regime to manipulate the ballots by attributing additional votes to the SPS.[28]

---

24 Jasna Dragović-Soso, 'The Impact of International Intervention on Domestic Political Outcomes: Western Coercive Policies and the Milošević Regime', in *International Intervention in the Balkans since 1995*, edited by Peter Siani-Davies (London and New York: Routledge, 2003), 122–3.

25 Research has shown that the hyper-inflation was staged by the regime in order to force citizens to spend their hard-currency savings on the foreign exchange market, which was controlled by the regime. See Mladjan Dinkić, *Ekonomija Destrukcije* (An Economy of Destruction) (Belgrade: Stubovi Kulture, 1995).

26 Mladen Lazić, 'Serbia: The Adaptive Reconstruction of Elites', in *Elites after State Socialism: Theories and Analysis*, edited by John Higley and Gyorgy Lengyel (Lanham, MD: Rowman & Littlefield, 2000), 123–40.

27 Dragović-Soso, 'Western Coercive Policies and the Milošević Regime', 123–5.

28 In view of the Kosovo Serbs' fervent partisanship for the SPS, it was very difficult for any domestic observers to control the polling stations in Kosovo (Thomas, *Serbia under Milošević*, 392–3).

Having endorsed the Dayton Agreement, which brought an end to the war in Bosnia in autumn 1995, Milošević temporarily relinquished nationalism to portray himself as a guarantor of peace in the region.[29] The international community hailed these developments by partly lifting the sanctions against the Federal Republic of Yugoslavia. As the perceived foreign threat diminished, the domestic political climate progressively eased, creating the opportunity for the opposition to seriously challenge the regime. In November 1996, the coalition 'Zajedno' (Together), which grouped the three major democratic opposition parties, won the local elections in all the major cities in Serbia. The authorities refused to recognise the electoral results, arguing that they should be cancelled owing to widespread irregularities. During the following three months, opposition parties and student organisations staged daily protests attended by hundreds of thousands of people across Serbia.[30] These events raised hopes among the opposition of an imminent collapse of the regime, which would have allowed Serbia to eventually move towards democracy. Nevertheless, these hopes were premature. Deprived of support from Western governments, who perceived Milošević as a guarantor of peace in the Balkans, the opposition failed to capitalise on the mass protests in order to topple the regime. The intervention of the OSCE's special envoy, Felipe Gonzales, led Milošević to admit defeat in most localities won by the opposition in February 1997. However, the central power remained intact. As the opposition gained control over the major urban centres, the Zajedno coalition dissolved over quarrels amongst the different party leaders. The increasing divisions and bickering among the democratic opposition parties allowed the regime to overcome its crisis of legitimacy and emerge victorious in the Serbian parliamentary[31] and presidential[32] elections in autumn and winter 1997.

The West's (absence of) reaction to the mass protests in Serbia suggests that the Milošević regime benefited from the tacit support of the international community, at least in the wake of the Dayton agreement. In the face of the regime's obvious attempt at manipulating the elections and repressing the protests, the OSCE's intervention effectively provided Milošević with a face-saving exit which allowed the regime to emerge practically unharmed from this crisis. The implicit approval of Milošević by Western policy-makers is further reflected in the participation of

29 Kesić, 'Serbia after Milošević', 99–100.

30 Thomas, *Serbia under Milošević*, 285–315; Cohen, *Serpent in the Bosom*, 251–9.

31 The parliamentary elections of September 1997, which were boycotted by a large section of the democratic opposition, saw the emergence of the SRS as the second largest parliamentary party with 82 out of the 250 seats. The government was formed by the SPS, SRS and JUL, and was therefore dubbed the 'red–black' coalition.

32 Since he could not legally have a third mandate as President of Serbia, Milošević arranged for the Federal Assembly to elect him to the post of President of Yugoslavia in July 1997. The Serbian presidential elections were won by his fellow SPS official, Milan Milutinović, in December 1997.

Western companies in the privatisation of several large state-owned companies in Serbia, which provided the regime with critical funds for buying social peace.[33]

The position of the West shifted dramatically following the eruption of violence in Kosovo in 1998, which led to the partial reintroduction of international sanctions towards the FRY. But once again, the spectre of war and the international isolation played into the hands of Milošević. As the clashes between Serbian security forces and the Kosovo Liberation Army intensified and the NATO countries threatened to intervene, the regime could once again draw on the well-established mechanisms of national mobilisation against the 'foreign enemy' in order to rally support among the population. Instead of undermining the regime, the seventy-eight-day NATO bombing campaign carried out in spring 1999 generated patriotic unity against what was widely perceived as foreign aggression.[34] It also allowed Milošević to strengthen his control over the levers of power and settle accounts with domestic opponents by closing down independent media, suppressing the autonomy of the university, and purging the judiciary and security sectors.[35] During the bombing, the regime closed ranks and increased repression against the opposition, notably by physically eliminating political opponents and critics. And while the withdrawal of the Serbian army and administration from Kosovo discredited the regime in the eyes of many of its supporters, the NATO intervention also undermined the pro-Western stance of the democratic opposition.

Serbia came out of the Kosovo war with an increasingly authoritarian and isolated regime. The increased clampdown on opposition groups and the frequent occurrence of high-profile assassinations of people who represented a potential threat to the regime created a climate of fear and insecurity.[36] The indictments raised by the ICTY against high-ranking Yugoslav political and military officials, including Milošević, for war crimes perpetrated in Kosovo reduced the chances for peaceful regime change.[37] At the same time, the widespread despair and political apathy of a population facing deteriorating living conditions provided little hope for renewed political mobilisation that could topple the regime. Nevertheless, the

33 The most important contract concerned the sale of Telekom Srbija to Italian and Greek companies, which was arranged by the former Tory Foreign Secretary and Director of the National Westminster Bank, Douglas Hurd ('Milošević Will Target Britain', *BBC News*, 3 July 2001).

34 Cohen, *Serpent in the Bosom*, 333–4.

35 Dragović-Soso, 'Western Coercive Policies and the Milošević Regime', 127–30.

36 These included the murders of paramilitary chief and underworld boss Željko Ražnatović Arkan and the former communist official and Serbian President Ivan Stambolić. The SPO leader Vuk Drašković survived two attempts on his life by the Serbian State Security Service in 1999 and 2000 ('Milošević Aides Found Guilty of Yugoslav Political Assassination', *New York Times*, 19 July 2005).

37 According to Cohen, most Serbian opposition leaders believed that the ICTY indictment of Milošević had complicated any chance for his negotiated exit from power. (Cohen, *Serpent in the Bosom*, 407).

country's deep isolation and profound economic decay made Milošević's rule unsustainable in the long run.

2. '5 October': Between Rupture and Continuity

The regime of Milošević was toppled in a wave of mass protests that followed his defeat at the Yugoslav presidential elections on 24 September 2000. Milošević's overthrow marked the beginning of a new era for Serbia, as well as the emergence of a distinctive model of transition to democracy. Indeed, Serbia's departure from authoritarianism has become a prime example of 'electoral revolutions' which combine electoral contests and mass protests in bringing down authoritarian-pluralist regimes.[38] This model was earlier applied in Slovakia and Croatia, where the authoritarian rulers acknowledged their defeat at the elections straight away, without the opposition having to resort to mass protests as in the case of Serbia. It was subsequently emulated in various parts of the former Soviet Union, in a wave of protests that have been dubbed 'colour revolutions'.[39]

In the 2000s, electoral revolutions became the main approach to democratic breakthroughs in those post-communist countries that remained in the grey zone between fully-fledged democracy and outright dictatorship.[40] But while this model has proved effective at dislodging authoritarian electoral regimes, it nonetheless imposes substantial limitations on the possibilities for achieving a radical break with the past. Indeed, an exit through the polls allows former political elites to maintain a degree of legitimacy and participate in political life after regime change. Moreover, the institutional continuity with the previous regime allows the incumbent elites to uphold their positions and obstruct reforms.

In this section, I examine the modalities of the transition away from authoritarianism in Serbia in autumn 2000. '5 October' was a defining moment for Serbia's transition to democracy. Indeed, this event largely delineated the parameters of regime change and shaped the context in which international judicial intervention took place. In view of this, I briefly describe here the fall of Milošević and discuss the compromises made with the incumbent elites in the wake of his overthrow.

---

38 Valerie Bunce and Sharon Wolchik, 'Defining and Domesticating the Electoral Model: A Comparison of Slovakia and Serbia', in *Democracy and Authoritarianism in the Post-Communist World*, edited by Valerie Bunce, Michael McFaul, and Kathryn Stoner-Weiss (Cambridge: Cambridge University Press, 2009), 134–54.

39 These revolutions took place in Georgia, Ukraine and Kyrgyzstan. See Mark Beissinger, 'Structure and Example in Modular Political Phenomena: The Diffusion of Bulldozer/Rose/Orange/Tulip Revolutions', *Perspectives on Politics* 5:2 (2007): 259–76.

40 Bunce and Wolchik, 'A Comparison of Slovakia and Serbia', 135.

A. The Bulldozer Revolution

In view of the disastrous socio-economic situation and the severe international isolation imposed on Yugoslavia following the NATO bombing campaign, the removal of Milošević became a necessity for improving the population's calamitous living conditions. In 1999, Yugoslavia was the poorest country in Europe, with about half of the population at the level of bare survival, and twenty per cent living in extreme poverty.[41] However, in spite of this dire state of affairs, the prospects for change seemed gloomy. Public opinion polls conducted at the end of 1999 revealed that, despite being dissatisfied and fearful for the future, the population was generally apathetic and politically passive. While 60 per cent of the population did not trust the regime and state institutions, half of the respondents did not trust the opposition.[42] In those circumstances, a divided opposition still did not stand a chance against Milošević.

Considering the state of public opinion and the earlier failures at bringing the regime down, the unification of the Serbian opposition parties clearly constituted a precondition for the removal of Milošević. By 1999, two groups of parties had emerged on the political scene: the Alliance for Change which was centred around the Democratic Party (DS) and the Alliance of Democratic Parties which was essentially composed of minority parties.[43] Following the end of the NATO bombing campaign, these two opposition blocks jointly held a number of rallies throughout Serbia, demanding the resignations of Milošević and both federal and republican governments. The unification of the opposition was completed with the establishment of the Democratic Opposition of Serbia (DOS) in January 2000 at the initiative of the Serbian Renewal Movement (SPO), which was the most influential opposition party at that time. On this occasion, the leaders of the 16 most important opposition parties agreed upon a joint strategy for obtaining early general elections, which led to the organising of a series of rallies in the spring of that year.[44]

To everyone's surprise, Milošević proceeded with changing the Yugoslav constitution in July 2000 and calling for early presidential elections to be held at the same time as the local and federal parliamentary elections scheduled for 24 September 2000. These constitutional amendments provided for the direct election of the Yugoslav president, who had until then been appointed by the federal legislature. In addition, the reform provided for the deputies in the Federal Assembly's upper chamber, the House of Republics, to be elected by direct vote instead of by the assemblies of Serbia and Montenegro.[45] This move effectively weakened the position of Montenegro's government, which had ideologically broken with Milošević in 1996, by preventing it from exercising control over the

41 Cohen, *Serpent in the Bosom*, 407.

42 Ibid.

43 CESID, 'Guide through Electoral Controversies in Serbia', July 2000, 79–80.

44 Ibid.

45 Cohen, *Serpent in the Bosom*, 402–4.

twenty seats allocated to Montenegro in the House of Republics.[46] As a result, the Montenegrin authorities decided to boycott the elections and declared void all acts of federal bodies made without the participation of their representatives. Finally, the electoral legislation enacted along with the new constitution transferred the two electoral units from Kosovo to the Serbian units of Prokuplje and Vranje, which contained large numbers of displaced persons from Kosovo who traditionally supported Milošević.[47]

The decision to modify the constitution and call for early presidential elections can be attributed to several factors. This reform primarily allowed Milošević, whose term in office was due to expire in July 2001, to run for two more terms and thus potentially stay in power until 2009.[48] The shift to a direct election of the Yugoslav president probably derived from Milošević's desire to increase his legitimacy abroad by showing that he remained a very popular and influential politician in Serbia. According to the former opposition leader Vesna Pešić, Milošević thus sought to challenge the international isolation and the ICTY indictment by demonstrating that he had the support of the Serbian population.[49] Moreover, the former Yugoslav President probably believed that he could still reap the majority of votes at a time when the regime was boasting about its victory over Western colonialism and its success in rebuilding the country.

The call for early presidential elections provided the opposition with the opportunity to challenge Milošević directly at the polls. The DOS coalition put forward Vojislav Koštunica, the leader of the Democratic Party of Serbia (DSS), as candidate for the elections. Although the DSS was a marginal opposition party throughout the nineties, Koštunica was deemed to stand the highest chances of defeating Milošević for several reasons. First of all, the DSS leader represented a moderate nationalist option which combined democratic principles with the defence of Serbian national interests.[50] Indeed, Koštunica was overtly critical of Western intervention in the Balkans, in particular with regard to Kosovo, but he also recognised the need to overcome the country's isolation. As a result, the DSS leader was deemed capable of covering a broad ideological spectrum and thus attracting voters who had previously opted for the SPS or SRS. Secondly, in view of his distance with regard to the West, Koštunica was largely spared from the slander

46 Indeed, instead of being appointed by the parliamentary majority in Montenegro, the deputies in the Upper Chamber would thereafter be split between the different parties according to the share of votes obtained at the elections. For Montenegro's schism with Milošević, see below.

47 Cohen, *Serpent in the Bosom*, 405.

48 It also made the removal of the president from office almost impossible (Cohen, *Serpent in the Bosom*, 403–4).

49 Personal interview with Vesna Pešić, former leader of the GSS, on 5 August 2009.

50 Cohen, *Serpent in the Bosom*, 430–35.

campaign which depicted opposition leaders as foreign henchmen.[51] Furthermore, unlike Drašković and Djindjić, the leaders of the SPO and the DS respectively, Koštunica had never become acquainted or negotiated with Milošević. As a result, he held the image of an uncompromising and incorruptible democrat, who was not tied to the West and could therefore safeguard Serbian national interests. Indeed, public opinion polls carried out in June 2000 suggested that Koštunica was the second most trusted leader after Milošević and that he could defeat Milošević if he were backed by a united opposition.[52]

For the first time since the introduction of pluralism in 1990, the opposition parties stood together, with the exception of Drašković's SPO who refused to endorse Koštunica and put forward its own candidate for the presidential elections.[53] This effectively turned the elections into a plebiscite on the rule of Milošević. However, considering the widespread distrust in the opposition, the political parties could hardly mobilise voters and achieve electoral victory on their own. In this context, civil society actors came to play a major role in rallying different segments of Serbian society. The student movement Otpor, which was formed in reaction to the regime's crackdown on the university in 1998, played a particularly important role in overcoming the fear and apathy that paralysed Serbian society.[54] Through its provocative actions against the regime, Otpor helped mobilise public opinion, particularly youth, against an increasingly repressive regime. In addition, the DOS coalition could rely on the support of the independent media, most of which were under the control of the municipalities that had fallen to the opposition in 1997.[55] It also benefited from the support of a large NGO network that promoted voter turnout and provided electoral oversight. These activities were coordinated and supported by Western donors who deployed a major democracy-assistance effort in Serbia from mid-1999 to late 2000.[56]

Following months of intense campaigning by opposition parties, student movements, NGOs and independent media for the electorate to oust Milošević at the polls, Koštunica and the DOS coalition achieved tremendous success at the elections. The opposition parties claimed victory in the first round of the elections, as Koštunica was reported to have won 52.54 per cent of the votes

---

51 Personal interview with Dragoljub Mićunović, DS executive and former Speaker of the Yugoslav Parliament (2000–2003), on 19 August 2009.

52 Cohen, *Serpent in the Bosom*, 412.

53 Ibid., 413.

54 For an analysis of Otpor's role in the removal of Milošević, see Slobodan Naumović, 'Otpor! et la "révolution électorale" en Serbie' (Otpor! and the 'Electoral Revolution' in Serbia), *Socio-anthropologie* (2009), 23/24: 41–73.

55 Eric Gordy, 'Serbia's Bulldozer Revolution: Conditions and Prospects', *Southeast European Politics* 1:2 (2000): 80.

56 Thomas Carothers, 'Ousting Foreign Strongmen: Lessons from Serbia', *Carnegie Endowment Policy Brief* 1:5 (2001): 1–7.

while 35.01 per cent were attributed to Milošević.[57] These results were challenged by the regime, which maintained that the DOS candidate won less than 50 per cent of the votes and called for a run-off between Koštunica and Milošević to be held two weeks later. The opposition responded by launching a campaign of civil disobedience and organising strikes, protests and roadblocks throughout the country. The wave of protests culminated in a mass rally which brought hundreds of thousands of people to the streets of Belgrade on 5 October, a day after the authorities had abruptly cancelled the presidential election of September 24. The protesters soon overpowered the police forces and took control over the parliament, the national television centre, and several other media outlets, as well as the headquarters of the SPS.[58] Deprived of the support of the army and security forces, which refused to intervene, Milošević was forced to step down and hand over power to Koštunica, who was sworn into office as president of Yugoslavia on 7 October 2000.

B. Transitional Compromises

The 'Bulldozer Revolution' that overthrew Milošević was surprisingly bloodless bearing in mind the violent and repressive policies that characterised his rule. Prior to the elections, the opposition leaders had unequivocally called for a peaceful transition to democracy, pledging that there would be no revanchism against the representatives of the former regime.[59] Following the events of 5 October, peaceful transfer of power was achieved at the cost of a series of compromises with the incumbent elites, which substantially influenced the process of regime change.

Institutional continuity and political cohabitation

The compromises with the former regime were set out on 6 October, when Koštunica secretly met with Milošević and the army Chief of Staff, Nebojša Pavković, on the initiative of the Russian Foreign Minister, Sergei Ivanov, who had arrived in Belgrade on that same day. The subject of this meeting remains a secret to this day. Koštunica and his associates claim that their discussion concerned exclusively the peaceful transfer of power, which materialised in Milošević recognising his

---

57 These results were based on the ballot count of the opposition parties and independent observers which monitored the elections (Cohen, *Serpent in the Bosom*, 438).

58 These events were dubbed 'Bulldozer Revolution' because the protesters used a wheel loader to charge the television building.

59 For a detailed account of the events that took place on 5 October 2000, see Dragan Bujošević and Ivan Radovanović, *The Fall of Milošević: The October 5th Revolution* (New York and Basingstoke: Palgrave Macmillan, 2003).

defeat and resigning shortly after this meeting.[60] As part of the deal, the Milošević family was ostensibly given some sort of political asylum in Russia, where his son immediately fled with large sums of money illicitly acquired during the previous decade. There were also unsubstantiated rumours that Koštunica promised Milošević that he would not be extradited to the ICTY.[61]

After securing Koštunica's presidential victory, the DOS coalition needed to assert its control over the executive. Since the functions of the Yugoslav president were limited to commanding the army and exerting an essentially symbolic role in foreign policy, the opposition needed to gain control over the Serbian and Yugoslav governments in order to actually rule the country. Although the DOS coalition won the federal legislative elections in Serbia, the parties of the former regime still retained a majority in the Federal Assembly thanks to the boycott of the elections by the Montenegrin ruling Democratic Party of Socialists (DPS).[62] The intention to preserve and reform the Yugoslav Federation and the urge to rejoin the club of international organisations led the DOS leaders to form a coalition government with Milošević's former ally in Montenegro – the Socialist People's Party (SNP) – instead of calling for new elections. While this deal extended the life of the Yugoslav Federation, it nonetheless came at a high cost. Indeed, the enduring influence of the SNP in the federal government later turned out to be a major obstacle to cooperation with the ICTY and the reform of the military.

The DOS coalition was also compelled to make a compromise with Milošević's SPS in order to take over control of the Serbian government, which constituted the most powerful branch of the executive. Although the elections had left the Serbian parliament unchanged, the Serbian government led by the SPS and SRS had lost any semblance of legitimacy following the events of 5 October. While the socialists were under no obligation to let early elections take place, they allegedly did so in exchange for the guarantee that the new government would not take supra-legal revenge on them or on their assets.[63] Following the removal of Milošević from power, the DOS coalition agreed to form a provisional Serbian government with the SPS and SPO until the early parliamentary elections scheduled on 24 December 2000. This provisional

60 Personal interview with Slobodan Samardžić, former advisor to President Koštunica, on 29 July 2009.

61 Vesna Pešić, 'Rekonstrukcija petooktobarskih zbivanja na osnovu memoarske i stručne literature' (Reconstruction of 5 October Events on the Basis of Memory and Expert Literature) in *Razvoj Demokratskih Ustanova u Srbiji – Deset Godina Posle*, edited by Dušan Pavlović (The Development of Democratic Institutions in Serbia – Ten Years After) (Belgrade: Heinrich Böll Foundation, 2010), 28.

62 Indeed, the pro-Milošević Montenegrin opposition Socialist People's Party won 19 of Montenegro's 20 seats in the Chamber of Republics and 28 seats in the 138-member Chamber of Citizens (Cohen, *Serpent in the Bosom*, 439).

63 Damjan Krnjević-Mišković, 'Serbia's Prudent Revolution', *Journal of Democracy* 12:3 (2001): 107.

government – colloquially called the 'three-headed' government – provided joint rule by the former regime and the new democratic coalition. Indeed, each function in government was shared by representatives of the three parties and decision-making was to be based on consensus.[64] At the same time, the Serbian President Milan Milutinović, who came from the SPS and was indicted by the ICTY for war crimes perpetrated in Kosovo, was allowed to remain in office until the end of his term in January 2002.[65]

In view of the deep divergences between these political parties, the cohabitation between the opposition and the former regime was highly dysfunctional and most decisions were taken informally at the level of the DOS coalition.[66] Nevertheless, participation in the provisional government allowed the SPS to preserve some degree of political legitimacy and authority. More importantly, it allowed the former regime to obstruct important reforms at a critical juncture and thus erode the momentum for a radical break with the past. Indeed, the SPS impeded the dismissal, requested by the DOS, of the head of the State Security Service, thus allowing the security structures of the former regime to reorganise and destroy evidence of wrongdoing in the three months following the overthrow of Milošević.[67]

This state of affairs generated ample frustration and discord within the DOS coalition. The provisional 'three-headed' government was allegedly established on the initiative of Koštunica, who insisted on respect of the existing legal framework and institutional procedures.[68] While this policy allowed for the peaceful transfer of power, it effectively prevented the dismantling of the former regime's security apparatus. As a matter of fact, Koštunica refused to resort to extra-legal measures in order to dismiss the State Security Chief, as requested by his coalition partners within the DOS. This led to the emergence of early divergences from the 'soft' approach to transition advocated by Koštunica among the DOS leaders who sought a radical break with the former regime.[69] These differences later proved to be insurmountable, which led to the fragmentation of the DOS coalition. However, bearing in mind that he was the only elected representative of the DOS coalition and, as the man who defeated Milošević, the most popular politician in the country, Koštunica's influence and political preferences prevailed in the early stages of regime change.

---

64 MIlića Uvalić, *Serbia's Transition: Towards a Better Future* (Basingstoke: Palgrave Macmillan, 2010), 118–19.

65 Milutinović surrendered to the ICTY shortly after the end of his term in office in January 2002. He was acquitted of all charges in February 2009.

66 Pešić, 'Rekonstrukcija petooktobarskih zbivanja', 27.

67 Uvalić, *Serbia's Transition*, 119; Pešić, 'Rekonstrukcija petooktobarskih zbivanja', 27.

68 Personal interview with Žarko Korać, leader of the Social Democratic Union and former Deputy Prime Minister in the DOS government, on 24 April 2009.

69 Vesna Pešić, 'Rekonstrukcija petooktobarskih zbivanja', 32; Personal interview with Momčilo Grubač, Yugoslav Minister of Justice 2000–2001, on 7 May 2009.

The safeguarding of the security apparatus

In addition to making compromises with the political representatives of the former regime in order to get hold of the executive, the DOS leaders struck a series of deals with the members of the security apparatus. Indeed, the opposition leaders had established contacts with representatives of the security sector prior to the events of 5 October in order to ensure that the armed forces would not interfere in the mass protests or attempt to assassinate the DOS representatives.[70] In this context, the DS leader Zoran Djindjić established links with the Special Operations Unit (JSO) which belonged to the Serbian State Security Service and effectively acted as Milošević's Praetorian Guard. On the other hand, Koštunica took advantage of his presidential function in order to forge a close relationship with the military.[71] He thus chose to keep in office the incumbent army Chief of Staff and the Chief of the Military Security Agency, which provoked indignation among the remaining DOS leaders. As a result of these deals, the Milošević-era security apparatus remained practically intact during the initial phase of the transition.

The opposition's compromise with the security structures of the former regime can be attributed to several factors. As noted above, the decision to negotiate with the main security actors was primarily motivated by the concern that the regime might resort to the use of force in order to prevent political changes. These fears proved to be substantiated, as there are reports that Milošević ordered the army to intervene on the night of 5–6 October.[72] The opposition's compromises with the incumbent security actors were thus essentially made out of necessity. According to Tim Edmunds, the DOS did not have the political confidence or the resources to take on Milošević's powerful security structures.[73] In this context, the subsequent maintenance of those structures can be imputed to both the lack of a clear strategy towards the security sector and the need to secure control and support within the state administration.[74]

In addition, the decision to preserve the existing security structures appears to have been partially driven by concern for the stability and integrity of the state. Upon settling in, the new Yugoslav authorities had to face an insurgency by an Albanian separatist guerrilla group in the Preševo valley, a region on the border with Kosovo. In those circumstances, reshuffling the army command was seen to be too delicate a task, as this could have affected the morale of the troops and the

70 Miloš Vasić, *Atentat na Zorana* (The Assassination of Zoran) (Belgrade: Politika, B92, Vreme, Narodna Knjiga, 2005), 16–30.

71 Timothy Edmunds, 'Intelligence Agencies and Democratisation: Continuity and Change in Serbia after Milošević', *Europe–Asia Studies* 60:1 (2008): 33–4.

72 This order was turned down by several high-ranking generals (Pešić, 'Rekonstrukcija petooktobarskih zbivanja', 29).

73 Edmunds, 'Intelligence Agencies and Democratisation', 34.

74 Personal interview with Miroslav Hadžić, Professor of Global and National Security at the University of Belgrade, on 26 August 2008.

operations on the ground.[75] On top of this, Koštunica's decision to keep the military executive in office was rationalised by the need to seek Montenegrin approval prior to reshuffling the army command.[76] Since the Montenegrin government continued to boycott the Yugoslav institutions, such approval could not be granted.

Finally, the deals struck separately by various opposition representatives with security actors may have been motivated by the DOS leaders' desire to secure a power base within the security sector in anticipation of subsequent political struggles among themselves. Indeed, the DOS was a heterogeneous coalition whose representatives disagreed on almost everything but the removal of Milošević. In those circumstances, it was to be expected that the DOS leaders would subsequently compete for power. Therefore, the compromises made on 5 October allowed both Koštunica and Djindjić to gain the allegiance of different segments of the security sector, which constituted a major asset for building up political influence in the post-Milošević era.

These relationships established in the early phase of regime change led to the building of enduring alliances between sections of the civil and security sectors, which effectively hindered the reform of the armed forces. As a result, the transitional authorities could not establish full control over the security apparatus for years after the removal of Milošević. Indeed, the subsequent reforms of the security sector were essentially limited to changes among the low-ranking personnel. According to Miroslav Hadžić, the new elites thus effectively accepted the reorganisation of Milošević's repressive apparatus as a replacement for reform.[77] In the long run, this state of affairs limited the capacity of the Serbian authorities to arrest war crimes suspects and made the transfer of indictees to the ICTY a potential risk for domestic stability.

***

All things considered, the overthrow of Milošević appears to have materialised as a result of both popular mobilisation (at the elections and protests) and defection within the ranks of the regime.[78] However, the 'Bulldozer Revolution' was by

75 Personal interview with Ivan Vujačić, DS executive and former Yugoslav Ambassador to the US, on 17 July 2009.

76 Personal interview with Slobodan Samardžić.

77 Miroslav Hadžić, 'Izvorni Razlozi za Reformu' (The Genuine Reasons for Reform) in *Reforma vojske – Iskustva i izazovi* (Reform of the Army – Experiences and Challenges), edited by Miroslav Hadžić (Belgrade: CCMR, 2003), 112–17.

78 The downfall of Milošević was largely imputed to the shift of allegiance of the economic elites who had completed the primary accumulation of capital in the nineties. Accordingly, these tycoons had a vested interest in establishing stability and putting an end to the country's international isolation in order to advance their economic interests. See Mladen Lazić 'Nacrt za istraživanje savremenih društvenih promena u Srbiji' (Framework for the Study of Contemporary Social Changes in Serbia) in *Konsolidacija demokratskih ustanova u Srbiji*, edited by Pavlović, 13–37.

no means a 'pacted' transition. Indeed, 5 October was certainly not a coup since the armed forces defected only after the regime's electoral fiasco and the staging of mass protests by the opposition. While the regime was weakened, it still had considerable assets and would certainly not have crumbled without the 'push' of the opposition.[79]

Nevertheless, the peaceful transfer of power was achieved at the cost of a series of compromises with the representatives of the former regime and the incumbent security actors. The political compromises embodied in the Serbian 'three-headed' provisional government significantly watered down the revolutionary momentum and prevented a clear break with the past. They also allowed the representatives of the former regime to transcend regime change by maintaining a semblance of legitimacy, thus getting the opportunity to participate in politics in the new democratic regime. More importantly, the deals struck with security actors led to the maintenance of the old structures of power, which would constitute a major source of instability for the transitional authorities.

3. Challenges of Consolidation: Political Polarisation and Precarious Stateness

Throughout the former communist states of Central and Eastern Europe, the process of democratic consolidation was driven by Euro-Atlantic integration. In those countries, the societal consensus over the basic national and foreign policy issues, as well as the absence of enduring conflicts over state sovereignty, allowed the successive governments to proceed with tackling the challenges of the 'triple transition' at a relatively early stage.[80]

In the Serbian case, the transition away from authoritarianism did not lead to the prompt emergence of a consensus over the country's geopolitical orientation or the establishment of a stable political environment which would allow for rapid democratic consolidation. The divisive legacy of Milošević's rule and the pervasiveness of political forces that embodied the former regime acted as major obstacles to political reform. In addition, the sovereignty of the Serbian (Yugoslav) state was continuously challenged by separatism in Montenegro and Kosovo, while its legitimacy was hampered by the war crimes legacy. In those circumstances, the processes of democratisation and Europeanisation proved to be much more difficult in Serbia than in most CEE countries. In this section, I develop an account of democratic consolidation in Serbia by focusing on two key

---

79 Bunce and Wolchik, 'A Comparison of Slovakia and Serbia', 153.

80 Claus Offe, 'Capitalism by Democratic Design? Democratic Theory Facing the Triple Transition in Eastern Europe', *Social Research* 58:4 (1991): 865–92; Milada Anna Vachudova, 'Democratisation in Postcommunist Europe: Illiberal Regimes and the Leverage of the European Union', in *Democracy and Authoritarianism in the Postcommunist World*, edited by Valerie Bunce, Michael McFaul, and Kathryn Stoner-Weiss, 82–106.

challenges faced by the successive democratic governments: political polarisation and the 'stateness' problem.[81]

A. Elite-Pacting and Party Politics

The Democratic Opposition of Serbia (DOS), which brought down Milošević and took over the reins of power, was a heterogeneous political coalition grouping eighteen parties of different ideological orientations. These parties shared the common aims of removing Milošević from power, implementing democratic and economic reforms and reintegrating Serbia into the international community.[82] While this common platform provided the DOS coalition with a sense of unity, the divergences among its constitutive parties were nonetheless considerable. According to the former leader of the Civic Alliance of Serbia, Goran Svilanović, the failure to make a radical break with the former regime in the wake of 5 October resulted from the fact that the opposition parties had substantially different views on Milošević's rule:

> In order to bring about change, in order to create a majority, it was necessary to assemble all those who were against Milošević's national policy since the beginning, plus those who actually supported this policy but were disappointed with its outcomes, so they saw him as someone who could no longer realise this policy, plus those who thought that the cost of realising this policy was too high. ... In order to bring about change, all this had to be assembled, and all this together does not entail a substantial abandonment of that policy. This in fact explains why there was no '6 October'. ... So Milošević was removed, there was a consensus on that, but there was no consensus that his policy was fundamentally wrong.[83]

Besides ruling out a radical break with the past, the lack of consensus over Milošević's legacy also undermined the coherence and unity of the DOS coalition at an early stage, owing notably to foreign pressures for cooperation with the ICTY. As shown in this section, the rivalry among the new elites opened the way for the lasting polarisation of the Serbian political scene, which acted as a major obstacle to the institutional reforms necessary for the consolidation of democracy.

---

81 For a definition and discussion of the 'stateness' problem in democratic consolidation, see Juan J. Linz and Alfred Stepan, *Problems of Democratic Transition and Consolidation* (Baltimore and London: The Johns Hopkins University Press, 1996), 16–37.

82 Vladimir Goati, *Partijske borbe u Srbiji u postoktobarskom razdoblju* (Party Struggles in Serbia in the Post-October Period) (Belgrade: Friedrich Ebert Stiftung and Institute of Social Sciences, 2006), 225.

83 Personal interview with Goran Svilanović, former leader of the Civic Alliance of Serbia (GSS) and Foreign Minister 2000–2003, on 23 May 2009.

Political rivalry and institutional instability

The DOS coalition consolidated its rule through the parliamentary elections of December 2000, which brought it 176 out of the 250 seats in the Serbian parliament (see Table 1 in Appendix). This overwhelming parliamentary majority brought hopes that the DOS could proceed without encumbrance with the implementation of reforms and the adoption of a new constitution. The DS leader, Zoran Djindjić, was elected Prime Minister on the basis of an earlier agreement between the DOS leaders. The remaining cabinet positions were distributed among the DOS representatives according to a coalition agreement struck prior to the elections.[84]

This distribution of power generated considerable frustration within the DSS which was allocated 45 seats in parliament, but only two positions in the Serbian government. Since Koštunica had won the Yugoslav presidential elections, his party experienced an exponential increase in popularity and party membership. Indeed, after the downfall of the Milošević regime, many SPS and SRS supporters switched allegiance to the DSS because of its ideological proximity in terms of attitudes towards the international community and the ICTY.[85] Public opinion polls carried out in 2001 showed that the DSS was by far the most popular party as it had the support of 29.8 per cent of the electorate. The DS came second with 14 per cent of support, while the SPS and SRS respectively had the support of 9.6 and 7.4 per cent of the electorate.[86] In view of this, there was a substantial discrepancy between the DSS's popularity and its representation in government. This led the DSS to demand a government reshuffle in mid-2001, which was opposed by the remaining parties of the DOS coalition.[87]

The DSS's frustration with its share of power exacerbated the latent tensions between this party and the DS, which was the most influential entity within the DOS coalition. These tensions emanated essentially from radically different views on the pace, scope and modalities of the reforms to be implemented. As noted above, the DSS, embodied in the Yugoslav president Koštunica, advocated a policy of gradual reforms within the legal and institutional framework inherited from the former regime, which they labelled 'legalism'.[88] This policy necessarily implied a degree of continuity with the former regime, as it did not call into question the legitimacy of institutions and political parties associated with Milošević. On the

84 Goati, *Partijske borbe u Srbiji*, 226.

85 Vladimir Goati, 'Partije Srbije od 1990 do 2002 u komparativnoj perspektivi' (Parties in Serbia from 1990 to 2002 in Comparative Perspective) in *Partijska scena Srbije posle 5 Oktobra 2000* (The Party Scene in Serbia after 5 October 2000), edited by Vladimir Goati (Belgrade: Friedrich Ebert Stiftung and Institute of Social Sciences, 2002), 9–45.

86 Goati, *Partijske borbe u Srbiji*, 227.

87 Ibid.

88 Vojislav Koštunica, 'Pravna država i prav(n)i reformizam' (The Legal State and Legal (Real) Reformism), *Nova srpska politička misao*, special issue 1(2001), 147–56; personal interview with Slobodan Samardžić.

other hand, the DS, led by the Serbian Prime Minister Djindjić, stood for a radical break with the former regime, even if this had to be done at the cost of infringing the legal and institutional procedures which they considered illegitimate. This was a policy of discontinuity which sought to achieve a rapid modernisation of the Serbian state.[89]

These irreconcilable views on the transformation of the Serbian state called into question the coherence and unity of the DOS coalition at an early stage. Djindjić's position as Prime Minister and influence over his coalition partners initially allowed him to proceed with the implementation of reforms envisaged by the DS regardless of the opposition of the DSS. Indeed, decision-making on the most important issues was transferred from state institutions to the DOS presidency, where small parties allied to the DS had disproportionate weight.[90] This state of affairs was obviously against the interests of the DSS, which increasingly advocated the disbanding of the DOS coalition and the establishment of a 'genuine party system'.[91] Koštunica and his party openly distanced themselves from the rest of the DOS coalition following the transfer of Milošević to the ICTY, which was engineered by Djindjić in June 2001. According to most observers, this event constituted the breaking-point between the DSS and the rest of the DOS (see Chapter 3). The split within the ruling coalition was formalised in August 2001 as the DSS withdrew from the Serbian government on the basis that the government was failing to tackle organised crime.[92]

The withdrawal of the DSS did not undermine the DOS government, which could still rely on a narrow majority in parliament. However, it did put an end to the unity of the so-called 'democratic bloc', which imposed substantial constraints on the implementation of reforms promoted by Djindjić, who increasingly resorted to extra-governmental institutions and decrees in order to bypass parliament.[93] The DSS increasingly sought to discredit the government by publicly accusing the DOS of corruption and links with the criminal underworld. At the same time, the DOS coalition attempted to undermine the authority of the DSS, notably by withdrawing that party's parliamentary seats in the summer of 2002. As a result of this premature electoral competition among the new elites, the DOS government was prevented from carrying out institutional reforms necessary for the consolidation of democracy. In view of the opposition of the DSS and the parties emanating from the former regime, the Serbian authorities were unable to

---

89 Zoran Djindjić, 'Adrenalin za promene' (Adrenaline for Change), *Nova srpska politička misao*, special issue 1(2001), 87–94; Goati, *Partijske borbe u Srbiji*, 228.

90 Kesić, 'Serbia after Milošević', 107–8.

91 Koštunica, 'Pravna država', 155–6.

92 This decision followed the assassination of a state-security official – Momir Gavrilović – after a visit to President Koštunica, which led to a series of mutual accusations between the DS and DSS. Out of the 17 parties that formed the DOS coalition, the only one to side with Koštunica was New Serbia (NS) (Goati, *Partijske borbe u Srbiji*, 227).

93 Kesić, 'Serbia after Milošević', 108.

introduce a new constitution and substantially reform the judiciary, security and media sectors.[94] Moreover, the quarrels and scandals that plagued the political elites generated widespread disillusion and political apathy among the population, as illustrated by the failure to elect a new Serbian president owing to insufficient turnout in autumn 2002.[95]

The political struggle between the DSS and the rest of the DOS turned into an institutional conflict as the different sides increasingly resorted to the use of security agencies under their command in order to undermine their opponents. As noted above, the transitional compromises struck in the wake of 5 October led to the establishment of clientistic relationships between the new political elites and the incumbent security personnel.[96] While the army and the Military Security Service were loyal to President Koštunica, the Prime Minister Djindjić benefited from the support of the police and, until November 2001, the Serbian State Security Service (See Chapter 3). These competing security structures, which remained staffed with Milošević's cronies and were heavily linked to the criminal underworld, exploited the divisions among the political elites in order to strengthen their positions and obstruct the reform of the security apparatus. During 2001 and 2002, the intelligence agencies played a particularly important role in the outbreak of a series of scandals through which both sides sought to discredit each other.[97] But Djindjić's commitment to tackling organised crime and cooperating with the ICTY turned large segments of the security apparatus against his government and himself. This tragically resulted in the assassination of the Serbian Prime Minister in March 2003 by former members of the State Security Service (see Chapter 3).

The government responded swiftly to this attack by declaring a state of emergency and implementing the police campaing known as 'Operation Sabre', which sought to deal a blow to organised crime and purge state institutions of rogue elements. Besides arresting the prime suspects in the assassination of Djindjić, this massive crackdown on organised crime brought to light the close connections between criminals, state institutions and political elites.[98] This led to a massive purge of the judiciary and the arrests of thousands of people. At the same time,

---

94 Mladen Lazić, *Promene i Otpori* ('Changes and Resistance') (Belgrade: Filip Višnjić, 2005), 132.

95 According to Serbian electoral law at that time, an election could only be validated if turnout exceeded 50 per cent of the population.

96 Edmunds argues that politicians were reluctant to tackle the reform of the sector, both because of their own divisions and weaknesses and for fear of a backlash from within the agencies themselves. In his view, the delays in reforming the security apparatus resulted from the practical recognition on the part of the government itself of the limits of its own authority rather than from a desire to compromise with, or incorporate, the old Milošević elites (Edmunds, 'Intelligence Agencies and Democratisation', 36–7).

97 Pešić, 'Rekonstrukcija petooktobarskih zbivanja', 33–8.

98 Vjeran Pavlaković, 'Serbia Transformed? Political Dynamics in the Milošević Era and After', in *Serbia since 1989*, edited by Ramet and Pavlaković, 39–40.

the authorities established special institutions for the prosecution of organised crime and war crimes, which spurred investigations into political murders under Milošević and greatly increased the ability of the domestic judiciary to tackle war crimes (see Chapter 5). During this period, the army and security services were brought under tighter civilian control, while the rogue elements were disbanded. These reforms were made possible by the transformation of the Federal Republic of Yugoslavia into the State Union of Serbia and Montenegro, which allowed the DS to take control over the army (see below).

The assassination of Djindjić and 'Operation Sabre' led to renewed popular support for the DOS government and its reformist policies. However, this increase in popularity soon gave way to cynicism and disillusion as the government got embroiled in corruption scandals and accusations of abuse of power.[99] Koštunica's DSS, which was left without any position in government as a result of the establishment of the State Union of Serbia and Montenegro, increasingly acted in conjunction with the SPS and SRS in undermining the government.[100] The attacks of the opposition and the internal squabbles which emerged as a result of the leadership void eventually led to the collapse of the DOS coalition in autumn 2003.

Polarised pluralism as an impediment to political change

As shown above, the split between the DSS and the DOS coalition led to the emergence of a tripolar party system on the Serbian political scene shortly after the removal of Milošević. Indeed, the absence of any semblance of reform within the SPS and SRS, which clung to the national-populist discourse of the former regime, protracted the dichotomy between 'un-democratic' and 'democratic' parties. At the same time, the break-up of the DOS led to the emergence of a reformist bloc grouped around the DS and a national-conservative option embodied in the DSS.[101]

As a result of these developments, the Serbian party system increasingly bore features of 'polarised pluralism'.[102] Indeed, during most of the post-October period, the Serbian party system was characterised by the presence of anti-system parties, the existence of bilateral and irresponsible oppositions, and the absence of political consensus over fundamental issues among political elites.[103] The anti-system parties were embodied in the SPS and SRS which considered the political order illegitimate since they regarded the 5 October events as a 'violent coup'

99 Kesić, 'Serbia after Milošević', 115–16.

100 Goati, *Partijske borbe u Srbiji*, 234.

101 Zoran Stojiljković, 'Partijska scena Srbije' (The Party Scene in Serbia) in *5 godina tranzicije u Srbiji* (5 Years of Transition in Serbia), edited by Srećko Mihajlović (Belgrade: Friedrich Ebert Stiftung and Socijaldemokratski klub, 2005), 96.

102 For the concept of 'polarised pluralism', see Giovanni Sartori, *Parties and Party Systems: A Framework for Analysis* (Colchester: ECPR Press, 2005), 116–28.

103 Goati, *Partijske borbe u Srbiji*, 225.

and sought to restore the former regime.[104] In view of this, there was clearly no consensus on democracy being 'the only game in town' in the aftermath of the removal of Milošević. Consequently, the divergences between the parties emanating from the former regime and the DSS were greater than the differences between the DSS and the DOS, which greatly limited the capacity of the opposition to cooperate. By the same token, the capacity of the SPS and SRS to participate in government was extremely limited in view of their diminished electoral support and small coalition potential.

The early parliamentary elections held in December 2003 brought a radical shift in the balance of power on the Serbian political scene (see Table 2 in Appendix). The right-wing SRS, which had been practically wiped out two years earlier, emerged as the largest single party by obtaining almost one third of all parliamentary seats (82 out of 250). This political resurrection came mainly as a result of the Radicals' success in portraying themselves as champions of social causes. Indeed this party drew most of its support from socially disadvantaged categories that were the primary 'losers' of the transition, such as pensioners, low-skilled workers, and those populations living in deprived rural and semi-urban areas.[105] Koštunica's DSS came second with 53 parliamentary seats, which allowed it to claim a leading position within the democratic bloc. Out of the seventeen remaining parties that formed the DOS coalition, only the DS and G17 entered parliament with a similar number of seats (36 and 34 respectively). New Serbia (NS) and the Serbian Renewal Movement (SPO) had formed a pre-electoral coalition and won 22 seats. So did the SPS, whose electoral support thus declined further compared to the previous elections.

The revival of the SRS, which was perceived as a threat to democratic consolidation, allowed the DSS to play a central role on the Serbian political scene as a pivot between the parties emanating from the DOS coalition and those emanating from the former regime. Koštunica took advantage of this position to create a minority government composed of the DSS, SPO–NS and G17, with the support of the SPS in parliament. This political arrangement explicitly sought to exclude the DS from government as the DSS insisted on the need for discontinuity with the previous cabinet which it denounced for being corrupt and for infringing the rule of law in 'Operation Sabre'.[106] But excluding the DS required making a deal with the SPS, which came at a high political cost for the parties in government.

104 Public opinion polls show that this view was extensively shared by their supporters. In 2007, only 15 per cent of the followers of the SRS and 16 per cent of the supporters of the SPS considered democracy to be the optimal political order [Dušan Spasojević, 'Dinamika političkih rascepa u Srbiji 2000–2010' (Dynamics of Political Cleavages in Serbia 2000–2010) in *Partije i izbori u Srbiji – 20 godina* (Parties and Elections in Serbia – 20 years), edited by Čedomir Čupić (Belgrade: Friedrich Ebert Stiftung, Faculty of Political Sciences of the University of Belgrade and Centre for Democracy, 2011), 113].

105 Stojiljković, 'Partijska scena Srbije', 90.

106 Goati, *Partijske borbe u Srbiji*, 234.

Indeed, public opinion polls carried out three months after the establishment of the government show that the DS emerged as the second most popular party with 17.9 per cent of electoral support, while support for the DSS and G17 dropped to 10.4 and 4 per cent respectively.[107] These observations are corroborated by the victory of the DS leader, Boris Tadić, in the Serbian presidential elections over the SRS candidate Tomislav Nikolić in June 2004. The election of Tadić was a blow for the governing coalition, which put forward a common candidate who did not even make it into the second round. The presidential function allowed Tadić and the DS to act as a counter-weight to the policies and discourses deployed by the government.

These policies constituted in many ways a step backwards in comparison to the previous government, particularly with regard to cooperation with the ICTY, which was brought to a standstill owing to the opposition of the DSS, NS and SPS to the arrest and transfer of war crimes suspects to The Hague (see Chapter 3). The suspension of ICTY cooperation strained Serbia's relations with the international community. As a result of this, the US suspended financial and technical assistance to Serbia and practically reintroduced the 'outer wall' of sanctions by withdrawing their support to Serbia in international financial institutions. The EU also pressed the Serbian authorities to cooperate with the ICTY by conditioning progress in accession talks upon the transfer of indictees to the Tribunal. This deterioration in diplomatic relations with the West was accompanied by a drastic reduction in the inflow of foreign direct investment which was practically halved between 2003 and 2004.[108]

The introduction of the policy of 'voluntary surrender', which led to the transfer of 16 indictees between the end of 2004 and 2005 allowed for short-lived, but nonetheless significant, progress in terms of European integration (see Chapter 3). Indeed, the European Commission opened the door for the country's process of integration into the EU by adopting a positive Feasibility Study for Serbia-Montenegro in April 2005. At the same time, the Serbian Parliament adopted a National Strategy for Accession to the EU, which boosted the government's pro-European credentials.[109] Nevertheless, the failure to capture General Mladić and transfer him to the ICTY led to renewed suspension of EU accession talks in May 2006. This generated considerable friction within the government, which resulted in the collapse of the ruling coalition and the dissolution of parliament, after the major political parties had agreed upon enacting a new Serbian constitution in autumn 2006.[110]

107 Ibid., 239.

108 Ibid., 233–9.

109 Ibid., 245.

110 The new constitution was jointly crafted by the DSS, DS, SRS and SPS. It was extensively criticised for stating in the preamble that Kosovo was and should remain a part of Serbia, thus preventing any future recognition of Kosovo's independence by the Serbian authorities. Also, many irregularities were reported during the referendum, whose outcome

While the January 2007 parliamentary elections confirmed the supremacy of the Serbian Radical Party with 81 seats in parliament, they shifted the balance of power within the 'democratic bloc' towards the DS, which emerged second with 64 seats (see Table 3 in Appendix). Tadić's party prevailed over the 'Populist Coalition' grouping Koštunica's DSS and New Serbia (NS), which received 47 seats. After three months of painstaking negotiations, these two groupings formed a government together with the G17, which had got 19 parliamentary seats. In spite of the fact that DS held more parliamentary seats than the DSS, Koštunica was given the mandate to lead the new government. The DSS thus continued to exert disproportionate influence on the Serbian political scene by taking advantage of its pivotal position between the DS and G17 on the one hand and the SPS and SRS on the other.[111]

The new government resumed negotiations with the EU following the transfer of two indictees to the ICTY in June 2007 (see Chapter 3). However, Serbia's EU accession talks came to a new standstill as the EU conditioned the signing of the Stabilisation and Accession Agreement (SAA) upon the arrest of Mladić. While this represented a major setback for the government's European agenda, the most sensitive issue for the ruling coalition concerned the status of Kosovo, as the Kosovo Albanian authorities were set to declare independence.[112] Although there was a wide consensus amongst Serbian politicians that the 'defence' of Kosovo constituted a priority in terms of national interests, there were major differences with regard to how the government should respond to the forthcoming declaration of independence. While the 'Populist Coalition' suggested that Serbia should freeze diplomatic relations with all entities that recognised an independent Kosovo, including the EU, the DS and G17 considered that straining relations with the EU would be counter-productive.[113] Relations between the two factions deteriorated as Koštunica refused to support Tadić in his renewed bid for the Serbian presidency in January 2008. In spite of this, the DS candidate won a second mandate through a run-off in which his opponent from the SRS received a record number of votes.[114] As Kosovo declared independence on 17 February, the rift between the two political groupings within the ruling coalition increased, which resulted in the collapse of the government and the dissolution of parliament in March 2008.

---

was contested owing to extremely low turn-out (International Crisis Group, 'Serbia's New Constitution: Democracy Going Backwards', Policy Briefing No. 44, November 2006. Accessed on www.crisisgroup.org on 20 January 2011).

111 During the negotiations on the creation of a coalition government with the DS and G17, the DSS flirted extensively with the SRS. Most notably, the DSS voted for the SRS leader Tomislav Nikolić to become President of the Serbian Assembly, a post which he held for only five days in May 2007.

112 International Crisis Group, 'Serbia's New Government: Turning from Europe', 31 May 2007. Accessed on www.crisisgroup.org on 20 January 2011.

113 'Oštrenje i zaoštravanje' (Sharpening and Toughening Up), *Vreme*, 17 January 2008.

114 'Tadić Wins Serbian Presidential Race', *Balkan Insight*, 3 February 2008.

The 2008 elections as a turning point

The suspension of EU accession talks and the escalation in rhetoric over Kosovo generated renewed polarisation on the Serbian political scene. The split between the DS and DSS over Serbia's response to Kosovo's declaration of independence brought an end to the short-lived unity of the democratic bloc, just as the disagreement over cooperation with the ICTY had led to the break-up of the DOS coalition seven years earlier. However, unlike in 2001, this political crisis spurred political mobilisation, as illustrated by the record turnout at the 2008 presidential elections, in which 67 per cent of voters participated in the second round.[115]

The diametrically opposed positions of the leading political parties towards the EU effectively turned the parliamentary elections of May 2008 into a referendum on Serbia's European integration. On the one hand, the DSS advocated Serbia severing ties with the EU in response to the recognition of Kosovo by most member states. This position was shared by the SRS and, to a lesser extent, the SPS, which declared itself against European integration if that meant giving up Kosovo or transferring indictees to the ICTY.[116] On the other hand, the DS formed the coalition 'For a European Serbia' (ZES) with the G17, the SPO and several small parties. This political grouping argued that joining the EU would increase Serbia's chances of preserving Kosovo and improving the population's living standards. In other words, the DS-led coalition presented these elections as a referendum over the European perspective, bringing Kosovo and the EU on the same ticket.[117] The Liberal-Democratic Party (LDP) also had an explicitly pro-European stance, but it advocated a conciliatory policy towards Kosovo's independence.

The ZES coalition emerged victorious in the parliamentary elections, thus becoming the most powerful political grouping in the country with 102 seats in parliament (see Table 4 in Appendix). The SRS maintained a high profile by obtaining 78 seats, while the DSS-NS coalition experienced a significant decline by losing a third of its parliamentary seats compared to the previous elections. To everyone's surprise, the SPS made a small comeback by entering into coalition with the Party of Serbian Unity (SSJ) and the pensioners' party (PUPS). Finally, the LDP won 13 seats, which was not enough for creating a government with ZES. This electoral outcome did not produce any clear winner since the pro-European coalition did not have enough parliamentary seats to form a government, while the parties opposing EU integration suffered a significant electoral setback. Although the DSS attempted to forge a majority with the SRS and the coalition grouped around the SPS, the latter eventually decided to form a government with ZES in what constituted the most dramatic *volte-face* in contemporary Serbian

115 Eric Gordy, 'Serbia Chooses a Future, Just', *openDemocracy*, 5 February 2008. Accessed on www.opendemocracy.net on 20 May 2011.

116 Sofia Sebastian, 'Serbia's 2008 Parliamentary Elections: Domestic and Regional Dilemmas', FRIDE, 28 April 2008, 5. Accessed on www.fride.org on 20 May 2011.

117 Ibid.

politics.[118] This decision was largely informed by promises of support to a pro-European government by Western diplomats. These promises were substantiated by the EU's decision to sign the SAA with Serbia on the eve of the elections, which boosted the electoral prospects of the ZES and tipped the balance within the SPS-led coalition towards forming a pro-European government.

The victory of the ZES and the creation of a pro-European government with the SPS produced substantial change on the Serbian political landscape. Since October 2000, Serbia had experienced a distorted party system characterised by the existence of a permanent ruling political block derived from the parties that opposed the regime of Milošević and a permanent opposition formed of parties that represented the former regime.[119] While the SPS had provided support to Koštunica's first minority government in 2004, it could not fully take part in that government owing to the stigma associated with its role in the former regime.[120] Since it had lost power, the SPS experienced partial reform as the modernist factions within the party gradually took over leadership, especially following the death of Milošević in 2006. But while it formally endorsed European integration, the SPS never renounced the legacy of Milošević.

The creation of a coalition government with the ZES was therefore a very delicate move both for the DS and the SPS. This move was made even more controversial by the adoption of a joint Declaration of Reconciliation in which these two parties pledged to leave the divisive past behind for the sake of building Serbia's future prosperity.[121] The adoption of this Declaration was accompanied by flamboyant statements in which the DS leaders sought to create parallels between the deaths of Milošević and Djindjić, and between the SPS's role on the Serbian political scene in the nineties and that of the DS in the 2000s.[122] This political pact, which was portrayed as a basis for national reconciliation, thus allowed for the rehabilitation of the SPS and its establishment as a fully legitimate political actor in the democratic order. For the DS, this constituted a necessary evil for overcoming its dependency on the DSS, which had completed a radical shift to the right. The DS and the SPS sought to emphasise their newly discovered affinities by increasingly portraying themselves as left-leaning parties.

---

118 'Trnoviti put ka Nemanjinoj 11' (Spiny Path to Nemanjina 11), *Vreme*, 26 June 2008.

119 Srdjan Cvijić, '"Blocked Political System": Serbia 2000–2008', *Balkanologie* XI, nos. 1–2 (2008). Accessed on http://balkanologie.revues.org/index1293.html on 12 May 2011.

120 Personal interview with Slobodan Samardžić.

121 Democratic Party and Socialist Party of Serbia, 'Deklaracija o pomirenju' (Declaration of Reconciliation). Retrieved from http://b92.net/info/dokumenti/ on 9 June 2009.

122 'Tadić: Poštovati volju gradjana' (Tadić: The Will of the Citizens Must Be Respected), *B92*, 2 June 2008; 'Ruka pomirenjea socijalistima' (The Hand of Reconciliation to the Socialists), *Večernje Novosti*, 8 June 2008.

The transformation of the Serbian party system was further advanced through the break-up of the right-wing SRS in September 2008. The split within Serbia's biggest political party occurred as a result of deep divergences over EU integration between the hard-liners loyal to the party President and ICTY indictee, Vojislav Šešelj, and the more moderate Deputy President and acting leader, Tomislav Nikolić.[123] Nikolić, who supported the ratification of the SAA, broke away from the SRS and created the Serbian Progressive Party (SNS), which soon overtook the SRS in terms of political influence and public support.[124] In an attempt to enhance their democratic credentials, the SNS representatives subsequently sought to portray themselves as an explicitly pro-European conservative party, notably by renouncing the ideology of 'Greater Serbia' and acknowledging the massacre of Srebrenica.[125]

These developments brought an end to the dichotomy between 'former regime/nationalist–authoritarian' and 'former opposition/democratic' parties which had persisted on the Serbian political scene since the overthrow of Milošević. The Serbian party system increasingly bore a resemblance to 'moderate pluralism', characterised by relatively small ideological distance and bipolar coalitions on a left–right scale.[126] At the same time, these developments led to the emergence of a broad consensus on European integration among political actors. These observations suggest that, by the end of the 2000s, the Serbian political scene was in the process of stabilisation and 'normalisation' which constituted a major step towards democratic consolidation.

B. Problems of Stateness and the Prevalence of National Issues

The lengthy process of stabilisation and normalisation of the Serbian political scene is to a great extent imputable to problems of stateness and the prevalence of national issues on the Serbian political scene.[127] Slobodan Milošević rose to power in the late eighties with the promise to solve the Serbian national question. His policies not only fuelled secessionism and ethnic conflict in the region, but

123 'Radikalno raspadanje' (Radical Breakdown), *Vreme*, 11 September 2008.

124 Public opinion polls carried out by the Medium Galup group in February 2010 showed that the DS and SNS were the two most popular parties with 30.6 and 29.9 per cent of voting intentions respectively. Support for the SRS dropped to 8.3 per cent ('Mrtva trka DS I SNS, većina za EU' (Close Race between the DS and SNS, Majority for the EU), *NSPM*, 11 February 2010).

125 'SNS: Kraj ideje Velike Srbije' (SNS: The End of the Idea of 'Greater Serbia'), *B92*, 1 November 2008; 'Vučić: U Srebrenici se dogodio strašan zločin' (Vučić: A Terrible Crime Took Place in Srebrenica), *Blic*, 21 January 2010.

126 Spasojević, 'Dinamika političkih rascepa', 113–14.

127 Linz and Stepan define 'stateness' problems as 'profound differences about the territorial boundaries of the political community's state and profound differences as to who has the right of citizenship in that state' (Linz and Stepan, *Problems of Democratic Transition*, 16).

they also left Serbia in an institutional limbo. Indeed, Milošević's split with the Montenegrin authorities rendered the FRY dysfunctional, while Kosovo was under international administration with no prospect of being reintegrated into Serbia. Along with the war crimes legacy, the problems of stateness constituted the most important challenges for the transitional authorities. In the words of Goran Svilanović, these national issues dominated the agenda of every government in the 2000s:

> What were the issues for the government? For both Djindjić and Koštunica, and especially for Koštunica, who was Prime Minister in two governments, these were: relations between Serbia and Montenegro, the status of Kosovo, pressure from the ICTY, the Bosnian and Croatian genocide lawsuits, and Serbia not having a constitution. I have mentioned six priorities, among which there is no E for Economy and there is no E for EU. ... The situation now is that Montenegro is independent, Kosovo has declared independence around which a diplomatic battle is being waged, the Tribunal is near the end of its work, the constitution has been adopted, and the [Bosnian] genocide lawsuit has been adjudicated. It is only now that you have a situation in which the priority is the economy or the EU, after nine years! So Serbia is only now in a position in which any other Central European country was during the transition.[128]

The pervasiveness of national issues distracted the focus of politics from pressing socio-economic problems experienced by the population, which further contributed to political apathy and support for nationalist parties. In this section, I give a brief overview of Serbia's relations with Montenegro and the problems associated with Kosovo's status in the 2000s.

Relations with Montenegro

Milošević's rule left Serbia in a troubled relationship with its counterpart in the Federal Republic of Yugoslavia (FRY). Montenegro's ruling party, the Democratic Party of Socialists (DPS), ideologically broke off from Milošević and turned to the West after Milo Djukanović took over its leadership in 1996.[129] Milošević's unreserved support for Djukanović's rival, Momir Bulatović, whom he appointed Federal Prime Minister against Djukanović's will, led the Montenegrin authorities to withdraw from federal institutions. The Montenegrin government subsequently took over most of the functions of the federal institutions, and thus practically

128 Personal interview with Goran Svilanović.

129 Reneo Lukić, 'From the Federal Republic of Yugoslavia to the Union of Serbia and Montenegro', in *Serbia since 1989*, edited by Ramet and Pavlaković, 65.

functioned as a sovereign state.[130] As a result, the FRY became a dysfunctional state whose authority was effectively limited to Serbia.

As mentioned above, the Montenegrin ruling party boycotted the September 2000 federal elections in response to the constitutional amendments introduced by Milošević in July of that same year. According to Kenneth Morrison, the decision not to participate in elections alongside the DOS coalition was partly motivated by the fact that the DPS had a vested interest in Milošević's regime.[131] Indeed, the more undemocratic and repressive the leadership in Belgrade, the more support Montenegro would receive from Western powers. The Montenegrin authorities were thus extremely cautious about Koštunica – whom they did not recognise as legitimate President – as they realised that his election would create a push for restoring the authority of the federal institutions over Montenegro. Indeed, the DOS coalition adopted a platform on the reform of the FRY which provided for the establishment of a strong federal state with a single personality in international relations, a joint federal government and president, a single army, a single currency, and a common foreign policy.[132] On the other hand, the Montenegrin government wanted Serbia and Montenegro to constitute themselves into two independent sovereign states and establish a loose confederation with common defence, monetary policy and foreign policy. In view of these differences, the negotiations between Koštunica, Djindjić and Djukanović did not yield any results.

As the Montenegrin authorities threatened to organise a referendum on independence in 2002, the international community stepped in to assist Serbia and Montenegro in reaching an agreement over the reform of the FRY. While the Western Powers had previously supported the Montenegrin separation from the Milošević regime, they were overtly sceptical of Montenegro's independence.[133] In view of the high level of polarisation over this issue within Montenegro, the international community feared that a move towards independence could generate internal instability. Moreover, it was considered that this could also destabilise the region by encouraging other territories such as the Republika Srpska to seek independence and rush the secession of Kosovo, which would have had negative repercussions in Serbia. Therefore, the EU high representative Javier Solana was put in charge of conducting talks on the reform and preservation of the federal union between Serbia and Montenegro. These negotiations resulted in the signing of the Belgrade Agreement which provided the basis for the establishment of the State Union of Serbia and Montenegro in February 2003.[134] The State Union was

130 The only remnants of the FRY in Montenegro were the federal army and air traffic control. The Montenegrin authorities introduced the German Mark as the official currency in 1999 and subsequently switched to the Euro (Lukić, 'Serbia and Montenegro', 70).

131 Kenneth Morrison, *Montenegro: A Modern History* (London and New York: I.B Tauris, 2009).

132 Lukić, 'Serbia and Montenegro', 71.

133 Ibid., 78–9; Morrison, *Montenegro*, 188.

134 Lukić, 'Serbia and Montenegro', 80–83; Morrison, *Montenegro*, 189.

a loose confederation which consisted in a unicameral parliament composed of delegates from the republican parliaments, a president elected by parliament, and a Council of Ministers comprising five departments.[135] This was widely perceived as a temporary arrangement since the Belgrade Agreement allowed the member states to reconsider their allegiance to the union after three years.

During those three years, the Montenegrin DPS-led government stepped up its efforts towards independence. Although they formally consented to form a State Union with Serbia, the Montenegrin authorities clearly had no interest in surrendering aspects of sovereignty they had gained since 1997.[136] After the removal of Milošević, the DPS increasingly deployed a pro-independence rhetoric. Over the next few years, the authorities proceeded with crafting a Montenegrin identity that was expressly distinct from, and exclusive of, Serbian national identity.[137] This was achieved through various means such as the symbolic reintroduction of Montenegrin national symbols, the establishment of Montenegrin as a separate language, the promotion of independence by intellectual elites and state-controlled media, and economic discrimination against those opposing independence.[138] This policy led to deep polarisation on the Montenegrin political scene between supporters and opponents of independence, which was exacerbated by the organisation of a referendum in May 2006. As the Montenegrins opted for independence, Serbia reluctantly became an independent state – a status it had relinquished in the wake of World War I in order to create the Kingdom of Serbs, Croats and Slovenes.

Kosovo's status

The Serbian army, police and administration were driven out of Kosovo as a result of the NATO military intervention in June 1999. UN Security Council resolution 1244, which brought an end to the hostilities, provided for the establishment of a provisional international administration embodied in the UN Mission for Kosovo (UNMIK). This resolution also reaffirmed the sovereignty of the FRY over Kosovo, which aroused hopes in Serbia that Kosovo would be reintegrated into the structures of a democratic Serbian state as an autonomous province.[139] The overthrow of Milošević thus raised expectations among the Serbian public that Kosovo's status would be resolved in Serbia's favour, while

135 These 5 departments dealt with foreign affairs, defence, international economic relations, internal economic relations and the protection of minority and human rights.

136 Lukić, 'Serbia and Montenegro', 88.

137 In view of the deep cultural and ethnic ties between Serbia and Montenegro, Montenegrin identity was traditionally considered – and is still considered by a wide section of the population – complementary with Serbian identity.

138 Morrison, *Montenegro*, 191–9.

139 However, resolution 1244 could also be interpreted as limiting the focus on autonomy to the interim period preceding a final settlement to be adopted on the basis of the

Kosovo Albanians rejected the possibility of autonomy within Serbia and would not accept anything less than full independence.

Kosovo's status was kept off the political agenda in the immediate aftermath of the removal of Milošević as the EU did not want to destabilise Serbia and the US shifted focus to the Middle East following the 11 September attacks. After proceeding with the establishment of Provisional Institutions of Self-Government (PISG) in the province, the UN endorsed a 'Standards before Status' policy, according to which Kosovo needed to make progress in eight key areas before tackling the resolution of the province's status.[140] Nevertheless, increasing pressures from Kosovo Albanians who threatened to organise a referendum on independence raised the issue of Kosovo's status on the political agenda. Amid growing tensions, the Serbian Prime Minister Djindjić requested the return of the Serbian police and army to the province and called for the opening of negotiations on Kosovo's status.[141] Discussions on technical issues were initiated in autumn 2003, only to be suspended as a result of the March 2004 riots. In the worst wave of violence since the war, Kosovo Albanians staged a pogrom of the Serbian population which led to the killing of 19 people and thousands of injured and displaced persons, as well as the destruction of Serbian property and cultural sites.[142]

The realisation that the international administration could not contain the violence and protect the Serbian minority led to a change of attitude among Western diplomats. While the international community was initially eager to postpone the question of Kosovo's status and give consideration to the idea of substantial autonomy within Serbia, it was now determined to proceed with the resolution of Kosovo's status and inclined towards independence.[143] After conducting a review of the implementation of standards, the UN called for the initiation of status talks under the supervision of the Contact Group comprising seven countries.[144] Following 15 rounds of negotiations throughout 2006, the talks hit the stumbling-block of the two parties' irreconcilable positions. On the one hand, the maximum

'will of the people' (Marc Weller, 'The Vienna Negotiations on the Final Status of Kosovo', *International Affairs* 84:4 (2008): 661).

140 These areas were: the existence of effective, representative and functioning democratic institutions; the enforcement of the rule of law; freedom of movement; sustainable return of refugees and IDPs, respect for the rights of the communities; creation of a sound basis for a market economy; fair enforcement of property rights; normalised dialogue with Belgrade; transformation of the Kosovo Protection Corps (James Ker-Lindsay, *Kosovo: The Path to Contested Statehood in the Balkans* (New York: Palgrave Macmillan, 2009), 18–19).

141 'Djindjić Launches Battle for Kosovo', *IWPR*, 10 February 2003.

142 These riots were staged in response to the deaths of three Albanian boys, which were allegedly caused by local Serbs (Ker-Lindsay, *Kosovo*, 20).

143 James Ker-Lindsay, 'From Autonomy to Independence: The Evolution of International Thinking on Kosovo, 1998–2005', *Journal of Balkan and Near Eastern Studies* 11:2 (2009), 141–56.

144 These were France, Germany, Italy, the Russian Federation, the UK and the US.

that the Serbian authorities were ready to concede was a high level of self-rule described as 'more than autonomy, less than independence'. On the other, the Kosovo Albanians would not accept anything short of independence. As a result, the contact group encouraged the UN Special Envoy, Martti Ahtisaari, to prepare a comprehensive proposal for a status settlement. This proposal recommended independence for Kosovo, which was rejected by the Serbian parliament.

Since the political parties in Serbia generally shared similar views towards Kosovo, the question of the status was not a matter of contention in domestic politics. However, this changed in 2007 as it became clear that the negotiations had failed and that Kosovo would unilaterally declare independence. Kosovo's status subsequently took centre stage in Serbian politics, even if the fate of the province was effectively out of the control of the domestic politicians.[145] As mentioned above, the second Koštunica government fell as a result of divergences between the DS and DSS over Serbia's response to Kosovo's declaration of independence, proclaimed in February 2008.[146] Following the victory of the pro-European forces in the Serbian parliamentary elections in May 2008, the Serbian authorities attempted to challenge the legality of Kosovo's unilateral declaration of independence before the International Court of Justice. In a very narrow approach to the question, the Court ruled that the adoption of the declaration of independence did not violate international law, which was a major blow for Serbian foreign policy.[147] Belgrade and Pristina subsequently initiated a new round of talks over technical issues under the supervision of the EU, which took a leading role in the international civil presence in Kosovo.

Conclusion

Serbia arguably experienced the most difficult and complex transition in Central and Eastern Europe. Whereas most Central and East European countries proceeded with building democratic institutions and market economies during the nineties, Serbia went through a period of blocked transformation during which the incumbent elites retained power by establishing a nationalist-authoritarian regime embodied in the rule of Slobodan Milošević. Although this period saw the introduction of pluralist elections and a semblance of democratic institutions, the ruling SPS effectively held onto power by exerting tight control over the media and the state apparatus.

A genuine departure from authoritarianism occurred only following the overthrow of Milošević in October 2000. In the subsequent period, Serbia

145 Eric Gordy, 'Serbia's Kosovo Claim: Much Ado About…', *openDemocracy*, 2 October 2007. Accessed on www.opendemocracy.net on 20 May 2011.

146 'Kosovo MPs Proclaim Independence', BBC, 17 February 2008.

147 Florian Bieber, 'Kosovo, Serbia and Bosnia: After the ICJ', *openDemocracy*, 28 July 2010. Accessed on www.opendemocracy.net on 20 May 2011.

experienced a difficult and protracted process of democratic consolidation, which was afflicted by political polarisation and problems of stateness. The pervasiveness of the political forces that constituted the former regime and the divisions among the democratic bloc prevented the emergence of a basic consensus over the transformation of the Serbian state. The consequent political rivalry was coupled with institutional instability as a result of the lack of democratic control over the security sector, which remained unreformed in the initial stages of the transition. In addition, the process of democratic consolidation was further complicated by the prevalence of national issues on the political agenda, as the sovereignty and legitimacy of the Serbian state were called into question by the secessions of Montenegro and Kosovo.

In those circumstances, international judicial intervention in the post-Milošević period took place against a backdrop of political and institutional uncertainty. As will be discussed in Chapter 3, foreign pressures for cooperation with the ICTY fuelled domestic instability as this issue took centre stage in the confrontation between political elites and generated a backlash within the security sector. While there was a relative consensus among Serbian politicians regarding relations with Montenegro and – up to a certain point – the resolution of Kosovo's status, cooperation with the ICTY was an extremely contentious and divisive issue for most of the 2000s. Besides fomenting domestic instability, the prosecution of high-ranking state officials at the ICTY was perceived by many politicians as an additional challenge to the sovereignty and legitimacy of the Serbian state, which were already jeopardised by the problems of stateness cited above (see Chapter 4). Therefore, considering the sensitivity of this issue at home and the importance attached to it abroad, the war crimes legacy and cooperation with the Hague tribunal arguably constituted the greatest challenge for the Serbian transitional authorities.

Chapter 3
Regime Change and the Politics of Cooperation with the ICTY

Introduction

During the 1990s, the work of the ICTY was obstructed by the reluctance of the authorities in Serbia and Croatia to cooperate with the Tribunal. During the Bosnian and Croatian wars, the nationalist authoritarian regimes in Croatia and Serbia shielded war crimes suspects from prosecution, aside from a few exceptional cases (see Chapter 5). The Dayton Peace Agreement, brokered in autumn 1995, established the duty to cooperate with the ICTY for the warring parties, including the Federal Republic of Yugoslavia. The following year, the Tribunal signed a Memorandum of Understanding with the Yugoslav authorities which allowed the Prosecution to open an office in Belgrade. The subsequent transfer of Dražen Erdemović and Radoslav Kremenović to The Hague opened up a short-lived semblance of cooperation. However, Belgrade's relations with the Tribunal rapidly deteriorated with the advent of the Kosovo crisis. In response to charges of war crimes issued by the Tribunal against Slobodan Milošević and his closest associates, the regime increasingly denounced the ICTY as an instrument deployed by the West to demonise the Serbs and legitimise the 1999 NATO aggression against Yugoslavia.[1]

The overthrow of Milošević on 5 October 2000 created the conditions for the establishment of tangible cooperation between Yugoslavia and the ICTY. However, this cooperation materialised primarily as a result of intense international pressure and on several occasions came at a high political cost for domestic stakeholders.[2] The international community made cooperation with the ICTY a condition for Serbia's access to foreign aid and progress towards European integration. This policy of conditionality led to the arrest and extradition of 46 war crimes suspects, including almost the entire Serbian political and military leadership from the 1990s. But the success of this policy was nevertheless tarnished by the fact that

1 Vladimir Ilić, 'Tribunal u Hagu iz perspective Srbijanskog posrtaja pred globalizacijom' (The Hague Tribunal from the Perspective of Serbia's Faltering Steps towards Globalisation), in *Haški Tribunal: Naš nesporazum sa svetom* (The Hague Tribunal: Our Disagreement with the World), edited by Milivoj Despot and Vladimir Ilić (Belgrade: Helsinki Committee for Human Rights, 2001).

2 Victor Peskin, *International Justice in Rwanda and the Balkans* (New York: Cambridge University Press, 2008).

Serbia's cooperation with the Tribunal was sporadic and protracted. At the same time, ICTY conditionality deeply affected domestic politics in Serbia and, at times, led to serious setbacks for the country's prospects in terms of democratisation and Europeanisation.

In this chapter, I examine the dynamics between domestic political developments and state cooperation with the ICTY in Serbia from the overthrow of Milošević in October 2000 until the arrest of Ratko Mladić in May 2011. The objective is to trace the evolution of Serbian policy-making on ICTY cooperation during this period and examine the repercussions of the policies of conditionality on the ground. This analysis highlights the tensions arising between international requests for cooperation and competing domestic political agendas in order to understand the outcomes, as well as the domestic responses to ICTY conditionality.

1. Hague Conditionality and the Breakdown of the DOS Coalition (2001–2003)

The general enthusiasm produced by the downfall of Milošević among Western diplomats and policy-makers bestowed upon the new Yugoslav authorities the favours of the international community. This allowed for the rapid reintegration of the country into the United Nations and the international financial institutions in autumn 2000. The new authorities were given a 'period of grace' regarding cooperation with the ICTY for the coalition government to settle in and take control of the state apparatus before any requests for the arrest and extradition of war crimes suspects were made. But the introduction of Hague conditionality soon brought to light the deep divergences within the governing DOS coalition.

A. The Extradition of Milošević as Political Breaking-Point

In the first months following the overthrow of Milošević, cooperation with the ICTY was absent from the domestic political agenda. In his first speech on national television as President of Yugoslavia, Koštunica declared that there would be no retaliation against the members of the former regime and that the Hague tribunal did not rank high on his list of priorities.[3] During his presidential campaign, Koštunica had openly rejected the possibility of extraditing Yugoslav citizens, including Milošević, to the Hague tribunal, which he perceived as an instrument of American influence and NATO presence in the Balkans.[4] Similarly, in the run-up

3 'Prvo obraćanje Koštunice preko RTS-a' (Koštunica's First Address on National Television), *B92*, 6 October 2000. Koštunica (in)famously declared that, for him, 'The Hague is the ninth hole on the flute', a Serbian idiom meaning that something is the last priority.

4 'Koštunica: Milošević neće ići u Hag' (Koštunica: Milošević Will Not Go to The Hague), *B92*, 5 September 2000.

to the Serbian parliamentary elections of December 2000, Djindjić declared that those who had cooperated in the removal of Milošević from power would not be extradited to The Hague.[5] In the transitional context, these statements could have been interpreted both as attempts to appease the security apparatus and the military, and as rhetorical moves to gather the support of the electorate. Public opinion was indeed largely opposed to cooperation with the ICTY as a result of the former regime's propaganda which had depicted the Tribunal as a terrorist organisation.[6]

The emergence of the 'Hague Issue'

As foreign pressure for cooperation with the ICTY grew, the new authorities adopted divergent stances towards this – an issue which had become increasingly divisive in domestic politics. The Yugoslav President reiterated his lack of regard for the Tribunal during Carla Del Ponte's first visit to Belgrade in January 2001, when he barely accepted to meet her, and even then, only to express his objections to the work of the Tribunal. Koštunica did not conceal his deep-seated antagonism towards the ICTY, which he looked upon as a political tribunal biased against the Serbs. On the other hand, Djindjić tactfully supported the work of the Tribunal and pledged cooperation as far as his remit would allow.[7] The Serbian Prime Minister thus became the principal interlocutor of Tribunal officials in spite of the fact that foreign policy and cooperation with the ICTY were formally under the remit of the federal government. Djindjić was indeed aware that cooperation with the Hague tribunal was necessary for obtaining international support and legitimacy. On several occasions, he held secret meetings with the Tribunal's Chief Prosecutor, Carla Del Ponte, in order to assert his commitment to cooperation and to ease pressure from the Tribunal.[8] Del Ponte lobbied Western governments intensely to condition economic assistance to Yugoslavia upon cooperation with the ICTY. Her campaign was particularly successful in the United States, where Congress put in place an annual certification process for assessing Yugoslavia's cooperation with the ICTY. This certification, to be issued annually on 31 March, was made a condition for the delivery of financial assistance and US support to Yugoslavia in international financial institutions.

---

5 'Nove tehnologije umesto šljivovice' (New Technologies Instead of Šljivovica), *NIN*, 21 December 2000.

6 In 2001, 54 per cent of the public was opposed to cooperation with the ICTY (Belgrade Centre for Human Rights and Strategic Marketing, 'Public Opinion in Serbia: Attitudes towards the ICTY', July 2003. Retrieved from www.bgcentar.org.rs on 7 March 2010).

7 Carla Del Ponte and Chuck Sudetić, *Gospodja Tužiteljka: Suočavanje s najtežim ratnim zločinima i kulturom nekažnjivosti* (Madame Prosecutor: Confrontations with Humanity's Worst Criminals and the Culture of Impunity) (Belgrade: Profil knjiga, 2008), 99–104.

8 Ibid., 107–12.

Since the Serbian government was in desperate need of financial assistance in order to implement its programme of reforms, the introduction of the certification deadline brought the issue of cooperation to the very top of the domestic political agenda. What the Tribunal pressed for most explicitly was the arrest and transfer of Milošević and other war crimes suspects to The Hague. But the various representatives of the DOS coalition were divided with regard to this matter. Koštunica's Democratic Party of Serbia (DSS) in particular opposed the extradition of Milošević, arguing that he should face charges in Serbia. The idea of trying Milošević in Serbia initially provided a common platform for the DOS leaders, as it was also backed by Djindjić, who repeatedly appealed to the domestic judiciary to undertake proceedings against war crimes suspects in order to remove potential offenders from society.[9] There were even some suggestions by Tribunal officials that a chamber of the ICTY should be set up in Belgrade in order to try Milošević.[10] This initiative, dubbed 'The Hague on the Danube', was however immediately rejected by Del Ponte on the basis that it would have been difficult to guarantee the safety of witnesses in Belgrade and that such a concession would have triggered similar demands from other suspects. In addition, the inertia of the Serbian judiciary, which had a poor record in war crimes proceedings, raised serious doubts about the ability of the domestic institutions to try Milošević.

The opponents to the handover of war crimes suspects to the ICTY initially built their case around the lack of legislation on cooperation with international tribunals. The Yugoslav constitution explicitly prohibited the extradition of Yugoslav citizens to foreign countries. The authorities sought to circumvent this legal obstacle by drafting a law on cooperation with the ICTY which introduced the notion of 'transfer' to international tribunals as distinct from 'extradition'.[11] There was a consensus within the DOS coalition that the arrest and transfer of war crimes suspects to the ICTY should await the adoption of this law in the federal parliament.[12] However, its enactment was hampered by the DOS's coalition partner in the federal government – the Montenegrin Socialist People's Party (SNP) – which was opposed to the handover of Yugoslav citizens to The Hague. The SNP, Milošević's closest political ally during the nineties, stood firmly against the arrest and transfer of the former Yugoslav President. The government initially sidestepped this legal obstacle by announcing the transfer of those ICTY indictees

9 'Svi za saradnju, neki i za izručenje Miloševića' (All for Cooperation, Some Even for the Extradition of Milošević), *Danas*, 7 February 2002; 'Hag – ni "Da" ni "Ne"' (The Hague – Neither 'Yes' nor 'No'), *Večernje Novosti*, 16 February 2001.

10 This suggestion was made by the Deputy Prosecutor Graham Blewitt in early March 2001 ['Tribunal spreman da sudi Miloševiću u Beogradu' (The Tribunal is Ready to Try Milošević in Belgrade), *Danas*, 8 March 2001].

11 The phrase used in Serbian is 'predaja' which can be translated both as 'transfer' and 'surrender'.

12 Personal interview with Momčilo Grubač, Federal Minister of Justice 2000–2001, on 7 May 2009.

who did not hold Yugoslav citizenship, and whose extradition was therefore not proscribed by the constitution.[13] The authorities thus arrested Milomir Stakić, the former Mayor of Prijedor, on the eve of Djindjić's first visit to Washington. This move was severely condemned by Koštunica, who argued that any transfer to the Tribunal should await the adoption of appropriate legislation on this matter. Such a reaction on the part of the Yugoslav President brought to light the substantial divergences on this matter within the DOS coalition, even though Djindjić strove to maintain the unity of the coalition for the sake of political stability.[14]

In spite of these divergences, the Serbian authorities proceeded with the arrest of Milošević on the eve of the deadline for American certification of cooperation. The confusion surrounding this event generated a lot of controversy. According to the former head of the State Security Service, Goran Petrović, this arrest was carried out following an attempt by the State Security Service to take over Milošević's personal security in accordance with legislation previously enacted by the Serbian government.[15] This action coincided with the delivery of a court summons to the former Yugoslav President, who was under investigation for abuse of power and corruption. Both the members of the State Security Service and the representatives of the Serbian judiciary were prevented from entering Milošević's residence by the Yugoslav Army guard and Milošević's armed bodyguards and supporters. The former Yugoslav President eventually surrendered after a 36-hour-long standoff and protracted negotiations with representatives of the Serbian government.[16] The open clash between the Yugoslav Army and the State Security Service preceding the arrest of Milošević revealed the lack of control over the armed forces on the part of the transitional authorities. Although some protagonists suggested that the army's interference was orchestrated by Koštunica, Milošević's arrest was officially backed by all the leaders of the DOS coalition, including the Yugoslav President.[17] These developments led the American Congress to grant Yugoslavia the certification of cooperation with the ICTY. However, the US authorities conditioned their participation in an international donor conference for Yugoslavia scheduled for 29 June 2001 upon clear progress in cooperation with the Tribunal.

The arrest of Milošević on the basis of ordinary criminal offences rather than crimes against humanity amply contributed towards discrediting the possibility of a domestic trial for the former Serbian strongman. Despite the insistence of

13 'Počinje istraga o krivičnim delima protiv čovečnosti' (Investigation of Crimes against Humanity Begins), *Politika*, 16 February 2001.

14 'Hag cepa DOS' (The Hague is Tearing the DOS Apart), *Glas*, 28 March 2001.

15 Personal interview with Goran Petrović, Head of the Serbian State Security Service (January–November 2001), on 28 December 2012.

16 According to Vesna Pešić, Milošević accepted to surrender only after Koštunica and Djindjić had provided guarantees that he would not be transferred to the ICTY [Vesna Pešić, *Divlje društvo: kako smo stigli dovde* (Wild Society: How We Got Here) (Belgrade: Pescanik, 2012), 56–7.

17 'Svi saglasni o privodjenju' (All Agree to the Arrest), *Glas*, 1 April 2001.

the Yugoslav authorities that Milošević should be tried in Belgrade and allusions by some Western diplomats to such an option being conceivable, it became clear that his extradition to The Hague was inevitable. This was reinforced by the discovery of mass graves containing bodies of Kosovo Albanians across various parts of Serbia (see Chapter 4). The working group established by the Ministry of the Interior accused Milošević and several former political and military officials of having organised the displacement of these corpses from Kosovo in order to conceal the atrocities for which they were responsible.[18] But even in the face of such clear evidence of the atrocities committed, the domestic judiciary still failed to undertake any proceedings for crimes against humanity perpetrated by the former regime. It thus became obvious that without thorough reforms of the domestic judiciary and police, which remained staffed with Milošević-era executives and crippled by inertia, local courts were reluctant to carry out such proceedings, or even incapable of doing so.

This state of affairs, combined with increasing international pressure for cooperation with the ICTY, led to a change in attitude on the part of the new authorities towards the Tribunal. During an official visit to the United States in early May 2001, Koštunica committed himself to enacting a law on cooperation with the ICTY by the end of that month.[19] He subsequently declared that alignment with the international community would require difficult compromises with regard to the Hague tribunal, thus implying that he might eventually approve the transfer of war crimes suspects to the ICTY.[20] Koštunica's change of tone was nevertheless mitigated by his insistence on two-way cooperation between Belgrade and the ICTY: he requested that the Office of the Prosecutor (OTP) raise indictments against Croatian and Kosovo Albanian suspects on the basis of evidence provided by the Yugoslav authorities.[21]

On the other hand, Djindjić increasingly pressed for cooperation with the ICTY by resorting to utilitarian arguments. While recognising the need to adopt legislation on this matter, he emphasised that cooperation was a precondition for Serbia's full reintegration into the international community and for the receipt of foreign aid.[22] At the same time, the discovery of mass graves provided the proponents of cooperation with a moral argument for extraditing Milošević to The Hague. Serbian government officials increasingly talked about the need to 'face

18 'Leševi nestali u akciji "Dubina 2"' (Bodies Concealed in Operation 'Depth 2'), *Politika*, 25 May 2001.

19 'Zakon o saradnji sa sudom u Hagu do kraja meseca' (Law on Cooperation with the Tribunal until the End of the Month), *Politika*, 13 June 2001.

20 'Neophodno pravno utemeljiti saradnju sa Hagom' (Cooperation with The Hague Must Be Given Legal Framework), *Danas*, 28 May 2001.

21 'Koštunica uslovio izručenje Miloševića' (Koštunica Conditioned the Extradition of Milošević), *Danas*, 15 May 2001.

22 'Saradnja sa Hagom preduslov za medjunarodnu poziciju' (Cooperation with The Hague a Precondition for International Position), *Politika*, 31 May 2001.

the past' and prosecute the former leader in order to individualise guilt and clear the Serbian people of collective responsibility.[23] These claims were dismissed by the representatives of the former regime, who accused the authorities of staging the discovery of mass graves and of spreading misinformation in order to justify the extradition of Milošević.[24]

The failure of 'legalism' and the extradition of Milošević

Despite having set the adoption of a law on cooperation as a precondition for transfers to the ICTY, the DOS leaders remained unable to enact it owing to the continued opposition of the SNP. Without the support of their Montenegrin coalition partners, the DOS coalition did not have a sufficient majority to vote in this law in the federal parliament. In the face of this, Djindjić announced that his government would circumvent opposition in parliament by resorting to supra-legal means, but Koštunica insisted on the need for legislation that would regulate cooperation with the ICTY. The Yugoslav President, who had by then adopted 'legalism' and the respect of institutional procedures as his political marker, argued that cooperation with the ICTY must not impinge upon the implementation of the rule of law and democracy in Serbia.[25]

This situation largely contributed towards distorting the debate about the Hague tribunal by shifting discussions from the political to the legal sphere. Both supporters and opponents of cooperation with the ICTY increasingly resorted to legal arguments in order to justify their positions.[26] Government officials stated that Yugoslavia was bound to cooperate on the basis of its membership of the UN and its commitments under the Dayton and Kumanovo peace agreements. This argument was also advanced by the Tribunal officials and their local supporters. They considered that a law on cooperation with the ICTY was unnecessary since cooperation could be based on the direct application of the Statute of the Tribunal.[27] On the other hand, the opponents of cooperation with the Hague tribunal argued that any type of extradition was proscribed by the constitution which had primacy over international law in the Yugoslav legal system.

This 'battle' over the interpretation of the legislation implicated an array of lawyers and legal experts, who substantiated the claims put forward by the rival

23 'Još jedna masovna grobnica' (One More Mass Grave), *Danas*, 21 June 2001.

24 'Poslednja faza razbijanja Srbije' (Ultimate Phase in the Destruction of Serbia), *Politika*, 7 June 2001.

25 Sonja Biserko, 'Zoran Djindjić i Haški tribunal' (Zoran Djindjić and the Hague Tribunal), in *Zoran Djindjić: Etika Odgovornosti* (Zoran Djindjić: The Ethics of Responsbility), edited by Latinka Perović (Belgrade: Helsinki Committee for Human Rights, 2006), 234.

26 'Igrale se delije legalizma' (Heroes Playing at Legalism), *Danas*, 9 June 2001.

27 'Ni odlaganje predaje ni ustupanje slučaja Milošević' ('No Delay in Extradition or Transfer of the Milošević Case), *Danas*, 27 March 2001.

political groups. Besides Koštunica, the 'legalist' argument was also championed by the representatives of the former regime as a complement to their established anti-Western rhetoric, which depicted the Tribunal as an anti-Serbian institution. Shifting the debate to the legal field had several advantages for the opponents of the Hague tribunal. First of all, they knew that the adoption of a law on cooperation was highly unlikely owing to the opposition of the SNP. Secondly, even if such legislation were ever passed, it would be easily challenged by the Constitutional Court which was still staffed with Milošević's appointees. Under such circumstances, 'legalism' constituted a powerful strategy for obstructing cooperation with The Hague.

Pressed by the forthcoming donor conference, the DOS coalition opted to replace the draft law with a decree that would be adopted by the federal government without being approved by the Yugoslav parliament. Although replacing a law with a decree was legally dubious, this move sought to reconcile the Serbian government's urge to show proof of cooperation, and thereby guarantee the success of the donor conference, with Koštunica's insistence on 'legalism'. In the following days, the Serbian authorities initiated procedures for the transfer of Milošević on the basis of this legal act. But the application of the decree was immediately suspended by the Yugoslav Constitutional Court on the initiative of the SPS and a group of lawyers representing Milošević.[28] Faced with a legislative deadlock, the Serbian government took the decision to proceed with the handover of Milošević to The Hague on the eve of the donor conference on the basis of direct application of the Statute of the ICTY. This decision made use of Article 135 of the Serbian Constitution, which allowed the Serbian authorities to take action on issues that fall under the remit of federal institutions when these are deemed to act against Serbian interests. The reliance on this constitutional provision, which was introduced by Milošević in order to disempower the federal authorities of Socialist Yugoslavia, was legally questionable and arguably at odds with the rule of law.[29]

The extradition of Milošević on 28 June, which corresponds to the date of the historic Battle of Kosovo in 1389 and Milošević's most important political rally in 1989, marked a symbolic break with the former regime. Djindjić justified the government's move by challenging the legitimacy of the unreformed Yugoslav Constitutional Court and arguing that failure to cooperate with the ICTY would imperil economic recovery by generating renewed isolation for the country. In his own words, the government decided to implement the ideals of 'earthly' Serbia, rather than the ideals of Milošević's 'heavenly' Serbia, for the sake of future generations.[30] On the other hand, the extradition of Milošević

28 'Sudije naredile da se obustavi primena uredbe' (Judges Order Suspension of Decree), *Politika*, 29 June 2001.

29 Tibor Varady, 'Ambiguous Choices in the Trials of Milošević's Serbia' in *The Milošević Trial: An Autopsy*, edited by Timothy Waters (New York: Oxford University Press, forthcoming)

30 'Milošević u Hagu' (Milošević in The Hague), *Blic*, 29 June 2001.

was heavily condemned by Koštunica, who denounced this move as an attack on the constitutional order, the rule of law and the federal state.[31] The Yugoslav President condemned the government for reviving the most undemocratic aspects of Milošević's politics by promoting lawlessness and undertaking humiliating actions.[32] From that moment, Koštunica and the DSS increasingly distanced themselves from the rest of the DOS coalition and the Serbian government. At the same time, the representatives of the SNP pulled out of their coalition with the DOS, thereby provoking the fall of the federal government. Nevertheless, this measure proved to be only symbolic, as they formed a new cabinet with the DOS coalition shortly afterwards for the sake of preserving the Yugoslav federation and their positions in the federal institutions.

Milošević's extradition – political significance and implications

It is important to analyse the motives behind Djindjić's decision to transfer Milošević to The Hague and Koštunica's condemnation of this move in order to understand the political significance of this event. While it is generally believed that Djindjić traded Milošević for financial assistance, the handover of the former Yugoslav President was never explicitly made a condition for US participation in the donor conference. What the American authorities had requested was 'substantial improvement' in cooperation with the ICTY, which officially referred to the adoption of a law on cooperation that would allow for the transfer of indictees to The Hague.[33] And as the Yugoslav parliament failed to enact such a law, the Serbian government had no other choice but to extradite Milošević in order to ensure the success of the donor conference. But the motives for such a move were ideological, as well as material. There is no doubting that international economic and political support was a prerequisite for the implementation of the reforms envisaged by the government. On top of that, Djindjić and his entourage firmly believed that Serbia's political and economic development should be pursued through the country's integration in Euro-Atlantic institutions, and therefore sought to reinforce Serbia's ties with the West.

Besides these obvious motives, several additional factors may have tipped the balance in favour of Milošević's extradition. According to Del Ponte, Djindjić feared that Milošević could make a comeback on the Serbian political scene as the leader of the opposition.[34] Although he was officially confined to his residence after being ousted from power, Milošević had renewed his political activities by being re-

31 'Izručenje se ne može smatrati zakonitim' (Extradition Cannot Be Considered Lawful), *Blic*, 29 June 2001.

32 'Nije po ustavu, nekome se žurilo' (It is not Constitutional – Someone Rushed It Through), *Ekspres*, 29 June 2001.

33 'Vašington traži povećanu saradnju Beograda sa Hagom' (Washington Requests Increased Cooperation of Belgrade with The Hague), *Politika*, 16 May 2001.

34 Del Ponte and Sudetić, *Gospodja Tužiteljka*, 107–9.

elected as the President of the SPS and attending several meetings of his party before being arrested. In the months following his arrest, the question of his extradition to The Hague became the primary political issue in the country. This threatened to imperil the reforms sought by the government as it distracted media and public attention from more pressing socio-economic issues. By sending Milošević to The Hague, the authorities were ridding themselves of a potential threat and a continued sensitive issue on the domestic political agenda. The insistence of Serbian officials that the country needed to 'move on' and stop discussing Milošević's fate suggests that this was an important factor in the government's decision to extradite him.[35] To a certain extent, this interpretation substantiates the legalist claim that international tribunals are an effective way of removing 'spoilers' from domestic politics.[36]

Last but not least, the extradition of Milošević most certainly constituted an attempt to release the Serbian authorities from international pressure for cooperation with the ICTY. In his memoirs, the former Serbian Interior Minister claims that the DOS leaders were convinced that handing over Milošević would permanently solve the 'problem' of the Hague tribunal.[37] Accordingly, they believed that, in this way, the remaining war crimes suspects indicted by the Tribunal would be tried in local courts. From this perspective, the extradition of the former Serbian strongman amounted to a concession aimed at relieving Serbia of its duties regarding cooperation with the ICTY. Since Milošević had been let down by his former allies within the armed forces, his transfer to the ICTY did not represent a major challenge for the authorities.[38] Furthermore, the extradition of the former President failed to generate any mass protest that could destabilise the government. Therefore, the immediate risks associated with this operation were relatively low compared to the expected benefits in terms of international recognition.

In the end however, the domestic political cost of sending Milošević to The Hague proved to be unexpectedly high. The extradition of Milošević constituted the breaking point between the two main leaders of the DOS coalition, Zoran Djindjić and Vojislav Koštunica.[39] Koštunica's severe condemnation of this move revealed that the two leaders could no longer agree on issues of crucial importance for the

35 'Vreme je da prestanemo da se bavimo Miloševićem' (Let's Move On from Milošević), *Politika*, 30 June 2001.

36 Gary J. Bass, *Stay the Hand of Vengeance* (Princeton, NJ and Oxford: Princeton University Press, 2000), 284–310.

37 Dušan Mihajlović, *Povlenske magle i vidici* (The Fog and Views of the Povlen) (Belgrade: NEA, 2005), 97–8.

38 Note that Milošević's transfer to The Hague was nonetheless carried out in the greatest secrecy in order to avoid any interference from the army. Personal interview with Goran Petrović.

39 Mihajlović, *Povlenske magle*, 98; Vesna Pešić, 'Rekonstrukcija petooktobarskih zbivanja na osnovu memoarske i stručne literature' (Reconstruction of 5 October Events on the Basis of Memory and Expert Literature), in *Razvoj Demokratskih Ustanova u Srbiji – Deset Godina Posle* (The Development of Democratic Institutions in Serbia – Ten Years After), edited by Dušan Pavlović (Belgrade: Heinrich Böll Foundation, 2010), 33–5.

future of the country. While the divergences between Djindjić and Koštunica had been evident since the beginning, this episode turned their disagreement into open antagonism.[40] The Yugoslav president claimed that he had not been informed about the decision to transfer Milošević, while Djindjić and his entourage argued that this decision had been approved by all the DOS leaders, including Koštunica. The controversy on whether Koštunica had approved this move or not went on for years. While this question may seem trivial, it remains important in determining whether the extradition of Milošević was a substantial reason, or just an excuse, for the DSS leader to discredit the rest of the DOS coalition and distance himself from it.

Both hypotheses seem plausible, and they are not mutually exclusive. By June 2001, the deep ideological divergences between the DSS and the DS had materialised over concrete policy issues. It became obvious that Koštunica's 'legalism', which stood for the respect of existing laws and institutional procedures, was fundamentally at odds with Djindjić's reformist agenda. The Yugoslav President's insistence on the need for a law on cooperation with the ICTY before proceeding with extraditions reflected broader and deeper divergences regarding how the country should be ruled and how the reforms should be carried out. While he supported the country's integration into the European Union, Koštunica insisted that the establishment of the rule of law and the respect of state sovereignty were paramount for a successful transition.[41] Besides being distrustful towards the proceedings of the ICTY, which he considered to be biased against Serbs, Koštunica resented the Tribunal for impinging on the sovereignty of the Yugoslav state. He believed that the policy of conditionality was no longer justified, since Milošević had been removed from power, and proved to be much more intransigent in his dealings with Tribunal officials and Western diplomats than Djindjić. In this context, the extradition of the former Yugoslav President on the basis of a decree issued by the Serbian government was perceived as an aberration by Koštunica and his entourage. In the words of Slobodan Samardžić, the extradition of Milošević was 'the straw that broke the camel's back'.[42]

In addition, the manner in which Milošević had been transferred to the ICTY had directly undermined the authority of the Yugoslav President and the federal government. Koštunica, who had become the most popular politician in Yugoslavia after defeating Milošević in the elections, effectively had very limited political power. His role as President of Yugoslavia was mostly symbolic, while his party had very little actual say in the Serbian government. This explains why Koštunica insisted on dissolving the DOS coalition and on calling early elections that would

40 Personal interview with Slobodan Samardžić, former advisor to Koštunica and Minister for Kosovo 2007–08, on 29 July 2009; personal interview with Dragoljub Mićunović, President of the Federal Parliament 2000–2003, on 19 August 2009.

41 Vojislav Koštunica, 'Pravna država i prav(n)i reformizam' (The Legal State and Legal [Real] Reformism), *Nova srpska politička misao*, Special Issue 1 (2001): 147–67.

42 Personal interview with Slobodan Samardžić.

allow for the development of an 'authentic' party system.[43] The Yugoslav President was very critical of the way in which all important decisions for the country were taken within the DOS coalition, which he described as a 'political conglomerate'. Koštunica's break away from the DOS coalition was therefore not unexpected, and the extradition of Milošević may have been just the right opportunity to do it. According to Zoran Živković, who was then Minister of the Interior in the Federal Government, the Hague tribunal acted as a catalyst that accelerated the emergence of divergences within the ruling coalition:

> The first serious clashes within the coalition related to The Hague [tribunal]. Of course, the differences were much more substantial – they essentially concerned Serbia's national interests, the role and mission of democratic changes, everything which is at the core of the policies of these parties – these differences were significant. But this was the pretext. … The cleavage between the DS and the DSS had become a rift that lasted for several years, during which Koštunica was practically holding the handbrake on reforms.[44]

The episode of Milošević's extradition thus demonstrates how foreign pressure to cooperate with the Tribunal fed directly into the emerging domestic power struggles between two leading political factions incarnated by Zoran Djindjić and Vojislav Koštunica. The Chief Prosecutor, Carla Del Ponte, purposely played on the divisions within the transitional authorities in order to pursue her agenda. As Djindjić and Koštunica competed for foreign support, the policy of conditionality promoted by Del Ponte proved effective in enforcing cooperation. Nevertheless, this policy had an adverse impact on democratic consolidation in Serbia. By delivering Milošević, Djindjić had gained the support of the international community at the expense of domestic stability. The policy of conditionality generated political turmoil, which became the main obstacle to the implementation of reforms pursued by the government.

B. The 'Hague Issue' as a Source of Perpetual Instability

The rise of the Hague issue further up the political agenda amply contributed towards the fragmentation and polarisation of the Serbian political scene by crystallising the divergences and generating a split within the DOS coalition. In the days following the extradition of Milošević, the DSS formed into a separate group in the Serbian parliament and called for a new Serbian government to be formed. The split within the transitional authorities led to the emergence of two competing structures of power around Prime Minister Djindjić and President Koštunica respectively.

43 Koštunica, 'Pravna država', 155–6.

44 Personal interview with Zoran Živković, Federal Minister of the Interior 2000–2003 and Serbian Prime Minister 2003–04, on 7 May 2009.

The emergence of the anti-Hague lobby: the JSO mutiny

As he distanced himself from the rest of the DOS coalition, Koštunica created a kind of shadow government grouped around his presidential cabinet.[45] In his stand-off against the Serbian government, the Yugoslav president was increasingly perceived by the remnants of the former regime as a protector who would save them from any purges or reforms carried out by the DOS government. This was particularly conspicuous with regard to the army and the Military Security Agency, who put themselves at the service of Koštunica in order to preserve their interests.[46] The animosity between Djindjić and Koštunica thus created an opportunity for the incumbent elites to maintain their positions in the new order by capitalising on the ongoing power struggle. The intelligence agencies took advantage of this situation by playing a pivotal role in the outbreak of political scandals in which opposing factions mutually accused each other of engaging in abuse of power and corruption.[47] These sporadic quarrels turned into an open political crisis as the DSS withdrew from the Serbian government in August 2001. Although this did not result in the fall of Djindjić's government, it did officially bring an end to the unity of the transitional authorities, despite the fact that the DSS was still formally part of the DOS coalition. Koštunica thus joined the opposition to the Serbian government while remaining in power as president of Yugoslavia.

In those circumstances, cooperation with the ICTY became a wedge issue that was instrumental in the power struggle between different political factions. The former Foreign Minister, Goran Svilanović, describes the role of the ICTY in the political fragmentation and polarisation of the domestic political scene in the following terms:

> So the Tribunal did not engender this divide, it did not create it. It just clearly exposed the divergences that existed amongst us; it took us further apart politically, and led to a serious cleavage. This cleavage was then defined as the difference between Djindjić on the one hand and Koštunica on the other. … In practice, this meant that you had the Prime Minister on one side and the President on the other, and above them were power structures that included one intelligence agency against another, the tycoons and the media. But then [these] two structures entered into such a powerful confrontation that

45 Personal interview with Vesna Pešić, former leader of the GSS, on 5 August 2009.

46 Personal interviews with Žarko Korać, Deputy Prime Minister in the Serbian government 2001–03, on 24 April 2009 and Goran Petrović, former head of the Serbian State Security, on 28 December 2012.

47 Timothy Edmunds, 'Intelligence Agencies and Democratisation: Continuity and Change in Serbia after Milošević', *Europe-Asia Studies* 60:1 (2008), 35.

> even two men who knew each other very well were no longer able to control these processes.[48]

In opposition to Djindjić's reformist agenda, Koštunica increasingly drew on a patriotic discourse that emphasised the defence of national interests and state sovereignty. The Yugoslav president thus gained the support of nationalist circles in his efforts to dislodge the Serbian government. His political agenda coincided with the interests of the parties associated with the former regime (SPS and SRS), as well as rogue elements within the security sector and the criminal underworld. These structures were deeply interconnected and directly involved in war crimes and organised crime.[49] They thus had a vested interest in impeding cooperation with the ICTY and thwarting the reforms pursued by the Serbian government.

The implicit collusion between Koštunica and segments of the former regime in obstructing cooperation with the ICTY resulted in the emergence of a powerful anti-Hague lobby. This alliance transcended the dichotomy between the former regime and former opposition, which blurred the normative distinction between these two political groupings and thus eroded the political capital of the DOS coalition. Furthermore, the emergence of the anti-Hague lobby contributed to destabilising the Serbian government by substantially increasing the risks associated with ICTY cooperation. In the eyes of the former head of the State Security Service, the political context made the arrest and transfer of ICTY indictees highly perilous:

> In simple terms, something that is a banal operation in a situation where society, the state and the institutions are divided – so that on the one hand, there is the army and the President of the state, and on the other, the [State Security] Agency and the Prime Minister, who think differently and want different things – this is the most impossible situation, this is a 100 per cent security risk.[50]

This state of affairs became conspicuous during the mutiny of the Special Operations Unit (JSO) that followed the arrest of two ICTY indictees, Predrag and Nenad Banović, in November 2001. After arresting them, members of the JSO revolted for not having been informed that these two brothers had been indicted by the ICTY. In response to this 'manipulation', they demanded the resignation of Serbia's Interior Minister, Dušan Mihajlović, and the adoption of a law on cooperation with the ICTY. This change of mood within the JSO, which had until then been loyal to Djindjić, can be explained by the fact that its members felt directly threatened by these arrests since one of the Banović brothers had

---

48 Personal interview with Goran Svilanović, former Minister of Foreign Affairs 2000–2004, on 23 May 2009.

49 Personal interview with Miloš Vasić, journalist for the weekly *Vreme*, on 26 March 2009.

50 Personal interview with Goran Petrović.

been a member of that unit during the war in Bosnia.[51] This perceived threat was reinforced by rumours that the ICTY was inquiring into the actions of the JSO in the nineties and that the whole unit would be handed over to the Tribunal.[52] During her previous visit to Belgrade, the ICTY Prosecutor Carla Del Ponte had requested information about 200 individuals, including members of the JSO. This information had been leaked to the JSO unit as a list of prospective indictments.[53] In those circumstances, the arrest of the Banović brothers was apparently perceived by the members of the unit as a retraction of the deal they had struck with Djindjić prior to the overthrow of Milošević.

These motives were all the stronger for JSO leaders trying to protect their personal interests: many were involved in criminal activities and felt increasingly threatened by the government's attempts to tackle organised crime.[54] Furthermore, several members of the unit were directly involved in the murder of political opponents on behalf of the former regime. Establishing accountability for these political murders was a priority for the DOS government and the newly appointed head of the State Security Service, Goran Petrović.[55] The JSO's show of strength ostensibly sought to warn the authorities against any attempt to bring them to account for past crimes or interfere with their on-going criminal activities. The week-long mutiny of the JSO culminated with members of the unit blocking the highway with their armoured vehicles in the centre of Belgrade. On that same day, their former leader – Milorad 'Legija' Ulemek – was due to appear in court for the attempted murder of Vuk Drašković on the Ibar Highway in October 1999. This concurrence of events suggests that the unit's expedition to Belgrade was aimed at dissuading the authorities from arresting its former leader.[56]

The mutineers' demand for the adoption of a law on cooperation corresponded with Koštunica's standpoint on this matter. The Yugoslav President openly stood in support of the mutineers as he condemned the Serbian government for sending people to The Hague without any legal framework.[57] The Yugoslav Constitutional Court had permanently revoked the federal decree on cooperation with the

---

51 'Oružana Pobuna' (Armed Rebellion), *Vreme*, 15 November 2001.

52 '"Crvene Beretke" ne žele da hapse za Haški Tribunal' ('Red Berets' Do Not Want to Make Arrests for Hague Tribunal), *Politika*, 11 November 2001.

53 'Odbijena ostavka Mihajlovića' (Mihajlović's Resignation Rejected), *Večernje Novosti*, 15 November 2001.

54 Miloš Vasić, *Atentat na Zorana* (The Assassination of Zoran) (Belgrade: *Politika, B92, Vreme, Narodna Knjiga*; 2005), 75–95.

55 This is illustrated by the fact that the former head of the State Security Service, Rade Marković, and the perpetrators of the attempted murder of Vuk Drašković were arrested within a month following the inauguration of the DOS government and the appointment of a new leadership within the State Security Service. Personal interview with Goran Petrović.

56 Ibid.

57 'Koštunica: Ne možemo bez zakona' (Koštunica: We Cannot Go On Without a Law), *Glas*, 11 November 2001.

ICTY only a few days before the JSO staged their protest.[58] While there is no evidence to demonstrate that he was directly involved, Koštunica's support for the mutiny effectively gave legitimacy to the action of the JSO. The leader of the DSS went on to argue that it was legitimate for the unit members to protest in their uniforms and with their weapons, comparing it to doctors protesting in their gowns.[59] This significantly reduced the government's room for manoeuvre. As the most popular politician in the country, Koštunica was able to turn public opinion against the government. Moreover, his command over the army prevented the Serbian government from resorting to the military to resolve the crisis. For Goran Petrović, the JSO mutiny was the culmination of a long-prepared counter-revolution orchestrated by Koštunica:

> That was the logical consequence. So this anti-Hague, anti-European lobby, which is also ultimately anti-Serbian and anti-civilisation, is doing everything possible to stop [the process of reforms]. It sees which way the wind is blowing: that we are doing everything that needs to be done in the [State Security] Service and that this relentlessly targets them and [opposes] their interests. This is why, from the very beginning, right from the spring [2001], there was a special war led by Vojislav Koštunica and the Democratic Party of Serbia and this military–security element against the State Security Service. They also have resources, even greater than ours; they also have collaborators and journalists. So there is constant generating of crises, of criticisms of the government – there is the well-known story satanising Djindjić. But this satanising started right back in 2001: it targeted the [Serbian] government and particularly the [State Security] Service, which played a key role in the democratic changes and the establishment of order. ... So they had prepared the ground for carrying out the counter-revolution. When they realised that everything was ready, they carried it out.[60]

Whatever the motives and the political background of the mutiny, this episode brought to light the Serbian government's major weakness: its lack of control over the armed forces. While Djindjić initially adopted a firm stance towards the mutineers, he was eventually obliged to make a compromise with the leaders of the JSO because of the government's lack of coercive capacity. The Minister of the Interior, Dušan Mihajlović, and the Chief of the Public Security Service allegedly reported to the Prime Minister that they did not have the means to confront the JSO.[61] After a series of protracted negotiations, the government yielded to the JSO's request to replace the heads of the State Security Service, thereby relinquishing

---

58 'Neustavna uredba o saradnji sa Hagom' (Decree on Cooperation with The Hague is Anti-Constitutional), *Politika*, 7 November 2001.

59 Biserko, 'Zoran Djindjić', 241.

60 Personal interview with Goran Petrović.

61 'Oružana pobuna – deset godina kasnije' (Armed Rebellion – Ten Years Later), *Vreme*, 10 November 2001.

control over that institution.[62] In view of the unfavourable power balance, Djindjić refrained from dissolving the JSO and from seeking accountability for the mutiny 'for the sake of preserving stability within the country'.[63] These concessions would later prove to be fatal for the Serbian Prime Minister, as they paved the way for his assassination.

From that point on, the Serbian government was permanently exposed to the threat of a putsch within the armed forces. This menace was nurtured through an extensive campaign of disinformation orchestrated by the tabloid press, which was funded and controlled by the criminal cartel.[64] This campaign sought to instil the fear of extraditions to the ICTY within the armed forces in order to destabilise the government. In the days following the JSO mutiny, a list of 362 members of the police allegedly sought by the ICTY was published in the tabloid *Reporter*. This list was completely fabricated on the basis of official documents issued by the Ministry of the Interior, with no link whatsoever to the ICTY. Its purpose was clearly to stir up panic among the police, the only armed force that remained under the control of the Serbian government.[65] According to Zoran Živković, the manipulation of the fear of the ICTY within the armed forces created a major problem for the authorities:

> In that sense, exploitation of the Hague issue slowed down the process of reforms and was an insurmountable obstacle to their faster implementation. Because, of course, when someone spreads the fear within the police and the army that each and every member of those forces is going to end up in The Hague – all of them had indeed been in Kosovo, Bosnia or Croatia ... – and when a feeling is created that people are prosecuted there not for war crimes but [just] for being Serbs, this produces anxiety and discontent within those institutions. You cannot carry out a reformist policy without having reformed the armed forces or without having at least reached an advanced stage in the reform of that sector. Here, people were alarmed almost every day, [thinking] 'you will be the next one', regardless of whether they were generals or captains. So this created a lot of problems.[66]

62 Goran Petrović and his assistant, Zoran Mijatović, resigned and were replaced by Andrija Savić and Milorad Bracanović. The latter is suspected of having had close links with Milorad 'Legija' Ulemek and the 'Zemun clan' members involved in the murder of Zoran Djindjić (Miloš Vasić, *Atentat na Zorana*).

63 'Vlada smirila krizu, specijalci opstali' (Government Has Calmed the Crisis; the Special Unit Remains), *Politika*, 18 November 2001. Note that the former members of the JSO were put on trial for the 2001 mutiny in October 2012.

64 Personal interview with Miloš Vasić.

65 'Borba za policiju, rušenje Vlade Srbije' (Fight for the Police Seeks to Make the Government Fall), *Nedeljni Telegraf*, 28 November 2001.

66 Personal interview with Zoran Živković.

As well as spreading the fear of extraditions, the tabloid press played a crucial role in propagating the nationalist discourse deployed by the anti-Hague lobby.[67] This consisted mainly in denouncing cooperation with the ICTY as a betrayal of national interests by portraying war crimes suspects as heroes of the Serbian cause. The policy of conditionality played into the hands of the nationalist circles by reinvigorating the discourse of victimisation instilled by the former regime. The anti-Hague lobby was thus able to stir up public opinion against cooperation with the ICTY and create a social climate in which the arrest of war crimes suspects carried a high political cost. At the same time, opposition to the ICTY was instrumental in the revival of anti-Western rhetoric and the resurgence of right-wing parties, most notably the Serbian Radical Party (SRS).[68]

The law on cooperation and its limitations

The mutiny of the JSO brought the adoption of a law on cooperation with the ICTY back onto the political agenda, thereby further increasing tensions between the DSS and the rest of the DOS coalition. The DSS acted swiftly to put forward a proposal for the adoption of an outline law at the federal level that would allow the constitutive republics to adopt their own legislation regulating the process of cooperation, including the transfer of indictees to The Hague.[69] This initiative allegedly sought to resolve the impasse created by the SNP in the federal parliament, as the Montenegrins remained firmly opposed to the handover of war crimes suspects to the ICTY. The proposal was rejected by the representatives of the DOS coalition, who sought to keep this matter under the remit of the federal government, which was formally in charge of the country's foreign relations. The DOS leaders insisted that all the parties in power should share responsibility for cooperation with the ICTY, and that there was no reason for the Serbian government to take on all the 'dirty business'.[70] The DSS proposal was thus portrayed as an attempt by Koštunica to pass on the deeply unpopular issue of cooperation with the ICTY to the Serbian government.

Although this proposal was aborted from its inception, this attempt nonetheless provides valuable insight into the position of the DSS regarding cooperation with the ICTY. The draft law stipulated that the transfer of war crimes suspects must be approved by Serbian courts and government. Accordingly, the

67 Personal interview with Rajka Despotović, journalist for *B92*, on 1 April 2009.

68 Marlene Spoerri and Annette Freyberg-Inan, 'From Prosecution to Persecution: Perceptions of the International Criminal Tribunal for the Former Yugoslavia (ICTY) in Serbian Domestic Politics', *Journal of International Relations and Development* 11:4 (2008): 358–62.

69 'U Hag po zakonu?' (To The Hague in Accordance with the Law?), *NIN*, 22 November 2001.

70 'Poslanici DOS glasaće protiv' (DOS MPs Will Vote Against), *Danas*, 15 December 2001.

ICTY was put in the position of a litigant in the process of extradition before the domestic judiciary. Besides restricting the possibility of transfer, this proposal effectively gave primacy to domestic courts over the ICTY, which was in direct conflict with the Statute of the Tribunal.[71] The representatives of the DSS thus sought to partially restore the balance in favour of state sovereignty by entitling the domestic authorities to administer and control the process of extraditions.[72] In addition, by transferring cooperation with the ICTY to the republics, the draft law excluded the federal institutions from this process. This effectively meant that the draft law would not allow for the handover of military personnel or federal officials, or the opening of state archives requested by the Tribunal.[73] Finally, the enactment of the DSS proposal would in any case have been highly unlikely, as the Serbian constitution prohibited the extradition of Serbian citizens to a foreign institution. Therefore, the law would most probably have been challenged by the Constitutional Court, which would have further delayed the transfer of war crimes suspects to the ICTY and prolonged the political crisis within the ruling coalition.[74]

Debate on the adoption of a law on cooperation resumed at the beginning of 2002 as a result of renewed international pressure for cooperation. The deadline for American certification of cooperation with the ICTY, which remained a condition for the provision of financial assistance, was again set for 31 March. The Serbian government announced that it would once again proceed with extraditions on the basis of the Statute of the Tribunal if the law on cooperation was not enacted in time.[75] Serbian officials increasingly pressed the DSS and SNP to adopt a law that would allow for the transfer of war crimes suspects at the federal level. Tensions between the DS and the DSS heightened as Djindjić and Koštunica accused each other of undermining the adoption of the law on cooperation and exposing the country to international sanctions.[76] These quarrels deepened the political crisis as the DSS officially withdrew from the DOS coalition.

The law on cooperation with the ICTY was eventually adopted on 10 April 2002 with the support of the SNP, which thus sought to be cleared of responsibility for leading the country into renewed isolation on the eve of the parliamentary

---

71 'Zakon za spoticanje Tribunala' (Legislation to Hinder the Tribunal), *Glas Javnosti*, 18 December 2001.

72 'Sačuvati i suverenitet' (Sovereignty Should Also Be Preserved), *Glas Javnosti*, 18 December 2001.

73 'Poslanici DOS glasaće protiv' (DOS MPs Will Vote Against), *Danas*, 15 December 2001.

74 Ibid.

75 'Ako ne bude zakona, primeniće se Statut' (If There is No Law, the Statute Will Apply), *Politika*, 21 February 2002.

76 'Svadja u senci sankcija' (Quarrel in the Shadow of Sanctions), *Politika*, 2 April 2002.

elections in Montenegro.[77] The SNP consented to support the law on condition that it would only apply retrospectively to war crime suspects who had already been indicted by the ICTY. This provision was heavily criticised by the Tribunal representatives, who were still carrying out investigations involving high-ranking political and military officials. In spite of these criticisms, the DOS coalition had no choice but to accept the SNP's provision in order to see the legislation enacted.

The adoption of the law was preceded by a heated parliamentary debate between representatives of the ruling coalition and the opposition. The Deputy Prime Minister, Miroljub Labus, made the case for the adoption of the law by arguing that cooperation with the ICTY would dispel existing prejudice against Serbs as perpetrators of genocide by individualising responsibility.[78] This line of reasoning, which essentially advanced the need for accountability and truth, stood in sharp contrast to the utilitarian arguments that had been deployed by the authorities to justify the extradition of Milošević. This change of rhetoric reflected a wider effort on the part of the DOS leaders to establish cooperation with the ICTY on moral grounds. This is illustrated by Djindjić's bold statement on the eve of the enactment of the legislation:

> We could have complied with the demands for cooperation six months ago. But international public opinion would then have considered that we were doing so out of despair, not out of the belief that the Hague tribunal, in spite of its shortcomings, is an international institution which we recognise because we want to get to the truth, and we do not support the indictees in their struggle against The Hague. I think that we have undergone this catharsis.[79]

For the Serbian government, the adoption of the law on cooperation was a crucial step in shifting the debate on the ICTY from the political to the legal sphere. With this move, cooperation with the Tribunal was effectively institutionalised and the transfer of war crimes suspects reduced to a technical matter. However, a few minutes after the adoption of the law on cooperation, the former Minister of the Interior and Hague indictee Vlajko Stojiljković committed suicide on the steps of the Federal Parliament. This dramatic event was deplored by Koštunica and the representatives of the former regime who denounced it as an example of the destabilising effects of the ICTY.[80] Stojiljković's act of despair most probably resulted from the realisation that indictees could no longer escape being extradited to The Hague. In view of this new reality, six indictees, including Nikola Šainović and Dragoljub Ojdanić, the former Yugoslav Prime Minister and Army Chief

77 'Rasplet najteže krize' (Denouement of the Most Difficult Crisis), *Politika*, 9 April 2002.

78 'Narod nije odgovoran' (The Nation is not Responsible), *Blic*, 12 April 2002.

79 'Bez ikakvih uslovljavanja' (Without Any Conditionality), *Politika*, 5 April 2002.

80 'Koštunica: Opomena političarima i medjunarodnoj zajednici' (Koštunica: Warning to Politicians and the International Community), *B92*, 11 April 2002.

of Staff during the conflict in Kosovo, deliberately turned themselves in to the authorities.[81]

In spite of such noticeable progress, the authorities had failed to deliver the 11 remaining indictees, including General Mladić. Tribunal officials blamed the Yugoslav Army for protecting the Bosnian Serb general, who was allowed to walk about freely and even make public appearances.[82] These allegations were repeatedly denied by state officials, who claimed that they were unable to locate the Hague indictee. The DOS leaders however later confirmed that Mladić was under the protection of the army and that the Serbian government did not attempt to arrest him in order to avoid any clashes between the police and the military.[83] This information was confirmed by the Ministry of Defence, which nevertheless claimed that the army's contacts with Ratko Mladić were suspended after the adoption of the law on cooperation.[84] Besides this, the army was also sheltering Veselin Šljivančanin, an army officer indicted for war crimes perpetrated in Vukovar at the beginning of the war in Croatia. This was later confirmed by the DOS leaders as pictures of Šljivančanin hiding in army barracks were leaked in the press in 2004.[85]

Overall, this state of affairs demonstrates that the Serbian government's capacity to arrest and transfer war crimes suspects to the ICTY was extremely limited. In January 2003, government officials openly stated that they were unable to meet the demands of the international community because they simply did not have the capacity to arrest Mladić and Šljivančanin.[86] While Djindjić controlled the police, the army was under Koštunica's authority, and the State Security Service largely remained outside civilian control following the JSO mutiny.[87] In addition,

81 'Mrkšić i Martić danas u Hagu' (Mrkšić and Martić at The Hague Today), *Glas Javnosti*, 15 May 2002. In addition to Šainović and Ojdanić, these were Mile Mrkšić, Milan Martić, Momčilo Gruban and Vladimir Kovačević.

82 'Kanonada besa zbog generala Mladića' (Storm of Anger Because of General Mladić), *Večernje Novosti*, 21 October 2002.

83 'Rat zbog Mladića!' (War Because of Mladić!), *Kurir*, 30 June 2005; 'Mladićev čuvar na bolovanju' (Mladić's Protector is Off Sick), *Blic*, 21 July 2005.

84 At the time of writing, the extent to which the army sheltered Mladić was still unclear. In 2006, the authorities launched an investigation against five army officials, including the former Army Chief of Staff, Nebojša Pavković, and the former Head of the Military Intelligence Agency, Aco Tomić. They were suspected of sheltering Mladić in army barracks until 1 June 2002, and providing him with support until 5 May 2003 ['Tomić i Pavković skrivali Mladića?' (Did Tomić and Pavković Shelter Mladić?), *B92*, 7 November 2010].

85 'Veselin Šljivančanin bio u generalštabu' (Veselin Šljivančanin Was [Hiding] in the Headquarters), *Danas*, 11 November 2004.

86 'Ne možemo ispuniti zahtev SAD' (We Cannot Meet the Request of the USA), *Danas*, 23 January 2003; 'Strah od incidenata' (Fear of Incidents), *Večernje Novosti*, 27 January 2003.

87 Edmunds, 'Intelligence Agencies and Democratisation', 37–41. Note that, in early 2003, the Serbian government replaced the heads of the State Security Service

the Serbian authorities did not legally have the right to arrest military personnel since the army was under the remit of the federal authorities.[88] The police were only entitled to arrest them once they had retired. By remaining passive, the Yugoslav president was implicitly acquiescent to, if not supportive of, the army's obstruction of the arrest of war crimes suspects. Serbian government officials of the time later claimed they had informed Koštunica about Mladić's whereabouts – to no avail.[89] In her memoirs, Carla Del Ponte mentions being offered Mladić in exchange for amnesty for the army's Chief of Staff, Nebojša Pavković, and the Tribunal's support for Yugoslavia's integration into NATO and the EU.[90] This clearly demonstrates how powerful an obstacle the unreformed military and security structures were to cooperation with the ICTY.

The murder of Djindjić and 'Operation Sabre'

The assassination of Zoran Djindjić on 12 March 2003, in a terrorist act dubbed 'Stop The Hague', tragically epitomised the destabilising effects of Hague conditionality. While the motives for shooting the Prime Minister seem to have been primarily related to his attempt to tackle organised crime, the perceived threat of the Hague tribunal within the armed forces had created a political climate which made this action possible. The trial for the murder of Zoran Djindjić established that this action was planned and executed by a criminal group that included members of the state security apparatus and had been heavily involved in war crimes.[91] Throughout the trial, one of the chief architects behind the murder appeared to be Milorad 'Legija' Ulemek, the former commander of the JSO unit. It was established that the primary motive behind the assassination of the Prime Minister was the fear of being arrested for political murders committed by the gang on behalf of the former regime during the nineties. However, the assassination was carried out by a member of the JSO, who claimed to have done it out of fear that his unit would be dissolved and sent to The Hague. Manipulation by the anti-Hague lobby of the military's and state security's fear of extradition to the ICTY had thus created the conditions for the assassination of the Serbian Prime Minister.[92]

---

that had been appointed following the JSO mutiny in an attempt to regain control over this institution.

88 Personal interview with Miroslav Hadžić, Professor of Global and National Security at the University of Belgrade, on 26 August 2008.

89 *Blic*, 21 July 2005.

90 Del Ponte and Sudetić, *Gospodja Tužiteljka*, 155–6.

91 Vasić, *Atentat na Zorana*.

92 'Ulemeku i Jovanoviću po 40 godina' (Ulemek and Jovanović Get 40 Years Each), *B92*, 23 May 2007; 'Likvidirao sam ga zbog Haga' (I Killed Him Because of The Hague), *Blic*, 26 December 2004; Personal interview with Miloš Vasić.

The pervasiveness of a nationalist discourse that fuelled opposition to the ICTY and the persistence of unreformed security structures led to a political climate in which Djindjić's murder was even perceived as a patriotic act by some segments of society. The assassination occurred only weeks after the ICTY had issued an indictment against Vojislav Šešelj, the leader of the Serbian Radical Party, who voluntarily surrendered to the Hague Tribunal. Šešelj's pompous departure was marked by a media campaign that sought to discredit the government and bolster nationalist feelings. The SRS actually accused the authorities of having requested that Carla Del Ponte indict Šešelj in order to remove him from the Serbian political scene, while Koštunica denounced the government for acting as a local branch of the ICTY instead of defending national interests.[93] At his farewell rally, Šešelj declared that he was going to The Hague in order to defend his national ideals and stand up to the Tribunal. He then appealed to all Serbian patriots to unite in preventing further transfers to the Tribunal.[94]

In those circumstances, the assassination of Djindjić was interpreted by many as an attempt to halt the arrest and transfer of ICTY indictees.[95] Furthermore, his murder coincided with the establishment of the first government of the State Union of Serbia and Montenegro, which replaced the Federal Republic of Yugoslavia in February 2003.[96] As the government of the State Union was comprised of the ruling parties of the two constituent republics, the DOS coalition was due to inherit control of the Ministry of Defence from the Montenegrin SNP. In this context, a substantial motive for the assassination of the Prime Minister could have been to thwart the takeover of the army by the DOS coalition, and thus forestall the announced reforms of the military that would have facilitated the arrest and transfer of ICTY indictees.[97] Others have advanced that this murder constituted an attempt to reverse regime change and bring to power Vojislav Koštunica, who incarnated a nationalist, yet democratic, political option.[98] Nevertheless, all these interpretations remain pure speculation, as none of

---

93 'Podizanje optužnice zahtevala vlast' (Issuance of Indictment Requested by Authorities), *Politika*, 3 February 2003; 'Tribunal nije pri kraju svog rada' (Tribunal Not Yet Close to End of Its Work), *Dnevnik*, 25 February 2003.

94 'Idem u Hag da ja njima sudim' (I am off to the Hague to Judge Them), *Glas Javnosti*, 24 February 2003.

95 'Ubili premijera iz straha od Haga' (They Killed Prime Minister out of Fear of the Hague), *Glas Javnosti*, 7 July 2003.

96 The State Union of Serbia and Montenegro was inaugurated in February 2003 as a result of the agreement between the Serbian and Montenegrin governments on the reform of the Federal Republic of Yugoslavia. Vojislav Koštunica was replaced by Svetozar Marović as President of the State Union and a new government was created with representatives of the parties in power in both republics (See Chapter 2).

97 Personal interview with Ivan Andrić, MP for the LDP and former member of the Parliament's Defence and Security Committee from 2001 to 2003, on 27 August 2009.

98 Srdja Popović, *Nezavršeni proces* (The Uncompleted Trial) (Belgrade: Helsinki Committee for Human Rights in Serbia, 2007).

them can be proved to be true. Since the trial for the murder of Djindjić did not examine the political background of this event, the political motives behind the Prime Minister's assassination remain deeply contested.

This attack prompted an immediate response from the Serbian government, as well as a sudden renewal of public support for the DOS coalition. The authorities declared a state of emergency and launched a massive crackdown on organised crime through 'Operation Sabre'. The political conditions were more favourable than they had ever been to addressing the issue of war crimes. Having secured control over the federal institutions and neutralised the defamatory campaign of the tabloid press, which was censored during the state of emergency, the DOS leaders could proceed with cooperation with the ICTY without obstruction. The newly constituted Parliament of Serbia and Montenegro amended the law on cooperation by removing Article 39, which restricted its application to suspects who had been indicted before its adoption.[99] In their public appearances, the DOS leaders increasingly emphasised the need to obtain redress for victims and come to terms with the war crimes legacy, deploring the lack of domestic initiative in this respect. In June 2003, the government set up domestic institutions specialised in the prosecution of war crimes suspects in order to reclaim the transitional justice agenda (See Chapter 5).[100] The War Crimes Chamber and the Office of the War Crimes Prosecutor were created as part of a wider strategy to address the criminal legacy of the former regime, which also involved the creation of special institutions for tackling organised crime.

These developments opened the way to a new wave of transfers and substantial improvement in the government's dealings with the Tribunal. The handover of Jovica Stanišić and Franko Simatović, two former top executives of the State Security Service, showed that 'Operation Sabre' had significantly facilitated cooperation with the Tribunal. Stanišić and Simatović had been arrested in relation to Djindjić's murder and were subsequently transferred to the ICTY as the OTP had indicted them for their alleged involvement in war crimes in Bosnia and Croatia.[101] In her first visit to Belgrade after the assassination of Djindjić, Carla Del Ponte expressed her satisfaction with the attitude of the authorities and announced a new era of cooperation between the ICTY and Serbia and Montenegro.[102] The détente in relations between the Chief Prosecutor and the Serbo-Montenegrin authorities was given further impetus by the transfer of a case instigated by the ICTY to Serbian courts. Serbian officials hailed this

99 'Izbrisan član 39- moguća nova izručenja' (Article 39 Deleted – New Extraditions Now Possible), *Danas*, 15 April 2003.

100 'Hag u Srbiji' (The Hague in Serbia), *Politika*, 25 June 2003.

101 Carla Del Ponte claimed that the Serbian authorites had urged the OTP to issue the indictments against Stanišić and Simatović. This claim was denied by Serbian officials.

102 'Popuštanje Haškog zagrljaja' (The Hague Relaxes Its Grip), *Danas*, 24 May 2003.

decision as a step in the right direction for full cooperation with the ICTY to be achieved by the end of the year.[103]

Nevertheless, the momentum for the apprehension of ICTY indictees fizzled out with the dramatic arrest of Veselin Šljivančanin in June 2003. Šljivančanin was besieged by the police in his apartment during a visit to his family in a residential suburb of Belgrade.[104] As he put up resistance to the police, the operation turned into a ten-hour-long standoff that was further complicated by the intrusion of a group of protesters led by the leaders of the right-wing SRS, who sought to block the arrest. This turmoil can be explained by the concurrence of several factors. First of all, the police officer who was in charge of the arrest was a close friend of Šljivančanin, which significantly complicated his arrest.[105] This situation reflected the difficulty of arresting former military or police personnel in a country where the security sector is relatively small and its members closely interconnected. The fact that Šljivančanin was reported by one of his neighbours as having been at home for his birthday revealed a serious omission by the police, who claimed not to know his whereabouts.[106] Most obviously, the recurrence of such lapses indicates that the reluctance of security personnel to locate and arrest war crimes suspects constituted an institutional obstacle to cooperation with the ICTY.

The arrest of Šljivančanin was further complicated by the fact that he was one of the most popular officers in the Yugoslav Army. In the early nineties, Šljivančanin had been portrayed by the regime media as the 'Knight of Vukovar' after having led the assault on the Croatian town in the early stages of the war.[107] His indictment and potential sentencing thus dealt a severe blow to the perceived legitimacy of the Serbian campaign in Croatia. In the months preceding his arrest, the authorities appealed to Šljivančanin to surrender, pointing to the discovery of new evidence that could potentially have cleared him of responsibility.[108] According to this evidence, the war crimes perpetrated in Vukovar had been planned and executed by paramilitary units, some of which had been organised by the Serbian Radical Party. The SRS thus had a vested interest in obstructing the arrest of Šljivančanin,

103 This refers to the *Ovčara* case, in which lower-ranking members of the military and paramilitary groups were tried for the murder of 200 people taken out of the hospital in Vukovar after the town had fallen under the control of Yugoslav/Serbian forces; 'Sa Hagom – do kraja godine' (With The Hague – Until the End of the Year), *Večernje Novosti*, 20 May 2003.

104 'Hapšenje dugo osam godina i deset sati' (The Arrest That Lasted Eight Years and Ten Hours), *Dnevnik*, 14 June 2003.

105 Personal interview with Ivan Andrić.

106 'Uhapšen na rodjendan, prijavio ga komšija' (Arrested on his Birthday, Reported by his Neighbour), *Glas Javnosti*, 14 June 2003.

107 'Veselin Šljivančanin – Odbrana Viteza' (Veselin Šljivančanin – The Defence of the Knight), *Danas*, 24 February 2003.

108 'Šljivančanin nije kriv za Ovčaru?' (Šljivančanin Not Guilty for *Ovčara*?), *Dnevnik*, 16 April 2003.

especially since Vojislav Šešelj had also been indicted for war crimes perpetrated after the takeover of Vukovar.[109]

The scandal produced by this messy arrest led the authorities to step back in their attempts to capture war crimes suspects, thus bringing cooperation with the ICTY to a new standstill. Over the following days, the government adopted a measure that allowed for the provision of financial support to those indictees who surrendered to the authorities.[110] This move marked a turn in the DOS government's approach to ICTY cooperation: instead of carrying out arrests and extraditions, the authorities thus openly sought to encourage the surrender of war crimes suspects. This policy was imported from Croatia, where it had proved effective in alleviating the destabilising effects associated with the arrests of indictees. In the long run, however, this had a highly adverse impact on transitional justice in both countries, as it appeared that the states stood behind the indictees. Foreign Minister Svilanović points to the unintended consequences of a policy which he personally sponsored:

> What happened to us was the socialisation of crimes. This was initiated in Croatia, then our government started to do it, and then the Bosnians did it as well. The socialisation of crimes means that the war criminals have become 'ours' in domestic public opinion. I think that it started with Blaškić, the Croatian general, when Croatia created a fund to sponsor his defence. This was completely unnecessary, completely nonsensical: the defence is entirely funded by the Tribunal, which is why it [the Tribunal] is expensive. However, this is for the PR in fact, he [Blaškić] thus becomes 'ours' in Croatian public opinion. The government did it in order to cleanse itself in the eyes of the domestic public. ... Then we started doing the same thing. I was signing directives for the allocation of some funds to Šešelj's family and the families of all the others who were arrested. [It thus appeared] as if the government was funding them and their families.[111]

The financial incentives introduced by the government had an immediate effect on cooperation with the ICTY as they led to the surrender of two indictees over the next two months.[112] But while this policy effectively mitigated the political costs of cooperation with the ICTY, it also had negative repercussions on the Tribunal's ability to advance transitional justice in Serbia, which I discuss in further detail later in this chapter.

---

109 Personal interviews with Dragoljub Mićunović and Miroslav Hadžić.

110 'Džeparac za Haške optuženike' (Pocket Money for Hague Indictees), *Blic*, 15 June 2003.

111 Personal interview with Goran Svilanović.

112 These were Željko Mejakić and Mitar Rašević (Del Ponte and Sudetić, *Gospodja Tužiteljka*, 202)/

The indictment of the generals and the fall of the DOS government

By autumn 2003, the political capital amassed by the authorities in the aftermath of Djindjić's assassination was exhausted. The government was fraught with internal disputes and exposed to allegations of corruption and abuse of power orchestrated by the opposition. In this context, the ICTY's indictments against four army and police generals for war crimes committed in Kosovo dealt a final blow to the DOS coalition in October 2003.[113] These indictments directly undermined the government as they targeted the highest-ranking representatives of the armed forces: the acting Chief of Public Security and Deputy Minister of the Interior, Sreten Lukić, the former army Chief of Staff, Nebojša Pavković, and General Lazarević, who had commanded the troops in Kosovo during the NATO bombing campaign. The fourth indictee was Vlastimir Djordjević, the former Chief of Public Security under Milošević, who had fled to Russia after 5 October 2000.

The indictment of Lukić was particularly problematic for the government. Lukić had been appointed by the DOS government in early 2001, after the authorities had verified that he was not suspected of being involved in war crimes by the ICTY or by any Western government.[114] His indictment was thus perceived by the government as a retraction of the guarantees given by the Tribunal earlier on, which was deemed unacceptable. Furthermore, this indictment directly imperilled the government's control over the police. Indeed, Lukić's loyalty was crucial for securing the allegiance of the police during the initial stages of the transition. Besides conducting the arrest of war crimes suspects, he had played a major role in 'Operation Sabre', during which he had personally arrested Djindjić's murderers. In those circumstances, Zoran Živković, who inherited the position of Prime Minister, felt both practically and morally obliged to oppose Lukić's extradition to the ICTY. This opposition was compounded by Živković's frustration over the clumsy workings of the Tribunal:

> I said that I was not going to arrest this man because you told me that he was OK; now you are saying that he is not OK; this is not possible. Besides, there was an emotional element, which would not have been decisive without this substantial [reason]: it is that he personally arrested Zvezdan Jovanović (the murderer of Zoran Djindjić) with his own hands. He did not order it; he arrested him with his own hands. And third, she [Carla Del Ponte] came to me with a document inscribed "Zoran Živković, Prime Minister of the Federal Republic of Serbia and Montenegro". I told her "Madam, I am the Prime Minister of Serbia. The Federal Republic of Serbia and Montenegro does not exist and has never existed. There was a Federal Republic of Yugoslavia and there is a State Union

113 'Hag otpečatio optužnice protiv četvorice generala' (The Hague Unsealed Indictments against Four Generals), *Balkan*, 21 October 2003.

114 Personal interview with Zoran Živković.

> of Serbia and Montenegro. You have got the name and the surname right, the rest does not exist. I cannot accept that."[115]

The DOS government took the decision not to proceed with the arrests on the basis that it did not have the mandate to apprehend acting army staff and that the arrest of Sreten Lukić would destabilise the country and reduce the government's capacity to cooperate with the Tribunal. Government officials insisted on transferring the cases against the generals to local courts. This possibility was put forward by the US Ambassador-at-Large for War Crimes Issues, Pierre-Richard Prosper, who declared that the generals could be tried in Serbia, but only if Belgrade were to transfer Mladić to The Hague.[116] For this reason, the ICTY's indictments against the generals were perceived by many in Serbia as further pressure to arrest and hand over Ratko Mladić.[117] But the option of transferring the cases against the generals to Serbia was ruled out by the Chief Prosecutor, Carla Del Ponte, who did not approve of the dealings between Washington and Belgrade.[118]

According to Živković, the Serbian government had brokered a deal with the US authorities in June 2003 that allowed for CIA agents to monitor and supervise Serbia's attempts at arresting Ratko Mladić and Radovan Karadžić for a period of six months. At the end of the period, the US would put an end to Hague conditionality, regardless of whether the two fugitives were captured or not.[119] Under such circumstances, it seems likely that the Office of the Prosecutor issued these indictments at that precise moment in order to avert the implementation of the agreement between the Serbian and US authorities. Indeed, without the US policy of conditionality, the Tribunal's leverage over Serbia would have significantly diminished.

The timing of the indictments against the generals was particularly problematic for Živković's government, which faced a motion of no confidence that led to the calling of early elections for December 2003. These indictments provided the opposition with political ammunition to discredit the DOS government, which was denounced as being submissive and lacking a coherent approach towards cooperation with the ICTY.[120] At the same time, they contributed to weakening pro-European forces and reviving anti-Western resentment in Serbia by reinforcing the

---

115 Ibid.

116 Milanka Saponja Hadžić and Gordana Igrić, 'Srbija reaguje na zahtev za izrucenje Mladića' (Serbia Reacts to Request for Mladić's Extradition), *IWPR*, 24 October 2003.

117 'Politički pritisak na Vladu' (Political Pressure on Government), *Politika*, 22 October 2003.

118 Del Ponte and Sudetić, *Gospodja Tužiteljka*, 213–16.

119 This period was supposed to end in March 2004. The agreement was repealed by the Koštunica government a few weeks before this expiry date (Personal interview with Zoran Živković).

120 'Država bez politike prema Tribunalu' (State Left without Policy towards the Tribunal), *Glas Javnosti*, 24 October 2003; 'Dva aršina iste vlasti' (Double Standards of Same Government), *Večernje Novosti*, 24 October 2003.

view that the Tribunal was biased against Serbs. This standpoint was now implicitly shared by some DOS leaders, who deplored the fact that the Tribunal prosecuted Serbian political and military officials for command responsibility, while it had not indicted any Kosovo Liberation Army (KLA) leader on the same principle.[121] The indictments against the generals thus provided a major boost to the nationalist parties by placing the 'Hague issue' centre stage in the electoral campaign. This state of affairs is illustrated by the candidacy of four ICTY indictees, including two of the four indicted generals, on four different MP lists.[122]

***

The evidence presented in this section clearly shows that international judicial intervention interfered with regime change in the early stages of the transition in Serbia. Foreign pressures for cooperation with the ICTY fomented political polarisation and institutional upheaval, thus weakening the position of the reformist transitional authorities. External demands for justice were way above what Serbia's nascent democracy could take at that time. In retrospect, the extradition of Milošević was a shock to the political system, which created long-term instability. The external demands for justice were directly at odds with the transitional compromises that had allowed a peaceful transition from authoritarianism to take place. As they realised that the arrest of indictees fomented political turmoil and instability, the authorities increasingly shied away from carrying out arrests and instead strove to convince the indictees to surrender. Ultimately, the ICTY's indictment of the Chief of Public Security and Deputy Interior Minister, Sreten Lukić, put the DOS government in direct opposition to the Tribunal.

2. EU Conditionality and the Voluntaristic Model of Cooperation (2004–2006)

As discussed in Chapter 2, the parliamentary elections of December 2003 produced a massive shift in the power balance on the Serbian political scene. The right-wing Serbian Radical Party (SRS), whose leader, Vojislav Šešelj, was on trial at the ICTY, established itself as the largest single party in the country. Koštunica's Democratic Party of Serbia (DSS) came second, which allowed him to create a minority government in coalition with several smaller parties, thanks to the support of Milošević's Socialist Party of Serbia (SPS) in parliament. The

121 'Šta je sa optužnicama protiv Albanaca?' (What about Indictments against Albanians?), *Danas*, 25 October 2003. Note, however, that the ICTY indicted three low-ranking KLA members – Fatmir Limaj, Isak Musliu and Haradin Bala – in February 2003.

122 'Na poslaničkoj i Haškoj listi' (On Both MP and Hague List), *Borba*, 10 December 2003.

remnants of the DOS coalition that had regrouped around the Democratic Party (DS), now led by Boris Tadić, entered opposition.

A. ICTY Cooperation Called into Question

The remodelling of the political landscape after the elections led to a radical change in the policy of cooperation with the ICTY. Before even settling in as Prime Minister, Koštunica announced that the transfer of war crimes suspects to the ICTY would not be a priority for his government.[123] This view came across quite clearly in the coalition agreement between the parties that formed the new government, which stipulated that the authorities would not proceed with the handover of war crimes suspects indicted for command responsibility.[124] These developments alerted the US authorities, who had conditioned the renewal of the certification on cooperation over the transfer of the generals to The Hague. Koštunica dismissed US conditionality as an ultimatum and argued that the transfer of the remaining war crimes suspects would destabilise democratic institutions by spurring extremism. According to him, the only way to maintain domestic political stability while cooperating with the ICTY was to persuade the indictees to surrender to the Hague tribunal.[125]

Following the example of Croatia and Bosnia, the new Serbian Prime Minister insisted on establishing a 'reciprocal' model of cooperation. Accordingly, the government would enable war crimes suspects to be transferred to The Hague in exchange for a number of concessions from the Tribunal. In particular, Koštunica requested the transfer of a number of cases to domestic courts and the implementation of the right of indictees to remain free until the beginning of their trial.[126] The latter issue was critical in promoting the surrender of war crimes suspects. Until then, the Tribunal had not accepted the guarantees provided by the Serbian government for the temporary release of indictees who had surrendered. These requests for temporary provisional release had been successfully opposed by the OTP, which only supported the requests of indictees who were willing to cooperate with the Prosecution. This issue had constituted a permanent source of tension between the DOS government and the Chief Prosecutor. Indeed, the latter's refusal to allow the indictees to remain free until the beginning of their trial acted as a significant disincentive for the surrender of war crimes suspects.

The government's change of attitude towards the ICTY was embodied in the 'Law on the Rights of Indictees in the Custody of the ICTY and of Members of

123 'Izručenja tribunalu (ne)će biti prioritet' (Extraditions Will (Not) Be a Priority), *Glas Javnosti*, 3 January 2004.

124 'Socijalisti kucaju na otvorena vrata' (Socialists Knocking on Open Door), *Danas*, 4 February 2002.

125 'U Hag dobrovoljno' (Going to The Hague Voluntarily), *Blic*, 12 March 2004.

126 'Dvosmerna saradnja sa Hagom' (Two-Way Cooperation with The Hague), *Politika*, 3 March 2004.

their Families' that was adopted at the first sitting of the new parliament. This controversial law was put forward jointly by the representatives of the governing parties and those parties that had constituted the former regime (SPS and SRS). It provided for material support to the families of the indictees and legal assistance for all indictees, as long as these expenses were not covered by another source. The rationale behind this initiative was twofold. Officially, the provision of financial support was a humane gesture designed to provide the families of indictees with a stable income and the possibility to visit their relative during his trial in The Hague.[127] At the same time, legal support was meant to ensure the defence of national interests. Supporters of this law argued that the sentencing of state officials at the ICTY could have negative repercussions on the lawsuits initiated by Bosnia and Croatia against Serbia and Montenegro for genocide before the International Court of Justice (ICJ).[128] It was thus deemed expedient that the state should get involved in the defence of these indictees in order to safeguard its own interests.

In practice, this law was not really ground-breaking: the previous government had already introduced some form of financial assistance to those who surrendered and the Tribunal usually covered the legal expenses of all indictees. In addition, similar measures were already in place in Croatia, where the state was actively involved in the defence of Croatian indictees. But while the financial assistance introduced by the DOS government aimed exclusively at promoting the surrender of war crimes suspects, this law sought to extend the benefits to all Serbian indictees, regardless of how they were transferred to The Hague. The representatives of the opposition argued that the main beneficiary of this law would be Slobodan Milošević, whose legal expenses were not covered by the Tribunal since he refused to recognise the Court.[129] Therefore, this effectively meant that the Serbian tax payers would be covering the expenses of representatives of the former regime, who had illicitly built up substantial wealth during the nineties. In this respect, this law constituted a partial restoration of the former regime.

The most important aspect of this law was its symbolic significance: by providing support to Hague indictees, the state manifested its solidarity with the accused. This solidarity was allegedly based on the defence of common interest: clearing Serbia of responsibility for the war crimes committed in the nineties. By conflating the defence of the indictees with the defence of the state, the proponents of this law reinforced the perception that the Serbian nation and state were those being tried at the ICTY.[130] It thus appeared as if, by presenting themselves at

127 National Assembly of Serbia, '6th Session of the 1st Parliamentary Sitting', 30 March 2004, 235–40.

128 Bosnia and Croatia had instigated two separate lawsuits for genocide against the FRY before the International Court of Justice (ICJ) in 1993 and 1999 respectively (See Chapter 4).

129 National Assembly of Serbia, 30 March 2004, 241–4.

130 'JUKOM: Loša poruka gradjanima' (JUKOM: Wrong Message to Citizens), *Politika*, 31 March 2004.

the ICTY, the indictees were acting in the public interest. This reasoning was given further impetus by the looming threat of the genocide lawsuits, which, had Serbia been found guilty, would have involved the payment of significant monetary compensation. This legislation thus ostensibly sought to boost Serbia's identification with, and support of, ICTY indictees.

After ample controversy, the law was eventually suspended by the Serbian Constitutional Court.[131] Nevertheless, its initial adoption on the eve of the annual deadline for American certification of cooperation with the ICTY sent a clear message to the international community. Belgrade's change of mood towards the Hague Tribunal led the US administration to suspend economic aid for Serbia and Montenegro. This episode also revealed significant divergences regarding the 'Hague issue' within the ruling coalition. Although the draft law was put forward by the government, Koštunica's coalition partners subsequently distanced themselves from this initiative.[132] Both the G17 and the SPO pressed for cooperation with the ICTY in order to advance the government's pro-European agenda. The leader of the SPO, Vuk Drašković, who became the new Minister of Foreign Affairs of Serbia and Montenegro, stood out in his support for the Tribunal. Having survived two attempts on his life by Milošević's State Security Service, he repeatedly argued that cooperation with the Tribunal was a precondition for Serbia to come to terms with the crimes committed by the former regime. This standpoint stood in stark contrast to the rhetoric deployed by the Serbian government, which was devoid of any principled arguments. Despite pledging cooperation with the ICTY, Koštunica continually denounced the Tribunal for being biased against Serbs. It thus transpired that the only purpose of this cooperation was to avoid international isolation and enable Serbia to achieve integration into Euro-Atlantic institutions.

The victory of the DS candidate, Boris Tadić, at the presidential elections in June 2004 increased domestic pressure on the government to cooperate with the Tribunal. The new president insisted that cooperation with the ICTY was a priority and that the prosecution of war criminals was a precondition for reconciliation in the region.[133] In the following period, Tadić became the most outspoken proponent of the need to come to terms with the past and acknowledge past atrocities, especially the Srebrenica massacre. Tensions within the government also grew as the spectre of renewed isolation loomed over the country. The Foreign Minister's attempt to instigate the transfer of the four generals to the ICTY put to the test

131 'Van snage pomoć haškim optuženicima' (Assistance to Hague Indictees Suspended), *Danas*, 16 April 2004.

132 'Vuk i Labus ostavili Koštunicu na prvom zakonu' (Vuk and Labus Abandon Koštunica on First Piece of Legislation), *Balkan*, 31 March 2004.

133 'Saradnja s Hagom prioritet' (Cooperation with The Hague is a Priority), *Politika*, 12 July 2004.

the government's promise that it would not proceed with the arrest of indictees.[134] The SPS, which provided crucial support to Koštunica's cabinet in parliament, announced that it would cause the government to fall if it turned over the generals. But the Serbian authorities avoided this by invoking the former government's decision that the arrest and transfer of the generals would jeopardise national security.[135] What's more, the government's readiness to cooperate with the ICTY was further challenged by the disappearance of Goran Hadžić on the day that his indictment was delivered by the Tribunal to the Serbian authorities. As the Tribunal published photographs showing Hadžić's escape, it appeared that information about his indictment had been leaked to the former leader of the Croatian Serbs.[136] This scandal amply contributed to further discrediting the Serbian government in the eyes of the international community.

These developments led the government to reconsider its position towards cooperation with the ICTY. Instead of neglecting the Tribunal, Koštunica now recognised that this was the most important political issue faced by Serbia.[137] He announced that the government would devise a national strategy for cooperation with the ICTY based on consensus among political actors in Serbia. The Prime Minister's approach to cooperation with the Hague tribunal was largely informed by the conflicting demands of his political allies. While his coalition partners pressed for cooperation in order to advance the government's pro-European agenda, the SPS continually threatened to suspend its support for the minority government if it were to proceed with the extradition of ICTY indictees. Therefore, Koštunica put forward the policy of 'voluntary surrender' as the only plausible option for proceeding with the transfer of ICTY indictees to The Hague.[138] In summer 2004, the Serbian government secretly presented its strategy for the apprehension of war crimes suspects to the ICTY officials.[139] This strategy consisted in compelling the 'minor' indictees to surrender in order to isolate and arrest General Mladić. In view of that, the government launched a massive media campaign to pressure the indictees into surrendering. This initiative was backed by influential circles in Serbian society, including the Serbian Orthodox Church.

The announcement of the government's new strategy for cooperation with the ICTY failed to produce any immediate results. In late 2004, the European Union joined US efforts to enforce ICTY cooperation in Serbia by explicitly linking accession talks with the arrest and extradition of indictees. Indeed,

---

134 'Generali uzdrmali vladu' (Generals Have Destabilised Government), *Blic*, 3 July 2004.

135 'Nema dogovora' (There's No Deal), *Politika*, 9 July 2004.

136 'Hag objavio fotografije Gorana Hadžića' (Hague Publishes Pictures of Goran Hadžić), *Danas*, 23 July 2004.

137 'Haško pitanje' (The Hague Issue), *Politika*, 19 July 2004.

138 'Dobrovoljna predaja' (Voluntary Surrender), *Politika*, 6 September 2004.

139 Del Ponte and Sudetić, *Gospodja Tužiteljka*, 294–5.

the EU announced that it would not conduct the Feasibility Study for Serbia and Montenegro's integration into the EU without any clear sign of progress in Serbia's cooperation with the Hague tribunal.[140] This progress was to be assessed by the Chief Prosecutor, Carla Del Ponte, who conditioned her positive assessment of Serbia and Montenegro's improvement in cooperation with the ICTY upon the transfer of indictees. The surge in foreign pressure contributed to increasing tensions within the State Union, as the Montenegrin authorities denounced Serbia for obstructing the country's process of European integration. As a result, the Serbian authorities announced that they would proceed with the arrest of indictees if they refused to surrender. The government's policy of voluntary surrender finally bore fruit with the transfer of the Bosnian Serb Colonel Beara on 10 October 2004.[141]

B. The Policy of 'Voluntary Surrender'

The policy of 'voluntary surrender', which had produced its first results with the transfer of Colonel Beara, led to the handover of 16 war crimes suspects between October 2004 and September 2005. After a year-long break in cooperation with the ICTY, the coordinated pressure of the United States and the European Union induced Koštunica's government to take concrete steps. The EU's conditioning of the Feasibility Study upon the transfer of indictees to The Hague created a particularly significant incentive for the Serbian government, which had placed European integration at the top of its political priorities. EU officials expressly pushed for the handover of three generals (Lukić, Lazarević and Pavković) who were clearly within the Serbian authorities' reach.[142] Despite having been indicted by the OTP in October 2003, these generals remained free and regularly made public appearances, during which they restated their refusal to surrender and requested to be tried in Serbia. The transfer of these generals on the eve of the deadlines imposed by the EU showed that the Serbian government had become extremely responsive to EU conditionality.

The policy's key success factors

The success of the government's policy of 'voluntary surrender' can be explained by a combination of various factors. The ability of the government to convince war crimes suspects to surrender largely derived from the proximity of Koštunica's

140 'Gorka pilula nam ne gine' (We Cannot Escape the Bitter Pill), *Večernje Novosti*, 12 September 2004.

141 'Ljubiša Beara u Hagu' (Ljubiša Beara in The Hague), *Politika*, 11 October 2004.

142 'Generali u Hagu do Svetoga Save' (Generals in The Hague until Saint Sava's Day), *Blic*, 27 December 2004.

entourage with circles within the military and security sector.[143] During his tenure as president of Yugoslavia, Koštunica had established close links with the military establishment. After becoming Prime Minister, he appointed his former advisor, Rade Bulatović, as head of the Security Intelligence Agency (SIA).[144] This proximity with the security sector was not only based on personal networks, but also on ideological affinities. The government's appeals for indictees to surrender were framed in patriotic language that resonated deeply with the military.[145] The media campaign deployed by the authorities portrayed their surrender to the ICTY as a contribution to the defence of Kosovo and to Serbia's European integration. In other words, surrendering became a patriotic duty, a sacrifice for the nation. In return for their sacrifice, the indictees were given the status of heroes: they were received in Belgrade by the Prime Minister and accompanied to The Hague by government officials.

This is best illustrated by the surrender of General Lazarević, the former commander of Yugoslav forces in Kosovo at the time of the NATO bombing campaign, in January 2005. His surrender followed an intensive media campaign during which government officials appealed to the generals to continue to fulfil their duty to the state by leaving for The Hague. But even while requesting their surrender, state officials would at the same time openly proclaim these generals' innocence.[146] In view of the then forthcoming negotiations on the status of Kosovo, Lazarević's surrender to the ICTY was portrayed as his ultimate battle for the defence of Serbia's southern province. On the occasion of his departure, the Serbian Minister of Justice, Zoran Stojković, declared:

> In the face of foreign pressure and attempts to undermine the struggle for Kosovo and Metohija through pressures by the Hague tribunal, General Lazarević is fulfilling his duty as an honourable officer to the end.[147]

Surrendering to the ICTY was thus portrayed as a patriotic gesture, for which indictees received great public recognition. As the authorities denounced the policy of conditionality as holding Serbia hostage to the Tribunal, the 'voluntary surrender' of indictees was presented as a contribution towards releasing the country from the Tribunal's yoke and enabling Serbia to progress towards the EU.

---

143 Personal interview with Milan Parivodić, DSS Executive and Serbian Minister of Foreign Economic Relations 2004–07, on 27 June 2009.

144 The Security Intelligence Agency replaced the State Security Service in 2002.

145 Personal interview with Zoran Stojković, Serbian Minister of Justice 2004–07, on 25 August 2009.

146 'Nijedan general nije zločinac' (Not a Single General is a Criminal), *Dnevnik*, 31 December 2004.

147 'Vlada obećava pomoć' (The Government Pledges Support), *Politika*, 29 January 2005.

Besides public recognition, the indictees were provided with the legal and financial support of the state. The government took an active role in allowing the indictees to remain free until the start of their trial by providing guarantees to the Tribunal that they would appear in court as soon as their hearing began. The temporary provisional release of Jovica Stanišić and Franko Simatović, two Milošević-era intelligence chiefs, in somewhat shady circumstances was hailed as a sign that the 'reciprocal' model of cooperation advocated by the government was bearing fruit.[148] This claim was given further strength by the subsequent temporary provisional release of four high-ranking military and political leaders, including General Lazarević, in April 2005. Back in Serbia, the Tribunal's decisions substantially increased the credibility of Koštunica's model of cooperation with the ICTY, especially since the DOS government had previously failed to obtain the release of three of these four indictees who had surrendered in 2002 and 2003.[149] Most obviously, the possibility of remaining free until the beginning of their trial provided a substantial incentive for the indictees to surrender.

Their surrender was further motivated by the provision of generous financial assistance, which was mostly concealed from the public. Besides bestowing on the families of the indictees the financial assistance introduced by the DOS government, it is widely believed that the authorities bought several 'surrenders' with the support of pro-government tycoons. On some occasions, these transactions were made public, as in the case of General Lazarević, whose family was donated a car by the political party New Serbia, which formed part of the coalition government.[150] In most cases, however, these deals were kept secret. Human rights advocates and opposition representatives have denounced the government for bribing the most 'important' indictees by allegedly giving colossal sums in exchange for their surrender.[151] Still, for the majority of indictees, even the financial support legally provided by the government did represent a substantial relief: many of them were living in abject poverty because of being fugitives.[152]

148 The release of Stanišić and Simatović was fiercely opposed by the Office of the Prosecutor. There are serious allegations that their release was supported by the US authorities, with which Stanišić had cooperated throughout the nineties ('Serbian Spy's Trial Lifts Cloak on His CIA Alliance', *Los Angeles Times*, 1 March 2009).

149 These were Nikola Šainović, Dragoljub Ojdanić and Milan Milutinović ['Četvorica na slobodi do sudjenja' (Four Set Free until Trial Begins), *B92*, 14 April 2004].

150 'Nova Srbija poklonila 'Škodu' porodici Lazarević' (New Serbia Donated a 'Skoda' to Lazarevic Family), *Glas Javnosti*, 13 March 2005.

151 According to Vladimir Goati, the Koštunica government budgeted 500,000 euros for promoting voluntary surrender, on top of the 312,000 euros allocated for this purpose by the National Council for Cooperation with the ICTY (Vladimir Goati, *Partijske borbe u Srbiji u postoktobarskom razdoblju* (Party Struggles in Serbia in the Post-October Period) (Belgrade: Friedrich Ebert Stiftung and Institute of Social Sciences, 2006), 243).

152 Personal interview with Ivan Andrić.

Finally, one of the most important factors – if not the most important one – behind the success of this policy was the capacity of the government to coerce the indictees into surrendering to the ICTY. The loyalty of the military and intelligence agencies enabled the government to locate and, if necessary, arrest the indictees and portray their transfer as 'voluntary surrenders'. Apparently, this technique was implemented on the occasion of the first 'voluntary' surrender: ICTY officials claimed that the police had besieged Colonel Beara's house after they had reported his location to the Serbian authorities.[153] This was even more obvious in the case of Sreten Lukić, who was taken to The Hague in his pyjamas and slippers from his hospital bed, with a drip still stuck in his arm.[154] This method presented several advantages for the authorities. Portraying these arrests as 'voluntary surrenders' allowed the government to stay in power by dismissing allegations that it was arresting and handing over the indictees to The Hague, which would have resulted in the withdrawal of SPS's support for Koštunica's cabinet. At the same time, by proceeding with the arrests, the government was sending a clear message to the indictees that they would definitely be transferred to the ICTY, one way or another. It thus appeared more advantageous for the war crimes suspects to surrender, or to pretend to have surrendered, in order to benefit from the legal and financial support of the state.

The policy's outcomes: cooperation runs counter to transitional justice

In spite of its success in apprehending war crimes suspects, the policy of 'voluntary surrenders' actually ended up undermining the goals of transitional justice associated with the ICTY. By providing material and moral support to the indictees, this policy created some form of solidarity towards the indictees among the general public. As noted above, the provision of material aid by the state was superfluous since the Tribunal covers the expenses of the indictees' defence: its function was essentially symbolic. As the government stood behind the indictees, who were depicted as martyrs sacrificing themselves (once again) for their homeland, the public empathised with the indictees, whom many people now perceived as scapegoats. The former Minister of Foreign Affairs in the DOS government, Goran Svilanović, sums up the consequences of this policy in the following terms:

> So (here is) what has happened in fact: we have created a dynamic in which our war criminals have become 'ours'. The same is true for Croatian public opinion and that of Bosnia. As a result, none of the three public opinions are satisfied with the work of the Tribunal, none of them give majority support to the work of

153 'Artman: Pukovnik Beara uhapšen u Srbiji' (Artman: Colonel Beara Arrested in Serbia), *Danas*, 11 October 2004.

154 'Dobrovoljac u pidžami' (Volunteer in Pyjamas), *NIN*, 7 April 2005.

> the Tribunal... This is such a political setback, a dramatic setback, for the idea of international war crimes trials.[155]

This state of affairs is corroborated by empirical evidence. Public opinion polls carried out in 2005 show that two thirds of the Serbian population believed that the Tribunal was biased against Serbs.[156] While 66 per cent of the population supported cooperation with the ICTY for utilitarian reasons, only 17 per cent supported it for the sake of justice. The results for the previous years were similar as the DOS government also largely resorted to pragmatic arguments for cooperation, especially on the occasion of Milošević's extradition.

This distortion in the public's attitude toward cooperation is largely imputable to the policy of conditionality, which set the terms of cooperation with the ICTY on purely utilitarian grounds.[157] By conditioning financial aid and European integration upon cooperation with the Tribunal, the international community created the conditions for detaching the extradition of indictees from any notion of justice and truth. This discrepancy was reinforced by the government's policy of 'voluntary surrenders', which sought to decriminalise and glorify the indictees. Their transfer to The Hague was devoid of any discussion of war crimes, as the authorities and the press often refrained from even mentioning the charges which were imputed to these individuals. The media campaign deployed by the government depicted cooperation with the ICTY as an unfair 'international obligation' imposed on Serbia. This only further fed into the overriding notion of injustice associated with the Tribunal. Accordingly, transferring war crimes suspects to the ICTY was essentially framed as a necessary measure for enabling Serbia to achieve socio-economic advancement through integration into the EU.[158]

This pragmatic discourse allowed the government to proceed with cooperation while subverting the Tribunal's attempt at promoting public reckoning with the past in Serbia. Koštunica and his entourage shared a deep-seated antagonism towards the ICTY, which they blamed for distorting history by disproportionately imputing the responsibility for the war and war crimes to the Serbian side. By raising the profile of the indictees in the eyes of the Serbian public and associating their defence with the defence of state interests, the policy of 'voluntary surrenders' deliberately sought to undermine the narrative of the past promoted by the

155 Personal interview with Goran Svilanović.

156 Belgrade Centre for Human Rights and Strategic Marketing, 'Public Opinion in Serbia: Attitudes towards the ICTY', April 2005. Retrieved from www.bgcentar.org.rs on 7 March 2010.

157 See Jelena Subotić, *Hijacked Justice: Dealing with the Past in the Balkans* (Ithaca: Cornell University Press, 2009).

158 Personal interview with Vojin Dimitrijević, Director of the Belgrade Centre for Human Rights, on 1 July 2009.

ICTY. This intent clearly transpires through the testimony of Slobodan Samardžić, Koštunica's former advisor and DSS executive:

> I think that since the intentions of the Tribunal were obvious – these indictments were such that they incriminated the state and its history, the nation and its history – the state simply had to help out these people for these reasons. … Serbia simply had to be pressed up against the wall of shame through these judgments, like Nazi Germany in 1945, so that denazification could be implemented. … So it was difficult to have a normal attitude towards this. It would have been abnormal for someone to cooperate without questioning these demands when seeing what its [the Tribunal's] political goals were. These were really obvious, and ways were sought to absorb this pressure on the state and to turn this into a normal legal process.[159]

The policy of 'voluntary surrender' thus clearly sought to assuage foreign pressures for cooperation with the ICTY and, at the same time, neutralise the political goals of the Tribunal. This policy reconciled the government's deep-seated antagonism towards the ICTY and its pro-European agenda by producing a normative shift in cooperation. While the DOS government promoted surrenders to alleviate the destabilising effects associated with the arrest of indictees, the Koštunica administration openly stood behind the indictees in order to undermine the Tribunal's transitional justice agenda, to which it was ideologically opposed. This endeavour was underpinned by the fear – sensed by Serbian political elites across the board (see Chapter 4) – that the ICTY's efforts at de-legitimising the Milošević regime could undermine the legitimacy of the Serbian state. Furthermore, the policy of 'voluntary surrender' allowed Koštunica to satisfy both domestic and foreign pressures for cooperation, while keeping his government in office with the support of the SPS. This approach to ICTY cooperation was a matter of consensus among political elites, which amply contributed to reducing the destabilising effects associated with the Hague issue. Therefore, this policy reflected both the power balance between domestic political actors and the ideological preferences of the government at that time.

3. The Crisis and Exhaustion of the 'Hague Issue' (2006–2011)

By the end of 2005, the effectiveness of the 'voluntary surrender' policy was exhausted as the flow of transfers to The Hague came to an end. The two most important indictees, Radovan Karadžić and Ratko Mladić, remained at large, along with four other fugitives. After the arrest of the Croatian General Gotovina in December of that year, these were the last six indictees sought by the Tribunal. Serbia thus stood out as the only country that was failing to cooperate with the ICTY. As a

---

159 Personal interview with Slobodan Samardžić.

result, Tribunal officials were able to intensify their diplomatic efforts at pressuring the Serbian authorities to arrest and hand over the last remaining indictees.

A. ICTY Cooperation as a Source of Renewed Instability

The international community particularly pressed for the arrest and transfer of General Mladić, who was believed to be hiding in Serbia. The Serbian authorities repeatedly claimed that there had been no trace of the general since 2002, when he had supposedly been expelled from army barracks.[160] They argued that there was no evidence of Mladić being in Serbia, although they could not prove the contrary either. However, the highly publicised discovery of a network that allegedly provided intelligence and logistical support to Mladić suggested that the runaway general might still have been under the protection of the armed forces.[161] This suspicion was sporadically heightened by Foreign Minister Drašković, who repeatedly accused the intelligence agencies of protecting Mladić.[162] Even though these claims were immediately dismissed by representatives of the secret services and the military, doubts persisted on this issue. The arrest of a former Bosnian Serb officer who was allegedly helping Mladić hide in January 2006 still failed to produce any results.[163] These developments reinforced Western diplomats' conviction that there was no political will in Belgrade to arrest Mladić. Indeed, the Chief Prosecutor, Carla Del Ponte, claimed that the Serbian government was still attempting to convince Mladić to surrender instead of arresting him.[164] As a result, she lobbied for the EU to increase pressure on Serbia to cooperate with the ICTY.

Having set several deadlines for the apprehension of Mladić that had not been met by the Serbian government, the EU decided to suspend talks with Serbia on the Stabilisation and Accession Agreement (SAA) in May 2006.[165] This triggered a deep governmental crisis and a period of instability during which reforms of

---

160 'Pripadnici KOS čuvaju Mladića' (Members of KOS [military security] Are Protecting Mladić), *Blic*, 6 October 2005.

161 'Vukčević: Znamo ko pomaže Karadžiću i Mladiću' (Vukčević: We Know Who is Helping Karadžić and Mladić), *Politika*, 23 December 2005.

162 'Fajnenšel tajms: Drašković priznao da DB čuva Mladića' (Financial Times: Drašković Admits that the State Security Service is Protecting Mladić), *Danas*, 6 April 2005.

163 The War Crimes Prosecutor, Vladimir Vukčević, later claimed that the arrest of Mladić's protectors in 2006 was carried out by the State Security in order to obstruct the arrest of Mladić, who had been located by the authorities ['Imali smo Mladića u šaci' (We Had Mladić in Our Hands), *Vreme*, 14 October 2010].

164 These claims were later substantiated by Vladimir Vukčević who declared that, in 2006, the Head of the State Security Service proposed to the War Crimes Prosecution to negotiate the surrender of Mladić. This offer was subsequently repealed ['Bilo opstrukcija u vezi sa Mladićem' (There Were Obstructions with regard to Mladić), *B92*, 27 December 2010].

165 'Ozbiljna kriza Koštuničine vlade' (Koštunica's Government in Serious Crisis), *Vreme*, 4 May 2006.

state institutions were practically brought to a halt. The EU's decision came just three weeks before the Montenegrin referendum on independence, which sealed the fate of the State Union of Serbia and Montenegro. It provided a major boost to the secessionist parties, whose main argument was that an independent Montenegro would progress faster towards EU membership.[166] The break-up of the State Union on the eve of the negotiations on the future status of Kosovo was a major blow for Koštunica who had made the preservation of the country's sovereignty and integrity his priority. The beginning of the Kosovo talks in July 2006 set this issue at the top of the domestic political agenda. This led to a progressive radicalisation of the Serbian political scene, in which the Hague tribunal was instrumental.

The resurgence of the 'Hague issue' in domestic politics was prompted by the sudden death of Slobodan Milošević in the penitentiary unit of the ICTY in March 2006. The SPS and SRS rallied together in denouncing the Tribunal for the murder of the former President and requesting his rehabilitation through a state-sponsored funeral.[167] Milošević's death provided Serbian nationalists with additional grounds to demonise the Tribunal as a Western conspiracy and to request the suspension of cooperation with the ICTY. This campaign was opposed by state officials, who did not allow a state-sponsored funeral or the return of Milošević's family, who had sought exile in Russia in order to escape criminal proceedings in Serbia. Nevertheless, there was a consensus among political elites that the Tribunal bore responsibility for the fate of the former President, and that his death had further discredited the Tribunal in the eyes of domestic public opinion.[168] So did the verdict to the trial of Naser Orić, the former commander of Muslim forces in Srebrenica, who was condemned to two years' imprisonment, which he had already served while waiting for the trial. This sentence provoked a chorus of disapproval amongst Serbian officials, who considered Orić to be the main culprit for war crimes perpetrated against Serbs in Eastern Bosnia.[169]

The renewed mobilisation of those parties which formed part of the former regime in opposing cooperation with the ICTY led to a reconfiguration of party alliances on the political scene. While the SPS still supported Koštunica's minority government and was rhetorically in favour of the process of European integration, it was firmly opposed to the arrest and transfer of indictees to The Hague. Although its representatives approved the policy of 'voluntary

166 Personal interview with Slobodan Samardžić; see also Kenneth Morrison, *Montenegro: a Modern History* (London and New York: I.B Tauris, 2009), 214.

167 'Sahrana u Beogradu ili pada Vlada?!' (Funeral in Belgrade or Government Will Fall?!), *Dnevnik*, 13 March 2006.

168 See Janine N. Clark, 'The Death of Milošević: Exploring Public Reaction in Serbia', *Southeast European and Black Sea Studies* 7:4 (2007): 591–608.

169 'Tadić: Kazna kao za kradju u samoposluzi' (Tadić: Sentence Equal to Shoplifting), *Danas*, 1 July 2006.

surrender', they repeatedly stated that they would withdraw their support for the government if it proceeded with the arrest of General Mladić. Their position thus coincided with the standpoint of the SRS, who were opposed to any kind of cooperation with the Tribunal. Following the death of Milošević, the SRS, with the support of the SPS, put forward a parliamentary motion calling for a halt to cooperation with the ICTY.[170] Although the motion was not passed, it did revive the spectre of the 'anti-Hague lobby'. Both the SPS and the SRS denounced the European policy of conditionality as extortion that sought to pressure Serbia into relinquishing its claims over Kosovo. The SRS repeatedly appealed to General Mladić not to surrender and warned the authorities that his arrest would generate mass protests. Through their campaign of support to General Mladić, the Radicals clearly sought to increase the security risks associated with the potential arrest of ICTY indictees.

On the other hand, the DS adopted a much more collaborative approach towards the governing coalition. While his party was formally in opposition, President Tadić expressed his full support for the government's plans to arrest and transfer the remaining indictees to The Hague.[171] Consequently, the DS provided crucial support for the measures implemented by the government to this end. In April 2006, the parliament of Serbia and Montenegro finally adopted a law which allowed for the freezing of assets belonging to ICTY indictees who were at large.[172] The adoption of this piece of legislation had been delayed for a year owing to the opposition of the SPS. Its enactment was urged by the EU, which thus requested the Serbian government to demonstrate its commitment to cooperation with the ICTY.

Following the suspension of the SAA talks, the Serbian government developed an action plan for the arrest and transfer of the remaining indictees. This initiative came from EU officials who considered that the Serbian authorities should implement measures similar to those taken by the Croatian government in order to locate and arrest Ante Gotovina.[173] The main objective of this action plan was to coordinate the work of the civil and military intelligence agencies, whose rivalry was seen as the main obstacle to locating and arresting the ICTY indictees.[174] In addition, the action plan sought to facilitate the exchange of information with foreign intelligence agencies and prepare public opinion for the

170 'Radikalima podrška samo od socijalista' (Radicals Only Get Support from Socialists), *Politika*, 28 March 2006.

171 'Tadić: Podržaćemo Vladu u saradnji sa Hagom' (Tadić: We Shall Support the Government in Cooperating with The Hague), *Blic*, 24 March 2004.

172 'Haškim beguncima zakonom zamrznuta imovina' (Assets of Hague Fugitives Frozen by Law), *Dnevnik*, 8 April 2004.

173 'Pakovanje Mladića u hrvatski model' (Packaging Mladić according to Croatian Model), *Dnevnik*, 23 June 2006.

174 'Premijer u ponedeljak predstavlja plan' (PM Presents Plan on Monday), *Danas*, 13 July 2006.

arrest and extradition of Ratko Mladić. In the view of Tribunal officials, this last element was critical for demonstrating the government's commitment to arresting the fugitives. The Chief Prosecutor, Carla Del Ponte, maintained that there was no political will to arrest Mladić in Belgrade despite Serbian officials asserting their resolve to apprehend him.[175] The action plan was implemented by the Action Team for the Completion of ICTY Cooperation headed by the Minister for Human and Minority Rights Rasim Ljajić and the Special Prosecutor for War Crimes Vladimir Vukčević, who enjoyed the trust of foreign diplomats and ICTY officials.[176]

By autumn, the failure to deliver Mladić to the ICTY and to resume the SAA talks had eroded the credibility of the coalition in power. As a result, G17 withdrew from government, which led to the calling of early parliamentary elections in January 2007. In view of the increasing popularity of the SRS, the parties that cooperated under the DOS coalition formed a common front against the resurgence of radical nationalism. The renewed 'democratic bloc' led by the DS and DSS shared common views on key national issues such as the country's integration into the EU and the status of Kosovo.[177] In this context, cooperation with the ICTY was portrayed not only as a means to further the country's progress towards the EU, but also as a decisive element for improving the country's position in negotiations on the future of Kosovo.

The electoral campaign was once again tainted by the Hague issue as it coincided with the beginning of the trial of Vojislav Šešelj. In the run-up to the elections, the leader of the Serbian Radical Party (SRS) engaged in a one-month-long hunger strike in order to claim the right to represent himself at his trial. Šešelj, who had waited four years in the prison of the ICTY for his trial to begin, was protesting against the decision of the Tribunal's Chamber to appoint him a lawyer. This diverted the attention of the Serbian media and public towards the plight of the SRS leader, who was increasingly portrayed and perceived as a martyr.[178] The Tribunal's decision to impose a defence lawyer on Šešelj was unequivocally condemned by the Serbian political and cultural elite, which was already highly critical of the delay in the trial.[179] Although the Chamber eventually backed down by accepting Šešelj's requests, this episode further discredited the Tribunal in the eyes of the public by reinforcing the view

---

175 The US embassy cables released by Wikileaks revealed that Western diplomats believed that the Koštunica administration had no genuine intention of arresting Mladić and that it was giving him protection instead ['Otpor Koštunice kočio saradnju' (Koštunica's Opposition Hampered Cooperation), *B92*, 10 December 2010].

176 'Ljajić i Vukčević koordinatori' (Ljajić and Vukčević as Coordinators), *Glas Javnosti*, 19 July 2006.

177 'Sloga Vlade i Predsednika' (Government and President in Agreement), *Večernje Novosti*, 31 July 2006.

178 'Sud na infuziji' (The Court on a Drip-Feed), *NIN*, 30 November 2006.

179 'Vlada Srbije zabrinuta zbog štrajka lidera SRS' (Serbian Government Concerned about SRS Leader Strike), *Danas*, 2 December 2006.

that it was biased against Serbs, or at least incapable of carrying out a trial with respect for the rights of defendants. Most notably, Šešelj's hunger strike boosted the political campaign of the SRS, which stood out as the clear favourite in the elections.

B. Loose Conditionality, Democratic Consolidation and the Waning of the 'Hague Issue'

The domestic political developments in Serbia led the international community to reconsider and progressively relax the policy of conditionality.[180] The resurgence of radical nationalism embodied in the SRS was increasingly perceived as a threat to the country's democratisation and the region's stability. These concerns were reinforced by the failure of the negotiations on the future status of Kosovo. The resolution of this issue became a priority for international actors who sought to attenuate the negative repercussions in Serbia of Kosovo's progress towards independence by facilitating the country's integration into the Euro-Atlantic institutions. This change of policy resulted first of all in Serbia's accession to NATO's Partnership for Peace programme in November 2006. As in the process of EU integration, progress towards NATO membership was conditioned upon cooperation with the ICTY. Nevertheless, the US authorities decided to grant Serbia access to the Partnership for Peace in order to boost the pro-Western parties on the eve of the parliamentary elections.[181]

The loosening of EU conditionality

The EU's tough stance with regard to Hague conditionality was increasingly called into question in diplomatic circles, as a number of countries pressed for easing the pressure on Serbia. The main argument in favour of this move was that the suspension of the SAA talks was counterproductive because it had pushed Serbia further away from the EU, thus exposing the country to nationalist parties and Russian influence. Nevertheless, the loosening of the policy of conditionality was firmly opposed by the Netherlands and Belgium, which insisted on the arrest of Mladić. Ultimately, the EU member states reached a compromise by agreeing that the SAA talks could resume as soon as Serbia made a substantial improvement in cooperation with the ICTY. In other words, the arrest of Mladić was no longer a benchmark for cooperation, nor a condition for the resumption of EU talks.[182]

The EU's policy of conditionality was also the subject of a fierce polemic among representatives of civil society organisations, who were actively involved in the

---

180 Victor Peskin and Mieczysław P. Boduszynski, 'Balancing International Justice in the Balkans: Surrogate Enforcers, Uncertain Transitions and the Road to Europe', *International Journal of Transitional Justice* 1:23 (2011): 1–23.

181 Del Ponte and Sudetić, *Gospodja Tužiteljka*, 325.

182 Peskin and Boduszynski, 'Balancing International Justice in the Balkans', 15.

processes of transitional justice and democratisation in Serbia. While one group of NGOs insisted that the EU persist in conditioning SAA talks upon the arrest and extradition of Mladić, many prominent civil society activists considered that this policy had become counter-effective.[183] This view was based on the conviction that cooperation with the ICTY had to be an outcome rather than a precondition of Europeanisation. Accordingly, the successful implementation of transitional justice measures could only be carried out within a European framework.[184] The suspension of SAA talks acted against the process of Europeanisation in Serbia, which in turn reduced the prospects for cooperation with the ICTY. By cutting short Serbia's progression towards membership of the union, the EU had effectively lost its leverage on the Serbian authorities, who increasingly turned to Russia in their opposition to Kosovo's independence. These NGO activists thus appealed to the EU to relax its policy of conditionality in order to advance Serbia's Europeanisation, and thereby promote renewed cooperation with the ICTY.[185]

Critics also pointed to the temporal limitations of the policy of conditionality. The protracted length of ICTY conditionality was amply contributing towards creating a climate of political apathy that inhibited reforms in Serbia. Hague conditionality had been distracting the attention of the media and the public away from more pressing socio-economic issues for years. Under those circumstances, the successive governments were never able to present their policies on these key issues as public attention was constantly focused on national questions: the ICTY and Kosovo. This state of affairs was deplored by the former Foreign Minister, Goran Svilanović:

> You know, Nuremberg lasted for six months and this has been going on for ten years. You cannot have public opinion focused on this – whether someone has been arrested or not – for ten years, it is simply impossible. … This temporal dimension is important, it has lasted too long, public opinion cannot withstand it. So now you have a resigned public opinion. When you ask them if they support the arrests, they will say that they support them – but only out of resignation. When you ask them whether they condemn the crimes [of the indictees] – 'No, they are our people'. So this identification, this socialisation is still very important.[186]

As described by Svilanović, this has generated widespread disengagement from politics among the population, who have not been able to look forward

183 'O inicijativi nekih NVO' (About the Initiative of Some NGOs), *B92*, 5 April 2007.

184 Personal interview with Biljana Kovačević-Vučo, Director of the Yugoslav Committee for Human Rights, on 20 July 2009.

185 Personal interview with Sonja Liht, Director of the Belgrade Fund for Political Excellence, on 11 August 2009.

186 Personal interview with Goran Svilanović. Note that trial of the major war criminals before the International Military Tribunal (IMT) actually lasted 11 months, from November 1945 to October 1946.

to improvements in living conditions. According to a prominent Serbian NGO activist, cooperation with The Hague has turned into agony, with conditionality weighing heavily on Serbia's European prospects.[187]

The parliamentary elections of January 2007 confirmed the predominance of the Serbian Radical Party. Although the deputy leader of the SRS, Tomislav Nikolić, briefly acted as Speaker in Parliament, his party was not able to assemble a majority in order to form a government. Following months of painstaking negotiations, Koštunica formed a new cabinet with the Democratic Party (DS), which had come second in the elections after the SRS, and with the G17. The new government set the arrest and transfer of Ratko Mladić and of the remaining indictees to the ICTY at the top of its priorities.[188] The resolve of the Serbian authorities was confirmed through the arrest of Zdravko Tolimir two weeks after the establishment of Koštunica's new cabinet. This arrest was hailed as a sign of improvement in cooperation with the ICTY, thereby opening the door for the resumption of SAA talks between Serbia and the EU. Nevertheless, the allegations that Tolimir's arrest had been staged in Bosnia in order to clear the Serbian government of responsibility cast doubts about Koštunica's readiness to proceed with the arrest of Mladić.[189] The subsequent arrest of Vlastimir Djordjević, who was located in Montenegro by the Serbian intelligence agency, further raised hopes that Serbia might be on track to arrest all the remaining fugitives.[190] However, these expectations proved wrong as the flow of transfers to The Hague was once again interrupted.

Besides political will, the arrest of the remaining ICTY indictees required establishing firm control over the security agencies which were assigned the task of tracking down those fugitives. Towards this end, the Serbian government created the National Security Council in May 2007. This new body – which comprised the President, the Prime Minister, various ministers and the heads of the intelligence agencies – was mainly aimed at improving coordination between the Security Intelligence Agency (SIA), the military intelligence agencies[191] and the police.[192] The lack of coordination between these institutions was seen as one of the main

187 Personal interview with Sonja Liht.

188 'Niko ne zna gde je, ali moramo ga uhapsiti' (Nobody Knows Where He Is, but We Must Arrest Him), *Dnevnik*, 8 March 2007.

189 Del Ponte and Sudetić, *Gospodja Tužiteljka*, 339–41.

190 'Refik Hodžić: nadamo se da je ovo uvod u hapšenje ostale četvorice optuženika' (Rekfik Hodžić: We Hope this is the Prelude to the Arrest of the Other Four Indictees), *Danas*, 18 June 2006.

191 In 2007, there were two military intelligence agencies in Serbia: the Military Security Agency which operated within Serbia and the Military Intelligence Agency which operated abroad.

192 The subsequently adopted legislation on intelligence agencies also provided for improved parliamentary control over the agencies. See 'Law on the Bases of Regulating Security Services of the Republic of Serbia', *Official Gazette of the RS, No. 116/2007*, retrieved from www.bia.gov.rs on 6 April 2013.

obstacles to ICTY cooperation, which the authorities explicitly sought to tackle through this measure.[193] In practice, the creation of the National Security Council sought to shift the authority over the intelligence agencies from the Prime Minister to the President, who presided over the Council and appointed the coordinator of the intelligence agencies.[194] Control over the SIA, the most important security agency in Serbia, was a long-lasting bone of contention between President Tadić and Prime Minister Koštunica.[195] Since the management of the SIA was appointed by the government, Koštunica was able to exert direct influence over this agency throughout his mandate as Prime Minister. The establishment of the National Security Council reduced Koštunica's monopoly in this respect by allowing Tadić to exert a certain degree of control over the SIA.

In the public sphere, Ratko Mladić became the subject of a discursive battle between the pro-European parties in power and the nationalist opposition. On the one hand, President Tadić increasingly portrayed the arrest of Mladić as a moral necessity for Serbia and a prerequisite for reconciliation in the region. During an appearance on a Croatian TV programme, he stated that Mladić was the darkest page in Serbian history, while apologising for war crimes perpetrated by Serbs against Croats.[196] This emphasis on the moral aspect of cooperation with the ICTY was given further impetus by the domestic War Crimes Prosecutor, Vladimir Vukčević, who also acted as the coordinator of the action plan for the location and arrest of the remaining indictees. On the other hand, the Radicals increasingly used Mladić in their public display as a figure symbolising Serbian resistance to the West. One amongst many other actions undertaken by the SRS in this respect consisted in pasting 'Ratko Mladić Boulevard' posters in a street named after Zoran Djindjić in May 2007.[197] The SRS and SPS representatives openly opposed the transfer of the Bosnian Serb general to the ICTY, announcing that they would organise public protests in the event of his arrest. Most obviously, the purpose of this strategy was not only to mobilise nationalist support, but also to increase the risks and political costs associated with the arrest of General Mladić by creating an adverse political climate.[198]

The failure to arrest the four remaining fugitives led to renewed disruption in Serbia's progress towards the EU in autumn 2007. After the completion of the SAA

193 'Ključ za okončanje saradnje sa Hagom' (The Key for Completing Cooperation with The Hague), *Dnevnik*, 1 January 2007.

194 Predrag Petrović, 'Nadzor službi bezbednosti na Zapadnom Balkanu: Slučaj Srbija' (The Oversight of Security Agencies in the Western Balkans: the Case of Serbia), Belgrade Centre for Security Policy Working Paper. Retrieved from www.bezbednost.org on 6 April 2013.

195 The military intelligence agencies were significantly smaller than SIA since their mandate was limited to military personnel and military threats.

196 'Mladić najtamnija strana naše istorije' (Mladić is Darkest Page in Our History), *Blic*, 25 June 2007.

197 'Provokacija sa Mladićem' (Provocations over Mladić), *Blic*, 27 May 2007.

198 'Ne daju Mladića' (They Will Not Give Mladić Up), *Kurir*, 19 June 2007; personal interview with Biljana Kovačević-Vučo.

talks, the EU conditioned the signing of the agreement upon the arrest of Mladić.[199] However, Serbia's prospects of European integration were increasingly called into question by the Kosovo issue. The explicit support by several core European countries for the independence of Kosovo led the Serbian Prime Minister to turn his back on the EU. Koštunica made it clear that the EU would have to choose between Serbia and Kosovo, thus dismissing any attempts to facilitate Serbia's progress towards the EU as compensation for the loss of its southern province.[200] The profound disagreements between the DSS and the DS on how to respond to Kosovo's proclamation of independence led to the collapse of the Serbian government in March 2008.

While the Kosovo issue and attitudes towards EU integration constituted the central themes of the electoral campaign, the proceedings of the Tribunal once again impinged on domestic political debates. The acquittal of Ramush Haradinaj, the former leader of the Kosovo Liberation Army, produced a massive outcry in Serbia.[201] The fact that Haradinaj was acquitted as a result of the prosecution's inability to secure the most important witnesses, nine of whom were allegedly killed during the trial, turned this case into a scandal.[202] Koštunica was one of the Tribunal's strongest critics on this matter. He requested that the EU speak out on this verdict and state clearly whether the Hague tribunal was still 'a beacon of light for European values and the benchmark of European standards in the process of integration'.[203] In view of these circumstances, the EU decided to proceed with the signing of the SAA in order to boost pro-European parties at the elections, while making the implementation of the agreement conditional upon the transfer of Mladić. This decision amply contributed to the victory of the pro-European coalition organised around the DS. Furthermore, the prospect of European integration tipped the balance within the parties grouped around the Socialist Party of Serbia (SPS) in favour of a pro-European government with the DS, instead of forming a coalition with the SRS and DSS (see Chapter 2).

Democratic consolidation and the waning of the 'Hague issue'

The arrest of Stojan Župljanin, and especially of Radovan Karadžić, in the days following the inauguration of the new government signalled that the 'Hague

---

199 'Uhapsite Mladića, pa sporazum sa EU' (Arrest Mladić, Agreement with the EU Will Follow), *Glas Javnosti*, 27 October 2007.

200 'Koštuničin uslov Evropi-Kosovo ili Srbija?' (Koštunica's Alternatives Offered to Europe – Kosovo or Serbia?), *Politika*, 13 December 2007.

201 'Burna reagovanja na presudu Haškog tribunala' (Strong Reactions to Verdict of the Hague Tribunal), *Glas Javnosti*, 4 April 2008.

202 The Appeals Chamber subsequently ordered a partial retrial which, once again, ended with the acquittal of Haradinaj in November 2012.

203 'Koštunica: za Evropsku Uniju Tribunal je svetionik' (Koštunica: For the EU, the Tribunal is a Beacon of Light), *Politika*, 7 April 2008.

issue' was receding.[204] The circumstances under which Karadžić was found and arrested in Belgrade remain unclear. The fact that he had been living for years in the Serbian capital under the guise of a new-age alternative-medicine guru defied imagination.[205] In view of the countless theories around his arrest, it is difficult to say – and impossible to prove – whether Karadžić had been under the protection of the Serbian authorities or some rogue elements within the state security apparatus.[206] In any case, this arrest cleared any doubts about the commitment of the new government to cooperation with the ICTY.

Domestic reactions to the arrest of the former Bosnian Serb President reflected broader changes on the political scene resulting from the elections. On the one hand, the SPS announced that the government would fulfil its international obligations derived from the law on cooperation with the ICTY, even though they had fiercely opposed the adoption of this legislation in 2002. In spite of rhetorically distancing themselves from the arrest of Karadžić, the Socialists did not call into question their participation in government.[207] On the other hand, the DSS – which had voted for the law on cooperation with the ICTY and had transferred many indictees to The Hague – now rallied with the SRS in denouncing the arrest of Karadžić. Following the acquittals of Naser Orić and Ramush Haradinaj, Koštunica openly challenged the legitimacy of the Tribunal, and the DSS gave its full support to the protests organised by the SRS.[208]

The decision to suspend parliamentary procedures for three weeks suggests that the authorities feared that the nationalist opposition might capitalise on the arrest of Karadžić.[209] But the nationalist parties' failure to generate mass mobilisation led to the realisation that the Hague tribunal could no longer be exploited for domestic political gains. Although the SRS-led protests caused turmoil and resulted in the death of one person, the 'Hague issue' no longer represented a threat to domestic stability. While the arrest of indictees and the indictment of high-ranking officials

204 'Uhapšen Radovan Karadžić!', *B92*, 21 July 2008.

205 'Radovan Karadžić's New-Age Adventure', *The New York Times*, 22 July 2009.

206 Note that Karadžić was arrested four days after the appointment of a new management team at the Security Intelligence Agency. The diplomatic cables released by Wikileaks suggest that the Serbian government knew of Mladić's whereabouts in 2008 and that Tadić had complained to foreign diplomats about Koštunica's obstruction to the arrest of Mladić. The War Crimes Prosecutor, Vladimir Vukčević, also declared that 'there were obstructions to the arrest of Mladić until mid-2008' ['Beograd tačno znao gde je Mladić' (Belgrade Knew Exactly Where Mladić Was), *B92*, 9 December 2010; 'Depeša o nezadovoljstvu Tadića' (Cable on Tadić's Discontent), B92, 10 December 2010; *B92*, 27 December 2010].

207 'SPS: Saradnja sa Hagom mora biti dvosmerna' (SPS: Cooperation with The Hague Must Be Reciprocal), *Politika*, 22 July 2008.

208 'Narodnjaci će podržati protest Radikala' (National Coalition Will Support Protest of Radicals), *Politika*, 26 September 2008. After being sentenced to two years imprisonment in 2006, Naser Orić was acquitted by the Appeals Chamber in July 2008.

209 'Nisam prekinula skupštinu zbog hapšenja Radovana Karadžića' (I Did Not Interrupt Parliament because of the Arrest of Radovan Karadžić), *Press*, 23 July 2008.

had earlier caused major political crises and unrest within the armed forces, the consequences of Karadžić's arrest and transfer to The Hague were relatively limited. This demonstrated that the Serbian democratic institutions and political system had acquired enough maturity and stability to face up to the challenge of bringing the most important indictees to justice. At this point, cooperation with the ICTY effectively ceased to be a wedge issue in domestic politics.

Despite these developments, the EU did not immediately proceed with the implementation of the SAA as the Netherlands conditioned their approval of the application of the agreement upon the arrest of Ratko Mladić. Nevertheless, the Dutch authorities were increasingly isolated in their intransigence regarding this issue. Following the arrest of Karadžić, the core of diplomatic activity shifted from pressuring the Serbian authorities to cooperate towards trying to convince the Dutch government to approve the implementation of the SAA with Serbia.[210] At the same time, the new Chief Prosecutor, Serge Brammertz, endeavoured to de-politicise the issue and reduce tensions in relations between the ICTY and the Serbian government by acknowledging and supporting the efforts of the Serbian authorities to locate and arrest Mladić and Hadžić.[211] As doubts about the political readiness of the government to arrest the remaining indictees dissolved, conditionality was effectively reduced to a technical matter. This is illustrated by the EU's decision to proceed with the implementation and ratification of the SAA with Serbia in 2010, despite two indictees remaining at large.

On the domestic front, the deep transformation of the Serbian political landscape that followed the 2008 parliamentary elections generated a substantial shift in attitudes towards ICTY cooperation among political elites. The breakup of the SRS, and the transferral of its most influential members into a pro-European national party, the Serbian Progressive Party (SNS), substantially reduced domestic resistance to the arrest and transfer of indictees (see Chapter 2). The SNS leader, Tomislav Nikolić, who had staged protests against the arrest of Karadžić during his tenure at the SRS, now argued that Serbia should cooperate with the ICTY and appealed to Mladić to surrender.[212] Cooperation with the ICTY thus became a matter of consensus on the political scene, with the exception of the rump SRS, whose influence was substantially diminished.

Ultimately, the arrests of Mladić and Hadžić in 2011 were the result of both increased political resolve and improved institutional capacity to carry out these arrests. These achievements were attributed to the National Security Council and the Action Team for locating and arresting the ICTY indictees, whose work was coordinated by Tadić's chief of staff Miodrag Rakić.[213] The fact that these

210 Personal interview with Ivan Andrić.

211 'Srbija poboljšala saradnju sa Tribunalom' (Serbia Has Improved Cooperation with The Hague), *Danas*, 13 December 2008.

212 'Nikolić: Hapšenje Mladića obaveza', *B92*, 10 November 2010.

213 'Miodrag Rakić, jedan od ključnih ljudi u potrazi za Mladićem: čovek koji može da bude zadovoljan' (Miodrag Rakić, One of the Key Figures in the Search for Mladić: A

operations were led by Tadić's closest entourage suggests that this was a top priority for the Serbian President. Following these arrests, Tadić declared that the National Security Council only started to function properly with the creation of the new government in 2008. He argued that there was no 'consent' between the authorities and the security services under Koštunica and explained the failure to arrest Mladić earlier in the following terms:

> Out of the 16 years during which Mladić escaped justice, the first five fell within the rule of Slobodan Milošević, during which nothing was happening [in terms of cooperation with the ICTY]. Later, there was a period when Mladić was not actively protected, but there was an implicit consensus on not handing him over.[214]

Tadić's statement reinforced the view that the Serbian authorities had been turning a blind eye to Mladić for a long time. The Serbian President announced that the judicial authorities would investigate how Mladić had escaped justice and whether some state structures were involved in it. However, as of April 2013, these judicial proceedings were limited to members of Ratko Mladić's family and his personal entourage.[215] It is therefore impossible to determine at this stage whether the arrest of Mladić had been impeded by politicians or by institutional obstruction within the security apparatus.

What is more obvious is that the Serbian authorities unambiguously endorsed the transitional justice discourse on the occasion of these arrests. The capture of Mladić was personally announced by Boris Tadić at a highly mediatised press conference during which the Serbian President portrayed this event as a major step towards justice and reconciliation:

> Today we close one chapter of our recent history that will bring us one step closer to full reconciliation in the region. I believe that every other country must be responsible for closing their own chapters. All crimes have to be fully investigated and all war criminals must face justice. … We are doing this because we truly believe that this is in accordance with our law: this is because of our people, Serbs, this is because of the moral dignity of our country and our people; and this is crucially important in terms of reconciliation between people living in the region of South-East Europe and former Yugoslavia.[216]

Man Who Can Be Satisfied), *Danas*, 28 May 2011.

214 'Srbija došla do katarze' (Serbia Has Attained Catharsis), *Dnevnik*, 4 June 2011.

215 These proceedings may be extended in the future. In June 2012, the War Crimes Prosecutor Vladimir Vukčević declared that the former Chief of Staff of the Yugoslav Army Nebojša Pavković and the former head of the Military Security Agency Aco Tomić were suspected of having provided protection to Mladić ['I Aco Tomić medju jatacima' (Aco Tomić Was Also an Accomplice), *Blic*, 23 Jun 2012].

216 'Boris Tadić: Uhapšen je Ratko Mladić' (Boris Tadić: Ratko Mladić Has Been Arrested), YouTube video, 42:21, from a press conference televised by RTS on 26 May, 2011,

Similarly, Tadić articulated a highly moralistic rationale for the arrest of Hadžić by arguing that Serbia cooperated with the ICTY 'for the sake of Serbia's citizens, for the victims among other nations, for reconciliation and for the establishment of credibility among all societies in South-East Europe'.[217] This rhetoric was substantially different from the pragmatic discourses deployed by the DOS and Koštunica governments who essentially portrayed ICTY cooperation as a necessity in order to avoid isolation and allow for Serbia to join the EU. It is difficult to say whether these rhetorical moves reflected personal beliefs and values or whether they were shaped by different political circumstances. Most certainly, Tadić benefited from a more favourable political environment to fully embrace transitional justice than did Djindjić and Živković. Koštunica, on the other hand, seems to have been opposed to the notion of transitional justice projected by the ICTY out of principle.

These developments demonstrated that a 'soft' approach to conditionality, which takes into consideration political realities on the ground, eventually pays off. Above all, they showed that the pursuit of justice is a long-term process that is essentially conditioned by democratic consolidation. Throughout the 2000s, Mladić had enjoyed the protection of some segments of the armed forces and the political backing of nationalist elites. His arrest required more than mere political will. It required asserting civilian control over a criminalised security sector and building a consensus on cooperation with the ICTY among polarised political elites. These two elements demanded a profound transformation of the political system inherited from Milošević a decade earlier.

Conclusion

The evidence presented throughout this chapter clearly demonstrates that there was a trade-off between externalised justice and political stability in post-Milošević Serbia. International judicial intervention directly interfered with regime change by fomenting political polarisation and institutional upheaval in the early stages of Serbia's transition to democracy.

Indeed, foreign demands for justice were deeply at odds with the political arrangements that allowed for peaceful transition from authoritarianism. The pervasiveness of Milošević's political and institutional structures represented a major obstacle to ICTY cooperation. In the absence of political consensus on the modalities of ICTY cooperation among pro-democratic actors, foreign pressures for the arrest and extradition of indictees exacerbated political conflicts within the DOS coalition. The disagreements over this issue – particularly with regard to the extradition of Milošević – generated a split among the transitional authorities

posted by 'signatian', 26 May, 2011, http://www.youtube.com/watch?v=D4D8XoJn5X0 [Original in English].

217 'Tadić: Srbija završila sva najteža poglavlja sa Hagom' (Tadić: Serbia Has Completed All of the Most Difficult Chapters with The Hague), *Politika*, 21 July 2011.

which substantially diminished the government's ability to implement reforms and cooperate with the ICTY.

In addition, ICTY cooperation was actively obstructed by recalcitrant elements within the armed forces. While the military sheltered indicted army officers, the perceived fear of extradition to the ICTY within the security sector allowed the opponents to ICTY cooperation to mobilise important segments of the security apparatus against the government. The mutiny of the JSO and the assassination of Prime Minister Djindjić show that the transitional authorities were exposed to a real threat from remnants of the former regime, who could potentially reverse the process of democratisation. Ultimately, even the allegiance of the police – the only armed force loyal to the Serbian government – was put to the test by the ICTY's indictment of the current Deputy Minister of the Interior and Chief of Public Security. This episode revealed the deep contradictions between externalised justice and the transitional compromises entailed by regime change.

In order to alleviate the destabilising effects of ICTY cooperation, the Serbian authorities increasingly sought to promote the surrender of indictees through the provision of state-sponsored financial and legal assistance to those suspects who turned themselves in. This practice, first introduced by the DOS government, culminated with Koštunica's policy of 'voluntary surrender', through which the state practically stood behind the ICTY indictees. While this policy allowed for the peaceful transfer of a substantial proportion of indictees from Serbia to The Hague, it also considerably undermined the transitional justice agenda of the Tribunal by detaching the extradition of war crimes suspects from any notion of justice and truth. This episode shows that national authorities have the capacity to mitigate the tensions arising between international justice and domestic stability. However, such compromises may be achieved at the cost of de-legitimising international institutions and undermining the goals of transitional justice.

Most obviously, Serbia's cooperation with the ICTY was substantially driven by the policies of conditionality deployed by the US and, in particular, the EU. The linking of ICTY cooperation with Serbia's accession to the EU framed transitional justice within a wider political project that was appealing for the majority of the population and political elites. However, the effectiveness and outcomes of these policies of conditionality largely depended on political developments on the ground. The arrest of the last remaining fugitives was ultimately made possible by the reconfiguration of the Serbian political scene and the strengthening of government control over the armed forces, as a result of which cooperation with the ICTY was no longer a threat to domestic stability. This suggests that the pursuit of justice in transitional countries remains essentially conditioned by democratic consolidation, even in the event of international judicial intervention. The arrest and extradition of Karadžić and Mladić eight and eleven years after the removal of Milošević are reminiscent of the trials held in Latin American countries years, or even decades, after their transition from authoritarianism. The Serbian experience thus corroborates the view that the pursuit of justice is the consequence rather than the cause of the establishment of stable democratic order.

Chapter 4
International Justice, State Responsibility and Truth-Telling

Introduction

Within the framework of transitional justice, the processes of truth-seeking and truth-telling play a crucial role in promoting reconciliation and democratisation. Besides bringing closure to victims, the pursuit of justice involves a search for truth that ought to contribute to rebuilding divided communities through the establishment of a shared narrative about the past. Proponents of criminal justice believe that trials should be regarded as forums where former adversaries articulate competing accounts of past events.[1] Beyond the courtroom, these proceedings are deemed to promote public deliberation about the past which allows for the emergence of a shared collective memory of divisive events. Furthermore, the institutionalisation of conflicts through legal proceedings is supposed to foster democratisation by instilling civic norms in society. Criminal trials thus have a didactic mission.

Establishing the truth about the atrocities committed during the wars of Yugoslav succession was clearly one of the main objectives of the ICTY. The need to carry out war crimes trials at the international level was based on the premise that the wars of Yugoslav succession were a direct consequence of 'incitement to hatred and organisation of systematic violence by those in positions of leadership'.[2] It is widely believed that the nationalist elites stirred up antagonisms between ethnic communities by manipulating memories of atrocities committed during World War II, which had not been addressed in the post-war period.[3] In order to prevent this from occurring again in the future, the Tribunal sought to establish a record of the most outrageous crimes committed during the wars of Yugoslav succession. Truth-seeking and truth-telling thus constituted an essential aspect in the Tribunal's mission of contributing to the restoration and maintenance of peace.

1 Mark Osiel, *Mass Atrocity, Collective Memory, and the Law* (New Brunswick, NJ: Transaction Publishers, 1997), 79–104.

2 Payam Akhavan, 'Justice in The Hague, Peace in the Former Yugoslavia? A Commentary on the United Nations War Crimes Tribunal', *Hum. Rights Q.* 20:4 (1998): 765.

3 Martha L. Minow, *Between Vengeance and Forgiveness: Facing History after Genocide and Mass Violence* (Boston: Beacon Press, 1998), 11; Robert M. Hayden, 'Recounting the Dead. The Rediscovery and Redefinition of Wartime Massacres in Late- and Post-Communist Yugoslavia', in *Memory, History, and Opposition under State Socialism*, edited by Ruby S. Watson (Santa Fe: School of American Research Press, 1994), 167–84.

But despite its relative success in prosecuting war crimes suspects from the region, the Tribunal proved unable to establish an authoritative account of the past among the targeted communities. Public opinion polls carried out throughout the 2000s show that local populations mistrusted the ICTY and that people generally believed that the Court was biased against their community.[4] This state of affairs could be partly attributed to the remoteness of the Tribunal from its audience, as well as the complexity and length of its proceedings which rendered trials unintelligible to the average citizen. Nevertheless, there is a common view among analysts and commentators that the didactic potential of the ICTY was undermined by domestic elites in Serbia.[5] Indeed, the transitional authorities avoided addressing the issue of war crimes by reducing it to 'cooperation with the ICTY', which was primarily attached to Western conditionality. As noted in Chapter 3, the pragmatic approach to cooperation with the ICTY deployed by various governments in Serbia resulted in detaching the transfer of war crimes suspects to The Hague from any notion of justice and truth. At the same time, the pervasive influence of nationalist discourse undermined any attempt to face the past by reinforcing denial of past atrocities.

This chapter aims to analyse the attitudes of the Serbian political elites towards the war crimes legacy and to explore how international judicial intervention influenced truth-telling in Serbia. In the first instance, I seek to explain why the transitional authorities failed to address the atrocities of the former regime following the overthrow of Milošević. I examine the obstacles to domestic attempts at truth-telling by discussing the failure of the Yugoslav Commission for Truth and Reconciliation and the discovery of mass graves in Serbia. Secondly, by analysing elite perceptions of the Milošević trial, I enquire why the ICTY failed to promote public engagement with the past. I draw extensively on the interviews that I have carried out with Serbian political elites in order to show how this trial inadvertently inhibited truth-telling by instilling fears that the prosecution of high-ranking officials at the ICTY might substantiate the genocide lawsuit brought by Bosnia against Serbia before the International Court of Justice (ICJ). Finally, by analysing domestic debates on Srebrenica, I explore how the factual findings established by the ICTY influenced truth-telling in Serbia. The massacre of Srebrenica was singled out by the ICTY and the ICJ as the worst atrocity – amounting to genocide – perpetrated during the wars of Yugoslav succession. As such, it was the subject of continuous political contestation between the reformist

4 Mirko Klarin, 'The Impact of the ICTY Trials on Public Opinion in the Former Yugoslavia', *Journal of International Criminal Justice* 7:1 (2009): 89–96; also, see the public opinion polls regularly carried out by the Belgrade Centre for Human Rights in cooperation with Strategic Marketing and the OSCE Mission to Serbia at www.bgcentar.org.rs.

5 Jelena Subotić, *Hijacked Justice: Dealing with the Past in the Balkans* (Ithaca: Cornell University Press, 2009); Diane F. Orentlicher, 'Shrinking the Space for Denial: The Impact of the ICTY in Serbia', Open Society Justice Initiative Report, May 2008.

and nationalist elites in Serbia. I draw on these debates in order to examine how facts established at the ICTY were sanctioned or challenged by domestic elites.

1. The DOS Coalition and the War Crimes Legacy

Throughout the nineties, the Milošević regime exerted major influence over public opinion through the control of state-sponsored media. As a result, the Serbian public had a very limited and distorted perspective of the Yugoslav conflicts. Public opinion polls carried out in early 2001 revealed the extent to which the Serbian public was uninformed and distrustful regarding allegations of war crimes committed by the Serbian side.[6] Accordingly, only 53 per cent of the population believed that Sarajevo was under siege for more than a thousand days and only 48 per cent believed that a great number of Bosniaks were killed in Srebrenica. With regard to the conflict in Kosovo, only 33 per cent of the respondents believed that the Albanian population was displaced during the NATO bombings. On the other hand, most people knew and believed that war crimes were committed against Serbs: 90 per cent of the respondents believed that Croats had killed many civilians in the operations "Storm" and "Flash", and 88 per cent believed that Bosnian Muslims had imprisoned Serbs in concentration camps.

On the whole, the public had a blurred vision of the conflicts and an inconsistent opinion on the causes of, and responsibility for, the wars. Most respondents could not identify an event or a date associated with the beginning of the conflicts and people generally had no clear idea about the consequences of the wars in terms of the number of casualties, internally displaced people and refugees.[7] While most people primarily attributed responsibility for the violent break-up of Yugoslavia to the international community and the other nations of former Yugoslavia, Milošević was singled out as the main individual culprit for the wars. At the same time, Ratko Mladić and Radovan Karadžić were considered the two main defenders of Serbian national interests. Paradoxically, 30 out of the 48 per cent who acknowledged Srebrenica considered Mladić to be a hero.

In this context of widespread ignorance, denial and confusion about the atrocities committed during the wars, coming to terms with the war crimes legacy involved spreading knowledge and bringing about acknowledgment of atrocities committed in the name of Serbian 'national interests'. In this section, by focusing on the creation of the Yugoslav Commission for Truth and Reconciliation and the discovery of mass graves containing bodies of Kosovo Albanians buried in different parts of Serbia, I attempt to explain why the transitional authorities failed to perform this task.

---

6 Svetlana Logar and Srdjan Bogosavljević, 'Vidjenje istine u Srbiji' (The Perception of Truth in Serbia), *Reč* 62:8 (2001), 8–10.

7 Ibid, 32–4.

A. The Yugoslav Commission for Truth and Reconciliation

The idea of creating a Yugoslav Commission for Truth and Reconciliation originated from civil society even before Milošević was ousted from power. This initiative was promoted by the representatives of the Open Society Foundation (OSF) who considered that the South African Truth and Reconciliation Commission (TRC) could serve as a model for Serbian transition to democracy.[8] The OSF representatives in Serbia invited the chairman of the South African TRC, Alex Boraine, to advise the Serbian civil society groups and authorities on the creation of such an institution in Yugoslavia.

Following the overthrow of Milošević, this initiative was taken up by Goran Svilanović, the leader of the Civic Alliance of Serbia, which was well known for its liberal orientation and proximity to the human rights movement. Svilanović, who was appointed Foreign Minister within the Yugoslav government, suggested creating a truth commission in order to prepare public opinion for war crimes trials. He framed his proposal in the following terms:

> The basic idea with regard to this commission is the following: I think that our citizens are poorly informed about what has happened over the last ten years and that the wider public should now finally be given access to information. This could be achieved by using the media, but bearing in mind the way public attitudes towards the media have developed over the past decade, there is still a high level of distrust towards them. So I have come round to the idea that this information should be disseminated by people who enjoy the confidence and support of the public. I think that their role could be to provide facts about what happened, to talk openly about crimes committed in the name of 'Serbian national interests', 'Serbdom' and the 'great idea', but also about crimes committed against our Nation and the citizens of this country. ... My idea is simply to tell the truth about what happened and to change the mood of public opinion in our country. I believe that the more people are acquainted with what happened, the more interested they will be in seeking accountability – [and finding out] the names of those who committed these crimes. Obviously, the culprits must be punished.[9]

In spite of receiving the backing of the Foreign Minister, the possibility of creating a truth commission was only sporadically mentioned by the country's new leadership. This initiative was given further impetus by the requests for cooperation with the ICTY made by the international community to the new government. As they advocated the need for trying Milošević in Belgrade instead of The Hague, the Yugoslav authorities were asked to show proof of their willingness to address

---

8 Dejan Ilić, 'Jugoslovenska Komisija za Istinu i Pomirenje 2001–?' (The Yugoslav Commission for Truth and Reconciliation, 2001 – ?), *Reč* 73:19 (2005): 60–62.

9 'Otvorena sva vrata' (All Doors Open), *Vreme*, 16. October 2000.

the war crimes legacy. In this light, the creation of a truth commission was seen as a way of demonstrating the government's resolve to deal with this sensitive issue. But while this initiative was given support by some international organisations, such as the Council of Europe, it was made clear that a truth commission could not replace the Hague tribunal.[10] In view of this, the Serbian Prime Minister, Zoran Djindjić, suggested that such a commission should work in parallel with the ICTY in order to attenuate the flaws of the Tribunal. He criticised the indictments of the ICTY for systematically targeting members of the security forces who had taken part in the Serbian campaign in Kosovo and suggested that a commission should be created to overcome this problem:

> I have talked with people from the Hague tribunal. I have told them that my opinion is that this mechanical approach – whereby all those who participated in these operations are *a priori* presumed guilty and need to be proven innocent in The Hague – is a disaster. I think that we will find a solution. I think that we should create a commission in Serbia that will, in parallel with the Hague tribunal, investigate all these events and collate documentation that will show our version of these cases, of each incident. I think that we should do this immediately and that we should invite the experts from the international tribunal to establish the truth about all of this with us.[11]

This initiative eventually materialised with the creation of the Yugoslav Commission for Truth and Reconciliation by President Koštunica in late March 2001. This decision was based on the conviction that the disclosure of evidence on the national conflicts would contribute to truth and reconciliation within the country and among the nations of the region. The president appointed nineteen members of the commission, whose mission was to 'organise research into disclosing evidence of the societal, national and political conflicts that led to the war and to explore the causal chain of those events'.[12] In addition, the commission was requested to inform the public about its work and findings, and establish cooperation with similar commissions and institutions in the neighbouring countries and abroad.

The credibility of the commission was challenged from the start as two prominent intellectuals who were reputed for their opposition to Milošević and their commitment to the defence of human rights refused to take part in it. The historian Latinka Perović relinquished her appointment, criticising the unclear objectives and the state-sponsored nature of the commission, which, in her view, undermined

10 *Vreme*, 25 January 2001.

11 'Nove tehnologije umesto šljivovice' (New Technologies instead of Šljivovica), *NIN*, 21 December 2000.

12 United States Institute for Peace, 'Truth and Reconciliation Commission for Serbia and Montenegro: Presidential Decree, March 30, 2001'. Retrieved from www.usip.org on 20 August 2010.

its claims to impartiality.[13] At the same time, the human rights lawyer and activist Vojin Dimitrijević resigned as he considered the mandate of the commission unrealistic. Dimitrijević argued that the Commission's mission of analysing the historical processes that led to the emergence of national conflicts and establishing the causes of the wars was over-stretched and unfeasible.[14] According to him, creating a 'Great Truth' by establishing the context prior to disclosing the facts related to human rights violations would amount to an attempt to provide a rationale for the crimes that had been committed.[15] Instead, Dimitrijević suggested that the Yugoslav Commission for Truth and Reconciliation should focus exclusively on human rights violations. However, he warned that a Commission exclusively composed of Serbian citizens would not seem impartial in its attempt to establish the truth about events that took place throughout the former (Socialist) Yugoslavia. Therefore, Dimitrijević argued that the Yugoslav Commission should only deal with human rights violations perpetrated in the Federal Republic of Yugoslavia.[16]

The resignations of Perović and Dimitrijević dealt a serious blow to the legitimacy of the Yugoslav Commission for Truth and Reconciliation at its inception. The newly created institution was further challenged by the representatives of the human rights NGOs, who were critical both of the way the Commission was created and the mandate it was given. These dissensions were at the centre of the conference 'In Search of Truth and Responsibility – Towards a Democratic Future' which brought together representatives of the media, NGO activists and academics, as well as the country's main political leaders.[17] The human rights activists distanced themselves from the Commission, which they criticised for being established without any public debate or prior consultations within civil society.[18] They reiterated that the Yugoslav Commission for Truth and Reconciliation had neither the moral authority nor the capacity to investigate events that took place outside the Federal Republic of Yugoslavia. In their view, such an endeavour could only be carried out by a regional body comprising all the parties to the conflict. Complaints were also raised regarding the composition of the Commission, as some members were closely connected to the former regime. In view of this, the most radical critiques denounced the Commission's focus on

13 'Ostavke' (Resignations), *Vreme*, 19 April 2001.

14 Ibid.

15 'Teško i bolno suočavanje' (Difficult and Painful Reckoning), *Vreme*, 12 April 2001.

16 Vojin Dimitrijević, 'Izgledi za utvrdjivanje istine i postizanje pomirenja u Srbiji' (Prospects for Establishing the Truth and Achieving Reconciliation in Serbia), *Reč* 62, no.8 (2001): 69–74.

17 This conference was organised by B92. It was held on 18, 19 and 20 May 2001 in Belgrade. The proceedings of the conference are available on www.b92.net/trr/2001/diskusija/diskutanti_hronoloski.php.

18 'Bol, sporovi i sarkazam' (Pain, Disputes and Sarcasm), *Vreme*, 24 April 2001.

exploring the roots of the conflict as an attempt to exonerate the Serbian side for the bloody break-up of Yugoslavia.[19]

It also became clear that, besides confronting the hostility of human rights organisations, the Yugoslav Commission for Truth and Reconciliation did not have the support of the political elites. During the conference, Goran Svilanović clearly stated that the mission that was given to the Commission did not correspond to what he had suggested beforehand.[20] According to him, this commission differed from the truth commissions established earlier in Latin America and South Africa, as it primarily aimed at giving an assessment of the historical events in the former Yugoslavia in the previous decades. In his own words, this Commission constituted an attempt at creating a new version of the 'Serbian facet of the war'.[21] While he did not condemn this endeavour, Svilanović warned that the establishment of the Yugoslav Commission for Truth and Reconciliation did not imply amnesty for war crimes. The Foreign Minister argued that prosecutions were a precondition to reconciliation and that the Yugoslav Commission could only contribute to this process by working together with similar bodies established in Bosnia and Croatia.

The position of Prime Minister Djindjić was even more striking as he had clearly turned his back on the idea of a Commission that would work in parallel with the ICTY. Through his speech, the Serbian Prime Minister expressed his suspicion and reservations regarding demands to address the past while state institutions were being reformed and rebuilt.[22] In his view, initiating a widespread process of coming to terms with the past at an early stage in the transition could destabilise and imperil the reform of state institutions. Djindjić recognised that, in principle, this process should reinforce the legitimacy of state institutions by establishing responsibility for past wrongs in a systematic and undiscriminating manner. However, he argued that, in practice, opening up the issue of moral and institutional responsibility for past wrongs would reinforce opposition to the reform of those institutions. Therefore, the Prime Minister suggested that the state institutions should be stabilised before instigating a widespread process of coming to terms with the past:

> I am going to put forward a more conservative argument whose basic message is that, before anything else, at least one basic component of these institutions

19 Ilić, 'Jugoslovenska Komisija za Istinu', 65.

20 Goran Svilanović, speech given at the conference 'In Search of Truth and Responsibility – Towards a Democratic Future' in Belgrade on 19 May 2001. Accessed on http://www.b92.net/trr/2001/diskusija/index.php?lang=srpski&nav_id=42427 on 19 August 2010.

21 Svilanović was referring to a collection of essays written by the Serbian liberal intelligentsia. See Nebojša Popov, ed., *Srpska Strana Rata* (The Serbian Facet of the War) (Belgrade: Republika, 1996).

22 Zoran Djindjić, speech given at the conference 'In Search of Truth and Responsibility – Towards a Democratic Future' in Belgrade on 19 May 2001. Accessed on http://www.b92.net/trr/2001/diskusija/diskutanti_hronoloski.php on 19 August 2010.

> must be stabilised, the basic needs of the population must be satisfied and the legitimacy of this system (through its functioning) must be established, before this system can be burdened with such hazards as raising sensitive issues and instigating processes which involve calling into question something that was approved by most people, that was a core national belief, that is part of the mentality and would require a level of sacrifice from these people for them to face up to the facts, to acknowledge that they were wrong, that their fellow-citizens were wrong and that they may also have been responsible for allowing these wrongs to assume such proportions.[23]

Zoran Djindjić, who was seen as the leader of the liberal wing of the DOS coalition, thus opposed the idea of initiating a state-sponsored process of coming to terms with the past at an early stage as he believed that this would imperil the legitimacy of the nascent democratic institutions. The Prime Minister's standpoint epitomised the inherent tensions between the long-term aspirations of transitional justice to transform political communities and the short-term strategic considerations of regime change. For Djindjić, preserving the stability and legitimacy of state institutions was a priority, in spite of the fact that he acknowledged the need to expose the sources of violence and transform the predominant political values in Serbian society. While he supported the immediate prosecution of war crimes suspects, Djindjić cautioned that the domestic institutions were not capable of addressing the war crimes legacy on a large scale:

> I obviously do not think that if you have evidence that someone committed a war crime, you should wait until the end of the year in order to initiate legal proceedings. But neither is it realistic to expect us to have, before the end of the year, a judiciary that is relatively independent, relatively stable and in a position to address the difficult legacy of the past, or other institutions that would be in a position [to achieve this], as well as relative stability in society which would allow people to take on the level of uncertainty and discomfort that would emanate from them having to 'confront their own selves', their state of mind, their prejudices, their chauvinism, their daily racism, all present in our culture – this will require a certain amount of time and certain foundations which are invisible, but without which this structure cannot be stable.[24]

For the Serbian Prime Minister, transitional justice thus needed to await a certain level of democratic consolidation. Djindjić did not predict when domestic institutions would be ready to undertake the process of coming to terms with the past. Nevertheless, he suggested that this should be on the agenda once a consensus had emerged on the basic values and norms within society:

---

23 Ibid.

24 Ibid.

> I think that this society needs to reach an agreement on the basic values, on the principles of democratic procedure, on how priorities established in a democratic manner should then be implemented, and that all of this would form the foundation upon which to carry out the more difficult, controversial tasks, one of which is coming to terms with the past.[25]

Finally, Djindjić argued that it would be wrong to expect quick results in the domain of transitional justice. He sought to lower the expectations associated with institutional and societal reckoning with the past by pointing to the fact that this is a long and difficult process which could be undermined by 'quick fix' measures:

> Institutional reckoning with the past is a process that I have attempted to describe ... My intention has been to reduce the level of enthusiasm and say: this is a very difficult [task], not because we do not want [to achieve] it, but because this is the nature of society, every society is like that, and if we do it superficially and get quick results, these may not produce the right outcomes. This could be done superficially – we could send two or three [individuals] to The Hague, put two or three in jail, and then wash our hands and say: that is it, we are clean. I think that the change of system that I have talked about will require digging deeper ...[26]

Djindjić's speech clearly suggested that the newly created Yugoslav Commission for Truth and Reconciliation did not have the backing of the Serbian Prime Minister. Without the support of the political establishment and civil society, the Yugoslav truth commission was doomed to fail. Besides being assigned a vague and unmanageable task, the Commission did not have the practical means to carry out its work. Indeed, the Commission was given very little power: it did not have the authority to summon the wrongdoers and the victims to appear at the hearings.[27] Since its relationship with the judiciary was undefined and it did not have the power to grant amnesties, the offenders had no interest in cooperating with the Commission. Moreover, the budget of the Commission was very limited and its access to foreign funding was undercut by its bad reputation within civil society.[28] All in all, the Commission did not move from its starting point of defining its objectives and strategy during the two years of its existence. The Yugoslav Commission for Truth and Reconciliation was eventually extinguished in 2003

---

25 Ibid.

26 Ibid.

27 Jelena Pejić, speech given at the conference 'In Search of Truth and Responsibility – Towards a Democratic Future' in Belgrade on 19 May 2001. Accessed on http://www.b92.net/trr/2001/diskusija/index.php?lang=srpski&nav_id=51231 on 19 August 2010.

28 Jasna Dragović-Soso and Eric Gordy, 'Transitional Justice and Reconciliation in the Former Yugoslavia', in *New Perspectives on Yugoslavia*, edited by Dejan Djokić and James Ker-Lindsay (London: Routledge, 2011), 205–7.

through the transformation of the Federal Republic of Yugoslavia into the State Union of Serbia and Montenegro.

All things considered, one question that remains to be answered is why President Koštunica created this institution in the first place. Bearing in mind the ambiguous goals and the limited power given to the Commission, it is hard to believe that it was meant to confront Serbian public opinion with the atrocities committed during the war. In fact, Koštunica was noticeably opposed to the need for coming to terms with the past in Serbia. As a moderate nationalist, he did not conceal his disagreement with the demands for moral catharsis in Serbian society:

> So-called moral catharsis is often invoked in the discussions around The Hague [tribunal]. I do not know what that moral catharsis means. So many crimes have been committed through wars and throughout history, and nobody has ever thought of talking about catharsis. There can be no moral catharsis without the catharsis of those leading NATO officials who were responsible for the bombing of this country in 1999. That would be moral catharsis. Otherwise, we would have in this country a hypocritical and immoral catharsis which we are currently experiencing as a result of the demands of people who are legally and politically responsible, such as Wesley Clark, Madeleine Albright, Richard Holbrook.[29]

Koštunica thus equated the responsibility of the former Serbian regime with the responsibility of the other parties that took part in the war, especially the leading NATO countries. As a result, he did not believe that it was necessary to confront the Serbian public with the atrocities committed by the Serbian side, since the former adversaries did not undertake similar steps.

Bearing in mind that the Yugoslav Commission for Truth was created a few days before the deadline for American certification of cooperation with the ICTY, it seems reasonable to believe that the primary motive behind the creation of the Commission was to appease foreign pressure for cooperation with the Tribunal.[30] As mentioned above, the possibility of creating a Commission was being considered by the Yugoslav authorities as a way of demonstrating to the international community their willingness to address the war crimes legacy. In this light, it seems that the hasty creation of the Yugoslav truth commission was meant to make up for the lack of cooperation with the Hague tribunal at a moment when the authorities in Belgrade had not even carried out the arrest of Slobodan Milošević.

Besides appeasing the international community, it has been suggested that the Yugoslav Commission for Truth and Reconciliation was created in order to reconcile the opposed political factions within Serbian society.[31] According to this

29 'Mučna saradnja' (Painful Cooperation), *Vreme*, 5 July 2001.

30 This certification was a condition for the provision of US financial support to Yugoslavia (see Chapter 3).

31 'Prva spoticanja' (First Stumbles), *NIN*, 26 April 2001.

view, the Commission was meant to bridge the gap between the conflicting views on the wars of Yugoslav succession among the supporters of the former regime and the various opposition parties. Hence, the Commission's focus on the causes of the wars was meant to produce a historical narrative that would transcend political antagonisms and allow for the transformation of political relationships. This hypothesis is substantiated by the statements issued by the creator as well as the members of the Commission. Indeed, Koštunica personally insisted that the Commission explore the roots of the conflicts that followed the break-up of Socialist Yugoslavia.[32] While expounding the rationale behind the establishment of the Yugoslav truth commission, the Yugoslav President argued that this Commission was necessary in order to 'confront ourselves and reconcile us with ourselves'.[33] In a similar vein, the former coordinator of the Commission, Radmila Nakarada, suggested that the Commission was meant to contribute towards 'internal normalisation' and the establishment of 'a coherent collective identity'.[34] From this perspective, the Yugoslav Commission for Truth and Reconciliation could be perceived as an attempt to legitimise the transitional compromises brokered with the former regime, as had previously been done in South Africa and Latin America. However, in the Serbian case, this attempt was effectively blocked by the opposition of civil society and the refusal of two prominent representatives of the liberal intelligentsia to take part in the work of the Commission.[35]

B. The Discovery of Mass Graves

The discovery of mass graves containing bodies of Kosovo Albanians that had been re-buried in different parts of Serbia provides additional insight into the attitudes of the transitional elites towards truth-telling. The DOS leaders had been aware of the existence of these mass graves since early 2001. The ICTY Chief Prosecutor, Carla Del Ponte, was informed about this by the Serbian Prime Minister Djindjić during her first visit to Belgrade in January 2001.[36] Nevertheless, the new authorities decided to conceal this information from the public. This decision was taken during a meeting of the DOS coalition described by the former Foreign Minister Goran Svilanović in the following terms:

---

32 *Vreme*, 12 April 2001.

33 Ana Kranjc and Emilija Marinkov, 'Komisija za Istinu i Pomirenje' (Commission for Truth and Reconciliation), Student Papers Collection, Belgrade, 2008, 14. Retrieved from http://www.most.org.yu/RADOVI/komisija.pdv on 20 August 2010.

34 Radmila Nakarada, *Raspad Jugoslavije: Problemi tumačenja, suočavanja i tranzicije* (The Fall of Yugoslavia: Problems of Interpretation, Reckoning and Transition) (Belgrade: Službeni Glasnik, 2008), 169.

35 *NIN*, 26 April 2001.

36 Carla Del Ponte and Chuck Sudetić, *Gospodja Tužiteljka: Suočavanje s najtežim ratnim zločinima i kulturom nekažnjivosti* (Madame Prosecutor: Confrontations with Humanity's Worst Criminals and the Culture of Impunity) (Belgrade: Profil knjiga, 2008), 104.

> I remember some discussions regarding Batajnica: these are mass graves of Albanians from Kosovo which we discussed at an informal meeting attended by all of us. So Koštunica was leading the meeting, and Dušan Mihajlović – the Interior Minister – insisted: "My friends, I cannot sleep because of this. You do not know what this is. You do not know how many graves there are, how many people. This is terrible, we have to disclose it". So at that meeting, we gave our approval – I as Foreign Minister, Žarko Korać as Deputy Prime Minister, Mićunović as Speaker of Parliament – but Koštunica stood firmly against it, he wanted to downplay it and was not prepared to announce it to the public. And then Djindjić came and said: "Of course I approve – this [disclosing the information about the mass graves] should be done". But then, Mihajlović went on to say how many [graves] there were, and at that moment Djindjić said: "Wait, wait, what did you say? That many?! Forget about it, this is out of question. Who is going to be able to live with this? Now we will have to explain where these bodies came from, how come there are so many graves". So the picture is not that clear-cut. As soon as he realised how many there were, he said "There is no way. Who is going to present this to the public? Are you serious?" This is the human fear of responsibility, [the fear] of reckoning. This meant that, just when we thought that we had a majority against Koštunica, that was immediately called into question. You had both the President and the Prime Minister standing against you. In fact, he [Djindjić] said: "Leave it, this is negative publicity for the country, so negative that we cannot come out with it".[37]

This account is corroborated by the testimonies of several other former representatives of the DOS coalition. Nenad Čanak, the leader of the League of Social Democrats of Vojvodina, later revealed that, during this meeting, the Interior Minister, Dušan Mihajlović, announced that there were 17 mass graves across Serbia.[38] He added that one member of the government requested that this be kept secret, fearing that it could cause problems with foreign investments. On this evidence, it appears that neither Vojislav Koštunica nor Zoran Djindjić was willing to come out in public with the truth about war crimes committed by the Serbian side. According to Goran Svilanović, the primary factor behind the politicians' reluctance to reveal the atrocities was the fear of responsibility. He argues that the DOS leaders did not have the courage to expose the war crimes to the Serbian public, in spite of the fact that they were sincerely committed to cooperation with the ICTY:

> We never came out in the media – we as politicians who enjoyed wide support at that time – to describe what had happened in Vukovar, why Vukovar was such an

37 Personal interview with Goran Svilanović, Minister of Foreign Affairs 2000–04, 23 May 2009.

38 'U Srbiji postoji 17 masovnih grobnica' (There Are 17 Mass Graves in Serbia), *Glas Javnosti*, 29 October 2004.

> issue for the Croatian public. [As for] Srebrenica – we never opened up about it. We did not try to explain clearly, using video materials, documents, everything [we had], to convince the public that we should cooperate with the Tribunal because these crimes were so terrible that we had to face up to them and to reveal to the people what these crimes were. We did not do that. So this is primarily our fault; we were not ready for it; we clearly did not have the courage. In that sense, this applies to both Koštunica and Djindjić. This is simply the fear of responsibility.[39]

But besides possibly lacking political courage to publicise the truth about war crimes, it seems reasonable to believe that the two DOS leaders had deeper motives for avoiding this task. According to the testimonies of Svilanović and Čanak, it appears that Djindjić opposed the disclosure of mass graves because he feared that this could harm the country's reputation and undermine economic reforms. This line of reasoning fitted into his general conviction that instigating the process of coming to terms with the past at an early stage could impinge upon the stability and reform of institutions.[40] The Serbian Prime Minister had good reasons to believe that disclosing the truth about war crimes could destabilise the institutions of the state. Considering the compromises made with members of the former regime, he must have been aware that many of those who were directly responsible for these atrocities remained in positions of power. This hypothesis is given further impetus by the events that followed the 'discovery' of mass graves in spring 2001.

The information that the former regime had relocated the bodies of Kosovo Albanians across the country was brought to light by a local newspaper from eastern Serbia which published a story about the discovery of a refrigerated lorry full of human bodies found in the Danube in April 1999.[41] This event occurred during the NATO bombing campaign, at the height of the ethnic cleansing operations carried out by the Serbian forces in Kosovo. The authorities had immediately classified this case a state secret, and the discovery was consequently concealed from the public. The publication of this story had a snowball effect in the media, which speculated that several high representatives of the police were involved in this case.[42] The authorities responded by pensioning off a number of police officers, including the former Chief of Public Security Vlastimir Djordjević Rodja, and creating a task force for investigating the discovery of the refrigerated lorry. The results of the investigation revealed that Milošević had ordered the removal of the bodies of victims that could be used by the Hague tribunal to raise war crimes

39 Personal interview with Goran Svilanović.

40 Zoran Djindjić, speech given at the conference 'In Search of Truth and Responsibility'.

41 'Pukla državna tajna' (State Secret Laid Bare), *Večernje Novosti*, 3 May 2001. This information was initially published by the periodical 'Timočka krimi revija' from Zaječar.

42 'Vodena grobnica guta generalske položaje' (Aquatic Grave Engulfs Generals' Positions), *Ekspres*, 5 May 2001.

charges in March 1999. This task was allegedly assigned to the former Interior Minister, who passed it on to the Chief of Public Security Vlastimir Djordjević Rodja. It was later revealed that the corpses from the refrigerated lorry were reburied at a police special unit training centre on the outskirts of Belgrade. The Interior Ministry subsequently made public the existence of two other mass graves in different parts of Serbia.

From the outset, the feeble reactions of the political elites raised suspicions regarding their willingness to expose the truth about these mass graves. At first, politicians tended to ignore or downplay the importance of this macabre discovery. The Serbian Prime Minister Djindjić, for example, declared that the priority of his government was the fight against organised crime and that 'the casino and perfumery owners are much more dangerous than war criminals'.[43] Nevertheless, in view of the massive public dismay provoked by the discovery of the mass graves, government representatives were obliged to confront this issue. On several occasions, the DOS leaders rhetorically called for the need to face the past and establish accountability for past crimes. In this vein, the Interior Minister, Dušan Mihajlović, stated that this case would discredit the so-called 'patriots' and the thesis that Serbs did not commit crimes but were only victims during the wars of Yugoslav succession. Furthermore, he emphasised that the pursuit of individual accountability would clear the armed forces and the Serbian people from collective responsibility for war crimes.[44] At the same time, the Democratic Party stated that the mass graves were clear proof of the former regime's responsibility for war crimes and the Deputy Prime Minister, Žarko Korać, announced that the indictment against Milošević would be expanded to war crimes.[45]

But in spite of these bombastic announcements, the domestic judiciary failed to instigate any proceedings against those responsible for these crimes. The main reason for this was that this case implicated the police and army chiefs who were still in office. Indeed, the task force for investigating the mass graves was set up by the former coordinator of the Serbian police forces in Kosovo – Sreten Lukić – who was the current Chief of Public Security and Deputy Interior Minister in Djindjić's government. As the coordinator of the Serbian police in Kosovo during the war, Lukić was necessarily aware of, and involved in, the transportation of bodies to different parts of Serbia. Nevertheless, Lukić denied his responsibility by arguing that the police was under the command of the army during the NATO

43 'Tovar strave'(The Cargoof Horror), *Vreme*, 10 May 2001.

44 'Počela ekshumacija leševa iz hladnjače' (Exhumation of Refrigerated Lorry Bodies Started), *Politika*, 3 June 2001; 'Još jedna masovna grobnica' (One More Mass Grave), *Danas*, 21 June 2006.

45 'Leševi u "OVK" uniformama' (Bodies in 'KLA' Uniforms), *Večernje Novosti*, 4 June 2001; 'Leševi iz hladnjače zakopani na "13 Maju"' (Bodies from Refrigerated Lorry Buried at '13 May'), *Vreme*, 7 June 2001.

bombing campaign.[46] This claim was rejected by the army Chief of Staff, Nebojša Pavković, who maintained that the police bore responsibility for the mass graves. In other words, the police and the army started blaming each other for these crimes. The representatives of the Serbian government openly stood in support of Lukić, although they were aware that he had been the coordinator of the Serbian forces in Kosovo and that he might be on the list of suspects. Indeed, Prime Minister Djindjić boldly stated that Lukić was 'the best for the job, even though he was no angel'.[47]

In those circumstances, the police investigation did not move beyond the findings of the task group which only incriminated four top officials, among them Slobodan Milošević. The 'discovery' of mass graves was brushed under the carpet soon after the transfer of the former Yugoslav President to The Hague in late June 2001. Indeed, this issue suddenly disappeared from the public spotlight, while the related domestic judicial proceedings were allegedly obstructed by the police.[48] The sidelining of this issue reinforced the hypothesis that the government had unveiled the mass graves in order to justify cooperation with the ICTY and prepare public opinion for the extradition of Milošević.[49] While it is impossible to establish whether the information about the mass graves emerged spontaneously or whether it was purposely leaked to the public by the authorities, this episode clearly highlighted the risks attached to addressing the war crimes legacy. With the police and the army still under the command of personnel who had taken an active part in the former regime, pursuing accountability or disclosing facts about war crimes could destabilise the country and imperil the transition to democracy. As a matter of fact, the evidence collected at the mass graves sites in Serbia was used by the ICTY prosecution to raise indictments against both Nebojša Pavković and Sreten Lukić, which amply contributed to the fall of the DOS government in autumn 2003 (See Chapter 3).

***

Both the failure of the Yugoslav Truth Commission and the reluctant disclosure of the mass graves demonstrate that the Serbian transitional authorities did not have the will or the strength to come out with the truth about war crimes. While Koštunica appeared to be ideologically opposed to the idea of coming to terms with the past, Djindjić stood against truth-telling for pragmatic reasons. In view of the compromises made with the former regime, the Serbian Prime Minister had

46 'Lukić: MUP bio pod komandom VJ; Pavković: Čelni ljudi policije lažu' (Lukić: MoI Was under Army Command; Pavković: Police Executives Are Lying), *Politika*, 7 June 2001.

47 *Vreme*, 10 May 2001.

48 'Serbia: New Mass Grave Found', *IWPR*, 13 June 2002.

49 Personal interview with Milan Milošević, journalist for the weekly *Vreme*, on 8 April 2009.

good reasons to believe that any attempt to address the past would be obstructed by rogue elements within the state institutions. This is illustrated by the discovery of mass graves, which led to an open clash between the police and the army over responsibility for these crimes. The lack of a domestic initiative to address the past can thus be attributed both to the ideological preferences of the elite and to the modalities of the transition, which upheld institutional resistance towards disclosing the atrocities committed by the Serbian side during the wars.

2. The Trial of Milošević and the Bosnian Genocide Case

In the absence of a domestic truth-telling initiative, the task of informing the Serbian public about the war crimes perpetrated during the Yugoslav wars was passed on to the ICTY. According to former Foreign Minister Svilanović, the Serbian authorities expected the Tribunal would take on this task in return for the government's commitment to arrest and transfer the indictees to The Hague.[50] Considering the high political cost associated with this issue, the most liberal factions within DOS thus sought to outsource truth-telling to the ICTY.

The trial of Milošević constituted the test-case of the Tribunal's ability to perform its truth-telling mission.[51] Milošević was the highest-ranking politician to be brought before the ICTY. He was the only person whose indictment covered the conflicts in Croatia, Bosnia and Kosovo, which reflected the Prosecution's view that Milošević played a key role in the violent break-up of the former Yugoslavia. Last but not least, his trial is the only one that was broadcast live on domestic television and widely watched by the Serbian public. This allowed the Tribunal to have a direct impact on the domestic audience and thus perform its didactic function.

In this section, I first examine the reactions of the domestic elites to the trial of Milošević. I essentially focus on the domestic reactions to the beginning of the trial, since this is when it was most followed by the general public (and the elite). Indeed, national television suspended broadcasting of the trial three weeks after it started, which significantly reduced its audience during the remainder of the trial.[52]

50 Personal interview with Goran Svilanović.

51 In the Prosecution's opening statement, the Chief Prosecutor, Carla Del Ponte, stated: 'With the trial of this particular accused, we reach a turning point of this institution. The proceeding upon which the Chamber embarks today is clearly the most important trial to be conducted in the Tribunal to date. Indeed, it may prove to be the most significant trial that this institution will ever undertake. It is thus a trial that must inevitably mark the path towards the conclusion of the work of this Tribunal, even though that day is still some way off'.

52 The trial of Milošević was entirely broadcast on the private channel B92. While on average a quarter of the Serbian population watched the first three weeks of the trial, this figure dropped below 10 per cent of the population after national television stopped broadcasting it. This can be attributed both to the general decline in interest for the trial

I then turn to the effects of this trial on the attitudes of the political elite and assess the repercussions of this process on truth-telling in Serbia. I demonstrate how, in the context of the genocide lawsuit brought by Bosnia against Yugoslavia before the ICJ, Milošević's trial held deep implications in terms of state responsibility, which significantly conditioned the political elite's conduct with regard to cooperation with the ICTY and truth-telling.

A. Elite Perceptions of the Milošević Trial in Serbia

Slobodan Milošević was on trial for 66 counts of genocide, crimes against humanity, grave breaches of the Geneva conventions and violations of the laws and customs of war.[53] He was initially indicted on 24 May 1999, during the NATO bombing campaign against Serbia, for allegations of wrongdoing in Kosovo. The indictments for Croatia and Bosnia were issued in autumn 2001, following Milošević's transfer to The Hague. According to Carla Del Ponte, the Prosecution did not claim that Milošević had committed or even ordered any specific crimes. Instead, it sought to demonstrate that he devised a long-term strategy with the intent of perpetrating numerous crimes, which he implemented using his authority first as President of Serbia and then as President of Yugoslavia.[54] Indeed, Milošević was alleged to have played a key role in a joint criminal enterprise (JCE) whose purpose was the forcible and permanent removal of the majority of non-Serbs from large areas in Kosovo, Croatia and Bosnia and Herzegovina. In the case of Bosnia, it was alleged that the campaign of persecution was conducted 'with intent to destroy in part the Bosnian Muslim group as such', which amounted to genocide.[55] Milošević was indicted both for his participation as a co-perpetrator in joint criminal enterprise and his position of authority, which entailed effective control over the institutions and individuals perpetrating crimes in these areas.[56]

In November 2001, the Prosecution made the request for a joinder of the three indictments issued against Milošević. The OTP argued that these three indictments concerned the same transaction in the context of a common scheme, strategy or plan to create a 'Greater Serbia'. The Trial Chamber allowed for the Croatia and Bosnia indictments to be joined, but it rejected the joinder of the Kosovo indictment. This decision was based on the interpretation that the Kosovo indictment could not be considered to form part of the same transaction in view

---

and the smaller audience of B92 (Sources: Strategic Marketing Research and AGB Nielsen Media Research, Belgrade).

53 Gideon Boas, *The Milošević Trial: Lessons for the Conduct of Complex Criminal Proceedings* (Cambridge: Cambridge University Press, 2007), 1.

54 Del Ponte and Sudetić, *Gospodja Tužiteljka*, 144.

55 *Prosecutor v. Milošević*, 'Case Information Sheet', Case No. IT-02-54. Accessed on www.icty.org on 20 January 2011, 4–6.

56 Boas, *The Milošević Trial*, 81–90.

of the geographic and temporal differences with the two other indictments and the fact that it made no reference to 'Greater Serbia'. This decision was revoked by the Appeals Chamber which ruled that the three indictments formed part of the same transaction, whose long-term aim was to 'establish or maintain control by the Serb authorities over particular areas which were, or were once, part of the former Yugoslavia'.[57] Nevertheless – according to Carla Del Ponte – the judges of the Trial Chamber insisted that the trial begin with Kosovo.[58]

As a result of the joinder of the three indictments, the trial revolved around a loosely defined 'Greater Serbia' project allegedly endorsed by the accused. The Prosecution's case theory contained a significant flaw: it overlooked the fact that Kosovo still formed part of Serbia at the time when the alleged crimes were committed and that it could therefore not be alleged that Milošević was attempting to expand Serbia's borders, as inferred in the cases of Croatia and Bosnia.[59] Throughout the trial, the Prosecution held an ambivalent position towards the notion of 'Greater Serbia', whose definition evolved over the different stages of the case. While this theory was invoked prior to the trial to legitimise the joinder of the three indictments, it was downplayed in the opening statement of the Prosecution as Carla Del Ponte insisted that Milošević was exclusively motivated by a hunger for power. According to Boas, the Prosecution only clarified its position at an advanced stage of the trial by dissociating Milošević's espousal of a Serb-controlled state from which non-Serbs were to be removed from the ideological and historical notion of 'Greater Serbia' promoted by Serbian nationalists.[60]

The beginning of Milošević's trial in February 2002 generated massive interest in Serbia. The extensive coverage of the trial on local media was made possible through a project funded by the US and Dutch governments. The rationale behind this project was that Milošević could only have a fair trial in The Hague if people in Serbia were well informed about the proceedings in the courtroom.[61] In addition, there was a common belief among Western diplomats that the Milošević trial provided a unique opportunity to present the truth about the Yugoslav wars to the Serbian public and discredit nationalism.[62] But against all expectations, the

57 Ibid., 119–20.

58 Del Ponte and Sudetić, *Gospodja Tužiteljka*, 146–7; on the other hand, the former Yugoslav Foreign Minister claims that the trial started with Kosovo because the Prosecution was not ready for the Croatia and Bosnia cases in February 2002 (Personal interview with Goran Svilanović).

59 Personal interview with Vladimir Djerić, former senior legal advisor at the Ministry of Foreign Affairs and representative of the Serbian state before the ICTY and ICJ, on 23 July 2009.

60 Boas, *Milošević's Trial*, 91–2.

61 Personal interview with Ljiljana Smajlović, journalist for the weekly *NIN*, on 27 June 2009.

62 In this vein, the former UN rapporteur for human rights in former Yugoslavia argued that 'the images of fear presented by the Prosecutors fall on the Balkan societies

broadcasting of the trial actually had the opposite effect. Indeed, the trial proved to be highly popular as it is estimated that over half of the Serbian population watched the first four days of the proceedings.[63] However, instead of discrediting Milošević, the trial actually generated public support for the former Yugoslav President. When asked to rate Milošević's performance in the courtroom, over 41 per cent of the respondents gave him a 5 on a scale ranging from 1 to 5 where 5 is the upper mark. On average, people considered that Milošević deserved 2.5 as a political personality and 3.76 for his performance at the Hague tribunal.[64] This means that most of the people who had a low opinion of Milošević as a politician supported him at the ICTY.[65]

The public reactions to the trial of Milošević dealt a blow to the Serbian government. Prime Minister Djindjić, who had taken a serious political risk in arresting and extraditing the former Yugoslav president, denounced the conduct of the trial as an 'expensive circus'.[66] He expressed his indignation at the amount of money spent by the Prosecution on searching for 'insignificant witnesses', and added that the trial had put his government in a serious dilemma over cooperation with the ICTY and the transfer of war crimes suspects. The subsequent suspension of the live coverage of the trial on national television suggests that the authorities were anxious about the repercussions of the trial on public opinion. Officially, Radio Television Serbia (RTS) suspended the broadcasting for financial reasons.[67] But according to Ljubica Gojgić, who covered Milošević's trial for *B92*, this was a mere pretext, since the coverage of the trial on *RTS* (as well as *B92*) was funded through foreign donations. Instead, she argues that national television was pressured by the authorities to suspend broadcasting of Milošević's trial.[68]

Djindjić's reactions illustrate how the Serbian elites who sympathised with the aims of transitional justice and supported the ICTY were utterly disappointed with the conduct of the trial. With hindsight, many observers blame the trial's failure to communicate the truth about war crimes to the Serbian public on the

---

like a sledgehammer of truth' ('Dinstbir: Sudjenje Miloševiću je javna tribina' (The Trial of Milošević is a Public Forum), *Nacional*, 22 February 2002).

63 Strategic Marketing & Media Research Institute, 'Gledanost direktnih prenosa sudjenja Slobodanu Miloševiću u Hagu' (TV Ratings of the Live Broadcasting of the Trial of Slobodan Milošević in The Hague), 2002, 3.

64 Ibid., 7–8.

65 For a discussion of public reactions to the trial of Milošević in Serbia, see Eric Gordy, 'Rating the Sloba Show: Will Justice Be Served?', *Problems of Post-Communism* 50:3 (2003): 53–63.

66 Lenard J. Cohen, *Serpent in the Bosom: The Rise and Fall of Slobodan Milošević* (Oxford: Westview Press, 2002), 18.

67 'RTS obustavlja prenos sudjenja Miloševiću' (RTS Suspends Broadcasting of Milošević Trial), *B92*, 8 March 2002.

68 Personal interview with Ljubica Gojgić, journalist for *B92*, on 18 May 2009. According to Ljubica Gojgić, *B92* was also pressured by the authorities to suspend the live coverage of the trial, although to a lesser extent than *RTS*.

strategy of the Prosecution and the framing of the indictment. According to Vladimir Djerić, who advised the Foreign Minister on legal matters related to the ICTY, the Prosecution's decision to join the three indictments through the concept of 'Greater Serbia' had two effects.[69] On the one hand, it dramatically extended the length of the trial by increasing the amount of witnesses called and evidence covered in the proceedings, and on the other, it associated Milošević's indictment with his political project. Djerić argues that the indictment thus had an intrinsic political dimension:

> I think that, since it focused on Milošević's political project as a joint criminal enterprise, the indictment inevitably dealt with political issues: the suspension of autonomies, the break-up of Yugoslavia, who said or did what to whom, etc… At the end, it came to the concrete facts, but it started with this political part and was somehow based on the identification of the joint criminal enterprise with Milošević's political movement. As a result, it had to come onto political terrain.[70]

This 'political dimension' invoked by Djerić emerged in the Prosecution's opening statement. The Deputy Prosecutor, Geoffrey Nice, opened the trial by laying out a historical and political context in which the crimes imputed to Milošević took place. During the first two days of the trial, he presented a historical account which described Milošević's rise to power and portrayed him as the mastermind behind most of the atrocities that had plagued the former Yugoslavia.[71] For the former Yugoslav Foreign Minister Goran Svilanović, the opening statement of the Prosecution was a missed opportunity to show evidence of war crimes to the Serbian public. In his view, the Prosecution's emphasis on the concept of 'Greater Serbia' distracted the focus of the trial from the actual crimes imputed to Milošević:

> In fact, I was very disappointed with the indictment and the conduct of the case. First, this insistence on the idea of 'Greater Serbia' instead of what I expected, and I expected something else. I expected that – in view of the massive public attention to this key trial – it would start with the facts and that the indictment would describe in detail what occurred … because the entire Serbian public was watching and wanted to hear. And for two days, they did not hear anything about it: there was no mention of the victims' names or the names of the injured, nothing. I assumed that it would start from there, that it would start from the actual crimes and that at some point they would say 'now let us see if you are responsible for this'; that this part would be instructive and that it would form part of the evidence to be heard. Instead of this, the whole story revolved around the philosophy of Greater Serbia, which was not the theme of the trial. But at the

69 Personal interview with Vladimir Djerić.

70 Ibid.

71 Cohen, *Serpent in the Bosom*, 13–14.

> end, it turned out that this was in fact the theme of the trial, which is why the trial turned into a disaster in my view.[72]

Svilanović thus blamed the trial's failure to reveal the atrocities and open the question of war crimes in Serbia on the strategy of the Prosecution. He considered that the Prosecution had undermined its truth-telling mission by deliberating about Milošević's political ideas instead of directly addressing the crimes imputed to the former Yugoslav President. In his view, there was no room for establishing historical causality or judging political ideas at this trial:

> So in the end, to sum up, I am in fact very disappointed. I sincerely wanted to open the question of war crimes and to reveal all the crimes – and there were then a lot of crimes in which Serbs were victims – and to leave this for later for people who deal with these issues, not to deliberate about the political ideas that led to these crimes during the trial, but to have the crimes exposed in public. Instead of that, it was all about a political idea – and it is difficult to try a political idea – and less about crimes. In that sense, it was a disaster.[73]

The Prosecution's venturing onto political terrain played into Milošević's hands, as it gave him the opportunity to defend his political project in front of the Serbian audience. The former Serbian leader chose to represent himself since he did not recognise the Court as legitimate. But instead of defending himself against the accusations set in the indictment, Milošević deployed a political and historical counter-narrative in which the responsibility for the violent break-up of former Yugoslavia was imputed to the Western Powers and the political leaders of the other Yugoslav republics.[74] The broadcasting of the trial thus provided Milošević with the opportunity to communicate his political ideas to the Serbian audience. According to Vladimir Djerić, the increase in popular support for Milošević can partly be explained by the fact that many people in Serbia still supported some of these political ideas:

> If people who were watching the trial saw that Milošević defended a policy, they might have renewed their sympathy towards Milošević … because they shared that policy with him. They had still not renounced that policy, notwithstanding the fact that they might have dissociated themselves from Milošević. I am talking about the general public. This policy was in some aspects completely harmless, I mean harmless from the standpoint of criminal law, not in political terms. For example, over 99 per cent of the population and politicians here still

---

72 Personal interview with Goran Svilanović.

73 Ibid.

74 Vojin Dimitrijević, 'Kako ubediti javnost' (How to Convince the Public), *Pravda u Tranziciji*, 1 (2005). Accessed on www.pravdautranziciji.com/pages/article.php?id=38 on 27 October 2010.

> believe that the reintegration of Vojvodina and Kosovo into the structures of the Serbian state at the beginning of Milošević's rule was completely legitimate and that it was not unjust. But in the narration of the tribunal, this was the beginning, the nucleus from which the criminal enterprise emanated.[75]

The public empathy towards Milošević can further be explained by the fact that his trial began with the Kosovo conflict about which the Serbian public had strong feelings at the time. The mere fact that Milošević was first indicted for Kosovo during the NATO bombing campaign and that he was subsequently charged for Croatia and Bosnia created the impression that his indictment was a political move in line with the West's war effort against Serbia.[76] Furthermore, starting with Kosovo gave the former Serbian leader the opportunity to counter the Prosecution's argumentation by constantly pointing to the NATO bombing. The memories of the bombing were still fresh among the Serbian population in February 2002. The recollection of that traumatic experience obscured the crimes imputed to Milošević in the eyes of the Serbian public. For Goran Svilanović, the sequencing of the proceedings constituted another major mistake of the Prosecution:

> In addition, the trial started with Kosovo, which immediately put Milošević in the position that whenever they said 'Kosovo', he said 'NATO bombing'. And rightly so. Obviously, at that moment, everyone remembered the bombing in the Serbian public – literally everyone. But they did not know what happened in Kosovo – it is true that they did not know, or that very few people knew, what had happened, what crimes had been committed, and how. And at that moment, you had the public watching: they were talking about 'Greater Serbia' as if this were a crime. Why was it a crime? It was a political idea. Also, they were talking about Kosovo of course, but they were also talking about the bombing – he (Milošević) created a parallel story in which everyone who lived in Belgrade, Kruševac, Kraljevo, Niš, Novi Sad knew that it was terrible what happened to them, and they heard only this. So, it would have been logical for the process to start the way it all started: Croatia, then Bosnia, and then Kosovo.[77]

There was a widespread consensus among observers in Belgrade that the witnesses called by the Prosecution at the beginning of the proceedings amply contributed towards discrediting the trial in the eyes of the Serbian population. In order to show how everything started with Kosovo, the Prosecution initiated the proceedings by calling Mahmut Bakalli, a former communist apparatchik whose reputation was already tarnished in the eyes of the domestic audience. The subsequent testimonies

---

75 Personal interview with Vladimir Djerić.

76 Dimitrijević, 'Kako ubediti javnost'.

77 Personal interview with Goran Svilanović.

of Albanian victims who denied the existence of the Kosovo Liberation Army or the NATO bombing were easily rebuffed by Milošević.[78] The human rights activist and legal scholar Vojin Dimitrijević summed up his impressions in the following terms:

> The trial on Kosovo, the way it started, was really an *unmitigated disaster*, because they called some frightened Albanian witnesses who did not dare to say that there were NATO troops out there, who simply answered with 'jo' and 'po'... The only one who was more articulate was Bakalli, who was remembered as a high-ranking communist leader who had many mistresses, who was rich, and so on... Then he pretended that he had always been in favour of the independence of Kosovo, while he was in the communist nomenclatura. ... So while there was some interest, it was Kosovo. But when it came to the really clear-cut cases – that is Bosnia, where you cannot tell any Bosnian that he was an aggressor or an Ustasha – the interest dropped and Milošević had already recovered his popularity.[79]

Besides calling irrelevant witnesses, the Prosecution undermined its case by making blatant mistakes. Ljiljana Smajlović, who covered the Milošević trial for the weekly *NIN*, pointed to the anachronism committed by the Deputy Prosecutor, Geoffrey Nice, in his opening statement, when he argued that Milošević embraced nationalism in his Gazimestan speech because he realised that communism was over in view of what happened to Ceauşescu.[80] Nice was thus overlooking the fact that the Gazimestan speech took place five months before the overthrow of Ceauşescu, which could not have been forecast by anyone at that time. Smajlović argued that such basic mistakes, which were obvious to the wider public in Serbia, discredited the overly simplistic historical narrative deployed by the Prosecution.[81] In her view, it became clear that the Prosecution did not have sufficient knowledge of the historical and geographical context throughout the trial. This view is corroborated by Goran Svilanović, who depicts another blunder made by the British prosecutor:

> At one point, if I remember rightly, Milošević interrupted Nice, who was reading the indictment, and said: 'Excuse me, sir, you claim that I attempted to *conquer*, to occupy, Kosovo. You know what? Your government's position is that this is

78 Personal interview with Ljiljana Smajlović.

79 Personal interview with Vojin Dimitrijević, Director of the Belgrade Centre for Human Rights, on 1 July 2009.

80 Ljiljana Smajlović, 'The View from Belgrade', paper presented at the conference 'The Milošević Trial: An Autopsy' at Indiana University on 19 February 2010. Retrieved from www.law.indiana.edu on 22 April 2010.

81 Personal interview with Ljiljana Smajlović.

> currently part of my country. How can I conquer and occupy my own country?' This rendered the indictment absurd.[82]

Overall, there was a broad consensus among the Serbian liberal elites that Milošević's trial was a failure in terms of public relations. For Vojin Dimitrijević, the Hague tribunal underestimated the importance of communicating with the public in the targeted countries in order to have justice 'seen to be done'.[83] He argued that, unlike domestic courts, international tribunals needed to promote their public image in order to justify their existence. In view of the negative public perception of the ICTY in the targeted states, the Hague tribunal clearly failed to manage its public relations, although there was an attempt to address this problem through a belated outreach programme. At the trial of Milošević, the public relations aspect was neglected to the extent that the voice of the Deputy Prosecutor was dubbed by a Croatian speaker on the TV coverage of the proceedings, which gave uninformed viewers the erroneous impression that Milošević was being tried by a Croat.[84] In addition, the Serbian names were regularly mispronounced by the Deputy Prosecutor and the members of the Trial Chamber, which gave a ridiculous tone to the proceedings.

Some human rights activists in Serbia attributed this public relations failure to the attitudes of the Serbian political elites, whom they blamed for deliberately discrediting the trial.[85] They argued that the proceedings were ridiculed by the domestic media, which presented Milošević's trial as a 'talk show', while domestic commentators stood in support of Milošević. These accusations led to a heated polemic among members of the liberal intelligentsia over who bore responsibility for the war (crimes) and how Serbian society should address the past. This polemic, which took place on the pages of the weekly magazine 'Vreme' between August and November 2002, generated a rift within civil society that was formerly united in its opposition to the Milošević regime.[86] Besides deliberating on the reporting of the Milošević trial and discussing the NATO bombing campaign, the various sides engaged in the debate voiced competing views regarding what confronting the past entailed.[87] On the one hand, a group of human rights activists and public intellectuals considered that Serbs were collectively responsible for war crimes

---

82 Personal interview with Goran Svilanović.

83 Dimitrijević, 'Kako ubediti javnost'.

84 Personal interview with Vojin Dimitrijević.

85 Personal interview with Sonja Biserko, President of the Helsinki Committee for Human Rights in Serbia, on 3 July 2009.

86 This debate was later published in book form by the Serbian Helsinki Committee for Human Rights. See Latinka Perović, Sonja Biserko and Seška Stanojlović, eds, *Tačka razlaza* (The Parting of the Ways) (Belgrade: Helsinške sveske, 2003).

87 For a comprehensive analysis of the debate, see Jasna Dragović-Soso, 'The Parting of the Ways: Public Reckoning with the Recent Past in Post-Milošević Serbia', in *The Milošević Trial – An Autopsy*, edited by Tim Waters (New York: Oxford University Press, 2013).

perpetrated by Serbian forces and that coming to terms with the past essentially meant confronting those crimes committed in the name of the Serbian nation. On the other hand, another group, mainly composed of journalists and public intellectuals, argued that responsibility for war crimes was primarily individual and that reckoning with the past should encompass the crimes committed by all the sides involved in the wars. According to this view, insisting on 'Serb guilt' would be counter-productive, as it would play into the hands of nationalists by reinforcing discourses of self-victimisation.[88]

In spite of these disagreements, there was also a common view that, instead of discrediting Milošević and his aggressive nationalist policy, the trial had led to the political resurrection of the former Serbian leader.[89] Following his overthrow, Milošević's popularity hit rock bottom since he was literally wiped off the political scene overnight. However, Milošević's appearance at the Hague tribunal allowed him to acquire a new political role. Through the defence of his political project in Court, Milošević shaped and promoted his nationalist discourse in Serbia.[90] Paradoxically, while Milošević's rule was characterised by his absence from the public scene, his image became pervasive through his trial. For Goran Svilanović, the trial was clearly counter-productive in terms of reckoning with the past:

> I was absolutely shocked by the fact that Milošević's approval ratings among the domestic public increased from 9 per cent on the day of the opening statement to 19 per cent two weeks later. This means that not only did people in Serbia not face what happened, but, on the contrary, it turned out that the Tribunal generated renewed support for these political ideas. Because the crimes were left up in the air, they were perhaps legally substantiated, but on the PR front – this is what I think the Tribunal should have done [better] – it [the Tribunal] was a big failure. And it is not only a failure in Serbia.[91]

The former Foreign Minister adds that this state of affairs inevitably had an impact on the government's approach towards cooperation with the ICTY:

> I have given the example of Milošević's trial in order to show what happens: that in two weeks, his approval ratings increased by ten per cent. Now, that intimidates the government because you are in power and you know that you took the decision to extradite and that, two weeks after the beginning of the trial,

88 Ibid.

89 Smajlović, 'The View from Belgrade'.

90 Svetlana Slapšak, 'Kulturna Poetika: Milošević – Srbija' (Cultural Poetics: Milošević – Serbia), paper presented at the round table on the trial of Milošević organised by the Humanitarian Law Centre on 18 December 2005 in Belgrade. Retrieved from www.hlc-rdc.org/Publikacije/857.sr.html on 13 May 2009.

91 Personal interview with Goran Svilanović.

> public opinion has turned against you. So, at the next request for the arrest [of indictees], you think 'wait, do I really want to make an arrest? If the result is going to be the same, why should I do it?' And this is an additional reason why it became more and more difficult to arrest [war crimes suspects], because the overall effect of the trials was the increase in support for indictees, which led to the erosion of support for governments in Serbia, Croatia and Bosnia.[92]

The negative reception of Milošević's trial in Serbia thus clearly increased the reluctance of the domestic political elites to cooperate with the Hague tribunal. Indeed, Milošević's trial raised the political risks attached to ICTY cooperation by reinforcing domestic resistance towards the arrest and transfer of war crimes suspects. At the same time, it discredited the Tribunal in the eyes of the domestic political elites and thus further diminished their commitment to transitional justice. In the remainder of this section, I discuss the repercussions of this trial on the attitudes of the Serbian elites in order to bring out its negative consequences in terms of truth-telling.

B. International Trials and State Interests

The beginning of Milošević's trial sparked a debate within the DOS coalition about the defence of state interests in the prosecution of former state executives before the ICTY. This polemic was triggered by concerns that the claims set out in the indictment against Milošević might have had negative repercussions for the state. These considerations were essentially discussed behind closed doors, as they provoked unease among the members of the DOS coalition who wanted to dissociate themselves from Milošević. Nevertheless, this issue was brought out in public by the Speaker of the Yugoslav Parliament, Dragoljub Mićunović:

> There is an illegitimate fear in the ranks of the DOS that whoever raises the question of Slobodan Milošević's indictment in The Hague will automatically be listed among Milošević's defenders. But we cannot escape discussing the political qualifications coming from the Prosecutor. It cannot be assumed that one man committed genocide. These things happen as a result of state policy, they are implemented through a decision of the state. We have to see what is the individual responsibility out there, and what is – if there was genocide – the responsibility of the state. The interests of our state and Milošević's interests in this matter are not identical. In some aspects they overlap, while in others they diverge. While it may not be in Milošević's interest to elucidate all the facts related to the wars in the former Yugoslavia, this is clearly in the interest of the current Yugoslav authorities which did not have any influence on Milošević's policy. Therefore, I do not advocate that the state defend Milošević in The Hague, but that the state defend its own interests, that it help establish all the

92 Ibid.

> facts – not with the intention of minimising the crimes, but of elucidating them. But we have to start from the fact that this is not only his own business, but also ours.[93]

Mićunović's viewpoint was not a matter of consensus within the DOS coalition. The representatives of the Serbian government immediately rejected the possibility of involving the state in the proceedings of the ICTY. They argued that Milošević's trial was a matter of individual responsibility and that the state had fulfilled all its duties by extraditing him.[94] But while the DOS leaders publicly downplayed the importance of Milošević's trial, Mićunović's statement suggests that Serbian officials were anxious about the allegations of genocide imputed to the former President. The authorities in Belgrade had good reasons to fear that Milošević could be convicted for genocide since Bosnia and Croatia had instigated two separate lawsuits for genocide against Yugoslavia before the International Court of Justice (ICJ).[95] The *Bosnian Genocide* case was particularly problematic for the Yugoslav authorities since the ICTY had established that the Srebrenica massacre amounted to genocide in its verdict to the trial of Radoslav Krstić in August 2001.[96] This decision implied that Yugoslavia could have been found responsible for genocide at the ICJ if it were established that the authorities in Belgrade had command over the troops on the ground in Bosnia. According to Tibor Varady, the head of the legal team representing Yugoslavia before the ICJ, Milošević's conviction for genocide at the ICTY would have substantially reinforced the argument of the Bosnian side:

> For Serbia to be convicted of genocide, it was necessary to demonstrate that the Serbian authorities had the intent to commit genocide. This is very difficult to prove. ... Had Milošević been convicted of genocide, this high threshold in terms of proving genocidal intent would have been lowered. So, this would really have been a significant argument. This does not mean that Bosnia would have won the case as there were many other arguments. However, this would have significantly strengthened Bosnia's position, there is no doubt about that.[97]

93 'Odbrana države ili Miloševića' (The Defence of the State or of Milošević), *NIN*, 7 February 2002.

94 'Političari na muci' (Politicians in Trouble), *Vreme*, 12 February 2002.

95 The ICJ is the principal judicial organ of the United Nations, whose role is to settle disputes between states. The Court has no jurisdiction to try individuals for war crimes or crimes against humanity. However, it does have jurisdiction over state responsibility for genocide on the basis of the Convention on the Prevention and Punishment of the Crime of Genocide.

96 *Prosecutor v. Krstić*, 'Case Information Sheet', Case No. IT-98-33. Accessed on www.icty.org on 2 November 2010.

97 Personal interview, on 16 November 2012, with Tibor Varady, head of the legal team representing Yugoslavia, and later Serbia, before the ICJ.

Although these concerns were rarely voiced in public, the fear that Yugoslavia could be the first state ever held responsible for genocide substantially informed the attitude of the Serbian authorities towards cooperation with the ICTY and truth-telling. In the words of the former Deputy Prime Minister, Miroljub Labus, the *Bosnian Genocide* case was 'hanging like the sword of Damocles over Serbia'.[98] The DOS leaders expected that the genocide lawsuits – which were instigated during the Bosnian and Croatian wars – would be withdrawn following the overthrow of Milošević.[99] The perseverance of the Bosnian and Croatian leaderships in seeking compensation before the ICJ provoked ample frustration among the Serbian authorities. The former Yugoslav ambassador to Washington Ivan Vujačić recounts how disappointed the DOS leaders were with this state of affairs:

> Listen, for ten years, we told the story 'the responsibility is individual; when Sloba leaves, we have our friends who are going to help us reconstruct, and so on'. And now, they come and say 'that's all fine, here is a collective judgment for genocide'. What should we do? Kill ourselves? This would have been really foolish, this whole nation would have turned against the West for ever. In fact, they [the West] were supposed to thwart this Bosnian story, but they did not succeed for all sorts of reasons.[100]

The upholding of the genocide lawsuits before the ICJ undermined one of the key arguments for the pursuit of justice: the individualisation of responsibility. The authorities in Belgrade had largely resorted to this argument in order to justify the arrest and extradition of war crimes suspects to the Hague tribunal. Indeed, the government representatives repeatedly claimed that cooperation with the ICTY would remove the stigma of war crimes from the Serbian nation. They believed that the charges against Yugoslavia would be dropped once cooperation with the ICTY was established. However, their expectations did not materialise, which substantially discredited their rationale for cooperation. In the words of Goran Svilanović, who was one of the most ardent supporters of ICTY cooperation, the government was caught in a vice:

> The argument in support of cooperation is to eschew the responsibility of the nation as such. But in fact two legal processes are running in parallel and at the end you have a situation in which almost all those who were supposed

98 Personal interview, on 8 June 2009, with Miroljub Labus, former leader of G17 Plus and Deputy Prime Minister in the Yugoslav (2000–03) and Serbian (2004–06) governments.

99 For a discussion of the political context of the *Bosnian Genocide* case, see Vojin Dimitrijević and Marko Milanovic, 'The Strange Story of the Bosnian *Genocide* Case', *Leiden Journal of International Law* 21:1 (2008), 65–94.

100 Personal interview with Ivan Vujačić, DS executive and former Ambassador to Washington, on 17 July 2009.

> to be arrested were arrested and prosecuted, while on the other hand this did not lead to the withdrawal of the genocide lawsuit, which is a lawsuit against the state. But anyone who identified himself with that state saw it as a lawsuit against himself, against the nation, and this is how it was seen by the Serbian public. And at the end, you had a situation in which individual and collective responsibilities were running parallel.[101]

Besides undermining the underlying principle of ICTY cooperation, the genocide lawsuits before the ICJ lessened the commitment of the authorities to the pursuit of justice and truth. Svilanović's statement suggests that he personally saw the *Bosnian Genocide* case as an attempt to attribute collective responsibility to the Serbian nation through the establishment of state responsibility. During the interview, the former Yugoslav Foreign Minister openly stated that 'one of the factors which complicated [ICTY] cooperation was that no-one wanted to take the responsibility for contributing to the stigmatisation of the nation – in fact, of the state'.[102] The same observation emerges in the testimony of the former Yugoslav Minister of Justice Momčilo Grubač:

> Even those who were absolutely aware of the need for cooperation – we were all torn between our willingness to cooperate on the one hand, and the risks that all this involved in terms of state interests on the other. Unfortunately, it turned out that, in many cases that were processed at the ICTY, the thesis that the state was on trial – the collective, not the individuals – was somehow substantiated.[103]

While they supported the pursuit of individual responsibility for war crimes, the liberally oriented elements within government disapproved of the Bosnian genocide lawsuit out of conviction. Besides objecting to the principle of collective responsibility, they considered that this lawsuit could not achieve justice because it wrongly created a distinction between victims and perpetrators along state lines. This was one of the main reasons why Tibor Varady decided to represent Yugoslavia at the ICJ:

> I am personally convinced that these lawsuits were on the wrong track. ... The problem in lawsuits between states is that those who were the real actors in the conflict were not [the same as] the actors at the ICJ. The conflicts in Bosnia and Croatia were ethnic. ... What happens afterwards [is that] Bosnia-Herzegovina is the subject of international law. This state instigates the lawsuit. This means that General Krstić and General Mladić are on which side? On the side of the plaintiff, on the side of the victim. And the Kosovo Albanians, the Hungarians

101 Personal interview with Goran Svilanović.

102 Ibid.

103 Personal interview with Momčilo Grubač, Federal Minister of Justice 2000–2001, on 7 May 2009.

> from Vojvodina and all those Serbs who were anti-war demonstrators are on the side of the alleged culprit. So, it is very difficult to achieve justice in this case.[104]

Ironically, some of the leading figures of the opposition to Milošević in the nineties were now called to testify at the ICJ in defence of the Serbian state. Dragoljub Mićunović, who was the first president of the DS in the early nineties, recounts his testimony:

> I went there as a witness of the defence and I testified that genocide involves the planned destruction of a nation or race, that Serbia has never passed any legislation that would be discriminatory against anyone, nor has the government adopted such a decision. I do not deny the crimes committed there by the Army of Republika Srpska or I do not know who – this is a different matter. I defended Serbia. So, there was no official stance. Whether some paramilitary unit committed crimes, this is a different thing, but this cannot be the responsibility of the government or the State.[105]

These concerns for state interests had a direct impact on the conduct of the Serbian authorities towards the ICTY and their attitudes towards disclosing the truth about war crimes in public. This was particularly the case during the Milošević trial, since he was the only high-ranking Serbian state official indicted for genocide. In order to safeguard state interests, the Yugoslav authorities requested to have a permanent observer at Milošević's trial.[106] However, this request was turned down by the Trials Chamber, which considered that states should not have formal representatives in the courtroom.

The state also provided significant support for the defence of Milošević, although this was kept secret from the public. During the trial, many commentators suspected that Milošević was given secret information by the intelligence agencies in view of the evidence he displayed in his cross-examination of witnesses.[107] This hypothesis proved to be true, as it was later revealed that Milošević was given support by the military Commission for Cooperation with the ICTY, which had been set up in order to collect evidence for the defence of Serbian indictees. This Commission was created in spring 2001, at a time when the Ministry of Defence was under the control of the Montenegrin SNP. It was abolished in April 2003, after the Democratic Party took control over the Ministry of Defence following

104 Personal interview with Tibor Varady.

105 Personal interview with Dragoljub Mićunović, DS executive and former Speaker of the Yugoslav Parliament (2000–2003), on 19 August 2009. The Army of Republika Srpska was the military force of the self-proclaimed Bosnian Serb Republic during the Bosnian war.

106 Personal interview with Vladimir Djerić.

107 'B. Kovačević-Vučo: Neko obavešten sprema Miloševića' (B. Kovačević-Vučo: Milošević Gets Intelligence Support), *Politika*, 27 February 2002.

the transformation of the Federal Republic of Yugoslavia into the State Union of Serbia and Montenegro. It is therefore difficult to assess whether this Commission was deliberately created by the transitional authorities, or whether it constituted a remnant of the former regime that escaped civilian control. However, the following statement by Dragoljub Mićunović suggests that at least some leaders of the DOS coalition approved of its work:

> I thought so, and I think that a lot had been done for that purpose – not so transparently and publicly – but that Milošević had ample support in terms of documentation. You noticed it in the way he defended himself there. This means that he was given access to archives, military documents, records – anything he needed. This was somehow done through these military channels and through this (domestic) war crimes court; he benefited from support in this respect. On the other hand, he did not want this support to be public because he wanted to keep his distance from the state that had sent him there. The same applies for Šešelj. It was only a matter of how to do it, and I think that this discrete manner was more useful for the state and the individuals, so that it did not turn into a media story.[108]

Mićunović's avowal clearly shows that the Serbian political elites were aware of, and acquiescent to, the support provided to Milošević. While it seems plain that the former President had access to official documents and other evidence in order to prepare his defence, it remains unclear to what extent the state was actually involved in this process. The fact that this support was provided secretly suggests that the state did not act as an impartial observer in this trial. This hypothesis is given further impetus by the fact that the Yugoslav authorities were reluctant to disclose secret documents that might have negative repercussions for the country in the *Bosnian Genocide* case.

Indeed, the question of access to secret military and state archives led to a significant deterioration in the relationship between the OTP and the authorities in Belgrade in the second half of 2002. In order to convict Milošević for genocide, the Prosecution needed to prove the involvement of the Serbian state and its leaders in the war and crimes in Bosnia. Therefore, the OTP requested access to the transcripts of the meetings of the Supreme Defence Council (SDC) – Yugoslavia's top decision-making body, composed of the highest-ranking political and military officials. According to Carla Del Ponte, the Yugoslav authorities rejected the OTP's request because they feared that these documents would reveal Milošević's involvement in Bosnia and Croatia, and thus substantiate the genocide lawsuits.[109] In October 2002, the ICTY Chief Prosecutor denounced the attitude of the Yugoslav officials in her address to the UN Security Council:

108 Personal interview with Dragoljub Mićunović.

109 Del Ponte and Sudetić, *Gospodja Tužiteljka*, 154–5.

> Military archives are closed to us, even in investigations where Serbs are the victims. The pattern is clear, and it may well be explained by an admission, made at one time but not since repeated, that nothing would be provided to the Tribunal if it might compromise the position of the FRY before the International Court of Justice, where Bosnia and Croatia seek the payment of war reparations. A quite improper consideration.[110]

In order to gain access to the SDC transcripts, the Trial Chamber issued a binding order to the authorities in Belgrade at the request of the Prosecution. The Yugoslav officials challenged the decision of the Trial Chamber by officially arguing that the Prosecution's request for blanket access to the archives was unacceptable.[111] However, unofficially, the Yugoslav authorities conditioned the handover of these documents on the provision of protective measures that would guarantee their secrecy.[112] These measures were contained in *Rule 54 bis* of the ICTY Rules and Procedures, which allowed a state to request protective measures for some documents 'on the grounds that disclosure would prejudice its national security interests'.[113] According to Carla Del Ponte, Belgrade's request for protective measures was based exclusively on the fear that the disclosure of the SDC transcripts would have negative repercussions for Serbia and Montenegro in the genocide lawsuits before the ICJ. In her memoirs, the former Chief Prosecutor recounts a meeting with the Yugoslav Foreign Minister:

> I requested Svilanović to hand over these documents. He refused, declaring – as he did so many times during our unofficial meetings and in the press – that these documents must not be seen by the judges of the International Court of Justice who were deciding upon the lawsuits brought by Croatia and Bosnia and Herzegovina against the Federal Republic of Yugoslavia, the precursor of the State Union of Serbia and Montenegro. Svilanović later declared that the government would give access to these documents only if the Appeals Chamber provided for 'protective measures', so that they would be cited only in closed sessions before the judges of the Hague tribunal, but not in public, as they would thus get to the International Court of Justice.[114]

---

110 Office of the Prosecutor of the ICTY, 'Address by the Prosecutor of the International Criminal Tribunals for the Former Yugoslavia and Rwanda, Mrs. Carla Del Ponte, to the United Nations Security Council', 30 October 2002. Accessed on www.icty.org/sid/8056 on 9 November 2010.

111 'Ne postoji pravo na opšti uvid u arhive' (There is No Right to Blanket Access to Archives), *Danas*, 20 December 2002.

112 Del Ponte and Sudetić, *Gospodja Tužiteljka*, 172.

113 ICTY, 'Rules of Procedure and Evidence', Rev. 43, 22 July 2009. Accessed on www.icty.org on 10 November 2010.

114 Del Ponte and Sudetić, *Gospodja Tužiteljka*, 200.

Driven by the urgent need to produce these documents during the prosecution phase of the Milošević trial, the Prosecution eventually agreed not to oppose Belgrade's request for protective measures on condition that these remain 'reasonable' and 'well-founded'.[115] As a result, the Trial Chamber for the Milošević case granted protective measures for the SDC transcripts which stipulated that parts of these documents be kept secret. However, the Prosecution subsequently challenged this decision as it considered that Belgrade's request could not be justified in terms of 'national security interests' stipulated in *Rule 54 bis*. The OTP's spokesperson Florence Hartmann later revealed that the Trial Chamber granted the protective measure in order not to damage Serbia's position in the *Bosnian Genocide* case before the ICJ.[116] According to her, the Serbian authorities were successful in arguing that an ICJ conviction would undermine peace and stability in the region and thus compromise 'vital national interests'. Hartmann concludes that the ICTY judges 'preferred the presumed stability of a country over the interests of justice and the truth, yielding to the watchword of international relations'.[117]

The relevance of the SDC transcripts remains the subject of ample controversy amongst the protagonists and observers of the Milošević trial. On the one hand, some members of the Prosecutorial team argue that these documents clearly demonstrate Serbia's involvement in, and responsibility for, war crimes in Bosnia, including the genocide in Srebrenica.[118] On the other hand, others suggest that this material shows that the Yugoslav and Serbian authorities did not have effective control over the Bosnian Serbs, thus contradicting the Prosecution's theory that Milošević was the mastermind behind the atrocities in Bosnia.[119] This polemic was further stirred by the fact that the ICJ did not request Serbia to produce these documents when ruling on the *Bosnian Genocide* case. Indeed, the Court rejected Bosnia's request for the production of unedited versions of the SDC transcripts on the basis that it had enough documentation and evidence on the relationship between the authorities of the FRY and the Republika Srpska and on the matter of

115 Ibid., 200–203.

116 Florence Hartmann, 'Vital Genocide Documents Concealed', Bosnian Institute, 2008. Accessed on www.bosnia.org.uk on 11 November 2010. See also Florence Hartmann, *Paix et châtiment* (Peace and Punishment) (Paris: Flammarion, 2007), 116–22. Hartmann was convicted of contempt of court by the ICTY in 2009 for disclosing this information.

117 Hartmann, *Paix et châtiment*, 120.

118 Del Ponte and Sudetić, *Gospodja Tužiteljka*, 336–8; Hartmann, 'Vital Genocide Documents Concealed'.

119 Marko Prelec, 'Justice, Truth and Peace at the Hague Bourse', paper presented at the conference 'The Milošević Trial: An Autopsy' at the Maurer School of Law, Indiana University, on 19 February 2010. Retrieved from www.law.indiana.edu on 22 April 2010.

control and instruction.[120] Nevertheless, critics have denounced this decision as a failure to disclose the truth and deliver justice.[121]

While the legal and historical implications of the SDC transcripts remain contested, it seems plausible that the authorities in Belgrade sought protective measures for these documents out of fear of their repercussions on the *Bosnian Genocide* case before the ICJ. This hypothesis is further corroborated by the testimony of the former ambassador to Washington, Ivan Vujačić:

> It is well known that we requested that documents should not go to that Court [ICJ], and that was respected as far as I know. Because we behaved naively: we withdrew our lawsuits against Bosnia and Croatia, thinking: 'let's make a compromise, we are friends, we are different now'. [They responded:] 'No, you withdraw your lawsuit, but we will not'. In that case, the documents that we handed over to the Hague tribunal were going to be sealed. This is a true story. This is a very real reason why cooperation with regard to documentation was made more difficult. Nobody wants to put his head in the guillotine and to pull [the blade down] – that is not very normal.[122]

The politicians' fear that the trial of Milošević might have negative repercussions for the state thus had a very tangible impact on cooperation with the ICTY and truth-telling. Since the Serbian state was being sued in parallel with its former president, the Serbian elites opted to conceal from the public any evidence that could potentially hinder state interests. Paradoxically, the members of the legal team representing Serbia before the ICJ believed that the SDC transcripts did not contain evidence showing Milošević's responsibility for genocide. According to Tibor Varady, while these transcripts might have been an additional proof of the support provided by the authorities in Belgrade to the Bosnian Serbs, it is unlikely that they contained evidence of genocidal intent on the part of the former Yugoslav leadership.[123] Varady suggests that Serbian decision-makers did not understand the distinction between these two elements and that they sought to restrict anything that might have harmed the country's reputation:

---

120 *Application of the Convention on the Prevention and Punishment of the Crime of Genocide* (Bosnia and Herzegovina v. Serbia and Montenegro), Judgment of 26 February 2007, paras 205 and 206. Retrieved from http://www.icj-cij.org/icjwwwidocket/ibhyframe.htm on 20 January 2011. Hereafter cited as ICJ Judgment.

121 Marko Milanovic, 'State Responsibility for Genocide: A Follow-Up', *The European Journal of International Law* 18:4 (2007): 669–94; Richard J. Goldstone and Rebecca J.Hamilton, 'Bosnia v. Serbia: Lessons from the Encounter of the International Court of Justice with the International Criminal Tribunal for the Former Yugoslavia', *Leiden Journal of International Law* 21:1 (2008), 95–112.

122 Personal interview with Ivan Vujačić.

123 Personal interview with Tibor Varady.

> A state does not want to publish something that harms its reputation. ... Therefore, this was not only about not being convicted for genocide, but [about] not being compromised. And many of those who were in the Serbian government did not perfectly understand these differences – whether this was about condemning Serbia or whether it was just about genocide. ... They wanted to restrict anything compromising, just as the Americans did not give everything. ... They also feared personal responsibility, [they thought] "what if something happens? Then, it is better not to give something that might not be dangerous than to be personally responsible". We told them "give everything that you think is harmless". This is what a lawyer says to a party. Had we seen these documents, we might have told them that there was nothing harmful [there]. But we did not even try to see them. Someone may have, I did not.[124]

In line with this train of thought, the Director of the National Council for Cooperation with the ICTY, Dušan Ignjatović, considered that requesting protective measures was a perfectly legitimate action to which many other countries – including the 'Great Powers' – resorted in their cooperation with the Hague tribunal.[125] Nevertheless, such actions clearly undermined the Tribunal's purpose of establishing and communicating the truth. The authorities' recourse to such measures also suggests that Serbian officials were increasingly reluctant to reveal to the public atrocities committed by the Serbian side. Instead of promoting truth-telling in Serbia, the trial of Milošević thus had the opposite effect: it further discouraged the political elites from disclosing the truth and addressing the war crimes legacy.

Besides sealing off the question of Serbian responsibility for war crimes in domestic politics, the fear of state responsibility provided a powerful argument to the opponents of cooperation with the ICTY. The spectre of collective responsibility was constantly nurtured by the representatives of the SPS and SRS, who equated Milošević's trial with the trial of the Serbian nation. Following the change of government in 2004, Koštunica drew on the defence of state interests in order to justify his tougher stance towards cooperation with the ICTY, as well as the provision of state support to the Hague indictees.[126] During this period, the policy of 'voluntary surrender' sought to portray war crimes suspects as heroes defending Serbian national interests at the ICTY. The linkage of state interests with the fate of ICTY indictees was thus instrumental in producing a normative shift in cooperation and undermining the goals of transitional justice (See Chapter 3). Therefore, whether it was genuine or simply rhetorical, the concern for state interests deeply affected the Serbian government's policies towards cooperation with the ICTY and truth-telling throughout the 2000s.

---

124 Ibid.

125 Personal interview with Dušan Ignjatović, Director of the National Council for Cooperation with the ICTY, on 10 June 2009.

126 'Hag velika obaveza' (The Hague is a Great Duty), *Politika*, 3 April 2004.

***

In contrast to the expectations of transitional justice advocates, the trial of Slobodan Milošević did not bring about reckoning with war crimes within Serbian society. Instead, the broadcasting of the trial reinforced negative public perceptions of the ICTY and discredited the Tribunal in the eyes of the liberal elite. Besides, in view of the *Bosnian Genocide* lawsuit, Milošević's trial raised genuine concern among the Yugoslav/Serbian authorities about state interests in the prosecution of former high-ranking officials. This concern for state interests led to the tacit provision of state support for the defence of Milošević. More importantly, it clearly reduced the room for truth-telling, as illustrated by the sealing of the SDC transcripts.

The interview data and analysis presented in this section shows how externalised justice and the way it was executed actually provoked a negative and unanticipated response within Serbia and amongst elites. Rather than engendering truth-telling and having a positive impact on regime change, the trial of Milošević and its conduct is shown to have compromised the ICTY and incriminated the Serbian state, thereby undermining the efforts of those within the new regime committed to the pursuit of justice. The tenor of the prosecution and, in particular, the requisitioning of state documentation linked the trial with the *Bosnian Genocide* lawsuit that was before the ICJ. As far as the authorities were concerned, the handing-over of state documentation jeopardised the safeguarding of 'state interests' and threatened the international reputation and legitimacy of the Serbian state.

After all, cooperation with the ICTY and the handing-over of Milošević to The Hague was supposedly based on the pursuit of an individual rather than on collective responsibility, and was conditional upon the separation of the two issues. Had Serbia been the first state ever held responsible of genocide, it would have suffered a massive loss of international legitimacy, besides potentially having to pay substantial monetary compensation to Bosnia and Herzegovina. In this context, international justice's potential for promoting truth-telling and regime change was clearly diminished. In the remainder of this chapter, I examine the dynamics between regime change, state interests and truth-telling by focusing on the issue of Srebrenica.

3. Srebrenica and the Politics of Acknowledgment

The policy of 'voluntary surrender' introduced by the Koštunica government in 2004 induced a substantial shift in official attitudes towards the war crimes issue. As discussed in Chapter 3, this policy consisted in providing financial and legal assistance to ICTY indictees and raising their public profile in order to encourage their surrender. While this policy boosted the transfer of war crimes suspects to The Hague, it also undermined the ICTY's truth-telling agenda by decriminalising the indictees and detaching their extradition from any notion of justice and truth. Indeed, the transfer of indictees to The Hague was devoid of any discussion of war crimes, as the authorities and the media refrained from even mentioning the charges which were imputed to these individuals. Unsurprisingly, public opinion polls showed a stark decline in public knowledge of war crimes during the period 2001–05.[127]

In view of these political developments, the domestic human rights community mobilised to promote the truth about war crimes committed by the Serbian side during the wars of Yugoslav succession. Several NGOs instigated programmes for 'facing the past' specifically designed to spread knowledge of war crimes and war crimes trials among the Serbian public.[128] These human rights organisations were particularly active in countering denial and promoting acknowledgment of Srebrenica in the months preceding the tenth anniversary of the massacre in July 2005. This NGO campaign largely contributed towards raising the issue of Srebrenica on the domestic political agenda. But instead of opening a debate on the war crimes legacy, the issue of Srebrenica became the subject of heated political contestation.

This section looks at how facts established at the ICTY were sanctioned or challenged by the domestic political elites. The massacre of Srebrenica was singled out as the worst atrocity of the Yugoslav wars by the ICTY, which defined it as genocide. Moreover, as the biggest massacre perpetrated on European soil since World War II, Srebrenica became a worldwide symbol of war crimes. As a result, the Serbian authorities were pressed to condemn this atrocity in order to demonstrate their willingness to address the past. However, this move was strongly opposed by the nationalist parties, who continually challenged the significance of Srebrenica. Indeed, the initiative for the adoption of a parliamentary resolution condemning Srebrenica failed on two occasions before materialising in March 2010. Besides analysing the competing discourses surrounding the debate on Srebrenica, I examine the factors that have eventually led to official acknowledgment of the Srebrenica genocide and assess the implications of this deed for Serbia's process of coming to terms with the war crimes legacy.

A. The NGO Campaign and the Politicisation of Srebrenica

Given that the Serbian authorities were reluctant to address the war crimes legacy, the task of advancing the truth about the war crimes committed by the Serbian side was taken on by domestic human rights organisations. Essentially composed of Belgrade-based intellectuals, most of these NGOs derived from the anti-war

127 Belgrade Centre for Human Rights, 'Public Opinion in Serbia: Attitudes towards the Hague Tribunal', 2005. Accessed on www.bgcentar.org.rs on 20 July 2009.

128 These programmes were implemented by human rights NGOs such as the Humanitarian Law Centre (HLC), the Helsinki Committee for Human Rights (HCHR), and the Lawyers' Committee for Human Rights (YUCOM).

movement and the opposition to the Milošević regime in the nineties.[129] Besides actively taking part in the removal of Milošević, these organisations played an important role in collecting and disseminating evidence of atrocities committed during the wars of Yugoslav succession. They thus substantially contributed towards efforts to prosecute war crimes suspects at the ICTY and before domestic courts following the change of regime.

In addition, the domestic human rights organisations sought to advance the process of 'facing the past' in Serbian society by exposing and denouncing the atrocities committed by the Serbian side during the wars. These programmes consisted primarily in organising conferences and media campaigns informing the public about the work and findings of the ICTY.[130] Besides disseminating evidence of war crimes, the human rights NGOs adopted an openly confrontational attitude towards the authorities in response to the government's policy of 'voluntary surrender'. This new approach was inaugurated in December 2004, when the Humanitarian Law Centre (HLC) caused a storm by accusing government representatives and senior police officials of orchestrating a cover-up of war crimes perpetrated by Serbian forces in Kosovo.[131] The HLC called upon the government to set up a commission of inquiry to elucidate the incineration of Albanian victims, allegedly carried out by the Serbian forces in order to conceal atrocities perpetrated during the Kosovo war. But these demands were simply ignored by the government, which remained silent on this issue.

In February 2005, a coalition of five NGOs announced that they would coordinate their activities and draw up a new strategy for promoting the truth about war crimes.[132] These organisations endorsed positive propaganda in order to pressure the political elites and public opinion into facing up to the atrocities committed by the Serbian side during the wars. The NGO coalition particularly focused its activities on countering the denial of Srebrenica in the months preceding the tenth anniversary of the massacre. The issue of Srebrenica was until then largely absent from political debate in Serbia. While mainstream politicians tended to avoid this issue, the massacre of Srebrenica was continually denied and downplayed by nationalist circles represented by the SRS and SPS. In those circumstances, the NGO campaign clashed directly with the militancy of right-

129 Bojan Bilić, *We Were Gasping for Air: [Post-]Yugoslav Anti-War Activism and Its Legacy* (Baden-Baden: Nomos, 2012).

130 For example, the Humanitarian Law Centre organised a column entitled 'The Hague among Us' in the newspaper *Danas* between April 2004 and June 2005. The HLC also organised a series of conferences at which the findings of the ICTY were presented in partnership with the Tribunal's outreach programme.

131 'Secret Police in Kosovo Cover-Up', *B92*, 30 December 2004.

132 These organisations were the Humanitarian Law Centre, Civic Initiatives, the Lawyers' Committee for Human Rights, the Youth Initiative for Human Rights and the Helsinki Committee for Human Rights. See 'Jočić i Bulatović koče istinu o Mačkatici' (Jočić and Bulatović Inhibit the Truth about Mačkatica), *Danas*, 4 February 2002.

wing organisations that celebrated the 'liberation' of Srebrenica and glorified General Mladić.[133] In response to this appalling denial of the massacre, eight NGOs appealed to the Serbian Parliament to adopt a resolution acknowledging and condemning the Srebrenica genocide.[134] The draft resolution put forward by the NGOs called upon the Serbian state to distance itself from the Srebrenica genocide by acknowledging that this crime had been committed in the name of the Serbian nation.[135] While this proposal was endorsed by two independent MPs, the possibility of adopting such a resolution was immediately rejected by the leading DSS on the basis that Serbia could not take responsibility for Srebrenica.[136]

The NGO campaign was given further impetus by the broadcasting of a tape showing the execution of six young Bosniaks from Srebrenica by a Serb paramilitary unit called the 'Scorpions'. The tape, which had originally been obtained by the Humanitarian Law Centre and shown at the trial of Milošević in The Hague, came as a stark wake-up call for politicians and public opinion in Serbia.[137] The authorities immediately proceeded with the arrest of the members of the Scorpions unit and the political elites unequivocally condemned this horrendous crime.[138] For the first time, the Serbian government recognised the need for facing the past and expressed its full support for war crimes prosecutions. The Serbian President and leader of the Democratic Party (DS), Boris Tadić, went even further, stating that this crime had been committed in the name of the Serbian nation and announcing that he would attend the commemoration of the tenth anniversary of Srebrenica.[139]

The broadcasting of the 'Scorpions tape' raised the initiative for the adoption of a parliamentary declaration on the political agenda. However, the various political parties had divergent views on what this resolution should consist of. While they all considered that the responsibility for war crimes should be individualised, the political parties disagreed on how Srebrenica should be interpreted and whether

---

133 The confrontation between human rights activists and right-wing organisations culminated at the public seminar on Srebrenica organised by the right-wing student organisation Nomokanon on 17 May 2005. See 'Cene uvreda i pljuvanja' (The Cost of Insult and Slander), *Vreme*, 26 May 2005.

134 The five NGOs mentioned above were joined by the Belgrade Circle, the Centre for Cultural Decontamination and the organisation Women in Black.

135 'Odreći se zločina'(Rejecting the Crime), *Večernje Novosti*, 28 May 2005.

136 'Dilema da li priznati zločin'(Dilemma over Acknowledging the Crime), *Danas*, 28 May 2005.

137 For a thorough analysis of the impact of the 'Scorpions tape', see Ivan Zverzhanovski, 'Watching War Crimes: The Srebrenica Video and Serbian Attitudes to the 1995 Srebrenica Massacre', *Southeast European and Black Sea Studies* 7:3 (2007): 417–30.

138 'Policija munjevito uhapsila "Škorpione"' (Police Have Hastily Arrested 'Scorpions'), *Glas Javnosti*, 3 June 2005.

139 'Pokloniću se žrtvama Srebrenice'(I Will Bow to the Srebrenica Victims), *Večernje Novosti*, 3 June 2005.

it should be emphasised as the gravest war crime. Over the following weeks, the main political actors engaged in a heated debate over the content of the declaration to be adopted in parliament. On the one hand, the DSS, SRS and SPS stood for the adoption of a declaration condemning all war crimes committed during the wars of Yugoslav succession.[140] These parties argued that the responsibility for war crimes is individual and that the Serbian state had nothing to do with the atrocities committed in neighbouring countries. In addition, they rejected the distinctive nature and scope of the Srebrenica massacre, which they only mentioned in their draft declaration as an example of war crime along with the crimes committed by the Bosniak forces in Bratunac.[141] This initiative was opposed by another group of parties centred around the DS, which insisted that the parliamentary declaration should specifically condemn the Srebrenica massacre.[142] While they acknowledged that all sides in the war had committed atrocities, these parties argued that the killing of thousands of men in Srebrenica had become a symbol of war crime throughout the world.[143] Therefore, they put forward a declaration condemning all war crimes, with special emphasis on Srebrenica.

After two weeks of negotiations among political parties, the initiative to adopt a parliamentary resolution was abandoned as a result of the irreconcilable positions of these two political blocs.[144] While the political parties mutually blamed each other for this outcome, the parliament's failure to adopt a resolution condemning Srebrenica can be attributed to several factors. First of all, the political representatives of the former regime embodied in the SPS and SRS had a vested interest in obstructing acknowledgment of Srebrenica and – in general – of war crimes committed by the Serbian side. Since these parties were in power during the nineties and since they directly took part in wartime activities, recognition of Srebrenica being genocide would have exposed them to the risk of being held politically responsible for it. This, in turn, would have further undermined their legitimacy as political actors in a democratic regime. Besides, these political representatives bore the risk of being held personally responsible for war crimes. At the height of the debate on the adoption of a parliamentary resolution, the acting leader of the SRS, Tomislav Nikolić, was accused of being directly involved in war crimes by the Director of the HLC, Nataša Kandić. While these accusations

140 'Većina za osudu svih zločina' (Majority for Condemning All Crimes), *Politika*, 14 June 2005.

141 On 12 July each year, the Serbian community commemorates the victims of the war crimes perpetrated in Bratunac by the Bosnian Muslim forces stationed in Srebrenica during the war.

142 The view of the DS was supported by several small parties: the Serbian Renewal Party, the Social Democratic Party and G17 Plus.

143 'Osuda na rečima'(Condemnation Pledges), *Večernje Novosti*, 15 June 2005.

144 'Skupština Srbije neće doneti deklaraciju o osudi zločina' (Serbian Parliament Will Not Vote Resolution Condemning Crimes), *Danas*, 15 June 2005.

proved to be unsubstantiated, they effectively constituted an attempt to disqualify the Radical leader from political life.[145]

Secondly, besides having a vested interest in opposing acknowledgment of Srebrenica, these parties ideologically stood against the idea that war crimes had been committed in the name of the Serbian nation. In this respect, the positions of the SRS and SPS concurred with those of the leading DSS, which, despite having opposed the regime of Milošević, displayed an overtly nationalist outlook on the wars of Yugoslav succession.[146] While these parties acknowledged that war crimes had been committed by the Serbian side, they rejected the view that these atrocities formed part of a wider campaign of ethnic cleansing orchestrated by the Serbian leadership. Instead, they insisted that these were the deeds of individuals, and had no connection whatsoever with the Serbian state. This standpoint is reflected in the testimony of the former Minister of Justice Zoran Stojković:

> Nobody disputes the fact that what took place in Srebrenica was a war crime. I am not looking to go into who had the greater number of victims, but I have had the opportunity to see the material that was collected. On this list of nine thousand dead, you have people who are currently living in America and who are still coming over. Therefore, when you look beneath the surface, this was a war crime [and not a genocide], and it means that individuals should be held accountable.[147]

The allegation that Srebrenica amounted to genocide was counter to this view since it presumed that this massacre was planned with intent to destroy in part the Bosniak ethnic group. Therefore, the initiative to adopt a parliamentary resolution condemning all war crimes sought to deny that Srebrenica was genocide and portray it as an ordinary war crime among others. Although the DSS, SRS and SPS formed an overwhelming majority in parliament, they refrained from putting through their resolution, as this would have generated controversy and embarrassment at home and abroad. Nevertheless, the content of this resolution was reproduced in a statement issued by Koštunica's government on the eve of the commemoration of Srebrenica.[148]

---

145 In response to these accusations, Nikolić instigated legal proceedings against Kandić who was later found guilty of defamation. This ruling was subsequently annulled by the Court of Appeal. See Human Rights Watch, 'World Report 2010 – Serbia', retrieved from www.hrw.org/world-report-2010/srbija-0 on 18 May 2012.

146 Indeed, Prime Minister Koštunica insisted on condemning all war crimes committed during the wars of Yugoslav succession on the basis that Serbs were the greatest victims of the conflict ('Osuda svih zločina' (Condemnation of All Crimes), *Politika*, 25 June 2005).

147 Personal interview with Zoran Stojković, Serbian Minister of Justice 2004–06, on 25 August 2009.

148 'Vlada izjednačeno osudila zločine' (Government Has Condemned Crimes Equally), *B92*, 7 July 2005.

Finally, Parliament's failure to condemn the Srebrenica genocide can partly be attributed to the fear among political elites that this would have generated negative consequences for Serbia in the *Bosnian Genocide* lawsuit before the International Court of Justice. This fear was substantiated by Serbia's legal representatives before the ICJ, who declared that the recognition by the Serbian authorities that genocide had been committed in Srebrenica would hinder their case.[149] As a member of the legal team, Tibor Varady considered that the acknowledgment of Srebrenica should only be considered as part of a settlement with the Bosnian authorities:

> Look, when I took over these legal cases as the leader of the legal team representing first the FRY, then Serbia and Montenegro, and then Serbia, I actually thought that a peaceful settlement was very likely and very logical. ... Now, the recognition of the genocide in Srebrenica before the decision [of the ICJ] would of course make sense only as part of an agreement. Because, if only Serbia recognised [genocide], this would obviously strengthen the position of the other side if that other side went on with the dispute. So, as the representative of Serbia, I was talking about acknowledgment of that horror in Srebrenica as part of a deal, an agreement. Because, otherwise, this would have been advising against the interests of Serbia – I was in the [legal] expert team after all.[150]

The politicians' fear of the ICJ ruling was further reinforced by the inflammatory statements issued by human rights activists following the broadcasting of the Scorpions tape. Indeed, the Director of the HLC, Nataša Kandić, claimed that this footage was clear proof of Serbia's involvement in the Srebrenica genocide,[151] while the President of the Serbian Helsinki Committee for Human Rights, Sonja Biserko, stated that Serbia committed genocide all over Bosnia and attempted to do the same in Kosovo.[152] As a result, the NGO declaration was perceived by most politicians as a resolution holding the Serbian state responsible for Srebrenica, thus exposing it to an adverse ruling of the ICJ. The NGO representatives thus inadvertently contributed towards reinforcing political resistance to the acknowledgment of Srebrenica by alienating the most reformist politicians, while exacerbating discourses of denial and self-victimisation nurtured by nationalist parties.[153]

---

149 'Udaraju nam žig genocida' (They Are Imputing Genocide to Us), *Večernje Novosti*, 24 June 2005.

150 Personal interview with Tibor Varady.

151 'Prikazan video zapis o ubijanju muslimana iz Srebrenice'(Footage of Killing of Srebrenica Muslims Displayed), *Danas*, 2 June 2005.

152 'Biserko: Srbija izvršila genocid u BiH' (Biserko: Serbia Committed Genocide in BiH), *Politika*, 25 June 2005.

153 For further elaboration on this, see Mladen Ostojić, 'Facing the Past While Disregarding the Present? Human Rights NGOs and Truth-Telling in Post-Milošević Serbia', in *Civil Society and Transitions in the Western Balkans*, edited by Vesna

In the context of the *Bosnian Genocide* lawsuit, no political party was ready to acknowledge that Srebrenica was genocide, even less to accept responsibility for it. Even the DS, which insisted on specifically condemning the Srebrenica massacre, did not refer to it as genocide.[154] At the same time, the DSS, SRS and SPS rejected the possibility of singling out Srebrenica altogether on the basis that this would necessarily imply that Serbia bore responsibility for the massacre. They accused the NGOs of orchestrating an 'anti-Serbian' campaign aimed at undermining the legitimacy and sovereignty of the Serbian state.[155] Accordingly, the allegations that Serbia was involved in Srebrenica and bore responsibility for genocide were aimed at preparing the ground for the suspension of the Republika Srpska and the granting of independence to Kosovo.[156] By opposing the adoption of a parliamentary resolution on Srebrenica and insisting that all war crimes be condemned, the nationalist parties portrayed themselves as defenders of the Serbian state, whose integrity was challenged by the claims of the NGOs.

Instead of opening a debate on the war crimes legacy, this failed attempt to acknowledge and condemn Srebrenica generated renewed nationalist mobilisation in Serbia. Besides discrediting the demands of the human rights groups, the nationalist circles centred around the SRS launched a counter-campaign denouncing war crimes committed against Serbs. Following the same methods previously used by the NGOs, they organised public conferences and broadcast footage of war crimes committed against Serbs in order to 'disprove the collective responsibility of the Serbian nation'.[157] In addition, the nationalist political and intellectual elites increasingly challenged the singularity of the Srebrenica massacre. Over the next few months, they orchestrated a broad media campaign aimed at contesting the facts established by the Hague tribunal and downplaying the scale and importance of the atrocities perpetrated by the Serb forces in Srebrenica.

The denial of the genocide in Srebrenica was articulated around three broad lines of argument. First of all, the claim that Srebrenica amounted to genocide was contested by denying the existence of a planned operation with genocidal intent. According to this argument, this fictitious scenario was made up by the Bosnian Muslim leadership in conjunction with their Western allies in order to justify military intervention against Bosnian Serbs.[158] Secondly, the scale of the atrocity

---

Bojičić-Dželilović, James Ker-Lindsay and Denisa Kostovicova (Basingstoke: Palgrave MacMillan, 2013), 230–47.

154 *Večernje Novosti*, 15 June 2005.

155 'Zaustaviti kampanju NVO protiv Srba' (Stop the NGO Campaign against Serbs), *Glas Javnosti*, 25 June 2005.

156 'Priprema za ukidanje Republike Srpske' (Preparation for the Suspension of the Republika Srpska), *Nacional*, 6 June 2005.

157 'Nikolić: Odgovor na satanizovanje Srba' (Nikolić: Response to the Satanisation of Serbs), Politika, 8 July 2005.

158 See, for example, 'Žrtve scenarija smišljenog u Sarajevu' (Victims of Scenario Devised in Sarajevo), *Politika*, 2 July 2005; 'Masakr ili genocid' (Massacre or Genocide),

was contested by drawing on a variety of informal expert reports and unofficial investigations. These reports sought to refute the possibility that Srebrenica constituted genocide – or even an 'outstanding' war crime – by minimising the number of victims and portraying the massacre as a manipulation orchestrated by the international community.[159] Finally, and most importantly, the significance of Srebrenica was counter-balanced by referring to the war crimes committed against Serbs in the nearby municipality of Bratunac. This relativisation of war crimes provided a justification for the Srebrenica massacre, which was thus portrayed as a consequence of the atrocities perpetrated by the Bosnian Muslim forces stationed in Srebrenica against local Serbs. In addition, the fact that the Serbian victims were overlooked by the international community, which actively participated in the commemoration of Srebrenica, was exploited by the nationalists in order to generate a feeling of injustice and self-victimisation. These sentiments were subsequently reinforced by the lenient sentencing of Naser Orić, the leader of the Muslim forces in Srebrenica, who was condemned to two years' imprisonment by the ICTY in July 2006.[160]

As a result of these developments, the Serbian political class and public opinion were deeply polarised with regard to this issue. While the Serbian President, Boris Tadić, attended the tenth anniversary commemoration of the Srebrenica massacre on 11 July 2005, the SRS leaders attended the commemoration in the nearby town of Bratunac on the day after. By drawing a parallel between these two events, the Serbian nationalists effectively sealed any debate about the singularity of Srebrenica and responsibility for this massacre. They thus watered down the effect of the Scorpions tape, which eventually failed to generate genuine public deliberation about war crimes committed by the Serbian side. Looking back at these developments a year later, Nataša Kandić reluctantly admitted that most of the advances in terms of reckoning with war crimes achieved through the broadcasting of the Scorpions tape had been reversed owing to the lack of political will to address this issue.[161]

***

The NGO campaign and, especially, the Scorpions tape successfully raised the war crimes issue on the political agenda and sensitised public opinion about the atrocities committed by the Serbian side. In this respect, the Serbian President's attendance at the tenth anniversary of the Srebrenica genocide marked a turning-

---

Večernje Novosti, 5 July 2005; 'Paralela sa Faludžom' (A Parallel with Fallujah), *Politika*, 3 August 2005.

159 See, for example, 'Sumnje u zvaničnu verziju' (Doubts in the Official Version), *Politika*, 1 July 2005; 'Velika laž – 8000 ubijenih' (Huge Lie – 8,000 killed), *Večernje Novosti*, 13 July 2005.

160 Orić was subsequently acquitted by the Appeals Chamber in July 2008.

161 'Daleko od katarze' (Far from Catharsis), *Politika*, 11 July 2006.

point in the acknowledgment of Serbian war crimes. However, the failure to adopt a parliamentary resolution on Srebrenica highlighted the domestic political resistance to reckoning with Serbian atrocities. As discussed above, this resistance was conditioned both by the balance of power on the domestic political scene and the fear that acknowledgment of the Srebrenica genocide might generate negative repercussions for Serbia in the *Bosnian Genocide* lawsuit before the ICJ.

The Srebrenica massacre thus became the subject of heated political contestation between liberal and nationalist elites. While the most ardent human rights activists claimed that Serbia committed genocide, the nationalist political and intellectual elite sought to deprive Srebrenica of its singular character and portray it as an 'ordinary' war crime among others. This politicisation of Srebrenica foreclosed the opening of any genuine debate about war crimes within Serbian society by generating further polarisation on this issue.

B. The Srebrenica Resolution: Acknowledgment without Reckoning?

The issue of Srebrenica was brought back onto the Serbian political agenda by the ruling of the ICJ in the *Bosnian Genocide* case in February 2007. The ICJ cleared Serbia from direct responsibility and involvement in the Srebrenica genocide, but it ruled that Serbia had breached the genocide convention by failing to prevent the genocide and to bring perpetrators to justice.[162] The Serbian political elites gave mixed reactions to this decision. On the one hand, the parties related to the former regime (SPS and SRS) hailed this decision as proof that Serbia did not take part in the war in Bosnia and that the former Serbian leadership was not responsible for the atrocities perpetrated there. However, they condemned the fact that the Court had endorsed the ICTY's view that Srebrenica amounted to genocide, which they saw as a conspiracy aimed at de-legitimising the Republika Srpska.[163] On the other hand, while the representatives of the DS and DSS welcomed the ICJ's decision to clear Serbia of genocide, they regretted the fact that the country was found guilty of breaching the genocide convention and pushed for cooperation with the ICTY to improve. The reaction of President Tadić was especially significant as he explicitly blamed Milošević's regime for disgracing the Serbian state and appealed to parliament to adopt a resolution condemning Srebrenica, in order to show compliance with the ICJ ruling.[164] Finally, the human rights organisations deplored the Court's decision, which they perceived as a blow to transitional justice and reconciliation in the region.[165] Indeed, several NGO representatives

162 ICJ Judgment. For a discussion of the legal aspects of the ICJ decision, see the special issue of the European Journal of International Law 18:4 (September 2007).

163 'Stranačka reagovanja' (Political Parties' Reactions), *Politika*, 27 February 2007.

164 'Tadić: Skupština mora da donese deklaraciju o Srebrenici' (Tadić: Parliament Must Adopt Srebrenica Resolution), *Politika*, 27 February 2007.

165 'Presuda negira priču o genocidnom narodu' (Ruling Denies Genocidal Nation Theory), *Politika*, 27 February 2007.

had earlier called upon the international community to support Bosnia's claims, arguing that establishing Serbia's responsibility for genocide was a precondition for Serbian society to face the past.

Despite the fact that Serbia was effectively cleared of genocide by the ICJ ruling, Tadić's initiative for the adoption of a parliamentary resolution on Srebrenica failed to generate the necessary support. Indeed, the main political parties held onto the positions adopted two years earlier. Once again, the DSS, SRS and SPS denied Srebrenica was genocide and requested that parliament condemn all war crimes. In this light, the SRS and SPS put forward two separate but similar draft resolutions which differed only in wording and the emphasis on different events.[166] Besides the DS, the initiative to explicitly condemn Srebrenica only benefited from the support of the newly created Liberal-Democratic Party (LDP) and a coalition of small parties from Vojvodina.[167]

In those circumstances, Tadić's appeal for the adoption of a parliamentary resolution on Srebrenica could not materialise. Although the DS emerged as the second biggest political party (behind the SRS) after the parliamentary elections of 2007, it did not have enough power to push through the adoption of such a resolution in parliament. Moreover, this initiative coincided with negotiations for the creation of a new government between the DS and DSS. Since these two parties held opposite views on the issue of Srebrenica, it seems likely that the DS dropped the demand for the adoption of a parliamentary resolution in order to prevent this contentious issue from undermining the creation of a government with the DSS. As Koštunica was given a mandate to form the new government, the issue of Srebrenica once again fell into oblivion. Therefore, although there were no longer reasons to fear that acknowledgment of the Srebrenica genocide could have adverse consequences for the Serbian state, the adoption of a resolution on Srebrenica in parliament was made impossible by the domestic political power balance.

It is only at the beginning of 2010 that the initiative for the adoption of a parliamentary resolution on Srebrenica was revived by President Tadić. This time, both external and domestic political conditions were favourable to this initiative. Indeed, the reconfiguration of the Serbian political scene that followed the parliamentary elections of May 2008 produced a significant shift in the power balance among political parties. The landslide victory of the political grouping

166 The draft resolution put forward by the SRS in 2007 condemned all war crimes, with an emphasis on the crimes perpetrated against Serbs and the crimes against peace committed by NATO. In addition to this, the proposal of the SPS stated that responsibility for the wars lay on the secessionist policies of the former Yugoslav republics and demanded the suspension of trials of high-ranking officials at the ICTY.

167 The LDP put forward a proposal which explicitly sought to acknowledge the responsibility of the Serbian state for breaching the genocide convention, while the coalition from Vojvodina drafted a resolution condemning all war crimes, with special emphasis on Srebrenica.

associated with the DS and the formation of a pro-European government with the coalition grouped around the SPS finally allowed Tadić to push for the passing of a resolution on Srebrenica in parliament.

While he anticipated domestic resistance to this initiative, the Serbian President argued that the establishment of the truth and the acknowledgment of past atrocities constituted a precondition for reconciliation in the region. He added that the adoption of a resolution condemning Srebrenica was an ethical deed which sought to transform societal values by promoting the respect of individual rights and European norms.[168] Such statements exemplified Tadić's increasing espousal of the transitional justice discourse. Whether this was motivated by EU accession or genuine will to improve relations with neighbouring states, the Serbian President set regional reconciliation and cooperation at the top of his political agenda. Tadić distinguished himself by repeatedly condemning Serbian war crimes[169] and regularly paying respect to victims of atrocities.[170]

The deeper motives and the timing of this renewed initiative for condemning Srebrenica can be attributed to several factors. Some observers suggested that Tadić's initiative needed to be contextualised within Serbia's attempt to challenge the legality of Kosovo's independence before the ICJ.[171] Accordingly, the Serbian authorities sought to demonstrate compliance with the Court's earlier decision in the *Bosnian Genocide* lawsuit in order to support their bid for the ICJ's advisory opinion on Kosovo's declaration of independence.[172] There were also rumours that the adoption of the Srebrenica declaration was urged on by the West in order to reanimate Serbia's process of European integration.[173] Indeed, the ratification of the Stabilisation and Accession Agreement (SAA) between Serbia and the EU was blocked by the Netherlands, which insisted on the arrest and transfer of Ratko Mladić to the ICTY before they would give their consent to this agreement. Bearing in mind that the European Parliament had itself voted a resolution condemning the Srebrenica genocide in January 2009, Tadić's initiative was seen by many as an

168 'Tadić: Rezolucija – etički iskorak' (Tadić: The Resolution – An Ethical Step Forward), *B92*, 15 January 2010.

169 Among other things, Tadić apologised to Croatian citizens, during a live show on Croatian television, for the crimes committed by Serbian forces; he declared that Mladić was the darkest page in Serbia's history (See Chapter 3).

170 President Tadić attended the tenth and fifteenth anniversary commemorations of Srebrenica and issued an official statement on every anniversary of the massacre, thus recognising it as a symbol of war crimes.

171 'Stranke o deklaraciji o Srebrenici' (Political Parties on Srebrenica Resolution), *B92*, 11 January 2010.

172 Serbia had successfully lobbied for the UN General Assembly to request an advisory opinion on the legality of Kosovo's declaration of independence in September 2008 (See Chapter 2).

173 'Srpska osuda Srebrenice naručena sa Zapada?' (Serbian Condemnation of Srebrenica Ordered from the West?), *Deutsche Welle*,12 January 2010.

attempt to assuage the EU's demands for Serbia to address the war crimes legacy.[174] Finally, the initiative to adopt a resolution on Srebrenica should be seen in the light of the diplomatic efforts to restore closer ties between Serbia and Bosnia, in which Turkey played a major role. The Bosnian leadership explicitly requested that the Serbian authorities acknowledge the Srebrenica genocide before improving their relations with Belgrade.[175] In this light, it seems obvious that Tadić's appeal for the adoption of a resolution on Srebrenica on the eve of a joint visit by the Bosnian and Turkish foreign ministers was not a coincidence.

Bearing in mind the divergent positions on the issue of Srebrenica among the ruling coalition – and the political elites in general – the initiative for the adoption of a resolution once again became the subject of lengthy negotiations among political parties. Since the coalition grouped around the SPS insisted on condemning all war crimes, Tadić suggested that parliament adopt two separate resolutions – one that would explicitly condemn Srebrenica and another one that would denounce war crimes perpetrated against Serbs.[176] This proposal manifestly resulted from a compromise with the SPS, which no longer opposed the adoption of a resolution on Srebrenica. This change of mood among the Socialists can be explained by the party's overall effort to portray itself as pro-European. Although the SPS never renounced its Milošević-era heritage, the party's new leadership clearly sought to make a break with the past by 'reconciling' itself with the democrats and forming a pro-European government (see Chapter 2).

Besides condemning the crime, Tadić's initiative aimed at establishing a consensus about Srebrenica by gathering the widest possible support among the opposition. The initiative was welcomed by the LDP, which stood for an explicit condemnation of the Srebrenica genocide. Surprisingly, the representatives of the newly created Serbian Progressive Party (SNS) also announced that they were willing to participate in the making of the resolution.[177] The renegade Radicals, who had become the second most important political party in the country, thus substantially changed their attitude towards Srebrenica, which they now explicitly condemned as a 'terrible crime'.[178] On the other hand, the representatives of

174 Jasna Dragović-Soso, 'Apologising for Srebrenica: The Declaration of the Serbian Parliament, the European Union and the Politics of Compromise', *East European Politics* 28:2 (2012), 163–79.

175 'Silajdžić: Srbija se nije izvinila' (Silajdžić: Serbia Has Not Apologised), *B92*, 9 December 2009.

176 'Tadić: Dve rezolucije o žrtvama rata' (Tadić: Two Resolutions on War Victims), *B92*, 12 January 2010.

177 'Različiti stavovi o rezolucijama' (Different Stances towards the Resolutions), *B92*, 24 January 2010.

178 With regard to this, the Deputy President of the SNS and former Secretary-General of the SRS Aleksandar Vučić performed a remarkable about-turn by arguing that he had not been allowed to speak about Srebrenica while he was in the SRS ['O Srebrenici nisam mogao da pričam u SRS' (I Could Not Talk about Srebrenica in SRS), *Blic*, 23 January 2010].

the DSS and the SRS stuck to their earlier positions by rejecting altogether the possibility of voting for a resolution on Srebrenica and insisting on one resolution condemning all war crimes.

Although most political parties now agreed on the need to adopt a resolution condemning Srebrenica, they still held divergent views on how the massacre should be denoted. While the coalition grouped around the SPS and the SNS rejected the possibility of defining Srebrenica as genocide, the LDP refused to vote for a resolution referring to anything but genocide.[179] The representatives of the DS attempted to circumvent this problem by arguing that the parliament was not entitled to give a legal qualification to this crime. In line with this, the government ultimately put forward a resolution which did not explicitly define Srebrenica as genocide, but instead referred to the ruling of the ICJ.[180] As this wording did not satisfy the LDP and the SNS, the resolution on Srebrenica was only passed by the slim majority that was the governing coalition.

The long-awaited official acknowledgment and condemnation of the Srebrenica genocide came about both as a result of the relatively positive outcome of the *Bosnian Genocide* lawsuit for Serbia and as a consequence of the reconfiguration of the domestic political scene. Since the ICJ had cleared Serbia of genocide, the state authorities had no further reasons to fear that this move could have adverse repercussions for the Serbian state. However, as the ICJ established that Serbia had nonetheless breached the genocide convention, the official acknowledgment of Srebrenica was seen as a necessary step towards improving Serbia's image abroad. In view of this, the ruling of the ICJ provided an additional motive for the adoption of a parliamentary resolution on Srebrenica.

Paradoxically, the adoption of this resolution was made possible by the SPS, which had earlier embodied the regime of Milošević and promoted denial of war crimes. This turn of events can be explained by the fact that the representatives of the SPS had no further reasons to fear that the acknowledgment of Srebrenica could jeopardise their political legitimacy or expose them to the risk of being held responsible for it. Indeed, since they had entered into government with the DS, the Socialists had established themselves as a fully legitimate political party in the

179 'Genocid preteška reč za SPS' (Genocide Too Hard a Word for SPS), *Blic*, 19 January 2010.

180 Besides condemning the crime perpetrated in Srebrenica, the resolution expressed 'condolences and apologies to the families of the victims because not everything was done to prevent this tragedy'. The resolution also provided support to Serbia's efforts to cooperate with the ICTY and capture Ratko Mladić, and appealed to the states of former Yugoslavia to pursue the process of reconciliation and condemn crimes committed against Serbs [See National Assembly of the Republic of Serbia, 'Deklaracija Narodne Skupštine Srbije o osudi zločina u Srebrenici' (Declaration of the National Assembly of Serbia Condemning the Crime in Srebrenica), accessed on www.parlament.gov.rs on 7 January 2011].

post-Milošević democratic era. In this context, endorsing the Srebrenica resolution could only increase their standing as a constructive pro-European party.[181]

This shows that the acknowledgment of Srebrenica was premised on a political compromise that effectively exonerated the former elites from moral and political responsibility for war crimes. Until and unless this had been achieved, the war crimes issue was subject to fierce politicisation and contestation, which prevented the emergence of any consensus on this topic. With the establishment of a new 'pact' embodied in the Declaration of Reconciliation between the DS and SPS, the former elites were effectively amnestied for all the wrongs committed during the nineties. Indeed, by choosing to put the past behind them and be forward-looking, the Serbian political elites decided to push aside the criminal legacy of Milošević's regime. In this context, the political potential of the Srebrenica resolution was significantly reduced. Instead of opening the way for a re-examination of Milošević's legacy, the resolution limited itself to condemning the crime, as well as the 'social and political processes' that allowed the genocide to take place, without even mentioning who perpetrated this massacre.[182] Such a vague and neutral message clearly sought to foreclose any further examination of the political and moral responsibility of the former regime.

In those circumstances, the acknowledgment of Srebrenica hardly reflected or facilitated reckoning with war crimes in Serbia. Indeed, the parliamentary resolution was drafted by the political parties behind closed doors, which inhibited any public debate about war crimes. Public opinion polls showed that only 20.6 per cent of the population supported a resolution on Srebrenica, while 46.2 per cent were in favour of a resolution condemning all war crimes.[183] This lack of support for the resolution shows that the official acknowledgment of Srebrenica was not the result of societal reckoning with war crimes, but rather a top-down initiative assumed by the political elites. At the same time, the fact that only 36 per cent of the population was in favour of handing over Mladić to the ICTY six months after the adoption of the Srebrenica resolution suggests that this did not bring about increased awareness of war crimes perpetrated by the Serbian forces.[184] Human rights activists had warned that the resolution would have no effect whatsoever on reckoning with war crimes unless its message was

---

181 The quest for legitimacy could also explain the SNS's rhetorical support for condemning Srebrenica. In this light, it turns out that Koštunica's ideological opposition to the acknowledgment of Srebrenica exceeded that of the Socialists and former Radicals.

182 The resolution condemned 'all social and political processes that gave rise to the social belief that one's national goals can be achieved through the use of force or physical aggression towards members of other nations and religions' (Republic of Serbia, 'Deklaracija Narodne Skupštine').

183 'Za rezoluciju 20.6 odsto gradjana' (20.6 per cent of Citizens in Favour of the Resolution), *B92*, 3 February 2010.

184 'Većina za EU ali pod "našim" uslovima' (Majority for the EU, but On 'Our' Conditions), *Danas*, 27 October 2010.

disseminated in society.[185] Since there had been no such effort, critics argued that the adoption of the resolution was a political manoeuvre rather than a genuine truth-telling initiative.[186]

Besides failing to engage the public, the resolution did not succeed in establishing a consensus about Srebrenica among the political elites. By avoiding explicitly defining Srebrenica as genocide, the resolution left room for challenging and denying the nature of this crime. As a result, the nature and scope of the Srebrenica massacre remained contested by the nationalist political and intellectual elites. In addition, the adoption of a second resolution condemning war crimes perpetrated against Serbs produced an ambivalent message.[187] Indeed, it seemed as if parliament had thus denounced all war crimes against Serbs and one war crime against the 'others'.[188] Such a message can hardly fit into a transitional justice agenda of reckoning with past wrongs. In this context, critics have argued that the Srebrenica resolution was meant to assuage foreign demands for acknowledging Serbian war crimes, while the declaration on war crimes against Serbs was for 'domestic use'.[189] The Srebrenica resolution has also been denounced as an attempt at condemning war crimes in order to safeguard the ideology that produced them in the first place. Nevertheless, many observers considered that this ambiguous message was the maximum that could be achieved out of a political compromise between the DS and the coalition around the SPS.[190] In the light of this, the ambiguous wording of the Srebrenica resolution and the adoption of a second resolution condemning war crimes against Serbs seem to reflect the political reality on the ground rather than a deliberate strategy of denial.

Although it had a relatively limited impact at home, the adoption of the resolution on Srebrenica was eagerly welcomed abroad. Indeed, this move was hailed by the international community as an important step in Serbia's process of coming to terms with the past and a significant contribution to reconciliation in the region.[191] The acknowledgment of Srebrenica effectively boosted the prospects for reconciliation by opening the door to the establishment of closer ties between Belgrade and Sarajevo. In the following months, the political leaders from the region

185 'Srebrenicu u nastavni program' (Srebrenica in the School Curriculum), *Danas*, 1 April 2010.

186 Dragović-Soso, 'Apologising for Srebrenica'.

187 This resolution was adopted by the Serbian parliament less than six months after the Srebrenica resolution. 'Usvojena deklaracija o zločinima nad Srbima' (Declaration on Crimes against Serbs Adopted), *Večernje Novosti*, 14 October 2010.

188 Personal interview with Žarko Marković, Belgrade Centre for Human Rights, on 30 December 2010.

189 'Opozicija protiv "srpske" deklaracije' (The Opposition against the 'Serbian' Resolution), *Danas*, 4 May 2010.

190 'Deklaracija maksimum vladajuće koalicije' (Resolution is the Maximum [Possible] for the Governing Coalition), *Danas*, 1 April 2010.

191 'Evropska Unija pozdravlja deklaraciju o Srebrenici' (EU Welcomes Resolution on Srebrenica), *Politika*, 1 April 2010.

showed increased political will to overcome the divisive legacy of the Yugoslav wars. Throughout 2010, the Serbian, Bosnian, Croatian and Montenegrin presidents participated in a series of meetings and attended various commemorations aimed at expressing apologies and showing mutual respect for war crimes victims.[192] Most obviously, these diplomatic efforts at promoting reconciliation need to be seen in the light of these countries' broader political circumstances and their European integration agendas.[193] Nevertheless, there is no doubt that the acknowledgment of Srebrenica by the Serbian parliament contributed to these developments. In this respect, the adoption of the Srebrenica resolution constituted a significant step towards reconciliation and cooperation in the region.

Amid all these observations, it is obviously too early to judge whether and how the adoption of the Srebrenica resolution will affect reckoning with war crimes in Serbia in the long run. Human rights activists generally agree that significant progress towards the acknowledgment of Serbian war crimes was made in the 2000s.[194] Whereas the issue of Srebrenica used to be taboo and Serbian war crimes openly denied during the nineties and early 2000s, by the end of the decade this was no longer the case, even in nationalist circles. Although the nature of the crime remained contested and relativised, the fact that a horrendous massacre had been committed by the Serb forces had become widely accepted.[195] Indeed, public opinion polls show that, in 2010, 55.2 per cent of the population believed that a crime had been committed in Srebrenica,[196] against only 37 per cent in 2004.[197] While this constitutes only a partial success, it is nonetheless fairly impressive in view of the short period under consideration. As the German example shows, societal reckoning with war crimes is a long-term process which spans decades.[198]

---

192 This increased diplomatic activity was launched on the tenth anniversary of the Igman initiative in June 2010. It was notably marked by Boris Tadić's attendance at the fifteenth anniversary of Srebrenica on 11 July and at the commemoration of war crimes committed by Serbian forces in Vukovar on 4 November.

193 Croatia's newly elected President Ivo Josipović contributed greatly to these diplomatic efforts by officially apologising for Croatia's conduct during the war in the Bosnian parliament and paying tribute to the victims of Croatian war crimes.

194 Personal interviews with Biljana Kovačević-Vučo and Vesna Pešić.

195 Jelena Obradović-Wochnik thus argues that 'the process of denial in Serbian society demonstrates a re-examination of certain events and, as such, represents a first step in the long process of understanding and acknowledging the past' (Jelena Obradović-Wochnik, 'Knowledge, Acknowledgment and Denial in Serbia's Responses to the Srebrenica Massacre', *Journal of Contemporary European Studies* 17:1 (2009): 61–74).

196 *B92*, 3 February 2010.

197 Belgrade Centre for Human Rights and Strategic Marketing Research, 'Public Opinion in Serbia: Attitudes towards the ICTY', August 2004. Retrieved from www.bgcentar.org.rs on 7 March 2010.

198 Alf Ludtke, '"Coming to Terms with the Past": Illusions of Remembering, Ways of Forgetting Nazism in West Germany', *The Journal of Modern History* 65:3 (1993): 542–72.

In view of this, a definitive verdict on the significance of the Srebrenica resolution will have to await future researchers.

Conclusion

This chapter has sought to explore the repercussions of international judicial intervention on truth-telling in Serbia. The analysis presented above shows a mixed picture which highlights the tensions arising between the ICTY's truth-telling mission and domestic efforts to preserve the stability and legitimacy of state institutions.

These tensions were particularly conspicuous during the trial of Milošević, which ended up having an adverse effect on truth-telling on the ground. In addition to further discrediting the Tribunal in the eyes of the local population, this trial also reduced the commitment of the Serbian liberal elites to cooperating in the pursuit of justice and truth. Not only were those elites utterly disappointed with the conduct of the trial, but they also feared that the charges brought against Milošević could substantiate the genocide lawsuit brought by Bosnia against the Serbian state before the ICJ. Paradoxically, while the transitional authorities had transferred Milošević to the ICTY in order to restore Serbia's international standing, his trial threatened to undermine the very legitimacy of the Serbian state. As a result, the Serbian authorities sought to restrict access to critical evidence in order to protect what they saw as vital state interests. Instead of opening the way for truth-telling, this process thus did quite the opposite.

These observations suggest that there is a potential trade-off between externalised justice and domestic truth-telling, which is indicative of the deep contradictions between the goals of transitional justice. While international tribunals seek to individualise responsibility in order to promote reconciliation, the Milošević trial demonstrated that the prosecution of high-ranking officials could imply state responsibility for genocide. As a result, the distinction between individual and collective responsibility became blurred in the eyes of many politicians, as well as of the wider public. Most importantly, those political elites who once opposed Milošević and played a key role in bringing him down now had a vested interest in disproving the allegations of genocide raised against him. International judicial intervention thus reduced the room for truth-telling in Serbia as it alienated those elites that were most committed to the pursuit of justice and truth.

On the other hand, the official acknowledgment of Srebrenica by the Serbian authorities demonstrates that the ICTY had partly achieved its mission of establishing facts about atrocities perpetrated during the Yugoslav wars. However, this success was premised on that account's compatibility with political developments on the ground. As discussed above, the adoption of the Srebrenica resolution came about both as a result of the relatively positive outcome of the *Bosnian Genocide* lawsuit for Serbia and as a consequence of the reconfiguration of the domestic political scene. Once Serbia had been cleared of complicity in genocide, acknowledgment of Srebrenica could only improve the legitimacy of the Serbian state. At the same time, the establishment of a new political pact which effectively rehabilitated the former elites diminished domestic resistance to the acknowledgment of Srebrenica. Ironically, instead of discrediting Milošević's regime, this move contributed towards restoring the legitimacy of his former party. Under such circumstances, the acknowledgment of Srebrenica could hardly contribute to genuine reckoning with the past.

These mixed outcomes indicate that the success of international justice in promoting truth-telling is conditioned by domestic political circumstances in target states. The ICTY's narrative of the past has been accepted to the extent that it does not challenge the legitimacy of political actors on the ground. Indeed, the symbolic status of Srebrenica was only recognised once its acknowledgment no longer posed a threat to state institutions and influential elites. On the other hand, the Prosecutor's argument that the former Serbian leadership constituted a joint criminal enterprise aimed at creating a 'Greater Serbia' remains widely denied. To be sure, the ICTY's failure to bring the Milošević trial to an end and the acquittals of the former heads of the Yugoslav Army and the Serbian State Security substantially undermined the Prosecution's narrative.[199] Regardless of the Tribunal's decisions in the remaining cases, this interpretation will most likely remain negated for the foreseeable future in view of its adverse implications for the Serbian state and its political elites.

199 Note that the Prosecution filed its notice of appeal in the case of the former officials of the Serbian State Security Jovica Stanišić and Franko Simatović on 28 June 2013.

Chapter 5
Domestic War Crimes Trials

Introduction

One of the main goals associated with transitional justice is the (re-)establishment of the rule of law in post-authoritarian and post-conflict states. This is seen by many as the most tangible and significant contribution of transitional justice policies to democratisation processes. Indeed, the pursuit of justice for past human rights abuses is meant to instil norms of accountability by demonstrating that no-one will be above the law in the new democratic order. In addition, the prosecution of past offenders aims at contributing towards the long-term development of institutional mechanisms that will foster respect for the rule of law. In this vein, transitional justice advocates have argued that international judicial intervention is instrumental in promoting judicial and security reforms in the targeted states, as well as building the capacity of the domestic judiciary.[1]

Restoring the rule of law in the former Yugoslavia constitutes an intrinsic part of the ICTY's mission.[2] Indeed, the Tribunal was established in the first place as a response to the inability and unwillingness of the domestic judiciaries to penalise violations of international humanitarian law.[3] It is only after the overthrow of Milošević in Serbia and the ending of the Tudjman era in Croatia that the political conditions for carrying out fair and impartial war crimes trials before domestic courts were met. In this context, the 'Completion Strategy' adopted by the Tribunal in 2003 gave a major impetus to the prosecution of war crimes suspects in local courts by providing for the transfer of intermediate- and lower-level indictees to national jurisdictions. As part of this strategy, the ICTY and the international community encouraged and supported the establishment

1 Rachel Kerr and Eirin Mobekk, *Peace and Justice: Seeking Accountability after War* (Cambridge: Polity Press, 2007), 7–8.

2 Eric D. Gordy, 'Postwar Guilt and Responsibility in Serbia: The Effort to Confront It and the Effort to Avoid It' in *Serbia since 1989: Politics and Society under Milošević and After*, eds Sabrina P. Ramet and Vjeran Pavlaković (Seattle and London: University of Washington Press, 2005), 168–9.

3 Croatia is the only state in which war crimes trials have been systematically carried out since the outbreak of the war. However, during the nineties, these prosecutions almost exclusively targeted ethnic Serbs and, for the most part, did not meet the elementary standards of due process.

of specialised institutions for the prosecution of war crimes suspects in Bosnia, Croatia and Serbia.[4]

The Serbian authorities proceeded with the creation of special institutions for the prosecution of war crimes following the adoption of the Law on Organisation and Competence of Government Authorities in War Crimes Proceedings in July 2003. This legislation provided for the establishment of a War Crimes Chamber (WCC) within the Belgrade District Court, as well as an Office of the War Crimes Prosecutor (OWCP) and a special unit for investigating war crimes within the police.[5] These newly created institutions were widely praised by international and domestic observers for their professionalism in the conduct of war crimes trials.[6] Between 2003 and 2011, the WCC completed 26 cases involving 69 people, while another 7 cases were underway, involving 37 defendants.[7] Bearing in mind that the overwhelming majority of defendants were Serbs, most observers considered that the domestic judiciary had become the principal vector of transitional justice in Serbia. This view was reinforced by the fact that the War Crimes Prosecutor, Vladimir Vukčević, played a key role in cooperation with the Hague tribunal since he had been put in charge of the Action Team for the arrest of the last few ICTY indictees.

This chapter seeks to examine the work of domestic institutions in prosecuting war criminals in the period between 2003 and 2011 by looking at three different aspects that I consider essential for understanding the scope and significance

4 These institutions have taken different forms. In Bosnia, the Office of the High Representative proceeded with the creation of an internationalised War Crimes Chamber in 2005. In Croatia, the authorities established four investigative centres for war crimes in Osijek, Rijeka, Split and Zagreb. Nevertheless, most war crimes trials in Croatia have been taking place before County Courts, depending on where the crimes were committed. For an overview of war crimes trials in the former Yugoslavia, see Jasna Dragović-Soso and Eric Gordy, 'Transitional Justice and Reconciliation in the Former Yugoslavia' in *New Perspectives on Yugoslavia*, eds Dejan Djokić and James Ker-Lindsay (London: Routledge, 2011), 197–200.

5 The WCC and OWCP are competent for prosecuting criminal offences against humanity and international law as set forth in the Penal Code of Socialist Yugoslavia, as well as offences recognised by the ICTY Statute. These institutions have jurisdiction in proceedings for war crimes perpetrated on the territory of the former (Socialist) Yugoslavia, regardless of the citizenship, nationality, race or religious background of the perpetrator and victim alike (OSCE Mission to Serbia, 'Law on Organisation and Competence of Government Authorities in War Crimes Proceedings', retrieved from www.osce.org/serbia/18571 on 30 July 2009).

6 The establishment of these institutions has been largely supported by the international community, most notably the US Embassy in Belgrade and the OSCE, which provides expertise and capacity-building for the WCC and the Office of the War Crimes Prosecutor (Personal interview with Ivan Jovanović, legal advisor on war crimes at the OSCE mission in Serbia, on 2 July 2009).

7 As of March 2011, only 12 out of the 26 completed cases constituted final judgments approved by the Supreme Court. These cases concerned a total of 2,590 victims. Data retrieved from www.tuzilastvorz.org.rs on 17 March 2011.

of these trials. These three aspects are: the war crimes trials' relation to regime change; their contribution to transitional justice; and their implications in terms of regional cooperation. Therefore, I first examine to what extent the work of the WCC and the War Crimes Prosecution was influenced by the domestic political and institutional context. In doing so, I explore the attitudes of the political elites towards these institutions and how their work was conditioned by the situation within the justice and security sectors. Secondly, I examine to what extent the work of the WCC and the War Crimes Prosecution fitted into the transitional justice agenda, especially with regard to promoting truth-telling. For this purpose, I analyse the discourse deployed by the War Crimes Prosecutor and consider the criticisms of domestic war crimes trials made by various human rights NGOs. Finally, I explore the extent to which these institutions specialised in prosecuting war crimes constituted a form of 'juridified diplomacy'.[8] I thus look at the role of these institutions in restoring the sovereignty and legitimacy of the Serbian state, with a particular focus on the controversies surrounding the prosecution of Bosniak and Kosovo Albanian war crimes suspects.

1. Regime Change and War Crimes Prosecutions

Under Milošević's rule, the Serbian judiciary remained extremely unresponsive to the numerous reports and evidence of war crimes perpetrated during the wars of Yugoslav succession. Although Yugoslav legislation provided for the prosecution of breaches of international humanitarian law, domestic war crimes trials were sporadic, incidental and biased. Indeed, the Serbian courts only processed a handful of cases, which were ridden with procedural flaws.[9] This state of affairs reflected the disastrous situation of the country's judicial system, which was afflicted by corruption and kept under tight control by the regime.

The situation improved slightly in the aftermath of Milošević's removal from power. The local courts instigated several cases for atrocities committed by Serbian forces in central Serbia and Kosovo, which demonstrated a clear improvement in the conduct of war crimes trials.[10] Nevertheless, the scope of war crimes prosecutions

8 I borrow this concept from Gerry Simpson who defines it as 'the phenomenon by which conflict about the purpose and shape of international political life (as well as specific disputes in this realm) is translated into legal doctrine or resolved in legal institutions' [Gerry Simpson. *Law, War and Crime: War Crimes Trials and the Reinvention of International Law* (Cambridge: Polity Press, 2007), 1].

9 Humanitarian Law Centre, 'Report on Transitional Justice in Serbia, Montenegro and Kosovo 1999–2005', 2006, 31.

10 These were the *Sjeverin* and *Podujevo* cases. The first concerned the abduction, torture and killing of 16 ethnic Bosniaks from Sandžak, a region in southwest Serbia, by members of the paramilitary group 'Avengers' on 22 October 1992. The second is related to the killing of 14 Kosovo Albanian civilians and the wounding of five children by members

before domestic courts remained extremely limited. This was primarily due to the fact that local courts lacked the capacity and the competencies to investigate complex war crimes cases, which often involved dozens, or even hundreds, of perpetrators and victims throughout the former Yugoslavia.[11] The inertia of the Serbian judiciary generated considerable frustration among the political elites, who had hoped that domestic war crimes trials would reduce foreign pressure for cooperation with the ICTY and allow for the transfer of cases to Serbian courts. But the government's calls for the judiciary to come to grips with the war crimes legacy fell on deaf ears. As a result, the possibility of holding Milošević's trial in Belgrade was discredited, which amply contributed to the notion that there was no alternative to the transfer of war crimes suspects to The Hague (see Chapter 3).

It was only after the creation of specialised institutions for prosecuting war criminals and the adoption of the ICTY's Completion Strategy in 2003 that the Serbian judiciary took on the task of systematically prosecuting war crimes suspects. These developments not only provided for the transfer of cases and material from the ICTY to domestic courts, but they also allowed for greater initiative and efficiency in the investigation and prosecution of war crimes by the Serbian judiciary. In this section, I first explore the motives for the creation of these institutions and examine to what extent their work was influenced by political developments during the period 2003–2010. I then turn to the influence of institutional factors on war crimes trials by looking at how the work of the WCC and the War Crimes Prosecution was affected by the situation within the police and the Serbian Supreme Court.

A. Political Attitudes towards Domestic War Crimes Trials

The coincidence between the establishment of special institutions for prosecuting war crimes suspects and the announcement of the ICTY's Completion Strategy raises the difficult question of whether these institutions were created as a result of domestic initiative or foreign intervention. Since it is impossible to establish what would have happened in the absence of international judicial intervention, an approximate and tentative answer to this question can only be given by gauging the different factors that contributed to the creation of these special institutions. After doing so, this section examines the extent to which these institutions were subject to political pressures from domestic elites.

---

of the 'Scorpions' unit in Podujevo on 28 March 1999 (HLC, 'Report on Transitional Justice 1999–2005', 31–2).

11 Personal interview with Žarko Marković, Belgrade Centre for Human Rights, on 30 December 2010.

The establishment of special institutions for prosecuting war crimes

The DOS government announced the creation of institutions specialised in the prosecution of war crimes suspects in April 2003, one month after the assassination of Prime Minister Djindjić.[12] This move formed part of a broader strategy to address the criminal legacy of the Milošević era which also involved the establishment of specialised institutions for tackling organised crime.[13] Indeed, the assassination of Djindjić led to the realisation that the persistence of criminal structures derived from the former regime represented an immediate threat to the democratic order. While 'Operation Sabre' dealt a significant blow to the criminal underworld, it became clear that it was necessary to develop long-term mechanisms for addressing the criminal legacy of the former regime. Since these criminal structures were deeply embedded within the institutions of the state, their neutralisation required the creation of novel institutions that would acquire substantial autonomy and expertise in the fight against organised crime and the prosecution of war crimes.[14]

From this perspective, it appears that the creation of specialised institutions for prosecuting war crimes formed part of a state-building effort instigated by the transitional authorities and accelerated by the assassination of the Serbian Prime Minister. Accordingly, the emergence of these institutions is primarily attributable to the resolve of the reformist political elites whose endeavour benefited from foreign support. This view is corroborated by the testimony of the War Crimes Prosecution's spokesman, Bruno Vekarić, who asserts that the DOS government was genuinely committed to addressing the war crimes legacy:

> I was in Djindjić's government at that time, so I can tell you first-hand that Zoran's reformist government definitely recognised the need for Serbia to come to terms with its dark past. Because you see, we cannot talk about European integration, about economic gains, without being ready to clear up what we did in the previous period. When I say 'we', I mean Serbia. (…) On the basis of the idea that Djindjić and his team endorsed, the Živković government, along

12 'Vlada priprema specijalni zakon za ratne zločine' (Government is Preparing Special Law on War Crimes), *Politika*, 16 April 2003.

13 This involved the creation of a Special Department for Organised Crime within the Belgrade District Court as well as a Special Prosecutor for Organised Crime and a Special Unit for Tackling Organised Crime within the Interior Ministry. The special institutions for prosecuting war crimes and organised crime are often referred to in the media as the 'Special Court', although they do not formally constitute a separate court.

14 There is a direct relationship between organised crime and war crimes in the former Yugoslavia. Indeed, these conflicts were characterised by widespread looting and smuggling, to the extent that these activities constituted a key element in the motives and strategies of the belligerents. This relationship provided an additional argument for prosecuting war criminals, most of whom carried on with their criminal activities after the war. See Eric D. Gordy, 'Serbia after Djindjić: War Crimes, Organised Crime, and Trust in Institutions', *Problems of Post-Communism* 51:3 (2004): 10–17.

> with international actors, supported the creation of specialised institutions that would deal with the issue of war crimes. Why is this important? Because this constituted a new approach to the war crimes issue, which was detached from the criminal environment alongside the issue of organised crime. This is very important because it provides unique credibility.[15]

This evidence suggests that the transitional authorities had already envisaged establishing an institutional mechanism for addressing the past before Djindjić's assassination. While the former Serbian Prime Minister shunned the creation of the Yugoslav Truth Commission, he repeatedly called for the domestic judiciary to investigate and prosecute war crimes.[16] But the scarcity of war crimes trials before domestic courts soon led to the realisation that the Serbian judiciary was unable to process such cases, in spite of the prevailing political will to do so.[17] The specificity and complexity of war crimes prosecutions required changing the existing legislation and developing competencies in this field. In view of this, the Law on Organisation and Competence of Government Authorities in War Crimes Proceedings allowed for the implementation of the ICTY statute in national courts. This legislation also facilitated the conduct of war crimes proceedings by allowing for witnesses to testify by video link and by introducing the status of cooperating witness.[18] At the same time, the establishment of the WCC and the War Crimes Prosecution created the conditions for developing expertise in the application of international criminal law. The creation of specialised institutions was particularly significant in easing the transfer of knowledge and material from the ICTY to the domestic judiciary and creating a pool of professionals specialised in the prosecution of war crimes.[19]

While this state-building effort was clearly instigated and carried out by the domestic political elites, there is no doubt that this endeavour was to a great extent driven by international judicial intervention. Indeed, the creation of specialised institutions for prosecuting war crimes was publicly justified both by the need for addressing the past and by the desire to recover state sovereignty in relation to the ICTY. These two motives transpire in the argumentation provided by the Serbian

---

15 Personal interview with Bruno Vekarić, spokesman of the Office of the War Crimes Prosecutor, on 26 May 2009.

16 Note that although he did not endorse the Yugoslav Truth Commission, Djindjić suggested that mechanisms for addressing the past should be established once the stability of state institutions was secured. See Zoran Djindjić, speech given at the conference 'In Search of Truth and Responsibility – Towards a Democratic Future' in Belgrade on 19 May 2001. Accessed on http://www.b92.net/trr/2001/diskusija/diskutanti_hronoloski.php on 19 August 2010.

17 Personal interview with Vladimir Djerić, former senior legal advisor at the Ministry of Foreign Affairs and representative of the state before the ICTY and ICJ, on 23 July 2009.

18 HLC, *Report on Transitional Justice 1999–2005*, 27–9.

19 Personal interview with Žarko Marković.

Minister of Justice, Vladan Batić, during the parliamentary debate that preceded the adoption of the Law on War Crimes:

> We simply have to get rid of the burden of the past, to undergo catharsis which involves recognising that some of our nationals or citizens have committed crimes in our name. Also, we must say that all that has happened with the Hague tribunal has been a necessary evil, something that nobody wanted, a debt from the past, something that the current government has had to accept as a choice between two evils: cooperation with the Hague tribunal or additional isolation, additional sanctions.[20]

While admitting that the domestic judiciary had failed to address the war crimes issue, the Justice Minister emphasised his dissatisfaction and frustration with the work of the ICTY. According to him, the creation of specialised institutions for prosecuting war crimes suspects constituted a remedy for this 'necessary evil':

> So the Hague tribunal is something that is imposed, that nobody wanted, that is not the expression of anybody's will, sympathy or love. I who am telling you this have had lengthy and unpleasant communication, correspondence and conversation with the Hague tribunal, namely with the Chief Prosecutor of the Hague tribunal. It is unclear whether we had enough maturity as a state to be able to prosecute war crimes on our own. I believe that we have now, and that we have a credible judicial system to deal with the unfortunate burden of an ugly past.[21]

Batić's speech suggests that the special institutions for prosecuting war crimes were to a great extent created in reaction to the Hague tribunal. Indeed, the transitional authorities sought to restore the legitimacy and sovereignty of the Serbian state, which had been taken away in response to the failure of the domestic judiciary to prosecute war crimes. The newly created institutions for prosecuting war crimes were thus assigned the task of demonstrating that the Serbian state had acquired sufficient democratic maturity to come to grips with the war crimes legacy. In light of this, the ICTY's Completion Strategy greatly contributed towards the establishment of these institutions by opening the way for the transfer of cases to national courts. In the previous period, this possibility had been ruled out by the Chief Prosecutor, Carla Del Ponte, who had insisted on the transfer of indictees to the ICTY.[22] Therefore, we can infer that the establishment of specialised institutions for prosecuting war crimes came about as a result of the interplay between external incentives and domestic political circumstances.

---

20 National Assembly of Serbia, 9th Parliamentary Sitting, 27 June 2003, 234–5.

21 Ibid.

22 Personal interview with Momčilo Grubač, Minister of Justice in the Yugoslav Federal Government 2000–2001, on 7 May 2009.

Political pressures on the OWCP

In spite of being home-grown institutions, the WCC and OWCP did not always benefit from the support and approval of the domestic political elites and government. Shortly after their establishment, the existence of these institutions was called into question by the newly elected Koštunica government. Upon his appointment, the new Minister of Justice Zoran Stojković announced that the special institutions for organised crime and war crimes would be disbanded on the basis that these institutions created unnecessary income disparities within the judicial system and that any court should be able to process these cases.[23] Although the government did not proceed with abolishing these institutions, it drastically reduced their funding. In April 2005, the War Crimes Prosecutor, Vladimir Vukčević, complained that the budget of the OWCP was cut by a third, which left them without basic utensils such as paper and staples.[24] In those conditions, the functioning of the War Crimes Prosecution relied almost entirely on American donations and support from the ICTY.

Tension between the Koštunica administration and the OWCP intensified in December 2004 as a result of the government's pressure on the War Crimes Prosecutor to raise indictments against the four generals sought by the ICTY (see Chapter 3). Indeed, the Justice Minister publicly blamed the War Crimes Prosecution for having conceded important cases to the ICTY by failing to generate indictments.[25] These attacks sought to push the OWCP to indict the four generals in order to ease foreign pressure for their extradition to The Hague. As explained in Chapter 3, Koštunica ruled out the arrest and transfer of ICTY indictees during his first mandate as Prime Minister. Instead, he promoted the voluntary surrender of war crimes suspects and insisted on the transfer of cases to domestic courts. The government's strategy consisted in undercutting the authority of the Hague tribunal by arguing that the domestic judiciary had the ability to prosecute war crimes suspects. In the words of the OWCP spokesman, Bruno Vekarić, this institution became an excuse for hindering ICTY cooperation:

> There was a lot of empty talk after the change of government. It was as if someone were trying to justify the existence of these institutions. As if we had to show that we are capable of prosecuting here, that "we are better than the Hague [tribunal]". Therefore, a parallel was created with the Hague [tribunal], but this was a mere political pretext. (…) They were insisting that we exist to prosecute

23 'Najavljeno ukidanje specijalnog suda' (Special Court Suppression Foreshadowed), *Glas Javnosti*, 30 March 2004.

24 'Optužnice za Batajnicu do kraja godine' (Indictments for Batajnica before the End of the Year), *Nedeljni Telegraf*, 13 April 2005.

25 'Mnogo su se uspavali' (They Are Too Lethargic), *Blic*, 12 December 2004.

> war criminals in Serbia. This was a challenge to the Hague [tribunal]; we were *de facto* [used as] a kind of pretext.[26]

In order to maintain its integrity and independence, the War Crimes Prosecution had to draw on the support of foreign actors. According to Bruno Vekarić, Western diplomats intervened in order to fend off an attempt by the government at removing the War Crimes Prosecutor, Vladimir Vukčević:

> We were very well placed, primarily in relation to the international community. Our authority was such that there was no political force that could wipe us out. Stojković, Koštunica's Minister of Justice, attempted it at first. (…) I would remind you that in December 2004, a proposal for the removal of Vukčević was circulated in parliament, where the Radicals and the DSS wanted to replace him because he did not want to raise an indictment against the generals who are now in The Hague. That was a cheap political trick, to raise an indictment against the generals here while the politicians thought about what they were going to do with it – whether to cooperate or not. Since he refused [to do] it, as someone who was completely independent and knowing the consequences that could ensue, the initiative for his replacement was instigated. The SRS and DSS had a majority then, so he could easily have disappeared. This was primarily prevented by international actors: various delegates from the White House and the EU went straight to Koštunica to tell him that this was not a message a democratic state ought to send.[27]

Foreign actors thus played a key role not only in providing material support to the special institutions for prosecuting war crimes, but also in ensuring those institutions a substantial level of autonomy in relation to the domestic political elites. During this initial period, the War Crimes Prosecutor deplored the fact that the OWCP's authority was greater abroad than at home.[28] Nevertheless, the international prominence of that institution largely contributed towards its acceptance at home. Indeed, the Koštunica administration soon realised that the OWCP played a key role in communication with the ICTY. Moreover, it became clear that the special institutions for prosecuting war crimes constituted an asset enabling cases to be transferred to the domestic judiciary, which was central to the government's idea of 'two-way cooperation' with the Tribunal. As a result, the Koštunica government gradually changed its stance towards the OWCP by providing public support and enacting legislation to facilitate domestic war crimes trials.

Relations between the executive and the special institutions for prosecuting war crimes improved particularly following the establishment of the DS–DSS

---

26 Personal interview with Bruno Vekarić.

27 Ibid.

28 'Možemo da sudimo i Šešelju' (We Can Prosecute Even Šešelj), *Vreme*, 16 December 2004.

government in 2007. Indeed, the DS, personified by President Tadić, constituted the greatest source of support for the OWCP on the domestic political scene.[29] The new government substantially increased material support for the War Crimes Prosecution, whose budget almost doubled between 2006 and 2008.[30] But in spite of these positive developments, the authority and legitimacy of the special institutions for prosecuting war crimes was substantially challenged by right-wing politicians. Throughout 2006 and 2007, the representatives of the SRS launched a series of attacks on the OWCP, which they accused of exerting pressure on witnesses to testify at the trial of Vojislav Šešelj in The Hague. According to them, the OWCP was conducting interrogations on behalf of the ICTY and the cases brought before the WCC were meant to fabricate evidence and produce witnesses against Šešelj. Through this slander campaign, the Radicals sought to discredit the special institutions for prosecuting war crimes by portraying them as an extension of the ICTY in Serbia. They also sought to intimidate the employees of those organisations by launching verbal attacks against the representatives of the War Crimes Prosecution in parliament and the media.

In view of the high number of SRS members directly involved in the cases brought before the WCC, it seems obvious that the Radicals had a vested interest in obstructing war crimes prosecutions.[31] By orchestrating public attacks against the OWCP, the SRS representatives sought to create a political climate unfavourable to war crimes trials. They went as far as to call for the lynching of the War Crimes Prosecutor, who was subsequently regularly targeted by death threats emanating from extremist groups. The representatives of the OWCP reluctantly admitted that these political pressures had an impact upon the work of the domestic judiciary. Although they repeatedly claimed that they had the capacity to process any high-level war crimes suspect, it was later revealed that the OWCP had rejected Carla Del Ponte's offer for them to prosecute Šešelj.[32] Bearing in mind the influence and behaviour of his political party, the transfer of the SRS leader to the WCC was deemed too risky. This evidence shows that the capacity of the special institutions for prosecuting war crimes suspects was substantially constrained by political actors. In such circumstances, domestic war crimes trials were inevitably limited in their scope and attainments.

Apart from being constrained by the activism of right-wing politicians, the work of the special institutions for prosecuting war crimes suspects was also

---

29 Personal interview with Bruno Vekarić.

30 Belgrade Centre for Human Rights, 'Monitoring and Reporting on Activities of Judicial Institutions in Serbia in the Field of Organised Crime, War Crimes, Discrimination and Domestic Violence', 2008. Hereafter cited as Belgrade Centre for Human Rights (2008).

31 The first two major cases processed by the WCC, *Ovčara* and *Zvornik*, involved former paramilitaries associated with the SRS ['Vekarić: Radikali se plaše naših predmeta' (Vekarić: Radicals Fear Our Cases), *Danas*, 30 May 2007].

32 'Del Ponteova nudila Šešelja' (Del Ponte Offered Šešelj), *Politika*, 15 September 2009.

affected by the wider political context. Most notably, the political crisis that followed Kosovo's declaration of independence had direct repercussions on domestic war crimes trials. In view of the increased political tensions, the families of Kosovo Albanian victims refused to come to Belgrade to follow the trials.[33] The Humanitarian Law Centre (HLC) also reported that, during this period, in spite of being in possession of enough evidence, the War Crimes Prosecution refrained from raising indictments against Serbs suspected of having committed crimes in Kosovo. While these allegations were rejected by the OWCP representatives, they overtly admitted that the political situation engendered stagnation with regard to the opening of new cases, owing in particular to the fact that the police were unlikely to investigate war crimes perpetrated in Kosovo.[34]

The political conditions for the work of the WCC and OWCP improved substantially following the creation of a pro-European government in 2008. As a sign of increased political resolve to address the war crimes legacy, the post of Justice Minister was filled by the former Secretary of the OWCP, Snežana Malović. The special institutions for prosecuting war crimes thus received full backing and support from the authorities, which increased their powers and reduced their exposure to political pressures. Nevertheless, the capacity of these institutions remained limited by scant resources. In 2007, the War Crimes Prosecutor, Vladimir Vukčević, complained that the annual budget of the OWCP was smaller than the salary of the Chief Prosecutor, Carla Del Ponte.[35] The underfunding of these institutions caught the attention of the European Commission, which called for the strengthening of the OWCP's capacity.[36] While the Prosecution's budget was subsequently increased, its capacity remained very limited. Indeed, the OWCP was staffed by eight deputy prosecutors who simultaneously conducted investigations on war crimes in Bosnia, Croatia and Kosovo. But the lack of capacity of the WCC, which consisted of only five judges and two trial chambers, was even more problematic. Under these conditions, this institution could only conduct 7 or eight trials at the same time and issue two or three verdicts per year.[37] Therefore, while the domestic legitimacy and authority of the WCC and the OWCP had been substantially reinforced, the work of these organisations remained hampered by financial hardships and limited capacity.

33 'Političari otežavaju beogradska sudjenja za ratne zločine' (Politicians Hinder Belgrade War Crimes Trials), *IWPR*, 15 February 2010.

34 'Politika vrši pritisak na pravosudje' (Politics Exerts Pressure on Judiciary), *Danas*, 27 February 2008.

35 'Mladić mora u Hag ne zbog Evrope, nego zbog našeg obraza' (Mladić Must Go to The Hague, Not because of Europe, but for the Sake of Our Honour), *Dnevnik*, 25 April 2007.

36 Commission of the European Communities, 'Serbia 2008 Progress Report', 2008, 15.

37 Personal interview with Žarko Marković.

B. Institutional Challenges to the Prosecution of War Crimes Suspects

In spite of being independent, the newly created institutions for prosecuting war crimes suspects were not wholly detached from the institutional environment in which they operated. Most notably, the OWCP relied heavily on the police to conduct investigations, whereas the rulings of the WCC were conditioned upon the approval of the Serbian Supreme Court. In this section, I explore the extent to which these exogenous institutions influenced the conduct and affected the outcomes of war crimes proceedings in post-Milošević Serbia.

The police

In Serbia, the police play a key role in investigating criminal offences, uncovering perpetrators and arresting suspects. In order to boost war crimes investigations, the Law on Organisation and Competence of Government Authorities in War Crimes Proceedings provided for the creation of a War Crimes Investigation Service (WCIS) within the Interior Ministry. This special unit within the police was meant to assist the OWCP in the instigation of war crimes proceedings. However, the belated establishment of the WCIS signalled early on that relations between the OWCP and the police would not be easy. Indeed, the unit only became operational in 2005, owing to difficulties in filling its ranks. According to the War Crimes Prosecutor, few policemen showed interest in joining the WCIS because there was no financial incentive to do so, while chances were high that the members of the unit would have to investigate war crimes committed by their colleagues.[38] When the unit was formed, it only comprised five policemen. Although this number increased to 10 in 2006 and 22 in 2007, the WCIS continuously faced significant material constraints, notably regarding office space.[39]

In spite of being specifically designed to investigate war crimes, the WCIS was repeatedly criticised by the representatives of the OWCP for lacking initiative and failing to instigate new cases. Indeed, the War Crimes Prosecutor complained on numerous occasions about the inertia of the WCIS, for, while the members of the unit responded to the demands of the OWCP, they were nonetheless reluctant to undertake investigations on their own.[40] In such conditions, the task of conducting investigations was essentially incumbent upon the OWCP. This had negative repercussions on war crimes proceedings by substantially limiting the number of cases processed by the OWCP.[41]

The WCIS's resistance to investigating war crimes can be partly explained by the lack of reforms within the police. Since most senior officers in the

38 *Vreme*, 16 December 2004.

39 Bogdan Ivanišević, 'Against the Current – War Crimes Prosecutions in Serbia', International Centre for Transitional Justice, 2007, 13.

40 *Nedeljni Telegraf*, 13 April 2005.

41 'Imali smo Mladića u šaci' (We Had Mladić in Our Hands), *Vreme*, 14 October 2010.

Serbian police had taken part in the conflicts during the nineties, there was deeply ingrained institutional circumspection – if not opposition – towards war crimes investigations. This problem was made worse by the fact that the WCIS was staffed with policemen who had assumed high-ranking positions during the Kosovo conflict. This incongruity was blatantly revealed by the appointment of Slobodan Borisavljević as head of the unit in January 2006.[42] Borisavljević was the former Deputy Chief of the Public Security Department under Milošević. His superior – Vlastimir Djordjević – was prosecuted by the ICTY for war crimes and crimes against humanity perpetrated in Kosovo. In view of his proximity to the former leadership, Borisavljević was deemed to know about the atrocities perpetrated by the Serbian forces in Kosovo. More importantly, bearing in mind his former position, he clearly had a vested interest in obstructing the uncovering of these crimes. In those circumstances, many commentators saw the appointment of Borisavljević as head of the WCIS as an overt attempt to obstruct the war crimes proceedings. Indeed, Borisavljević had been appointed to this position in spite of the War Crimes Prosecutor's opposition to this move.[43] This decision was reversed following the intervention of the ICTY Chief Prosecutor, Carla Del Ponte who expressly requested Koštunica to remove Borisavljević from the WCIS.[44]

Resistance towards war crimes proceedings within the police was most noticeable in the cases addressing war crimes perpetrated in Kosovo, owing to the fact that most of these cases incriminated active police officers. One of the primary tasks of the OWCP upon its inception was to investigate the killing of several hundred Kosovo Albanians whose bodies were found buried in mass graves in Belgrade and other parts of central Serbia in 2001 (see Chapter 4). In spite of the fact that these mass graves were investigated and used as evidence by the ICTY, the first case related to these events in a domestic court was opened only in April 2006 – five years after the discovery of the mass graves and over two years after the creation of the OWCP.[45] Both the representatives of the OWCP and independent observers attributed this delay in the proceedings to obstruction from the police.[46] Indeed, the War Crimes Prosecutor, Vladimir Vukčević, openly declared that the investigation was purposely hindered by the police:

42 'Borisavljević ponovo funkcioner MUP' (Borisavljević an MoI Official Again), *B92*, 19 January 2006; Note that the WCIS was also directed by a former high-ranking police official at the time of the Kosovo crisis – Gvozden Gagić – between 2004 and 2005.

43 'Vukčević bio protiv' (Vukčević Was Against), *Danas*, 21 January 2006.

44 'Dogovorena smena Slobodana Borisavljevića' (Removal of Slobodan Borisavljević Arranged), *Danas*, 8 February 2006.

45 This case concerned the killing of at least 50 Kosovo Albanian civilians by members of the Serbian Special Police Units in Suva Reka on 26 March 1999.

46 'Opstrukcija iz policijskih redova' (Obstruction from Police Ranks), *Danas*, 28 October 2005.

> Many active members of the police know about these crimes, so we cannot overlook the fact that there is obstruction at certain stages of the proceedings from those same institutions which are legally in charge of identifying perpetrators of war crimes. In such cases, evidence has been concealed and destroyed, and it is not easy for a Prosecutor to instigate proceedings with a flimsy indictment. We are at risk of legalising the crime, which we do not want to do.[47]

The OWCP eventually managed to make progress in this investigation, thanks to a change of legislation which allowed the War Crimes Prosecution to carry out interrogations without resorting to the police.[48] Still, the proceedings were thwarted by false testimony from members of the police who were alleged to have given false statements out of fear of, or solidarity with, their colleagues.[49] In addition, the War Crimes Prosecution had difficulty in getting access to critical information contained in the 'Kosovo and Metohija Dossier' – an archive of the Interior Ministry, which comprised police reports about wartime activities of the Serbian police in Kosovo.[50] The OWCP's requests for accessing this dossier were repeatedly turned down by the police on the basis that the files were in the process of 'systematisation'. The *Suva Reka* case ended with the conviction of four policemen, but the highest-ranking suspect and four other defendants were acquitted.[51] This verdict dealt a blow to the OWCP and the representatives of the families of the victims, who considered that the acquittal of the former commander of the Special Police Unit, Radoslav Mitrović, was scandalous.

Obstruction from the police was even more pronounced in the trial for the killing of the Bytyqi brothers. This case concerned the murder of three American citizens of Kosovo Albanian origin, who were arrested by the Serbian police after the end of hostilities for having illicitly entered the country.[52] After serving a fifteen-day prison sentence, they were taken to a police training camp in eastern Serbia where their bodies were subsequently found in one of the mass graves uncovered in 2001. The *Bytyqi* case was separated from the other Kosovo Albanian victims found in the mass graves upon the request of the American authorities, who pressed

47 'Najvažnija – Politička volja' (The Most Important Thing is Political Will), *NIN*, 13 July 2006.

48 'Prve optužnice za Batajnicu' (First Indictments for Batajnica), *Danas*, 27 October 2005.

49 Belgrade Centre for Human Rights (2008), 34–6.

50 Ivanišević, 'Against the Current', 14; Belgrade Centre for Human Rights (2008), 37.

51 In October 2010, the Court of Appeal ordered a retrial for one defendant who had been found guilty by the WCC ['Suva Reka: Trojci potvrdjena presuda' (Suva Reka: Verdict Confirmed for Three), *B92*, 12 October 2010].

52 The Bytyqi brothers had enlisted in the 'Atlantic Brigade' of the Kosovo Liberation Army (KLA) during the Kosovo campaign. They crossed the administrative border between Kosovo and central Serbia in an attempt to escort their Roma neighbours out of Kosovo.

the OWCP to speed up the inquiry.[53] Nevertheless, the investigation dragged on for three years as it came up against fierce resistance within the police. Indeed, most of the policemen who were present at the training camp at the time of the crime denied knowing of the internment of the Bytyqi brothers or the existence of the mass graves.[54] In addition, the OWCP was left without critical documentation concerning the suspects, as their files had mysteriously disappeared. In spite of the support provided by the American FBI, the OWCP fell short of identifying the main culprits.

The War Crimes Prosecution eventually raised an indictment against two policemen who were alleged to have taken the Bytyqi brothers from the prison where they were serving their sentence to the police camp where they were killed. The former commander of the training centre, who was suspected of being responsible for the killing, appeared in court as a witness. The trial thus overlooked those who ordered and executed the crime, focusing instead on two middlemen who were accused of having transported the victims. This state of affairs was heavily criticised by observers of the trial and the representatives of the victims' relatives, who considered that the high-level suspects were shielded from prosecution. The Director of the Humanitarian Law Centre, Nataša Kandić, accused the OWCP of carrying out an incomplete trial simply to satisfy the demands of the American authorities.[55] The War Crimes Prosecutor readily admitted that this case had an international dimension and that failure to resolve it could have disastrous implications for Serbia. But despite the OWCP's best intentions, the trial concluded with the acquittal of the two suspects. Following the issuing of the verdict in September 2009, the OWCP spokesman declared that this process was inhibited by a 'pact of silence' within the police.[56] The *Bytyqi* case thus bluntly demonstrated the capacity of the police to hamper war crimes proceedings and affect their outcome.

But the police also proved capable of preventing the initiation of war crimes proceedings. In March 2009, police unions and veteran organisations staged protests across south Serbia in response to the arrest of four former members of the Special Police Units (SPU).[57] These policemen were arrested after the Humanitarian Law Centre filed a complaint against 17 former members of the SPU who were alleged to have committed war crimes in Kosovo on the basis of testimonies provided by several former members of that unit. The protesters demanded the immediate release of the policemen, as well as the disclosure of the cooperating witnesses' identities. Many observers compared these demonstrations with the mutiny of the

53 'Asanacija državne tajne' (Cleaning-Up of State Secret), *Vreme*, 9 March 2006.

54 Belgrade Centre for Human Rights (2008), 36–8.

55 'Zavet ćutanja' (Vow of Silence), *Vreme*, 18 June 2009.

56 'Nastavak istrage u slučaju Bitići' (Bytyqi Case Investigation Continues), *B92*, 23 September 2009.

57 A fifth suspect – Radoslav Mitrović – was already in custody in relation to the *Suva Reka* case.

JSO which took place in 2001 in response to the extradition of war crimes suspects to The Hague (see Chapter 3). Oddly enough, the protesters received backing from the Interior Minister, who declared that the arrests had 'stirred unrest among policemen who took part in the conflict' and announced that the Ministry would provide legal support to the suspects because 'it was in its interest to prove their innocence'.[58] These declarations raised serious doubts about the resolve of the authorities to prosecute war crimes committed by the police. Left without political support, the OWCP saw the need to justify its moves by stating that '99 per cent of the policemen did their job honourably, defending Serbian interests in Kosovo and Metohija' and that the testimonies of the members of the police were valuable because they allowed a distinction to be made between those who had committed crimes and those who had not.[59] The suspects were eventually released two months after their arrest, which Nataša Kandić saw as an obstruction of justice:

> That was all organised, these protests were not spontaneous, they were controlled by the police. It appeared that the Prosecution made a good move. When we lodged our complaints, they demanded an investigation and incarceration – specifically with regard to Mitrović, who had just been acquitted in the trial for the war crime in Suva Reka, which was a big case. So they launched an investigation, but it appeared that something happened after two months – they were released from prison. I attended the inquiry once and I noticed that there was significant closeness between the prosecutors, the suspects, and their lawyers, so it was obvious to me that something was going on there.[60]

Two years after the arrest of the SPU members, the HLC released a report accusing the OWCP and the police of having exerted pressure on witnesses to withdraw their testimonies against the former policemen.[61] Furthermore, in what constituted a major blow to the OWCP's reputation, the War Crimes Prosecution was accused of being bribed into releasing the suspect.

This episode demonstrates that institutional resistance to war crimes prosecutions within the security sector acted as a barrier to war crimes trials. In spite of the political willingness and the judicial capacity to prosecute war crimes suspects, these proceedings were limited by the institutional environment in which they took place. The capacity of certain segments of the police to obstruct and

58 'Najavljeni novi protesti u Leskovcu' (New Protests Announced in Leskovac), *Danas*, 15 March 2009.

59 'Hapšenje policajca revoltiralo pripadnike MUP-a' (Arrest of Policemen Revolted MoI Members), *Politika*, 20 March 2009.

60 Personal interview with Nataša Kandić, Director of the Humanitarian Law Centre, on 12 August 2009.

61 Humanitarian Law Centre, 'Irregularities and Abuse of Power in War Crimes Proceedings in the Republic of Serbia', March 2011.

mobilise against war crimes proceedings thus significantly reduced the scope of the OWCP's work.

The judiciary

On top of being constrained by the police, the special institutions for prosecuting war crimes also faced obstructions within the judiciary sector. These hindrances were orchestrated by the now defunct Supreme Court of Serbia, which was the court of last resort in the Republic of Serbia until the reform of the judiciary carried out in 2009. Up till then, Serbia's highest judicial body repeatedly undermined war crimes proceedings by systematically overturning the rulings of the War Crimes Chamber.

Indeed, the Supreme Court took a series of controversial decisions which raised serious doubts about its impartiality with regard to war crimes trials. Besides ordering the retrial of all war crimes cases processed before ordinary courts, this institution overruled several judgments of the WCC. The most notorious decision of the Supreme Court concerned the nullification of the WCC's verdict in the *Ovčara* case in December 2006. This trial dealt with the massacre of over 200 Croatian prisoners by members of the Yugoslav Army and Serbian paramilitary units following the fall of Vukovar in November 1991. As the first case transferred by the Prosecution of the ICTY to the OWCP, it constituted a test-case for the Serbian judiciary. The conduct of the trial was hailed by the representatives of the victims and the domestic observers, who praised the judges for their efforts at clarifying the context in which the crime took place – a practice that was uncommon in domestic courts.[62] The WCC condemned 14 out of the 16 indictees to 231 years in prison, which was acclaimed as the beginning of a new era for the Serbian judiciary and the first sign of institutional reckoning with the past.[63]

In this context, the suspension of the *Ovčara* verdict by the Supreme Court was seen by many as an attempt to obstruct transitional justice.[64] This decision substantially undermined trust in the Serbian judiciary among victim groups, who refused to participate in the renewed process. According to the war crimes prosecutor, Vladimir Vukčević, this ruling also raised suspicions about the impartiality of the Supreme Court among foreign diplomats, thus inhibiting the

62 'Briljantno sudjenje po manjkavoj optužnici' (Brilliant Trial on a Deficient Indictment), *Danas*, 7 December 2005.

63 'Nataša Kandić: Novo poglavlje u srpskom pravosudju' (Nataša Kandić: New Chapter for Serbian Judiciary), *Danas*, 13 December 2005.

64 This view was upheld by most observers of the trial. The OSCE mission in Serbia identified some elements in the Supreme Court's decision as indicating possible political motives, although it did not find conclusive evidence that the decision was politically driven (Ivanišević, 'Against the Current', 18).

transfer of cases from the ICTY to the Serbian judiciary.[65] These suspicions were reinforced by the fact that the Supreme Court had never taken over a war crimes case in order to address the flaws that it had identified in the process, although it had the legal authority to do so. In the opinion of Žarko Marković from the Belgrade Centre for Human Rights, this simple fact clearly demonstrates that the Supreme Court sought to obstruct war crimes trials:

> The Supreme Court had the legal authority to order the retrial of every case that it suspended an indefinite number of times, but it also had the authority to take over the case and address the flaws identified in the process before the local courts. (…) It never did this. It would say that this was an uncommon practice and that it was provided by the law only in exceptional cases. If this was only exceptional, I do not see any more important case than *Ovčara*, where there were 200 victims (…) If in such situations you do not instigate legal proceedings and you do not aim at resolving the case in the best [possible] way, but evade responsibility and order a retrial three times, it is a clear sign of obstruction, or at least of a lack of will to deal with it seriously.[66]

This obstruction was orchestrated by the judges of the Supreme Court, who had been appointed during Milošević's rule. The failure to carry out lustration of the state institutions allowed Milošević's cronies to maintain their positions within the judiciary after the change of regime.[67] In 2007, four out of five judges of the War Crimes Chamber of the Supreme Court had been appointed before the removal of Milošević.[68] As a result, these institutions upheld the ideology of the former regime, which denied Serbian war crimes. Therefore, these hindrances did not come about as a result of political pressures, but rather were the product of the personal convictions of the judges presiding in the Supreme Court.[69] Indeed, the outcomes of the Supreme Court's rulings depended entirely on the composition of the Chamber which deliberated on war crimes cases. As the composition of the Supreme Court progressively changed, this institution adopted a more approbatory stance towards the rulings of the WCC. These positive developments were given further impetus by the judicial reform carried out in 2009, following which the Supreme Court was replaced by the newly-established Court of Appeal. Thus, the

65 'Ukidanje presude za Ovčaru produžava život Tribunalu' (Suspension of *Ovčara* Verdict Extends Life of Tribunal), *Blic*, 1 January 2007.

66 Personal interview with Žarko Marković.

67 The Serbian parliament passed a lustration law in June 2003, but this legislation was never implemented.

68 Human Rights Watch, 'Unfinished Business: The War Crimes Chamber in Serbia', 2007, 29.

69 Personal interview with Dragoljub Todorović, a lawyer affiliated with the Humanitarian Law Centre, on 29 December 2010.

obstructions to war crimes prosecutions within the judiciary seem to have been addressed at this stage.

The analysis presented above suggests that the special institutions for prosecuting war crimes were principally established in response to international judicial intervention and as a result of the inability of domestic courts to conduct war crimes trials. The creation of these novel and independent institutions proved highly successful in boosting the prosecution of war crimes suspects and facilitating the transfer of cases from the ICTY to the Serbian judiciary.

Nevertheless, the evidence also suggests that the functioning of the WCC and the OWCP was largely influenced by the political and institutional context in which these institutions operated. Indeed, the integrity and subsistence of these institutions were on several occasions jeopardised by domestic political elites, while the conduct and outcomes of war crimes trials were significantly affected by obstruction coming from the police and the Serbian Supreme Court. The special institutions for prosecuting war crimes thus operated within a political and institutional realm which clearly delineated the scope and potential of their work.

This political and institutional realm within which the WCC and the OWCP operated was itself conditioned by regime change. Both the improving political climate and the removal of obstructions within the judiciary came about as a result of democratic consolidation and institutional reform. We can thus draw a clear parallel between regime change and war crimes prosecutions. The scope and potential of war crimes trials in Serbia was likely to expand as democratic rule was consolidated and state institutions were reformed.

2. Domestic War Crimes Trials and Transitional Justice

In the analysis presented above, I argued that the special institutions for prosecuting war crimes were in large part established by the Serbian authorities in reaction to international judicial intervention. Indeed, the prosecution of war crimes suspects at the ICTY seems to have at least encouraged, if not triggered, the establishment of these institutions. This observation suggests that the Hague tribunal did to some extent achieve its mission of contributing towards re-establishing the rule of law in the targeted states.

Nevertheless, the prosecution and punishment of war crimes suspects at the ICTY did not constitute an end in itself. Throughout this book, I have suggested that the main rationale for international judicial intervention in the former Yugoslavia lies in the concept of transitional justice, according to which the search for justice ought to promote democratisation and reconciliation in post-authoritarian and post-conflict societies. In order to understand the repercussions of this intervention, it is therefore necessary to enquire whether, and to what extent, the Serbian institutions for prosecuting war crimes endorsed this agenda. In other words, the key question is whether these institutions existed only to satisfy the international community or whether they were proof of a genuine commitment to the principles of transitional justice.

In order to provide a tentative answer to this question, this section explores the degree to which the WCC and the OWCP sought to promote liberalising political change by confronting the Serbian public with the war crimes committed in their name. In Chapter 4, we saw that both the reformist political elites and the Hague tribunal largely failed to raise awareness in Serbian society about the atrocities committed by the Serbian side throughout the wars of Yugoslav succession. In those circumstances, the special institutions for prosecuting war crimes constituted the first institutionalised mechanism for truth-telling in Serbia. In the first part of this section, I examine the efforts of these institutions to promote reckoning with the past by analysing the activities of the WCC and the OWCP and assessing their impact on Serbian public opinion. I subsequently draw on the criticisms voiced by human rights organisations and experts monitoring the work of these institutions in order to discuss the limitations and shortcomings of domestic war crimes trials.

A. The WCC and the OWCP as Agents of Transitional Justice

The war crimes trials taking place before the WCC were closely monitored by domestic human rights organisations, international organisations and foreign embassies in Belgrade. The conduct of these trials was deemed to meet the highest standards of due process. Indeed, the judges of the WCC were widely praised for their impartiality, professionalism and respect for the rights of victims and suspects.[70] As a matter of fact, many observers considered that the war crimes trials in Belgrade were the best in the region. Furthermore, most of them believed that the WCC was the most important vector of transitional justice in Serbia. According to Dragoljub Todorović, a lawyer who represented the families of the victims in 11 war crimes cases, these trials constitute the most significant legacy of 5 October:

> This Court has shown good results – it has been objective and very professional. Perhaps the same could not be said for the Prosecution, but still, 90 per cent of the accused are Serbs and the victims are Muslims, Albanians and Croats. For me, it was unimaginable that this could function in Belgrade, but it has functioned very well, the trials have been excellent (…) All the cases completed have been successful, [the accused] have been given maximum sentences of twenty years in accordance with the penal code of Socialist Yugoslavia. (…) So this is the only explicit instance of reckoning with the past in Serbian society.[71]

70 Belgrade Centre for Human Rights (2008), 43; Diane F. Orentlicher 'Shrinking the Space for Denial: The Impact of the ICTY in Serbia', Open Society Justice Initiative, May 2008, 80–81.

71 Personal interview with Dragoljub Todorović.

This view was shared by most human rights organisations concerned with transitional justice. In its evaluation of the WCC, Human Rights Watch (HRW) argued that this institution plays a key role in disclosing the truth about war crimes to the Serbian public:

> The Serbian War Crimes Chamber is a critical forum for ensuring full accountability for the crimes committed during the Balkans conflicts in the 1990s. In addition to bringing to justice perpetrators in Serbia who might otherwise go unpunished, the trials are a means of educating the public about these crimes. Transparency and accountability are essential to help ensure these crimes do not occur in the future.[72]

The fact that the overwhelming majority of war crimes suspects brought to trial were ethnic Serbs supports the view that the special institutions for prosecuting war crimes were pursuing a transitional justice agenda. Indeed, 22 out of the 26 cases processed by the WCC by 2010 concerned Serb perpetrators. While this state of affairs was primarily imputable to the fact that Serb suspects were most easily accessible to the Serbian authorities, it nonetheless reflected a willingness on the part of the War Crimes Prosecution to expose and condemn the atrocities perpetrated by the Serbian side. Indeed, the representatives of the OWCP repeatedly argued that each side in the conflict should prosecute 'its own' war criminals because these crimes were committed in the name of their respective nations.[73] Accordingly, the war crimes trials before the WCC should have allowed people in Serbia to confront and denounce the atrocities committed by their fellow nationals. In view of this, the OWCP considered that a substantial part of its mission was to contribute towards allowing Serbian society to come to terms with the past.[74]

In addition to this, the objectives of the OWCP included: providing redress to war crimes victims, individualising responsibility and promoting the highest European and civilisational values.[75] These working principles suggest that the OWCP was firmly committed to furthering the transitional justice agenda in Serbia. Apart from exposing Serbian war crimes, the trials of Serbian suspects helped to bring the victims from the other sides into the public spotlight. Indeed, the families

---

72 HRW, 'Unfinished Business', 32.

73 'Ovde bolje sudjenje' (Prosecution Here is Better), *Večernje Novosti*, 5 November 2004; 'Svako da sudi svojima' (Each to Try Their Own), *Večernje Novosti*, 3 August 2005; 'Ne priznajem srpske zlocine' (I Do Not Recognise Serbian Crimes), *NIN*, 22 December 2005.

74 'Kosovo za 15 godina progutalo 9.500 žrtava' (Kosovo Has Swallowed 9,500 Victims in 15 Years), *Nedeljni Telegraf*, 7 November 2007.

75 Bruno Vekarić and Jasna Šarčević-Janković, 'Fifth Year Monograph of the Office of the War Crimes Prosecutor of the Republic of Serbia', Office of the War Crimes Prosecutor of the Republic of Serbia, 2008, 211.

of the victims attended several trials in Belgrade thanks to the assistance provided by the Humanitarian Law Centre, which had persuaded the victims to participate in the proceedings.[76] The authorities and media paid particular attention to the families of the victims from Srebrenica who came to attend the *Scorpions* trial which was instigated following the release of the tape showing the execution of six Bosniaks that shocked Serbian public opinion (see Chapter 4). President Tadić personally met the families of the victims in order to acknowledge their suffering and reiterate his support for the search for justice and reckoning with the past.[77] According to transitional justice advocates, such acts of recognition by the Serbian authorities were essential for restoring the dignity of victims and opening the way for reconciliation.[78]

Besides providing redress for victims, one of the topmost objectives of the OWCP was to individualise responsibility for war crimes. This goal was particularly emphasised by the War Crimes Prosecutor, Vladimir Vukčević, who insisted on the need to remove collective responsibility from the Serbian nation:

> Our principle is the individualisation of responsibility. The criminals are people with names – not "Serbs", "Croats" and "Muslims". I will always abide by this principle. In my view, this is patriotism: to recognise and punish wrongs, instead of concealing, relativising and denying crimes that are tormenting us like ghosts for the second generation already. By so doing, we are removing collective responsibility from the Serbian nation.[79]

By stressing the goals of individualising responsibility and removing guilt from the community as a whole, the representatives of the OWCP portrayed war crimes trials as being in the interest of the Serbian nation. This strategy contributed widely towards the acceptance and normalisation of war crimes trials in Serbia.[80] Indeed, public opinion polls showed significant public support for domestic war crimes trials, as opposed to the widespread antagonism towards the ICTY. In 2009, 57 per cent of respondents believed that the verdicts brought by the WCC against Serb war crimes suspects were fair and impartial.[81] At the same time, 70 per cent of the population believed that the ICTY was biased against

76 In view of the considerable distrust towards Serbian institutions among victim groups, many of them were reluctant to take part in the trials in Belgrade. The HLC could draw on its reputation to persuade the families of the victims to attend the trials and facilitate access to witnesses for the OWCP.

77 'Tadić primio porodice Srebreničkih žrtava' (Tadić Received Srebrenica Victims' Families), *Danas*, 24 December 2005.

78 Orentlicher, 'Shrinking the Space for Denial', 82–3.

79 'Krug Mladićevih pomagača sve uži' (The Circle of Mladić's Aides is Getting Narrower), *Politika*, 20 May 2007.

80 Orentlicher, 'Shrinking the Space for Denial', 83.

81 Belgrade Centre for Human Rights, OSCE Mission to Serbia, and Strategic Marketing Research, 'Views on War Crimes, the ICTY, and the National War Crimes

Serbs. It should therefore come as no surprise that 46 per cent of the population considered that war crimes suspects should be tried in their own countries, while only 8 per cent were in favour of trying them at the Hague tribunal.[82] This state of affairs demonstrates that, in spite of all the attempts of the SRS to discredit the WCC and the OWCP, these institutions proved successful in asserting their legitimacy among the Serbian population.

Finally, the intent to promote the highest European and civilisational values clearly shows that the OWCP assigned itself a didactic mission. This objective concurs with the belief among transitional justice advocates that war crimes trials ought to have a transformative impact on society. The representatives of the OWCP generally sought to pursue this agenda through their appearances in the media. Indeed, the Chief War Crimes Prosecutor, Vladimir Vukčević, and the OWCP's spokesman, Bruno Vekarić, took a leading role in publicly denouncing Serbian war crimes and disseminating the facts established in the trials. According to Ivan Jovanović from the OSCE Mission to Serbia, the representatives of the OWCP fully endorsed the discourse of transitional justice in their public appearances:

> The War Crimes Prosecution, and especially the Prosecution's spokesman, enters into that wider societal narrative when speaking in public. He has completely adopted the transitional justice discourse of redress for the victims, and so on. When, for example, they speak about people who are accused of war crimes being criminals, being involved in organised crime, of there being a close relationship between organised crime and war crimes, and that they are not patriots at all… that story goes much farther.[83]

While these observations suggest that the OWCP's officials had a truth-telling agenda, their outreach capabilities were nonetheless extremely limited. Until 2009, Serbian legislation did not allow for the broadcasting of trials.[84] As a result, the public did not have direct access to the proceedings in the courtroom and the testimonies of the victims. At the same time, media reports on domestic war crimes trials were generally limited and superficial.[85] Although the number of media excerpts about the War Crimes Prosecution almost doubled between 2004

Judiciary', April 2009. Retrieved from www.bgcentar.org.rs on 7 March 2010. Hereafter cited as 'Views on War Crimes', 2009.

82 Ibid.

83 Personal interview with Ivan Jovanović.

84 The legislation on war crimes proceedings was changed in December 2009 in order to allow for the broadcasting of war crimes trials, subject to the approval of the President of the Court. Nevertheless, as of 2011, no war crimes trial taking place before the WCC had been broadcast.

85 Personal interviews with Ivan Jovanović and Žarko Marković.

and 2008,[86] public opinion polls showed that the public was largely uninformed about the work of the special institutions for prosecuting war crimes. In 2009, only 21 per cent of respondents declared that they were informed about the work of the OWCP and over 70 per cent could not name one single case brought before the WCC.[87] At the same time, 50 per cent of respondents believed that the objective of these trials was to address impunity, promote peace and tolerance, and demonstrate that Serbian society was able to come to terms with war crimes and accept responsibility for the misdeeds of its members. This evidence suggests that even though there was very little knowledge about war crimes among the public, the message associated with those proceedings had to a certain extent sunk in.

The lack of public outreach was seen by most observers as the main impediment to domestic war crimes trials contributing to transitional justice. To a certain extent, this shortcoming was exogenous to the work of the special institutions for prosecuting war crimes. Indeed, the poor media coverage of war crimes trials was largely attributable to the general lack of interest in these proceedings among the public. In the absence of high-profile cases, the press was more interested in the War Crimes Prosecutor's role in the search for Mladić than in war crimes proceedings.[88] As a result, the idea that 'justice is not only to be done, but must be seen to be done' had not yet materialised.

B. Criticisms and Controversies: Limited Accountability and Reckoning

While the lack of public outreach constitutes a generic problem with war crimes trials that holds true for domestic proceedings as much as for the ICTY, the work of the Serbian institutions for prosecuting war crimes was subject to some more substantial criticism by human rights NGOs and commentators. These critiques cast doubt on the readiness of the WCC, and especially the OWCP, to ensure full accountability and expose the role of Serbian institutions in war crimes. In this section, I discuss this criticism and assess its implications for understanding the extent to which domestic trials contributed towards transitional justice.

Focus on low-level perpetrators

One of the main criticisms of war crimes trials taking place before the WCC was that they tended to focus exclusively on low-ranking perpetrators. This reproach was primarily addressed to the OWCP, which had the exclusive responsibility of putting together cases and bringing perpetrators to justice. The War Crimes Prosecution came under attack from various human rights NGOs that accused it of deliberately avoiding prosecuting middle-ranking army officers in order to

86 'Tužilaštvo za ratne zločine' (War Crimes Prosecution), Office of the War Crimes Prosecutor of the Republic of Serbia, PowerPoint presentation on CD, May 2009.

87 'Views on War Crimes', 2009.

88 Personal interview with Žarko Marković.

conceal connections between the executors of war crimes and the Serbian military and political authorities.[89] According to these observers, the OWCP thus sought to portray war crimes as sporadic and isolated incidents perpetrated by members of paramilitary units that had no affiliation with state institutions.

This problem was somewhat ambiguous since the ICTY had primacy over the prosecution of high-ranking suspects. This allowed the OWCP to argue that it could not reach higher levels of the hierarchy since almost the entire political and military executive of the former regime had been brought to trial in The Hague. However, critics pointed to the fact that there was an intermediate level of responsibility which had not been prosecuted at the ICTY and was not being put on trial at the WCC:

> They could go into the chain [of command] – this is probably a sound criticism and the HLC is certainly right about this – the question of the indictees' rank. I would say that there is a rift: the top rank is in The Hague, and the lowest is here. The middle-rank perpetrators, or the ones who are just below those in The Hague, are missed out. (…) There are high-ranking people whom the Hague [tribunal] has not indicted. This is certainly a sound criticism from the HLC. In the case of these indictments pointed out by the HLC, where they are prosecuting two persons for *Zvornik*, just like in the *Bytyqi* case, 80 per cent of the perpetrators are missing. There are many other players – from the army, the security services, politicians – who are simply not in the indictment.[90]

This discrepancy was particularly noticeable in the *Ovčara* case which dealt with the crimes committed by the Yugoslav Army and Serbian paramilitary units following the fall of Vukovar in November 1991. While the ICTY prosecuted three high-ranking army officers in relation to these crimes,[91] the OWCP's indictment focused on the immediate perpetrators who were identified as members of paramilitary units or members of the Territorial Defence.[92] Although they praised the conduct of the trial, the human rights NGOs criticised the indictment for being selective.[93] Indeed, the representatives of the families deplored the fact that the trial did not elucidate the responsibility of the Yugoslav People's Army (JNA) for this crime. In view of this, the Director of the HLC, Nataša Kandić, overtly

89 Humanitarian Law Centre, 'Transitional Justice in Post-Yugoslav Countries', 2006, 13; Ivanišević 'Against the Current', 8–10; *IWPR*, 15 February 2010.

90 Personal interview with Žarko Marković.

91 These three officers were Mile Mrkšić, Veselin Šljivančanin and Miroslav Radić.

92 The Territorial Defence was a military reserve force affiliated with the constituent republics of Socialist Yugoslavia.

93 *Danas*, 7 December 2005.

accused the War Crimes Prosecution of protecting the JNA officers by failing to indict them.[94]

The focus on immediate perpetrators constituted a common pattern in war crimes proceedings taking place at the WCC. This state of affairs could be attributed to several factors. First of all, as stated above, the OWCP operated in a political and institutional context which significantly limited its ability to pursue accountability. We have seen how in the *Bytyqi* case, the Prosecution was prevented by obstruction from the police from investigating and bringing to trial those responsible for the crime. At the same time, the OWCP was often exposed to severe political pressures which limited the possibilities for prosecuting high-level indictees, as illustrated by the War Crimes Prosecutor's refusal to have Šešelj's case transferred to Belgrade. In view of this, the most ardent critics considered that the War Crimes Prosecutor's independence was undermined by political discretion to such an extent that he was acting on behalf of the executive.[95]

Apart from being limited by the political and institutional context in which it operated, the OWCP also faced some legal and technical constraints that may have prevented it from going after the higher-ranking suspects. It was suggested that the focus on immediate executors of war crimes stemmed from the common view among prosecutors that they could not apply the doctrine of command responsibility in the form in which it exists in international law.[96] Although the doctrine of command responsibility was introduced into Serbian legislation in 2006, it could not be applied retroactively to crimes that took place in the nineties. Nevertheless, the War Crimes Prosecution proved able to circumvent this problem by using provisions within Serbian legislation that could act as a substitute for command responsibility. In the *Zvornik* case, for instance, the Prosecution indicted two middle-ranking officials for failing to prevent crimes which they knew, or had good reasons to know, were about to be committed. However, it was unclear whether these provisions in Serbian legislation could fully replace the doctrine of command responsibility as applied at the ICTY.[97]

The focus on low-level perpetrators was also imputed to a lack of technical competencies to investigate and establish hierarchical accountability. Several observers argued that the OWCP did not have the capacity to indict high-ranking suspects, in spite of being willing to do so. It was suggested that the War Crimes

94 'Jasna odgovornost JNA' (JNA's Responsibility is Obvious), *Dnevnik*, 2 December 2005.

95 'FHP: Prikriva se veza države sa zločinima' (HLC: Link Between State and Criminals is Being Concealed), *Danas*, 28 July 2006; *IWPR*, 15 February 2010.

96 Ivanišević 'Against the Current', 9. Command responsibility is the doctrine of hierarchical accountability which maintains that a person in a position of authority can be held accountable for a crime if s/he knew, or should have known, that individuals under his/her command had committed crimes and s/he failed to punish those crimes or to prevent future crimes from occurring.

97 Personal interview with Ivan Jovanović.

Prosecution did not have the resources and the expertise to establish the links between 'the trigger-pullers and the masterminds behind the scenes'.[98] According to Ivan Jovanović, the domestic judiciary lacked the competencies developed by the ICTY:

> I think that the Prosecution has room for indicting some people who are higher ranked than the current indictees. However, this is not only about having the resolve to indict someone. As a lawyer, you have to be sure that you have enough evidence against these persons. Now we are getting into the legal field. I think that the Hague tribunal and the system they have built up there – a variety of experts, of different analysts – are much more successful and better at demonstrating these complex structures of command and hierarchies, and establishing implicit responsibility, command responsibility or joint criminal enterprise than the domestic prosecutors in Serbia and Croatia.[99]

The task of prosecuting higher-ranking individuals was further complicated by the fact that it was very difficult for the Prosecution to find witnesses who would be willing to testify against their superiors. While the ICTY could indict high-ranking officials on the basis of their positions in office, the OWCP had to rely on cooperating witnesses to demonstrate the responsibility of the executor's superiors. However, as noted above, members of the police were often reluctant to cooperate with the Prosecution. In fact, they often gave false statements in order to conceal the responsibility of their peers. In those circumstances, the OWCP lacked both the evidence and the confidence to instigate cases against high-profile suspects. The OWCP's spokesman, Bruno Vekarić, argued that the Prosecution ran the risk of legalising war crimes if it instigated cases without substantial evidence:

> If we instigate cases hastily, and if we resort to "general truths"...Look, this is the case now with the 37th Battalion [of the Special Police Units] in Leskovac. Nataša [Kandić] filed a complaint from which we can single out two incidents at the most for which there is enough evidence to use them in court. We could indict all of them, but they would be acquitted and their crime – if they committed it – would be legitimised. This is the danger, if we resort to general truths and instigate cases hastily without sufficient evidence, they will be acquitted and no-one will ever be able to try them for this any more. Because they will have a paper saying that they are not guilty of something they may in fact have done. This is why I think that it is better to be patient and confident, and to build up these cases and instigate them once you are convinced that you have enough evidence for a conviction.[100]

98 Ivanišević, 'Against the Current', 11–12.

99 Personal interview with Ivan Jovanović.

100 Personal interview with Bruno Vekarić.

This standpoint suggests that the OWCP was rather cautious of instigating cases against high-ranking suspects. Some observers contended that the focus on low-ranking perpetrators stemmed from the prosecutorial strategy which sought to prosecute the 'small fry' first in order to establish its legitimacy.[101] This hypothesis was supported by some signs of progress towards putting on trial higher-level suspects in several cases. In November 2007, four former officers of the JNA were indicted for the massacre of 70 Croatian civilians in the village of Lovas during the offensive on Vukovar.[102] This was the first case in which members of the regular army forces were put on trial. At the same time, several policemen were indicted in the *Suva Reka* and *Bytyqi* case, including one middle-ranking officer. According to the Director of the Belgrade Centre for Human Rights, Vojin Dimitrijević, these developments showed that the prospects for prosecuting high-level suspects were improving:

> At the beginning, they did not want to touch the officers of the JNA for example. That was convenient in the *Ovčara* case, because three of them were in The Hague. However, now they are starting to in some [cases], like *Lovas*. This has indeed been very cautious, but they are starting to take out these people who were not volunteers or members of the Territorial Defence, but were an integral part of the state apparatus. (…) This is going slowly, but you have to understand that they are facing fierce resistance and that sometimes the expectations of the NGOs are too high in view of this human factor.[103]

This positive assessment raised hopes that the domestic war crimes trials would increasingly deal with those who had planned and ordered atrocities. But, as of 2011, attempts to prosecute higher-ranking suspects remained limited. In an interview for the OWCP's publication 'Justice in Transition', the WCC's judge, Olivera Andjelković, expressed her frustration over the fact that the indictments presented by the War Crimes Prosecution did not include the chain of command:

> We have cases in which some volunteers are prosecuted, which begs the question why their commanders are not there, in spite of the fact that we know their names. Why have they not been indicted, why have they not been investigated, and who protects these commanders? I am irritated by the implication and I do not agree that these were paramilitary formations because they had their commanders and they were integrated within the structures of the Territorial Defence or some other [structures]. I have the impression that there is a chain

---

101 Ivanišević 'Against the Current', 8.

102 'Od prebrojavanja krvnih zrnaca do istine' (From Counting Blood Cells to the Truth), *Danas*, 12 January 2008.

103 Personal interview with Vojin Dimitrijević, Director of the Belgrade Centre for Human Rights, on 1 July 2009.

> of command which has been avoided in the proceedings so far. Some higher structures have not yet been included in the war crimes trials.[104]

This blunt criticism of the OWCP reinforces the views expressed by human rights NGOs and observers monitoring war crimes trials. It also indicates that the indictments' focus on low-ranking perpetrators was a serious source of anxiety for the judges presiding over the proceedings. These concerns were all the more pronounced as some critics accused the special institutions for prosecuting war crimes of seeking to conceal the involvement and responsibility of the Serbian state in war crimes.

Covering up state responsibility

The war crimes trials taking place before the WCC were criticised by various human rights NGOs for obscuring the role of the Serbian state in the wars of Yugoslav succession and failing to establish the responsibility of its institutions for war crimes.[105] These criticisms essentially concerned the cases related to war crimes perpetrated during the war in Bosnia, in which the Serbian state did not officially take part. According to these organisations, the OWCP's indictments were purposely limited to members of paramilitary units and Territorial Defence in order to obfuscate the involvement of the Serbian police and military in these atrocities. The domestic war crimes trials were thus alleged to sustain the view that this was a civil war in which war crimes had been committed by non-state actors or military units associated with the local authorities.

This criticism was particularly emphasised by the Humanitarian Law Centre, whose director, Nataša Kandić, contended that there was an absolute consensus within the special institutions for prosecuting war crimes on protecting the Serbian state:

> I think that the trials are important, in spite of their narrow scope and small number. In my view, the problem is that there is an absolute consensus with regard to the immediate executors – no-one will protect them, everything will be flung at them – but there is an absolute consensus that nothing should cause damage to the institutions, that the state of Serbia should be protected. Establishing links between these crimes in order to show that they were committed with the knowledge of the state, and organised by it, is not permitted. This is so obvious.[106]

---

104 'Ratni zločini nisu incidenti' (War Crimes Are Not Incidents), *Pravda u Tranziciji*, December 2010. Accessed on www.pravdautranziciji.com on 25 March 2011.

105 Ivanišević, 'Against the Current', 10–11; Helsinki Committee for Human Rights in Serbia, 'Human Rights, Democracy and Violence – Annual Report 2008', 2009, 40; Humanitarian Law Centre, 'War Crimes Trials in Serbia', Transitional Justice Bulletin 1, 2007, 3.

106 Personal interview with Nataša Kandić.

This alleged effort to conceal the responsibility of the Serbian state was largely imputed to the fear that Serbia could be convicted of genocide in the lawsuit brought by Bosnia before the International Court of Justice (ICJ) (see Chapter 4). Indeed, there was a common view among observers that the judges presiding over the war crimes proceedings were taking into account the repercussions their decisions could have on the ruling of the ICJ.[107] In view of this, the most ardent critics overtly accused the special institutions for prosecuting war crimes of protecting 'criminal groups within institutions' instead of protecting victims.[108]

These criticisms were particularly pronounced in the *Scorpions* case, which was instigated following the disclosure of a tape showing the murder of six Bosniaks from Srebrenica by members of this unit at the trial of Milošević. As discussed in Chapter 4, the broadcasting of this tape in Serbia shocked public opinion and triggered a fierce polemic on Srebrenica among the political elite. It also led to the immediate arrest of five members of the Scorpions unit, who were brought to trial at the WCC. In view of the widespread public interest that it generated, the *Scorpions* case was perhaps the most important war crimes trial handled by the domestic judiciary. It was also the first domestic trial to deal with events related to the Srebrenica massacre, and was therefore deemed to constitute a test-case for the special institutions for prosecuting war crimes.

This trial generated ample controversy and polemic between the War Crimes Prosecution and the human rights NGOs. The human rights activists denounced the OWCP primarily for portraying the Scorpions as a paramilitary unit. They considered that there was enough evidence to show that this unit was under the control of the Serbian Interior Ministry at the time this crime was committed. Indeed, the indictment raised against the former chief of the Serbian State Security Service, Jovica Stanišić, at the ICTY stated that he was in command of the Scorpions unit during the offensive on Srebrenica.[109] In spite of this, the representatives of the OWCP claimed that there was no evidence showing links between this unit and the Serbian state. According to Nataša Kandić, the Prosecutor thus sought to obfuscate the crime in order to obscure Serbia's responsibility in the Srebrenica genocide.[110] Observers also criticised the indictment for defining the Bosnian conflict as civil war.[111] This was a common feature in domestic war crimes trials which irritated

107 Personal interviews with Ivan Jovanović and Žarko Marković. Note that both interviewees considered that the decisions made by the judges of the WCC could not have impacted significantly upon the ruling of the ICJ.

108 'Tužilac traži maksimalne kazne za "Škorpione"' (The Prosecutor Requests Maximum Sentences for the 'Scorpions'), *Politika*, 4 April 2007.

109 'Preko Ledenog do države' (Through 'Ledeni' to the State), *Politika*, 18 January 2006.

110 'Izmenjena optužnica za dvojcu "Škorpiona"' (Indictment Against Two 'Scorpions' Has Been Changed), *Danas*, 24 October 2006.

111 'FHP traži izmenu optužnice protiv Škorpiona' (HLC Requests Amendment of Indictment against Scorpions), *Danas*, 13 January 2006; this issue had already been raised in relation to the *Zvornik* case before the WCC (See Ivanišević, 'Against the Current', 10).

human rights activists. The Prosecution's stance on the nature of the Bosnian war allegedly contradicted the view that this was an international armed conflict, as established by the ICTY in the *Tadić* case. Nevertheless, this critique is somewhat contestable since the Hague tribunal did not consistently uphold this interpretation in its subsequent cases.[112]

The *Scorpions* verdict issued in April 2007 generated further discontent among the families of the victims and the observers of the trial. Only two of the five indictees got the maximum sentence of 20 years' imprisonment.[113] A third indictee received a lighter sentence of thirteen years for having admitted to the crime and apologised to the families of victims. The fourth was condemned to the minimum sentence of five years and the fifth was acquitted because the Court established that neither of them took part directly in the killings.[114] This part of the ruling was particularly contentious since the footage clearly showed that these two suspects had verbally abused the victims and that they knew that these men would be executed.[115] The indignation of the human rights activists and victims was reinforced by the disapproval of the political elites. Indeed, the Serbian President, Boris Tadić, deplored the light sentences issued by the Court, stating that the only adequate punishment for such crimes was the maximum sentence.[116]

The WCC's verdict was further criticised for dissociating this killing from the Srebrenica genocide. Indeed, the Court ruled that these events were unrelated in spite of the fact that the families of the victims testified that these men were taken from Srebrenica following its takeover by the Bosnian Serb forces.[117] In addition, the ruling stated that there was not sufficient evidence to show that the order for the execution of the victims was issued by the Bosnian Serb Army, although it was established that the unit was under the command of the regular forces of the Republika Srpska. These findings added to the notion that the Court's verdict was driven by a political agenda which sought to conceal the responsibility of the Serbian state for war crimes. As a result, the WCC was accused of creating a distorted historical narrative according to which war crimes were the deeds of

112 Personal interview with Ivan Jovanović; 'Sve manje ljudi okrvavljenih ruku biće na slobodi' (Even Fewer People with Blood on Their Hands Will Be Free), *Danas*, 20 January 2007.

113 'Škorpionima 58 godina zatvora' (58 Years in Jail for the Scorpions), *Politika*, 11 April 2007.

114 The OWCP had modified the indictment against these two defendants during the proceedings. They were accused of aiding and abetting instead of complicity, which was heavily criticised by observers.

115 Belgrade Centre for Human Rights (2008), 31–2; Ivanišević, 'Against the Current', 16.

116 'Ratni zločin kao pljačka banke' (War Crime Equal to Bank Robbery), *Danas*, 12 April 2007.

117 Nataša Kandić, Škorpioni: Od zločina do pravde (Scorpions: From Crime to Justice) (Belgrade: Humanitarian Law Centre, 2008), 716–19.

'isolated butchers' instead of being the outcome of a criminal policy implemented by the institutions of the state.[118]

Distorted historical narrative

The failure to prosecute the chain of command and highlight the responsibility of the Serbian institutions in war crimes led some observers to argue that the Serbian judiciary was creating a distorted historical narrative that was substantially at odds with the facts established by the ICTY.[119] The WCC and the OWCP were thus suspected of sustaining a flawed interpretation of the past which denied that the Serbian authorities had carried out and supported ethnic cleansing campaigns throughout the wars of Yugoslav succession. This was primarily reflected in the war crimes trials' tendency to portray perpetrators as former members of paramilitary units or individual transgressors within the regular army and the police.[120] This narrative contradicted the view that these crimes formed part of an overall strategy which sought to extend or maintain Serbian control over territories in Bosnia, Croatia and Kosovo, as suggested at the Hague tribunal.

The contrast between the WCC and the ICTY was particularly manifest in the case of Kosovo. While the ICTY found the former political and military leadership of the Federal Republic of Yugoslavia guilty of conducting a campaign of widespread terror and violence against Kosovo Albanians,[121] the WCC treated the war crimes perpetrated by Serbian forces in Kosovo as isolated incidents. According to Ivan Jovanović, this state of affairs was primarily imputable to reluctance on the part of the special institutions for prosecuting war crimes to challenge the dominant interpretation of the past:

> There are several reasons for this. One of them is that the judges, the courts and the Prosecution avoid mentioning some facts in their verdicts, or making some observations, which are taboo in this society or something towards which Serbs are generally antagonistic. For example, [in the case of] verdicts on Kosovo, such as *Suva Reka* – the deportation and mass killing of Albanians in Suva Reka – the

118 'Presuda Škorpionima politički motivisana' (Scorpions Verdict Politically Motivated), *Danas*, 13 April 2007; 'Kazna, pokajanje i oprost' (Punishment, Repentance and Pardon), *Evropa*, 10 January 2008.

119 'Za otmicu i ubistvo 17 Bošnjaka 75 godina zatvora' (75 Years' Imprisonment for the Abduction and Killing of 17 Bosniaks), *Danas*, 30 September 2003; 'Kandić: Sudovi ne poštuju hašku istinu' (Kandić: Courts Are Not Respecting the Hague Truth), *Press*, 9 September 2007.

120 *Danas*, 28 July 2006.

121 *Prosecutor v.* Šainović *et al.*, 'Case Information Sheet', Case No. IT-08-87. Accessed on www.icty.org on 6 March 2011.

> Court did not get involved in saying that this was not an isolated incident, that there were many cases like it, and that it was part of a systematic campaign.[122]

Jovanović notes that this was true for war crimes trials taking place in Croatia as much as for those conducted in Serbia. He argues that these differences in the narratives produced by war crimes trials result from the fact that national judiciaries are influenced by the existing frameworks for interpreting the past which prevail within their societies. According to him, the OWCP did not suggest that there was a plan for creating a 'Greater Serbia' simply because the Prosecutors did not believe in the existence of such a plan and because they did not consider that war crimes were committed with the intention of realising that plan.[123] For Vesna Pešić, a prominent political activist and sociologist, this state of affairs reflects the fact that the judiciary is always under the influence of the dominant ideology.[124] In her view, the local judges were still contaminated by the official interpretation of the past which held that Serbs conducted exclusively defensive wars throughout the nineties.

In addition to these ideological factors, the contrast between the narratives produced at the WCC and the ICTY was to a large extent attributable to the differences in the application of law in these two courts.[125] While the Hague tribunal delved into the political and historical context in order to assess the responsibility of the high-level suspects, the common practice in the Serbian legal system was to focus exclusively on the specific crimes imputed to the defendants. Therefore, the war crimes trials conducted before the WCC generally avoided looking at the broader context. This is partly due to the fact that there was a dominant view among legal professionals in Serbia that the domestic courts could not prosecute crimes against humanity because these were not included in the legislation at the time the crimes were committed.[126] As a result, the Prosecution had no incentive to examine the context in order to demonstrate that war crimes were part of a broad and systematic attack against the civilian population. Instead of this, each crime was treated separately, which reinforced the view that these were sporadic and unrelated incidents. At the same time, there was no need to discuss the broader circumstances in which the crimes took place since most trials dealt with low-ranking suspects. Indeed, the judges knew the context very well and they did not feel the need to explore it further in order to establish the responsibility of first-hand perpetrators.[127]

---

122 Personal interview with Ivan Jovanović.

123 Ibid.

124 Personal interview with Vesna Pešić, MP for the Liberal-Democratic Party, on 5 August 2009.

125 Personal interviews with Nataša Kandić, Jovan Nicić and Biljana Kovačević-Vučo.

126 Crimes against humanity were included in Serbian legislation in 2006 (Personal interview with Ivan Jovanović).

127 Personal interview with Žarko Marković.

In those circumstances, the truth-telling capacity of the domestic war crimes trials was extremely limited. In most cases, the demands of the victims' representatives for discussion of the broader context remained unanswered as the proceedings were restricted to assessing the evidence brought against the defendants.

***

This section sought to explore the extent to which domestic trials contributed to transitional justice in Serbia. The evidence presented above shows mixed results. While it appears that the special institutions for prosecuting war crimes sought to advance the transitional justice agenda, their capacity to do so seemed somewhat limited.

On the one hand, these institutions showed a firm commitment to exposing and punishing the atrocities perpetrated by the Serbian side. In addition to providing redress to the victims and individualising responsibility, they thus sought to promote liberalising political change by confronting the Serbian public with the atrocities committed in its name. On the other hand, the WCC and the OWCP were deemed unable and unwilling to bring higher-level suspects to justice, to expose the responsibility of state institutions and to challenge the dominant frameworks for interpreting the past – or at least they seemed very cautious about doing so.

This state of affairs was largely attributable to the political and institutional resistance to war crimes trials discussed in the first section of this chapter. However, the deficiencies in domestic proceedings also arose from the political discretion of the WCC and the OWCP, which seemed particularly keen to preserve the stability and legitimacy of state institutions. In such circumstances, the potential for domestic trials to expose the truth and promote reckoning with the past was inherently restricted to what was deemed politically and socially acceptable.

3. War Crimes Prosecutions and Juridified Diplomacy

One of the main motives behind the creation of the specialised institutions for prosecuting war crimes was the resolve to reassert Serbia's judicial sovereignty, which had been restricted through international judicial intervention. Indeed, as noted above, the creation of these institutions was in large part aimed at demonstrating to the international community that Serbia was prepared to prosecute war crimes suspects, and was capable of doing so. In conjunction with the adoption of the ICTY Completion Strategy, this constituted a key step in enabling cases to be transferred from the Hague tribunal to the domestic judiciary. As a result, the special institutions for prosecuting war crimes played a key role in restoring Serbia's legitimacy and reclaiming its jurisdiction over war crimes proceedings.

By virtue of their mission, the WCC and the OWCP were actively involved in diplomatic contacts with ICTY representatives and foreign officials. This was especially true for the War Crimes Prosecutor, who played a crucial role in the country's cooperation with the Hague tribunal, as well as in the re-establishment of closer ties with neighbouring countries. This intrusion of judicial institutions into political matters reflected a wider trend in international affairs which Gerry Simpson has named 'juridified diplomacy'. Simpson argues that the twentieth century was characterised by the increasing juridification of politics, which 'involves the translation of political conflict into legal doctrine, and, occasionally, the resolution of these conflicts in legal institutions'.[128] According to him, the emergence of juridified diplomacy essentially constituted an attempt to depoliticise contentious issues by displacing them into the judicial realm and thus 'rising above politics'.[129]

The establishment of international tribunals such as the ICTY constitutes a prime example of juridified diplomacy. Indeed, the Hague tribunal sought to pacify the former Yugoslavia by criminalising the political and military leaders from the region who were deemed responsible for the widespread violence and suffering undergone by the population. By adjudicating over the responsibility for war crimes, the ICTY was deemed to depoliticise this sensitive issue and open the way for reconciliation between former belligerents.[130] In this section, I examine the extent to which the Serbian institutions for prosecuting war crimes – in particular the OWCP –took over this project. I argue that the OWCP's engagement in deeply political matters constituted an attempt at depoliticising the war crimes issue by reducing it to an essentially legal and technical matter. This endeavour was primarily reflected in the OWCP's involvement in cooperation with the ICTY and its efforts at promoting reconciliation through collaboration with the judiciaries of the neighbouring countries. After illustrating this claim, I highlight the limits of juridification by discussing the controversies surrounding the prosecution of Kosovo Albanian and Bosniak suspects at the WCC.

A. Juridification and the Displacement of War Crimes Issues

Restoring the credibility of the Serbian judiciary and asserting its capacity to prosecute war crimes suspects constituted the primary task of the WCC and the OWCP. As noted above, these institutions were praised for their professionalism and impartiality by international and domestic observers. In particular, the OWCP became internationally prominent for its role in tackling impunity and restoring the rule of law in Serbia. In 2007, the Serbian War Crimes Prosecutor, Vladimir Vukčević, was presented with the prestigious Cran Montana Award for 'his

128 Simpson, *Law, War and Crime*, 132.

129 Ibid., 140. Simpson nonetheless acknowledges that 'often, though not always, these procedures prove to be disappointing precisely because law cannot entirely displace such differences'.

130 Payam Akhavan, 'Justice in The Hague, Peace in the Former Yugoslavia? A Commentary on the United Nations War Crimes Tribunal', *Human Rights Quarterly* 20:4 (1998), 737–816.

achievements in combating war criminals, his contribution to changing public opinion in Serbia, and dedication to the improvement of legal systems both in Serbia and regionwide'.[131] The OWCP thus became instrumental in rebuilding the image of the Serbian state. In view of this, the War Crimes Prosecutor came to play a major role in Serbia's foreign affairs. These political activities were especially pronounced in Serbia's cooperation with the ICTY and the re-establishment of closer ties with neighbouring countries.

The juridification of ICTY cooperation

The OWCP's dealings with the ICTY primarily concerned the transfer of cases and evidence from the Tribunal to the Serbian judiciary. Following the adoption of the ICTY Completion Strategy, Rule 11 *bis* of the Tribunal's Rules of Procedure and Evidence provided for the referral to national jurisdictions of cases for which the indictments had been completed by the Office of the Prosecutor (OTP).[132] In such cases, the domestic Prosecution was bound to follow the allegations stated in the indictment and the ICTY was entitled to monitor the entire investigative and judicial process. Nevertheless, as of 2011, only one case had been transferred to the Serbian judiciary under Rule 11 *bis*. This case concerned Vladimir Kovačević 'Rambo', who was indicted for the bombing of Dubrovnik and was later found unfit to stand trial owing to mental illness.[133]

The lack of referrals to the Serbian judiciary was imputed to the fact that most Serbian indictees were high-profile suspects who were deemed too important to be referred to domestic courts.[134] It is, however, most likely that the ICTY refrained from transferring indictees to Serbia owing to conflicting views on the principle upon which cases should be referred. According to Rule 11 *bis*, cases could be referred either to the State on whose territory the crime had been committed, or to the State upon whose territory the accused had been arrested, or to a State that had jurisdiction and was both willing and adequately prepared to accept the case.[135] If the first principle were applied, suspects arrested in Serbia and indicted for war crimes committed in Bosnia and Croatia could potentially have been referred to the judiciaries of those countries. The transfer of Serbian indictees to either Bosnia or Croatia would undoubtedly have generated considerable discontent and a potential backlash in Serbia.

131 'War Crimes Prosecutor Vladimir Vukčević Presented with the Prestigious Cran Montana Award', Office of the War Crimes Prosecutor, 26 October 2007. Retrieved from www.tuzilastvorz.org.rs on 10 March 2011.

132 ICTY, *Rules of Procedure and Evidence*, IT/32/Rev.45, 8 December 2010, 8–9. Retrieved from www.icty.org on 11 April 2011.

133 *Prosecutor v. Vladimir Kovačević*, 'Case Information Sheet', Case No. IT-01-42/2-1. Accessed on www.icty.org on 10 March 2011.

134 HRW, 'Unfinished Business', 21–2.

135 ICTY, *Rules of Procedure and Evidence*, 8–9.

This hypothesis is illustrated by the aborted initiative for the transfer of three former officers of the Yugoslav People's Army (JNA) who had been extradited to the ICTY by the Serbian authorities in order to stand trial for atrocities committed following the fall of Vukovar in 1991. In 2005, the OTP instigated the procedure for the referral of this case either to the Croatian or to the Serbian judiciary on the basis that the crimes were committed in Croatia and the suspects arrested in Serbia.[136] This provoked a fierce reaction from the Serbian judicial and political authorities, which announced that the transfer of the JNA officers to Croatia would jeopardise cooperation with the ICTY. At the same time, the Croatian authorities considered that they were entitled to get the case since this was one of the most serious crimes committed against their nationals. The Chief Prosecutor, Carla Del Ponte, eventually decided to withdraw the motion for the transfer of this case in view of the deep resentment this would necessarily have generated in one of the two countries.[137] On this basis, the OTP would probably have faced similar challenges with any attempt to transfer an indictee arrested in Serbia.

But although the ICTY referred only one indictment to the Serbian judiciary, it nonetheless provided ample evidence and support for the OWCP to instigate its own cases. The first two major cases brought before the WCC – *Ovčara* and *Zvornik* – were based on evidence collected by the OTP. However, in both cases, the investigation was supplemented and the indictment issued by the OWCP. Hence, while the ICTY had identified three suspects in each of these cases, the OWCP subsequently indicted 21 persons for *Ovčara* and 9 for *Zvornik*.[138] The ICTY also provided financial and political support for the OWCP to conduct investigations in Kosovo, notably in relation to the *Suva Reka* case.[139] Most importantly, the OWCP and the OTP signed a Memorandum in 2006 which allowed the Serbian War Crimes Prosecution to get access to the ICTY's database.[140] This not only provided the OWCP with valuable material for building new cases, but it also demonstrated the high level of trust and respect towards this institution among ICTY representatives.

This high level of trust and respect in the OWCP among foreign officials led the War Crimes Prosecutor to assume a key role in the arrest and extradition of indictees to The Hague. Indeed, as the flow of transfers made possible by the policy of voluntary surrenders came to an end, the ICTY representatives and EU officials became increasingly distrustful of Koštunica's readiness and capacity to deliver the remaining fugitives (see Chapter 3). They insisted on the deployment of new measures and lobbied for heavier involvement of the OWCP in the

136 'Del Ponte: Vukovarsku trojku ustupiti Hrvatskoj ili SCG' (Del Ponte: *Vukovar Three* Should Be Referred to Croatia or Serbia and Montenegro), *Danas*, 10 February 2005.

137 'Vukovar Case Decision Provokes Mixed Reactions', *IWPR*, 17 November 2005.

138 Personal interview with Bruno Vekarić.

139 *Vreme*, 16 December 2004; HRW, 'Unfinished Business', 22.

140 'Pristup Haškim podacima' (Access to The Hague Data), *Politika*, 16 July 2006.

search for the six suspects who still remained at large at that time.[141] As a result, Vladimir Vukčević became the operations coordinator for the implementation of the Government's Action Plan for Locating and Arresting the Hague Indictees, adopted in July 2006.[142] The War Crimes Prosecutor was put in charge of coordinating the work of the security services involved in the search for the indictees, as well as communicating with the ICTY. In addition to directing search operations on the ground, Vukčević thus became the principal interlocutor of the Tribunal representatives and foreign officials concerned with ICTY cooperation. Furthermore, he became one of the major proponents of ICTY cooperation in Serbia through his appearances in the media. Unlike the Koštunica administration, the War Crimes Prosecutor projected a distinctly principled rationale for the arrest and prosecution of war crimes suspects. As noted earlier, the OWCP turned out to be more prominent in the media for its role in the search for the Hague fugitives than for the war crimes proceedings before the WCC.

While the transfer of cases and evidence between the ICTY and the OWCP was primarily a judicial matter, the pursuit and arrest of Hague fugitives endowed the War Crimes Prosecutor with an essentially political mission. The appointment of Vladimir Vukčević as the coordinator of the Action Plan for the arrest of the ICTY indictees effectively constituted an attempt to depoliticise an issue that remained extremely sensitive both on the domestic and on the international front. Indeed, this Action Plan was aimed primarily at demonstrating the resolve of the Serbian authorities to arrest and extradite the remaining indictees at a moment when the EU had suspended the SAA negotiations with Serbia owing to the failure to deliver Mladić to the ICTY. It thus constituted an attempt to persuade both Western diplomats and the domestic audience that the arrest of Mladić and five other indictees was a purely technical matter, not a political one. However, considering the general antagonism towards the ICTY and the lack of consensus over the arrest and extradition of indictees in Serbia, this remained an extremely contentious issue in domestic politics.

In view of this, Vukčević's engagement in the search for the indictees was aimed at preventing the nationalist parties from further exploiting the issue of ICTY cooperation by displacing it from the political to the judicial sphere. As an unelected official, the War Crimes Prosecutor was immune to the political cost of promoting an agenda that remained widely unpopular among the population. Indeed, Vukčević could bear the responsibility of hunting the fugitives and promoting cooperation with the ICTY without fearing loss of popularity. While this further exposed him and the OWCP to the attacks of the SRS, it did not call into question his position or the existence of that institution. The political authorities thus partly outsourced the costs of ICTY cooperation to the judiciary while

141 *Danas*, 8 February 2006.

142 The Minister of Human and Minority Rights, Rasim Ljajić, was appointed as the 'politico-diplomatic' coordinator of the Action Plan. 'Ljajić i Vukčević koordinatori' (Ljajić and Vukčević Coordinators), *Glas Javnosti*, 19 July 2006.

reaping the benefits associated with the advancement of Euro-integration resulting from the transfer of indictees. Paradoxically, the opponents of cooperation also increasingly resorted to legalistic arguments by questioning the circumstances in which the arrests of Zdravko Tolimir and Radovan Karadžić were carried out.[143] This juridification of ICTY cooperation was instrumental in causing the Hague issue to recede on the Serbian political scene, as described in Chapter 3.

Regional judicial cooperation as a tool for reconciliation?

In addition to playing a key role in ICTY cooperation, the OWCP substantially contributed to the re-establishment of closer ties with neighbouring countries by promoting regional cooperation in the prosecution of war crimes. The Serbian War Crimes Prosecutor established a particularly close relationship with the Croatian and Bosnian State Prosecutors, which greatly facilitated the exchange of evidence and information between the judiciaries in the region. This collaboration was encouraged and supported by the international community – especially the US authorities and the OSCE – which brought the Prosecutors together at various forums and pressed them to assist each other.

According to some observers, regional cooperation in the prosecution of war crimes had become the cornerstone of transitional justice in the region.[144] Indeed, mutual legal assistance constituted a necessity for overcoming the obstacles faced by the national judiciaries in investigating and prosecuting war crimes, since, in most cases, the perpetrators and the victims lived in separate countries. In such circumstances, the Prosecutors often relied on the assistance of their foreign counterparts in order to gain access to witnesses and collect evidence. The OWCP therefore signed bilateral agreements regulating cooperation with the Offices of the Prosecutors of Bosnia and Croatia.[145] These agreements allowed for the exchange of information and evidence among Prosecutors on an informal basis, without having to go through lengthy procedures at the level of the Ministries of Justice.

As a result, the judiciaries of these countries cooperated successfully on a number of cases. Indeed, the Croatian State Attorney General assisted the OWCP by providing evidence and enabling witnesses to testify in the *Ovčara* and *Lovas* cases.[146] The OWCP returned the favour by providing assistance in the investigation of the *Lora* and *Osijek* cases processed in Croatia. It also collaborated with the Bosnian judiciary, notably by establishing a joint investigative team working on

143 In June 2007, the Radicals requested a parliamentary inquiry into the arrest of Tolimir amid allegations that he was kidnapped and transferred to Bosnia so that the authorities in Belgrade could avoid responsibility for his arrest. In the case of Karadžić, the representatives of the DSS and NS supported the SRS-led demonstrations in protest against the way in which Karadžić was arrested.

144 'Regional Cooperation Lift for War Crimes Justice', *IWPR*, 29 June 06.

145 HRW, 'Unfinished Business', 15.

146 Ivanišević, 'Against the Current', 30.

the *Zvornik* case with the Cantonal Prosecutor from Tuzla.[147] The Serbian War Crimes Prosecutor met up regularly with his Bosnian and Croatian colleagues in order to address problems and discuss further improvement in cooperation between their teams. In some cases, the three prosecutors reacted jointly to the public disclosure of war crimes. In August 2006, the broadcasting of footage showing war crimes perpetrated by Croatian and Muslim forces upon Krajina Serbs led Vladimir Vukčević to meet the Croatian and Bosnian Prosecutors in order to agree on the prosecution of those crimes.[148] The cooperation between these judiciaries was so promising that there were even talks on creating a regional Tribunal that would take over the work of the ICTY. Nevertheless, this initiative was never seriously considered owing to the lack of political support from domestic and international actors.[149]

Apart from helping to bring perpetrators to justice, regional cooperation in the prosecution of war crimes opened the way for the establishment of closer political ties between these countries. Domestic war crimes trials particularly helped advance the rapprochement of the Serbian and Croatian political elites by reducing mutual antagonism associated with the war crimes legacy. The OWCP's handling of the *Ovčara* case amply contributed towards this end. For years, the Croatian political elites have cultivated the remembrance of Vukovar as a symbol of Croatian martyrdom at the hands of the Serbian aggressor.[150] In view of this, the prosecution of those responsible for the *Ovčara* massacre by the WCC constituted a form of acknowledgment and redress for Croatian victims by the Serbian state. According to the War Crimes Prosecutor, Vladimir Vukčević, the *Ovčara* case opened the way for reconciliation between the two countries:

> The final verdict increased confidence, first between the judicial organs and then among the people, at least that is what I think. I have the impression that it is precisely this case which paved the way for the reconciliation of the Serbian and Croatian judiciaries. All the agreements and memorandums date back to the inception of that case.[151]

---

147 This measure was subsequently suspended by the Bosnian High Judicial and Prosecutorial Council on the basis that it did not accord with national legislation, nor with international agreements to which BiH is a party (Ivanišević, 'Against the Current', 31).

148 'Tužilaštva Srbije, Hrvatske i BiH pripremaju zajedničke akcije' (Serbian, Croatian and Bosnian Prosecutions Prepare Joint Actions), *Građanski list*, 10 August 2006.

149 HRW, 'Unfinished Business', 23.

150 Rose Lindsey, 'Remembering Vukovar, Forgetting Vukovar: Constructing National Identity through the Memory of Catastrophe in Croatia' in *The Memory of Catastrophe*, eds Peter Gray and Kendrick Oliver (Manchester, New York: Manchester University Press, 2004), 190–204.

151 'Vukčević: Procesuiranje slučaja *Ovčara* jača pomirenje i poverenje' (Vukčević: The Prosecution of the *Ovčara* Case Strengthens Reconciliation and Trust), *Blic*, 27 October 2010.

These claims were substantiated by the improvement in relations between Belgrade and Zagreb during Tadić's presidency. In November 2010, President Tadić attended the commemoration of the *Ovčara* victims along with his Croatian colleague, Ivo Josipović. The two presidents also paid their respects to Serbian victims killed by Croatian forces in Paulin Dvor, for which two persons were prosecuted by the Croatian judiciary. The fact that judicial cooperation on the prosecution of war crimes preceded these political acts suggests that domestic war crimes trials effectively laid the ground for the official acknowledgment of victims and the re-establishment of closer ties between Serbia and Croatia. In that sense, war crimes trials effectively contributed to reconciliation, as claimed by proponents of transitional justice. Indeed, by taking the lead in addressing the war crimes legacy, the national judiciaries sought to depoliticise this issue by displacing it from the political to the legal sphere. The OWCP and its regional counterparts thus took over the responsibility of addressing a sensitive issue that was obstructing the normalisation of political relations in the region. The juridification of the war crimes issue therefore contributed towards appeasing political tensions and antagonisms associated with the past.

But in spite of these positive developments, regional cooperation in the prosecution of war crimes was hampered by disagreements over competing jurisdictions in war crimes proceedings. This is largely due to the fact that the Bosnian, Croatian and Serbian legislations did not allow for the extradition of nationals to other countries. In this context, none of these judiciaries had access to the war crimes suspects who resided in, and held citizenship of, one of the neighbouring countries. This problem was aggravated by divergent views over which judiciary should have precedence in prosecuting war crimes suspects.[152] On the one hand, the Bosnian authorities insisted on the principle that perpetrators should be tried in the state where crimes were perpetrated. On the other hand, the Serbian War Crimes Prosecutor insisted on the principle that war crimes suspects should be prosecuted in the country where they were located. In view of this, the OWCP signed an agreement with the Croatian State Prosecutor which allowed for the transfer of cases between those two countries.[153] As a result of this agreement, the Croatian judiciary handed over six cases to the OWCP in July 2007.[154] This move was widely praised for tackling impunity by side-stepping the obstacle engendered by the extradition of war crimes suspects. Nevertheless, this type of cooperation was not implemented with Bosnia and Kosovo, and this gave rise to political tensions that I discuss in the remainder of this section.

---

152 'Sporno samo gde suditi osumnjičenima' (The Only Contentious Issue is Where to Try Suspects), *Danas*, 7 February 2007.

153 'Sporazum sa Zagrebom' (Agreement with Zagreb), *Blic*, 14 October 2006.

154 'Saradnja Srbije i Hrvatske u gonjenju ratnih zločinaca' (Cooperation between Serbia and Croatia in the Prosecution of War Crimes), *Politika*, 13 July 2007.

B. The Limits of Juridification: Competing Jurisdictions and Contentious Trials

Although the Serbian War Crimes Prosecution in principle espoused the idea that each country in the region should try its own nationals, it nonetheless sought to prosecute all those suspects within its reach, regardless of their nationality or ethnicity. The Law on Organisation and Competence of Government Authorities in War Crimes Proceedings gave the OWCP and WCC jurisdiction over all acts of war crime and genocide perpetrated in the former Yugoslavia, notwithstanding the nationality of the victims or perpetrators. The special institutions for prosecuting war crimes were thus established on the principle of 'territorially limited universal jurisdiction' which corresponded to the geographical and temporal jurisdiction of the ICTY.[155] This led the OWCP to prosecute and seek custody of several Kosovo Albanian and Bosniak suspects, generating political tension over the prosecution of war crimes in the region.

Juridified diplomacy and contested sovereignty: prosecuting Kosovo Albanian war crimes

While the War Crimes Prosecution established good cooperation with the Croatian and Bosnian judiciaries, its relations with the UNMIK mission in Kosovo were more difficult. Since the Serbian authorities had no effective control over Kosovo, the OWCP relied entirely on the support of the international administration for investigating war crimes perpetrated there. On a number of occasions, UNMIK provided logistical support to the OWCP for interviewing Kosovo Albanian witnesses of crimes perpetrated by Serbian forces. However, this assistance was deemed insufficient by the OWCP representatives, who claimed that they could not complete cases owing to UNMIK's failure to respond to their demands for access to witnesses in Kosovo.[156]

The OWCP's relations with UNMIK were particularly affected by the efforts of the Serbian authorities to arrest and prosecute former members of the Kosovo Liberation Army (KLA). This ambition was set out by the former Serbian Minister of Justice, Vladan Batić, who called for the War Crimes Prosecutor to take over the investigations against the former KLA leaders.[157] The Serbian officials thus sought to exert pressure on the ICTY and UNMIK to prosecute war crimes perpetrated against Serbs in Kosovo. Nevertheless, the international administration in Kosovo only undertook a very limited number of war crimes trials, which were plagued by delays and lack of capacity. Indeed, an OSCE report published in 2009 established that 'there has been a systemic failure to adjudicate war crimes cases' in Kosovo

155 Personal interview with Ivan Jovanović.

156 Ivanišević, 'Against the Current', 31–2.

157 'Naše tužilaštvo goniće Tačija, Čekua i Haradinaja' (Our Prosecution Will Try Thaçi, Çeku and Haradinaj), *Dnevnik*, 30 October 2003.

during the 2000s.[158] At the same time, UNMIK officials thwarted Serbian attempts to get KLA leaders extradited from third countries. The former KLA chief of staff, Agim Çeku, was thus arrested on a number of occasions on the basis of an international warrant issued by the Serbian authorities, only to be released upon the request of UNMIK representatives.[159]

The tensions between the OWCP and UNMIK heightened during the trial of the former KLA member Anton Lekaj before the WCC. Lekaj, who was arrested in Montenegro for car theft, was the first Kosovo Albanian to face war crimes charges in Serbia. He was suspected of having participated in the abduction, torture and killing of 13 persons attending a Roma wedding ceremony in the days following the retreat of the Serbian troops from Kosovo.[160] Six months after the beginning of the trial, the Chief of the UNMIK mission, Søren Jessen-Petersen, requested that the Serbian authorities suspend the proceedings against Lekaj on the basis that UNMIK had sole authority to prosecute war crimes perpetrated in Kosovo.[161] This demand provoked fierce reactions among Serbian politicians who rejected it as an attempt to assert Kosovo's sovereignty and shield former KLA members from accountability for war crimes. While politicians argued that Serbia still had formal sovereignty over Kosovo, the representatives of the OWCP claimed jurisdiction over this case on the basis of an earlier agreement with the UN which provided for suspects to be tried in the place where they were found. The conflict escalated as the UNMIK representatives turned down the OWCP's requests to examine witnesses.[162] This decision resulted in the almost complete suspension of cooperation between the OWCP and UNMIK which, according to the War Crimes Prosecution, affected the outcome of the *Lekaj* case.

Although contacts between the OWCP and the international administration subsequently resumed, the War Crimes Prosecutor repeatedly complained that cooperation in the prosecution of war crimes was hampered by the political tensions related to Kosovo's unresolved status. Indeed, the OWCP representatives denounced the international administration for postponing the prosecution of war crimes out of fear of provoking a nationalist backlash among Kosovo Albanians. They argued that impunity for Kosovo Albanian war crimes against Serbs reinforced domestic resistance to the OWCP's attempts to prosecute Serbian policemen suspected of war crimes in Kosovo.[163] The prosecution of war crimes perpetrated in Kosovo was indeed a politically sensitive issue in Serbia, as illustrated by the

158 OSCE, 'Kosovo's War Crimes Trials: An Assessment Ten Years On', May 2010, 6.

159 'Vekarić: Nema optužnice protiv Čekua' (Vekarić: No Indictment against Çeku), *Danas*, 7 March 2006.

160 Humanitarian Law Centre, 'Sudjenje za ratne zločine u Srbiji' (War Crimes Trials in Serbia), December 2007, 1–2.

161 'Petersen od Srbije traži Ljekaja' (Petersen Requests Lekaj from Serbia), *Danas*, 4 April 2006.

162 'Petersen bira svedoke' (Petersen Selects the Witnesses), *Politika*, 8 June 2006.

163 HRW, 'Unfinished Business', 20.

protests against the arrest of Special Police Unit members discussed above. In point of fact, impunity for atrocities perpetrated upon Serbs in Kosovo created an overwhelming sentiment in Serbia that the international community was shielding former KLA members from accountability. On the other hand, the prosecution of Kosovo Albanians before the WCC was interpreted as, and was possibly motivated by, a craving to reassert Serbia's sovereignty over Kosovo. This state of affairs demonstrates that, in the case of Kosovo, the juridification and depoliticisation of the war crimes issue was clearly limited by the absence of political settlement over Kosovo's status. Instead of addressing deep-seated controversies over the past, the prosecution of war crimes thus contributed to increasing political tensions in the context of a lasting conflict over Kosovo's claim to sovereignty.

Several additional trials were subsequently conducted against Kosovo Albanian suspects before the WCC.[164] These cases did not cause renewed tensions with the authorities in Kosovo, which suggests that there was increasing acceptance among international officials with regard to trying Kosovo Albanian war crimes suspects in Serbian courts. Nevertheless, cooperation between the Serbian judiciary and the administration in Kosovo remained problematic, despite the fact that the EULEX mission set the prosecution of war crimes as a priority. While there was some progress in exchanging information at the initial stages of the investigations, Kosovo Albanian witnesses remained reluctant to testify in Serbian courts. Moreover, the documentation provided by the Kosovo administration bore the stamp of the state of Kosovo which made it unusable in Serbian courts since Serbia did not recognise Kosovo's statehood.[165] Therefore, cooperation in the prosecution of war crimes was unlikely to improve until, and unless, a political settlement had been reached on Kosovo's status.

The politicisation of war crimes trials: seeking accountability for Bosniak war crimes

The limits of juridification in appeasing political tensions related to the war crimes issue in the region were further highlighted by the OWCP's efforts to prosecute for atrocities perpetrated against the Yugoslav People's Army (JNA) at the beginning of the war in Bosnia. The War Crimes Prosecution inherited two cases from the defunct Military Tribunal – the *Dobrovoljačka*[166] and *Tuzla Convoy* cases – which concerned attacks on the military convoys of the JNA during their withdrawal from Sarajevo and Tuzla in May 1992. The Serbian authorities claimed that these attacks constituted a violation of international law because the JNA officials and the Bosnian authorities had previously signed an agreement on the peaceful evacuation of the Yugoslav Army from Bosnian cities. In addition, the Bosniak

164 These were the *Orahovac group (Sinan Morina)* and *Gnjilane group* cases.

165 E-mail communication with Ivan Jovanović, 20 May 2011.

166 'Dobrovoljačka' (Volunteers) refers to the street in Sarajevo where the attack on the JNA convoy took place on 3 May 1992.

forces were alleged to have perpetrated atrocities on the wounded soldiers who were captured following the attack, and this amounted to war crimes.

Although the OWCP conducted investigations into these cases, the War Crimes Prosecutor declared on several occasions that he expected these crimes to be prosecuted in Bosnia where the suspects were located.[167] Indeed, the Bosnian judiciary had opened its own investigations into these cases and the OWCP offered to transfer all the evidence it had collated. However, cooperation on these matters never materialised owing to the failure of the Bosnian and Serbian judiciaries to reach an agreement, like the one signed between Belgrade and Zagreb, on the transfer of cases between the two countries. This state of affairs derived partly from the divergences mentioned above over which judiciary should have precedence in prosecuting the war crimes. While the OWCP representative maintained that suspects should be prosecuted by the state which arrested them, the Bosnian authorities held onto the view that perpetrators should be tried in the country where the crimes were committed. In those circumstances, the OWCP's initiative for creating joint investigative teams with their Bosnian counterparts working on these cases did not come to fruition.[168] In addition, the OWCP representatives claimed on several occasions that the Bosnian investigations into these cases were obstructed by political pressures from the Bosniak political elites.[169] As a result, the Serbian and Bosnian Prosecutions pursued their investigations separately.

The disagreements over jurisdiction in these cases led to an increase in political tensions following the arrest of Ilija Jurišić, a prime suspect in the *Tuzla Convoy* case, by the Serbian authorities. Jurišić was unexpectedly arrested at Belgrade airport in May 2007 while travelling to Germany. As a former high official of the Bosnian Interior Ministry, he was suspected by the OWCP of having given the order to attack the JNA convoy during its retreat from Tuzla. Jurišić's arrest and subsequent indictment for war crimes provoked substantial discontent in Bosnia, where many considered this to be a politicised process aimed at criminalising the Bosniak resistance to Serbian aggression.[170] The Bosnian judiciary, which provided assistance to the OWCP in collecting evidence and hearing witnesses, requested the transfer of Jurišić to Bosnia on the basis that he was a Bosnian citizen and that the crime of which he was suspected was committed in that country. This demand was rejected by the War Crimes Prosecutor, who claimed jurisdiction over this case owing to the fact that Jurišić was arrested in Serbia and that the

167 *Večernje Novosti*, 3 Aug. 2005; 'Sudjenja u državama osumnjičenih' (Trials in the Suspects' States), *Blic*, 18 September 2006.

168 'Ratni zločini i regionalna saradnja' (War Crimes and Regional Cooperation), *B92*, 10 March 2010.

169 Ibid.; 'Begunci ruže lice Srbije' (Fugitives Damage Serbia's Image), *Politika*, 8 July 2007.

170 'Reakcije zbog "Tuzlanske Kolone"' (Reactions to the 'Tuzla Column'), *B92*, 10 November 2007.

OWCP was entitled to try any war crime committed in the former Yugoslavia.[171] Moreover, Serbian legislation prohibited the extradition of any indictee suspected of a crime for which the sentence exceeds ten years, which allowed the Serbian authorities to rule out Jurišić's transfer to Bosnia on legal grounds. The WCC sentenced Jurišić to 12 years' imprisonment in September 2009, which triggered a wave of disapproval among Bosniak victim organisations and Serbian human rights NGOs.[172] The verdict was heavily criticised by the HLC, which claimed that the trial did not elucidate what happened in the attack on the JNA convoy in Tuzla and that the process was driven by the OWCP's urge to gain domestic support by showing that it also pursued justice for Serb victims.[173]

The political tensions associated with war crimes trials further increased in 2010 as a result of the arrest of the former member of the Bosnian Presidency, Ejup Ganić, in London on the basis of a Serbian arrest warrant.[174] The Serbian authorities requested the extradition of Ganić, who was one of the 19 Bosnian officials suspected by the OWCP of being responsible for the attack on the JNA convoy in the *Dobrovoljačka* case. This initiative added strain to the already tense diplomatic relations between Belgrade and Sarajevo. It also revived deep-seated antagonisms within Bosnia over responsibility for the war and accountability for war crimes. Indeed, the Bosniak political elites fiercely condemned this move as an attempt to castigate their resistance to Serbian aggression.[175] Ganić's supporters portrayed his arrest as an attempt to misrepresent the nature of the war, claiming that he would not get a fair trial in Serbia. On the other hand, the Bosnian Serb representatives supported the initiative for trying Ganić in Belgrade on the basis that the Bosnian judiciary had failed to prosecute war crimes committed against Serbs.

While this case was heavily mediatised and debated in Bosnia, the Serbian authorities sought to play down its political implications by portraying it as an exclusively legal matter in the remit of the judiciary. In an attempt to ease political tensions, President Tadić declared that Serbia would not oppose the extradition

171 Since most of the victims in this attack were citizens of Serbia, the Serbian judiciary could also claim jurisdiction over this case on the basis of the principle of passive personality, according to which states have, in the exercise of their sovereignty, jurisdiction over crimes committed against their nationals (Personal interview with Ivan Jovanović).

172 'Presuda Jurišiću izazvala razočarenje u BiH' (Jurišić Verdict Has Generated Disappointment in Bosnia), *Radio Free Europe*, 28 September 2009.

173 Humanitarian Law Centre, 'Trials for War Crimes and Ethnically and Politically Motivated Crimes in Post-Yugoslav Countries', 2008, 107–9.

174 The Serbian arrest warrant was enforced by the British authorities on the basis of a bilateral agreement on Mutual Legal Assistance between Serbia and the UK (*B92*, 10 March 2010).

175 'Različite ocene o hapšenju Ganića' (Different Views on the Arrest of Ganić), *B92*, 3 March 2010.

of Ganić to Bosnia if the Bosnian judiciary undertook proceedings against him.[176] He insisted that the location of the trial was irrelevant and that the only thing that mattered for the Serbian authorities was that Ganić face justice. This statement suggests that Serbia's request for the extradition of Ganić primarily constituted an attempt at pressuring the Bosnian judiciary to prosecute the *Dobrovoljačka* case. This hypothesis is substantiated by the testimony of Ivan Jovanović, who claims that the OWCP officials made various attempts at inducing their Bosnian colleagues to take over this case before starting their own investigation:

> The thing here is that the Serbian Prosecution ... shared evidence with the Bosnian Prosecution and waited until 2006 for Bosnia to undertake something with regard to *Dobrovoljačka*. When they saw that nothing was happening, they then decided to instigate [an investigation] and they are now saying "we want to take this to the indictment stage: we will not seek them out nor prosecute them, we want you to do something". So, in the case of *Dobrovoljačka*, the problem is not that Serbia insists on prosecuting them. The problem is that Serbia requests that someone deal with this case, but nobody else wants to do it apart from Serbia.[177]

Nevertheless, this initiative was severely criticised by Serbian human rights NGOs, who saw it as a blatant politicisation of war crimes trials. Indeed, Serbia's request for Ganić's extradition was denounced by some human rights activists as an attempt to create a balance in the prosecution of war crimes committed by the different sides in the conflict.[178] Others have alleged that, throughout these proceedings, the OWCP sought to gain legitimacy in Serbia by demonstrating a resolve to castigate war crimes perpetrated against Serbs.[179]

Serbia's request for the extradition of Ganić was eventually rejected by the Magistrates' Court in the City of Westminster in July 2010. This decision dealt a major blow to the OWCP and the Serbian state, not least because the District Judge, Tim Workman, ruled that Serbia's request was used for political purposes and, as such, amounted to abuse of the process of the court.[180] Indeed, the Bosnian side had successfully argued that the Serbian government was attempting to use these

176 'Tadić: Ganiću može da se sudi u BiH' (Tadić: Ganić Can Be Tried in Bosnia), *B92*, 15 March 2010; the Bosnian authorities had filed a request for the extradition of Ganić to Bosnia in order to counter Serbia's request.

177 Personal interview with Ivan Jovanović.

178 'Ganić Case Highlights Dispute Over Bosnia War's Causes', *IWPR*, 20 September 2010.

179 'Za slučaj "Dobrovoljačka" je nadležan Sud BiH' (The Court of Bosnia and Herzegovina Has Authority Over the 'Dobrovoljačka' Case), *Radio Free Europe*, 13 March 2010.

180 *The Government of the Republic of Serbia v. Ejup Ganić*, City of Westminster Magistrates' Court, 27 July 2010, paras 19 & 39. Retrieved from www.crimesofwar.org on 20 January 2011.

proceedings as a lever to secure Bosnia's approval of the Srebrenica declaration adopted by the Serbian parliament on 31 March 2010. The Serbian authorities allegedly promised to drop the request for Ganić's extradition in return for Bosnia's endorsement of the declaration, which was severely criticised for not referring to Srebrenica as genocide (See Chapter 4). The defence maintained that this blackmail was motivated by the desire of the Serbian government to legitimise the declaration and thereby give impetus to the country's integration into the EU. And, while these allegations were predictably rejected by the Serbian government officials, the War Crimes Prosecutor conceded that 'this was all done behind his back'.[181]

In addition to rejecting Serbia's demand as political blackmail, the verdict of the Magistrates' Court seriously undermined the credibility of the OWCP and the WCC. Indeed, the decision not to extradite Ganić was primarily based on the fact that both the ICTY and the Court of Bosnia and Herzegovina had found that there was no case against him. The judge considered that the OWCP did not provide any further evidence incriminating Ganić and that the prosecution was politically motivated.[182] These findings were largely based on the testimonies of two former High Representatives of Bosnia and Herzegovina as well as several UK-based academics, who testified that Ganić would not have a fair trial in Serbia and that these proceedings were aimed at giving a distorted view of the war in Bosnia. In addition, Judge Workman established that there had been no agreement between the JNA and the Bosnian authorities on the peaceful retreat of the Yugoslav Army, which undermined the claim that the attacks on the convoys in Sarajevo and Tuzla constituted violations of international law *per se*.[183]

The OWCP representatives imputed this outcome to the fact that Bosnia is widely perceived in international circles as the victim of the Yugoslav wars.[184] They argued that the ICTY and the Bosnian judiciary had not seriously investigated the *Dobrovoljačka* case and decried the witnesses produced by the defence as a powerful political lobby. On the other hand, the Bosniak officials claimed that these proceedings demonstrated Serbia's involvement in the war in Bosnia, which Belgrade had thus far officially denied.[185] Moreover, they requested the exoneration of Ilija Jurišić on the basis of the UK court's finding that no agreement had been reached on the peaceful retreat of the JNA troops.

181 'Vukčević: tvrdnje Ganića besmislene' (Vukčević: Ganić's Claims Are Unfounded), *B92*, 30 July 2010.

182 *Serbia v. Ganić*, para. 40.

183 Ibid. Para. 37.

184 'Ganić neće biti izručen Srbiji' (Ganić Will Not Be Extradited to Serbia), *B92*, 27 July 2010; *B92*, 30 July 2010.

185 'Ganić razmatra tužbu protiv Srbije' (Ganić is Considering Lawsuit against Serbia), *B92*, 26 August 2010.

A few months later, the Serbian Court of Appeal ordered the retrial of the *Tuzla Column* case and the release of Ilija Jurišić, who was allowed to return to Bosnia.[186]

This episode shows how attempts to prosecute war crimes can backfire. Instead of de-politicising the war crimes issue and opening the way for reconciliation, the OWCP's efforts to bring to justice Bosniak war crimes suspects had the exact opposite effect. Indeed, these initiatives exacerbated inter-ethnic antagonisms and brought controversies over the Bosnian war back onto the political agenda. These cases demonstrate the limits of juridified diplomacy in overcoming deep-seated divergences over the past. In spite of the overall consensus on prosecuting war crimes in the region, the domestic judiciaries had different views on which crimes should be prosecuted, who should be held accountable for them, and where these trials should take place. In the absence of agreement over these issues, on several occasions the domestic judiciaries transferred their litigation to foreign courts.[187] Paradoxically, the transfer of competencies to the local judiciaries was thus partially reversed. In those circumstances, the juridificiation of the war crimes issue not only failed to resolve political conflicts about the past, but it actually contributed to keeping those conflicts alive.

Conclusion

Domestic war crimes trials are the most tangible, and arguably the most significant, achievement of international judicial intervention in Serbia. By encouraging the creation of special institutions for prosecuting war crimes, the ICTY substantially contributed to transferring international legal norms to the Serbian judiciary and establishing the rule of law in Serbia. Besides taking over the lead in the prosecution of war crimes suspects, the WCC and the OWCP endorsed the transitional justice agenda of promoting liberalising political change and reconciliation. Indeed, these institutions showed a clear commitment to confronting Serbian society with the atrocities committed by Serb forces and addressing divisive political issues in the region by cooperating with the judiciaries of the neighbouring countries in the prosecution of war crimes.

186 'Tuzlanska kolona "ispočetka"' (The Tuzla Column 'from Scratch'), *B92*, 11 October 2010. According to Ivan Jovanović, this decision was not related to the outcome of the Ganić extradition case. Indeed, the Court of Appeal based its decision on the incomplete establishment of facts by the court of first instance (E-mail communication with Ivan Jovanović on 20 May 2011).

187 The controversy over the *Dobrovoljačka* case was revived in March 2011 with the arrest of the former Bosnian Army General Jovan Divjak in Austria on the basis of a Serbian warrant. Divjak is one of the 19 individuals suspected of the attack on the JNA by the OWCP, which requested his extradition to Serbia ('Divjak Arrest Exposes Balkan Prosecutor's Failings', *IWPR*, 15 Mar. 2011).

Nevertheless, the evidence presented in this chapter shows that the work of the domestic institutions for prosecuting war crimes was substantially informed by the tensions between the search for justice on the one hand and the concern for upholding political stability and legitimacy on the other. But while, in the case of the ICTY, these contradictions pitted the Serbian authorities against the Tribunal officials, the OWCP and the WCC incorporated concerns for stability and legitimacy in their pursuit of justice. This is illustrated by the Prosecution's decision, following the staging of protests that threatened to stir up instability, to pull back from prosecuting police members suspected of having committed war crimes in Kosovo. Similarly, the WCC judges' decisions to obscure the links between the paramilitaries and the state or to detach the Scorpions' killings from the Srebrenica genocide seem to be have been largely motivated by concerns for the legitimacy of the Serbian state. These examples suggest that the special institutions for prosecuting war crimes exercised significantly broader political discretion in their work than the ICTY. In such circumstances, the potential of domestic trials for bringing perpetrators to justice and challenging dominant frameworks for interpreting the past was inherently limited.

These limitations were to a great extent conditioned by the political and institutional context in which war crimes trials took place. The special institutions for prosecuting war crimes relied heavily on political support for ensuring their integrity and subsistence, as well as for asserting their legitimacy. At a more practical level, the OWCP and the WCC required institutional support in order to carry out war crimes proceedings successfully. As noted above, this political and institutional context was constantly evolving, thus widening or reducing the scope and potential of war crimes trials. In this respect, domestic institutions for prosecuting war crimes were no different from the ICTY, which relied heavily on Great Power support for its subsistence as well as for pressuring targeted states to cooperate. The work of the Tribunal was also to a certain extent informed by political convenience, as illustrated by the failure to investigate NATO war crimes in Serbia.[188] The difference is that in domestic proceedings, domestic political interests had more say than foreign ones.[189]

In this context, domestic war crimes trials were a mixed blessing for reconciliation in the region. The rapprochement between Serbia and Croatia during Tadić's presidency showed that the juridification of war crimes had the potential to depoliticise this issue, thereby contributing towards the re-establishment of closer political ties in the region. But, as the national judiciaries faced competing pressures from their immediate environments, they failed on several occasions

188 Carla Del Ponte openly admitted that the ICTY's Office of the Prosecutor did not conduct investigations against NATO because this was 'beyond the political universe in which the Tribunal was allowed to operate' [Carla Del Ponte and Chuck Sudetić, *Gospodja Tužiteljka* (Madame Prosecutor) (Belgrade: Profil knjiga, 2008), 68].

189 Note that the *Bytyqi* case, which was instigated at the request of the US authorities, shows that Great Powers did have some say in domestic war crimes proceedings too.

to 'rise above politics'. In those cases, juridified diplomacy proved incapable of bridging conflicting interpretations of the past or absolving war crimes trials of enduring political conflicts. Instead, war crimes prosecutions added fuel to the fire by increasing political tensions and reviving antagonisms over the war (crimes) legacy.

Conclusion: An Ambivalent Legacy

The beginning of the twenty-first century in Serbia was tainted by the legacy of the wars that ravaged the former Yugoslavia in the 1990s. The question of responsibility for war crimes weighed heavily on Serbia's prospects for democracy and aspirations to join the EU. This issue was brought to the top of the political agenda by Western demands for the prosecution of those deemed most responsible for the atrocities perpetrated during the Yugoslav wars. With the creation of the ICTY, the international community had mobilised unprecedented political and financial resources to bring to justice war criminals from the former Yugoslavia. The policies of conditionality deployed by the US and the EU created immense pressure on target states to cooperate with the Tribunal. For the Serbian authorities, this involved the formidable task of arresting and handing over 46 indicted individuals to the ICTY, including the highest-ranking political, military and security officials of the Milošević regime.

The conditioning of financial aid and European integration upon ICTY cooperation obliged the Serbian authorities to comply with the demands of the Tribunal regardless of whether the parties in power were sympathetic or antagonistic to it. The vivid memories of the UN embargo in the 1990s ruled out the possibility for any government to durably withhold cooperation at the cost of renewed isolation. For Serbian officials, the ICTY was an external variable to which they had to adjust. In the words of Prime Minister Djindjić, 'the Hague tribunal is like the weather forecast: since you cannot change it, the only thing you can do is to adapt to it'.[1] In practice, the Serbian authorities had the ability to occasionally negotiate and temporarily postpone ICTY compliance. Nevertheless, their room for manoeuvre with respect to the requests of the Tribunal was relatively small compared to the obstacles they faced at home. In the context of Serbia's fragile transition to democracy, Djindjić and his associates experienced tremendous difficulties in coping with foreign demands for justice.

The experiences of the DOS government set the parameters for Serbia's policy of cooperation with the ICTY. The political and institutional resistance encountered by the Djindjić administration in its initial attempts to comply with the Tribunal's orders led the authorities to adopt an overly cautious approach to this issue. In view of its capacity to foment political polarisation and generate upheaval within the armed forces, the Tribunal was increasingly perceived by the Serbian authorities as a potential threat to political stability and government authority. At

1 'Godišnjica atentata: Bio je brži od vremena' (The Assassination Anniversary: He Was Faster than Time), 11 March 2013.

the same time, the proceedings at the ICTY generated considerable frustration and disappointment within the government. The clear connection between the trial of Milošević and the Bosnian genocide lawsuit at the ICJ raised serious concerns over state interests in the prosecution of former high-ranking officials at the ICTY. The perceived conflation of individual and collective responsibility was not just construed by nationalist elites who sought to exploit the Tribunal for political gains. It was genuinely resented by those policy-makers who were most committed to the pursuit of justice and truth. As a result, Serbia's policy of cooperation with the ICTY in the post-Milošević period was driven by concerns for regime stability and state interests.

Considering its highly divisive and destabilising potential, cooperation with the ICTY required wide political consensus. While this consensus was largely built around the aspiration to join the EU, it was first and foremost premised upon the pacification of the Serbian political scene, which involved closing the book on the legacy of Milošević's rule. This was partly achieved through the adoption of conciliatory methods of compliance with the ICTY. The policy of 'voluntary surrenders' allowed the Serbian authorities to comply with the Tribunal's demands without generating turmoil and without touching upon the delicate issue of responsibility for war crimes. For the most part, however, the pacification of the political scene was accomplished through the rehabilitation of the parties emanating from the former regime and their acceptance as legitimate political partners. The restoration of the SPS through its support for Koštunica's minority government and, especially, its participation in a coalition government with the DS, allowed for the emergence of a consensus on ICTY cooperation for the sake of EU integration. Cooperation with the ICTY was thus premised on 'national reconciliation', which effectively absolved the representatives of the former regime from political responsibility for war crimes.

This paradox shows that, in the Serbian case, externalised justice and democratisation were two separate processes running in parallel. These two processes interacted in an asymmetrical fashion. While externalised justice has at times jeopardised democratisation, its overall impact on political developments on the ground was fairly limited. On the other hand, the arrest and transfer of indictees to the ICTY was very much conditioned upon the transformation of the Serbian political scene and the strengthening of democratic institutions. Rather than being a catalyst for democratisation, externalised justice was made possible by democratic consolidation on the ground. In this context, the outcomes of the policies of conditionality deployed by the US and the EU depended largely on domestic political dynamics. While, on the whole, these policies provided a major impetus for ICTY cooperation, they also generated turmoil and instability at key junctures. The Serbian case supports the view that there is a systemic tension between justice and stability in the early stages of transition, but that this relationship varies in accordance with the degree of democratic consolidation. This observation points to the importance of appreciating political circumstances on the ground when administering justice, rather than attempting to 'rise above politics'.

In view of the potential tensions between international justice and democratic consolidation, there is clearly a case for sequencing transitional justice efforts with domestic regime change processes. Naturally, the general validity of this principle needs to be checked against other instances of international judicial intervention.

The disconnect between the ICTY and Serbian politics was above all reflected in the Tribunal's failure to generate public engagement with the war crimes legacy in the aftermath of Milošević's downfall. The attitudes of the Serbian authorities in this respect ranged from outright denial, through disregard to partial acknowledgment of war crimes. These attitudes were shaped by both personal convictions and political expediency. Bearing in mind his nationalist views, Koštunica's opposition to the ICTY and the concept of transitional justice was hardly surprising. But Djindjić's attitude towards the creation of a truth commission and the disclosure of mass graves revealed a broader reluctance to address the war crimes issue. As in the case of ICTY cooperation, this reluctance to deal with the war crimes legacy at home primarily derived from concerns for political stability. In view of the transitional compromises that allowed for the safeguarding of Milošević-era military and security structures, the Serbian authorities were wary of undertaking any measures that could cause turmoil within the armed forces. Furthermore, they were aware of the fact that the lack of judicial capacity to deal with war crimes could only be compensated by the development of novel institutions, such as the War Crimes Chamber, which required substantial time and money.

The liberally oriented elites grouped around the DS had additional reasons to show scant regard for the war crimes issue. Talking openly about atrocities perpetrated by Serbian forces carried a high political cost in view of the deeply entrenched popular belief that Serbs were victims in the wars of Yugoslav succession and that the ICTY was an anti-Serb conspiracy. Any attempt to publicly denounce Serbian war crimes presented the risk of further exposing the DOS leaders, who had been disparaged as 'foreign henchmen' and 'traitors' during the nineties, to nationalist attacks. Instead of dealing with the past, Djindjić and his entourage deployed a forward-looking political agenda focused on addressing the most pressing socio-economic needs of the population. Their transitional justice policy was limited to cooperation with the ICTY, to which they relegated the delicate task of confronting the Serbian public with the war crimes committed by Serbian forces. But the conduct of the Milošević trial and its potential repercussions on Bosnia's genocide lawsuit against Serbia led the Serbian liberal elites to keep aloof from, and become increasingly distrustful towards, the Tribunal. Although the representatives of the DS and its allies sought to distance themselves from the former regime, they refrained from coming out in public with evidence incriminating it, in order to safeguard what they saw as 'state interests'. The collective nature of the genocide lawsuits before the ICJ undermined the ICTY's attempt at individualising responsibility and foreclosed any discussion on the former regime's responsibility for war crimes.

It is therefore not surprising that the official acknowledgment of the Srebrenica genocide by the authorities in Belgrade was conditioned upon the ICJ's exoneration of the Serbian state from responsibility for genocide. The ICTY was instrumental in prompting this acknowledgment insofar as it provided evidence upon which local human rights NGOs could draw in order to further the transitional justice agenda on the ground. This agenda was to a certain extent endorsed by President Tadić, who had made the improvement of relations with Bosnia and Croatia a priority. Tadić's open condemnation of Serbian war crimes and attendance at the commemorations in Srebrenica and Vukovar marked a significant shift in official attitudes towards the war crimes legacy. But the passing of the parliamentary resolution on Srebrenica in collaboration with the SPS illustrates the extent to which this 'break with the past' was politically expedient and superficial. Instead of reflecting a critical assessment of the Milošević regime's role and involvement in war crimes, the adoption of this resolution was made possible by the pacification of the political scene and the rehabilitation of the political elites associated with the former regime. Just as in the case of ICTY cooperation, the sanctioning of the facts established by the Tribunal was premised upon political forgiveness for past wrongs embodied in the 'national reconciliation' professed by the DS and the SPS.

The Serbian case thus illustrates what Bronwyn Leebaw portrayed as the 'irreconcilable goals' of transitional justice.[2] As Leebaw suggested, the long-term aspirations of transforming inherited values and political relationships by exposing political violence are at odds with the short-term goals of establishing stability and legitimating transitional compromises. In the case of Serbia, such tensions were exacerbated by the fact that transitional justice was enacted by an international tribunal which was detached from the local political context and had little consideration for political circumstances on the ground. While the ICTY sought to discredit the policies and practices associated with the Milošević regime, this, in practice, carried the risk of subverting Serbia's fragile transition to democracy and compromising the Serbian state. This is why even those political elites that were sympathetic to, and supportive of, transitional justice turned their backs on the Tribunal and refrained from openly addressing the war crimes legacy. Whether or not the ICTY could have alleviated these negative effects without jeopardising its integrity remains an open question. The attitudes of the Serbian authorities towards the ICTY were substantially informed by their disappointment and frustration with its performance, particularly with regard to the trial of Milošević. Some of this frustration could surely have been mitigated by more tactful diplomatic and public relations techniques on the part of the Tribunal. On the other hand, paying too much attention to local political concerns could have prejudiced, or even paralysed, the legal process. There is indeed a very thin line between prosecutorial discretion and judicial independence.

Without the endorsement of the Serbian democratic authorities, the prosecution of the former Serbian leadership at the ICTY could not generate any broader reckoning with the criminal policies of the Milošević regime in the aftermath of

2 Bronwyn A. Leebaw, 'The Irreconcilable Goals of Transitional Justice', *Human Rights Quarterly* 30:1 (2008): 95–118.

regime change. The ICTY Prosecution's account of the Yugoslav wars, which held that war crimes were in large part the result of a joint criminal enterprise designed and implemented by Serb political and military leaders, did not take root in Serbia. Instead, the Serbian official narrative portrayed war crimes as sporadic incidents carried out by rogue individuals and paramilitary groups. This narrative was nurtured by nationalist politicians who sought to minimise Serbian responsibility for war crimes. Whether intentionally or not, the war crimes trials held in Serbia reinforced this narrative by focusing on low-ranking perpetrators whose actions were detached from state institutions and government policies. Ultimately, the ICTY itself contributed to this perception of the Yugoslav wars through several controversial decisions, such as the acquittal of the former Yugoslav Army Chief of Staff Momčilo Perišić and that of the former Serbian State Security chiefs Jovica Stanišić and Franko Simatović. By exonerating these former Serbian state officials, the Tribunal left open to question the Milošević regime's responsibility for atrocities perpetrated in Bosnia and Croatia.

In these circumstances, the legacy of the ICTY seems ambivalent. On the one hand, the Tribunal was successful in bringing perpetrators to justice and prompting the Serbian authorities to instigate and institutionalise war crimes prosecutions at home, which is a considerable achievement in itself. On the other hand, the ICTY failed to establish an authoritative account of the Yugoslav conflicts and raise awareness about Serbian responsibility for war crimes. It is uncertain whether the facts established at the ICTY and the domestic war crimes prosecutions will, in the long run, bring about a change in public attitudes towards the war crimes legacy. The positive developments achieved under the Tadić administration in terms of acknowledging Serbian crimes were offset by the change of government in 2012: Serbia's new president, the former SRS – turned SNS – leader Tomislav Nikolić, openly challenged the ICTY's verdict that the Srebrenica massacre constituted genocide. He maintained that this was 'a terrible crime' committed by some individuals in the name of the Serbian nation, for which he sought pardon.[3] In an inflammatory speech given at the UN General Assembly in response to the acquittals of the Croatian generals Gotovina and Markač, Nikolić further denounced the ICTY as an anti-Serb court comparable to the Inquisition. In line with this change in rhetoric, the new Serbian government extended financial support to those indictees who had not surrendered to the ICTY as well as to those who had already been convicted.[4]

This reversal in official attitudes towards the ICTY suggests that, at least in the short run, the legacy of the Tribunal is likely to remain contested and contingent upon political circumstances on the ground. In the long run, however, the evolution of public attitudes towards the war crimes of the nineties will depend on broader societal developments that may or may not be informed by the ICTY's contribution.

---

3 'Serbian President Apologises for Srebrenica "Crime"', *BBC*, 25 April 2013.

4 'Ljajić: Više novca za Srbe u Hagu' (Ljajić: More Money for Serbs in The Hague), *B92*, 18 February 2013.

The record of previous international tribunals is inconclusive in this respect. The Nuremberg trials did little to engender German acknowledgment of the holocaust in the immediate post-war period. While subsequent war crimes trials played a more important role, they were only contributing factors in Germany's gradual reckoning with Nazi crimes, a process that spanned more than three decades.[5] In Japan, on the other hand, negative perceptions of the Tokyo Trials seem to have acted as a continuous impediment to settling the legacy of World War II.[6] The role of international criminal tribunals in shaping memories of traumatic events is therefore a subject that deserves further investigation. I hope this study will stimulate future researchers to undertake this task, with regard to the Balkans and elsewhere.

5 See Alf Ludtke, '"Coming to Terms with the Past": Illusions of Remembering. Ways of Forgetting Nazism in West Germany', *The Journal of Modern History* 65:3 (1993): 542–72; Jeffrey Herf, 'The Emergence and Legacies of Divided Memory: Germany and the Holocaust since 1945' in *Memory and Power in Post-war Europe*, edited by Jan Werner Muller (New York: Cambridge University Press, 2002); Tony Judt, *Postwar: A History of Europe since 1945* (London: Penguin, 2005).

6 Madoka Futamura, *War Crimes Tribunals and Transitional Justice: the Tokyo Trial and the Nuremberg Legacy* (Abingdon: Routledge, 2008).

Bibliography

Primary Sources

Interviews Conducted by the Author

Andrić, Ivan, MP for the LDP and former member of the Parliament's Defence and Security Committee (2001–03); Belgrade, 27 August 2009.

Bilandžić, Vladimir, Special Advisor on Confidence and Security-Building Measures at the OSCE Mission to Serbia; Belgrade, 26 December 2012.

Biserko, Sonja, President of the Helsinki Committee for Human Rights in Serbia; Belgrade, 3 July 2009.

Despotović, Rajka, journalist for *B92*; Belgrade, 1 April 2009.

Dimitrijević, Vojin, Director of the Belgrade Centre for Human Rights; Belgrade, 1 July 2009.

Djerić, Vladimir, former senior legal advisor at the Ministry of Foreign Affairs and representative of the Serbian state before the ICTY and ICJ; Belgrade, 23 July 2009.

Djurišić, Marko, President of the Democratic Party (DS) Executive Board; Belgrade, 11 June 2009.

Draškić, Maja, Professor of Law at the University of Belgrade and judge at the Constitutional Court of the Republic of Serbia; Belgrade, 13 April 2009.

Gojgić, Ljubica, journalist for B92; Belgrade, 18 May 2009.

Grubač, Momčilo, former Yugoslav Minister of Justice and judge at the Yugoslav Constitutional Court (2000–2001); Belgrade, 7 May 2009.

Hadžić, Miroslav, Professor of Global and National Security at the University of Belgrade and Director of the Centre for Civil-Military Relations; Belgrade, 26 August 2008.

Ignjatović, Dušan, Director of the National Council for Cooperation with the ICTY; Belgrade, 10 June 2009.

Jovanović, Ivan, National Legal Advisor on War Crimes at the OSCE Mission in Serbia; Belgrade, 2 July 2009.

Kandić, Nataša, Director of the Humanitarian Law Centre; Belgrade, 12 August 2009.

Korać, Žarko, leader of the Social Democratic Union and former Deputy Prime Minister in the Serbian government (2001–04); Belgrade, 24 April 2009.

Kovačević-Vučo, Biljana, former Director of the Yugoslav Committee for Human Rights (JUKOM); Belgrade, 20 July 2009.

Krasić, Zoran, MP for the SRS and head of the legal team for the defence of Vojislav Šešelj; Belgrade, 2 August 2009.

Labus, Miroljub, former leader of G17 Plus and Deputy Prime Minister in the Yugoslav (2000–2003) and Serbian (2004–06) governments; Belgrade, 8 June 2009.

Liht, Sonja, Director of the Belgrade Fund for Political Excellence; Belgrade, 11 August 2009.

Marković, Žarko, researcher at the Belgrade Centre for Human Rights; Belgrade, 30 December 2010.

Mićunović, Dragoljub, DS executive and former Speaker of the Yugoslav Parliament (2000–2003); Belgrade, 19 August 2009.

Milosavljević, Bogoljub, Professor of Law at Union University in Belgrade; Belgrade, 24 December 2012.

Milošević, Milan, journalist for the weekly *Vreme*; Belgrade, 8 April 2009.

Nicić, Jovan, legal advisor at the National Council for Cooperation with the ICTY; Belgrade, 20 August 2009.

Pajević, Milan, former advisor on Foreign Affairs to Deputy Prime Minister Miroljub Labus (2001–04), 18 June 2004.

Parivodić, Milan, former Serbian Minister of Foreign Economic Relations (2004–07); Belgrade, 27 June 2009.

Pešić, Vesna, former leader of the Civic Alliance of Serbia (GSS) and current MP for the LDP; Belgrade, 5 August 2009.

Petrović, Goran, Head of the Serbian State Security Service (January–November 2001); Belgrade, 28 December 2012.

Petrović, Predrag, Executive Director of the Belgrade Centre for Security Policy; Belgrade, 26 December 2012.

Samardžić, Slobodan, DSS executive, former advisor to President Koštunica and Minister for Kosovo (2007–08); Belgrade, 29 July 2009.

Senić, Vlajko, MP for G17; Belgrade, 17 June 2009.

Shattuck, John, United States Assistant Secretary of State for Democracy, Human Rights and Labour from 1993 to 1998; Budapest, 27 November 2012.

Smajlović, Ljiljana, journalist and President of the Serbian Association of Journalists; Belgrade, 27 June 2009.

Stojković, Zoran, former Serbian Minister of Justice (2004–07); Belgrade, 25 August 2009.

Svilanović, Goran, former leader of the Civic Alliance of Serbia (GSS) and Foreign Minister (2000–2003); Belgrade, 23 May 2009.

Todorović, Dragoljub, lawyer affiliated with the Humanitarian Law Centre; Belgrade, 29 December 2010.

Varady, Tibor, head of the legal team representing Yugoslavia (later Serbia and Montenegro and Serbia) before the ICJ; Budapest, 16 November 2012 and 10 April 2013.

Vasić, Miloš, journalist for the weekly *Vreme*; Belgrade, 26 March 2009.

Vekarić, Bruno, spokesman of the Office of the War Crimes Prosecutor; Belgrade, 26 May 2009.
Vojnović, Ilija, assistant to the Director of the International Republican Institute Programme for Serbia; Belgrade, 28 May 2009.
Vujačić, Ivan, DS executive and former Yugoslav Ambassador to the US; Belgrade, 17 July 2009.
Živković, Zoran, former Federal Minister of the Interior (2000–2003) and Prime Minister of Serbia (2003–04); Belgrade, 7 May 2009.

Newspapers, Periodicals, and Electronic Media

B92
Balkan
BBC
Blic
Borba
Danas
Deutsche Welle
Dnevnik
Ekspres
Evropa
Glas Javnosti
Građanski list
Guardian
IWPR
Kurir
Los Angeles Times
Nacional
Nedeljni Telegraf
NIN
Politika
Press
Radio Free Europe
Večernje Novosti
Vreme

Official Documents, NGO Reports and Public Opinion Polls

Belgrade Centre for Human Rights and SMMRI, 'Public Opinion in Serbia: Attitudes towards the International Criminal Tribunal for the former Yugoslavia (ICTY)', Belgrade, July 2003. Retrieved from www.bgcentar.org.rs on 7 March 2010.

Belgrade Centre for Human Rights and Strategic Marketing Research, 'Public Opinion in Serbia: Attitudes towards the ICTY', Belgrade, August 2004. Retrieved from www.bgcentar.org.rs on 7 March 2010.

Belgrade Centre for Human Rights and Strategic Marketing Research, 'Public Opinion in Serbia: Attitudes towards the ICTY', Belgrade, April 2005. Retrieved from www.bgcentar.org.rs on 7 March 2010.

Belgrade Centre for Human Rights, 'Monitoring and Reporting on Activities of Judicial Institutions in Serbia in the Field of Organised Crime, War Crimes, Discrimination and Domestic Violence', Belgrade, 2008.

Belgrade Centre for Human Rights, OSCE Mission to Serbia, and Strategic Marketing Research, 'Views on War Crimes, the ICTY, and the National War Crimes Judiciary', Belgrade, April 2009. Retrieved from www.bgcentar.org.rs on 7 March 2010.

Centre for Free Elections and Democracy (CeSID), 'Guide through Electoral Controversies in Serbia', Belgrade, July 2000.

Commission of the European Communities, 'Serbia 2008 Progress Report', Brussels, 2008.

Democratic Party and Socialist Party of Serbia, 'Deklaracija o pomirenju' (Declaration of Reconciliation). Retrieved from http://b92.net/info/dokumenti/ on 9 June 2009.

Helsinki Committee for Human Rights in Serbia, 'Human Rights, Democracy and Violence – Annual Report 2008', Belgrade, 2009.

Human Rights Watch, 'Unfinished Business: The War Crimes Chamber in Serbia', 2007.

Human Rights Watch, 'World Report 2010: Serbia', January 2011.

Humanitarian Law Centre, 'Report on Transitional Justice in Serbia, Montenegro and Kosovo 1999–2005', Belgrade, 2006.

Humanitarian Law Centre, 'Sudjenje za ratne zločine u Srbiji' (War Crimes Trials in Serbia), Belgrade, 2007.

Humanitarian Law Centre, 'War Crimes Trials in Serbia', Transitional Justice Bulletin 1, 2007.

Humanitarian Law Centre, 'Trials for War Crimes and Ethnically and Politically Motivated Crimes in Post-Yugoslav Countries', Belgrade, 2008.

Humanitarian Law Centre, 'Irregularities and Abuse of Power in War Crimes Proceedings in the Republic of Serbia', Belgrade, 2011.

International Court of Justice, *Application of the Convention on the Prevention and Punishment of the Crime of Genocide* (Bosnia and Herzegovina v. Serbia and Montenegro), Judgment of 26 February 2007, The Hague. Retrieved from http://www.icj-cij.org/icjwwwidocket/ibhyframe.htm on 20 January 2011.

International Criminal Tribunal for the former Yugoslavia, 'Rules of Procedure and Evidence', IT/32/Rev.45, 8 December 2010. Retrieved from www.icty.org on 11 April 2011.

International Crisis Group, 'Serbia's New Constitution: Democracy Going Backwards', Policy Briefing no. 44, November 2006. Accessed on www.crisisgroup.org on 20 January 2011.

International Crisis Group, 'Serbia's New Government: Turning From Europe', 31 May 2007. Accessed on www.crisisgroup.org on 20 January 2011.

Ivanišević, Bogdan. 'Against the Current – War Crimes Prosecutions in Serbia'. International Centre for Transitional Justice, 2007.

Kandić, Nataša, ed. *Škorpioni*: *Od zločina do pravde* (Scorpions: From Crime to Justice). Belgrade: Humanitarian Law Centre, 2008.

National Assembly of the Republic of Serbia. 'Deklaracija Narodne Skupštine Srbije o osudi zločina u Srebrenici' (Declaration of the National Assembly of Serbia Condemning the Crime in Srebrenica). Belgrade, March 2010.

National Assembly of the Republic of Serbia, 6th Session of the 1st Parliamentary Sitting, 30 March 2004, 235–40.

National Assembly of the Republic of Serbia, 9th Parliamentary Sitting, 27 June 2003, 234–35.

Office of the Prosecutor of the ICTY. 'Address by the Prosecutor of the International Criminal Tribunals for the Former Yugoslavia and Rwanda, Mrs Carla Del Ponte, to the United Nations Security Council'. The Hague, 30 October 2002. Accessed on www.icty.org/sid/8056 on 9 November 2010.

Organisation for Security and Cooperation in Europe (OSCE). 'Kosovo's War Crimes Trials: An Assessment Ten Years On'. Pristina, May 2010. Retrieved from www.osce.org/kosovo/68569 on 30 July 2009.

Organisation for Security and Cooperation in Europe (OSCE). 'Law on Organisation and Competence of Government Authorities in War Crimes Proceedings'. Belgrade, 2005. Retrieved from www.osce.org/serbia/18571 on 15 April 2011.

Prosecutor v. Krstić, 'Case Information Sheet', Case No. IT-98-33. Accessed on www.icty.org on 2 November 2010.

Prosecutor v. Milošević, 'Case Information Sheet', Case No. IT-02-54. Accessed on www. icty.org on 20 January 2011.

Prosecutor v. Šainović et al., 'Case Information Sheet', Case No. IT-08-87. Accessed on www.icty.org on 6 March 2011.

Prosecutor v. Vladimir Kovačević, 'Case Information Sheet', Case No. IT-01-42/2-1. Accessed on www.icty.org on 10 March 2011.

Sebastian, Sofia. 'Serbia's 2008 Parliamentary Elections: Domestic and Regional Dilemmas'. FRIDE, 28 April 2008. Accessed on www.fride.org on 20 May 2011.

Strategic Marketing & Media Research Institute (SMMRI). 'Gledanost direktnih prenosa sudjenja Slobodanu Miloševiću u Hagu' (TV Ratings of the Live Broadcasting of the Trial of Slobodan Milošević in The Hague). Belgrade, 2002.

The Government of the Republic of Serbia v. Ejup Ganić, City of Westminster Magistrates' Court, 27th July 2010. Retrieved from www.crimesofwar.org on 20 January 2011.

United States Institute for Peace. 'Truth and Reconciliation Commission for Serbia and Montenegro: Presidential Decree, March 30, 2001'. USIP Library, posted on 5 May 2009. Retrieved from www.usip.org on 20 August 2010.

Vekarić, Bruno and Jasna Šarčević-Janković. 'Fifth Year Monograph of the Office of War Crimes Prosecutor of the Republic of Serbia'. Office of the War Crimes Prosecutor of the Republic of Serbia, 2008.

Public Speeches, Memoirs and Other Publications

Del Ponte, Carla and Chuck Sudetić. *Gospodja Tužiteljka: Suočavanje s najtežim ratnim zločinima i kulturom nekažnjivosti* (Madame Prosecutor: Confrontations with Humanity's Worst Criminals and the Culture of Impunity). Belgrade: Profil knjiga, 2008.

Djindjić, Zoran. 'Adrenalin za promene' (Adrenaline for Change). *Nova srpska politička misao*, special issue 1(2001): 87–94.

Djindjić, Zoran. Speech given at the conference 'In Search of Truth and Responsibility – Towards a Democratic Future' in Belgrade on 19 May 2001. Accessed on http://www.b92.net/trr/2001/diskusija/diskutanti_hronoloski.php on 19 August 2010 on 19 August 2010.

Koštunica, Vojislav. 'Pravna država i prav(n)i reformizam' (The Legal State and Legal (Real) Reformism). Nova srpska politička misao, special issue 1(2001): 147–56.

Mihajlović, Dušan. Povlenske magle i vidici (The Fog and Views of the Povlen). Belgrade: NEA, 2005.

Pejić, Jelena. Speech given at the conference 'In Search of Truth and Responsibility – Towards a Democratic Future' in Belgrade on 19 May 2001. Accessed on http://www.b92.net/trr/2001/diskusija/index.php?lang=srpski&nav_id=51231 on 19 August 2010.

Smajlović, Ljiljana. 'The View from Belgrade'. Paper presented at the conference 'The Milošević Trial: An Autopsy' at Indiana University on 19 February 2010. Retrieved from www.law.indiana.edu on 22 April 2010.

Svilanović, Goran. Speech given at the conference 'In Search of Truth and Responsibility – Towards a Democratic Future' in Belgrade on 19 May 2001. Accessed on www.b92.net/trr/2001/diskusija/index.php?lang=srpski&nav_id=42427 on 19 August 2010.

Secondary Sources

Books and Articles

Adlana, Raquel. 'A Victim-Centred Reflection on Truth Commissions and Prosecutions as a Response to Mass Atrocities'. *Journal of Human Right* 5:1 (2006): 107–26.

Akhavan, Payam. 'Punishing War Crimes in the Former Yugoslavia: A Critical Juncture for the New World Order'. *Human Rights Quarterly* 15:2 (1993): 262–89.

Akhavan, Payam. 'Justice in The Hague, Peace in the Former Yugoslavia? A Commentary on the United Nations War Crimes Tribunal'. *Human Rights Quarterly* 20:4 (1998): 737–816.

Anonymous. 'Human Rights in Peace Negotiations'. *Human Rights Quarterly* 18:2 (1996): 249–58.

Armstrong, James D., Theo Farrell, and Helene Lambert. *International Law and International Relations.* Cambridge: Cambridge University Press, 2007.

Arthur, Paige. 'How "Transitions" Reshaped Human Rights: A Conceptual History of Transitional Justice'. *Human Rights Quarterly* 31:2 (2009): 321–67.

Barahona de Brito, Alexandra. *Human Rights and Democratisation in Latin America: Uruguay and Chile.* Oxford: Oxford University Press, 1997.

Barahona de Brito, Alexandra, Carmen Gonzales Enriquez, and Paloma Aguilar, eds. *The Politics of Memory: Transitional Justice in Democratising Societies.* New York: Oxford University Press, 2001.

Barkan, Elazar. *The Guilt of Nations: Restitution and Negotiating Historical Injustices*. New York and London: Norton, 2000.

Barker, J. Craig. *International Law and International Relations.* New York and London: Continuum, 2000.

Bar-Tal, Daniel. 'From Intractable Conflict Through Conflict Resolution to Reconciliation: Psychological Analysis'. *Political Psychology* 21:2 (2000): 351–65.

Bass, Gary J. *Stay the Hand of Vengeance: The Politics of War Crimes Tribunals.* Princeton and Oxford: Princeton University Press, 2000.

Beissinger, Mark. 'Structure and Example in Modular Political Phenomena: The Diffusion of Bulldozer/Rose/Orange/Tulip Revolutions'. *Perspectives on Politics* 5:2 (2007): 259–76.

Bell, Christine. 'Transitional Justice, Interdisciplinarity and the State of the "Field" or "Non-Field"'. *International Journal of Transitional Justice* 3:1 (2009): 5–27.

Bieber, Florian. 'The Serbian Opposition and Civil Society: Roots of the Delayed Transition in Serbia'. *International Journal of Politics, Culture, and Society* 17:1 (2003): 73–90.

Bieber, Florian. 'Kosovo, Serbia and Bosnia: After the ICJ'. *openDemocracy*, 28 July 2010. Accessed on www.opendemocracy.net on 20 May 2011.

Bilić, Bojan. *We Were Gasping for Air: [Post-]Yugoslav Anti-War Activism and Its Legacy*. Baden-Baden: Nomos, 2012.

Biserko, Sonja. 'Zoran Djindjić i Haški tribunal' (Zoran Djindjić and the Hague Tribunal), in *Zoran Djindjić: Etika Odgovornosti* (Zoran Djindjić: The Ethics of Responsibility) edited by Latinka Perović, 223–48. Belgrade: Helsinki Committee for Human Rights, 2006.

Blakesley, Christopher. 'Atrocity and Its Prosecution: The Ad Hoc Tribunals for the Former Yugoslavia', in *The Law of War Crimes: National and International Approaches*, edited by Tim McCormack and Gerry J. Simpson, 189–228. The Hague: Kluwer, 1997.

Bakić, Jovo. 'Extreme-Right Ideology, Practice and Supporters: Case Study of the Serbian Radical Party'. *Journal of Contemporary European Studies* 17:2 (2009): 193–207.

Boas, Gideon. *The Milošević Trial: Lessons for the Conduct of Complex Criminal Proceedings.* Cambridge: Cambridge University Press, 2007.

Borneman, John. 'Reconciliation after Ethnic Cleansing: Listening, Retribution, Affiliation'. *Public Culture* 14:2 (2002): 281–304.

Bujošević, Dragan and Ivan Radovanović. *The Fall of Milošević: The October 5th Revolution.* New York and Basingstoke: Palgrave MacMillan, 2003.

Bunce, Valerie and Sharon Wolchik. 'Defining and Domesticating the Electoral Model: A Comparison of Slovakia and Serbia', in *Democracy and Authoritarianism in the Post-communist World*, edited by Valerie Bunce, Michael McFaul, and Kathryn Stoner-Weiss, 134–54. Cambridge: Cambridge University Press, 2009.

Carothers, Thomas. 'Ousting Foreign Strongmen: Lessons from Serbia'. *Carnegie Endowment Policy Brief* 1:5 (2001): 1–7.

Carothers, Thomas. 'The End of the Transition Paradigm'. *Journal of Democracy* 13:1 (2002): 5–21.

Chandler, David. *From Kosovo to Kabul and Beyond: Human Rights and International Intervention.* London: Pluto Press, 2005.

Clark, Janine N. 'The Death of Milošević: Exploring Public Reaction in Serbia'. *Southeast European and Black Sea Studies* 7:4 (2007): 591–608.

Cohen, Lenard J. *Serpent in the Bosom: The Rise and Fall of Slobodan Milošević.* Oxford: Westview Press, 2002.

Collier, Ruth B. and James Mahoney. 'Adding Collective Actors to Collective Outcomes: Labour and Recent Democratisation in South America and Southern Europe'. *Comparative Politics* 29:3 (1997): 285–303.

Cvijić, Srdjan. '"Blocked political system": Serbia 2000–2008'. *Balkanologie* 11, nos 1–2 (2008). Accessed on http://balkanologie.revues.org/index1293.html on 12 May 2011.

Davis, Madeleine. 'Externalised Justice and Democratisation: Lessons from the Pinochet Case'. *Political Studies* 54:2 (2006): 245–66.

Dimitrijević, Nenad. 'Serbia After the Criminal Past: What Went Wrong and What Should be Done'. *International Journal of Transitional Justice* 2:1 (2008): 5–22.

Dimitrijević, Vojin. 'Izgledi za utvrdjivanje istine i postizanje pomirenja u Srbiji' (Prospects for Establishing the Truth and Achieving Reconciliation in Serbia). *Reč* 62:8 (2001): 69–74.

Dimitrijević, Vojin. 'Kako ubediti javnost' (How to Convince the Public). *Pravda u Tranziciji* 1, (2005). Accessed on www.pravdautranziciji.com/pages/article.php?id=38 on 27 October 2010.

Dimitrijević, Vojin and Marko Milanović. 'The Strange Story of the Bosnian Genocide Case'. *Leiden Journal of International Law* 21:1 (2008): 65–94.

Dinkić, Mladjan. *Ekonomija Destrukcije* (An Economy of Destruction). Belgrade: Stubovi Kulture, 1995.

Doorenspleet, Renske. 'The Structural Context of Recent Transitions to Democracy'. *European Journal of Political Research* 43:3 (2004): 309–35.

Dragović-Soso, Jasna. *Saviours of the Nation: Serbia's Intellectual Opposition and the Revival of Nationalism.* London: Hurst and Montreal: McGill–Queen's University Press, 2002.

Dragović-Soso, Jasna. 'The Impact of International Intervention on Domestic Political Outcomes: Western Coercive Policies and the Milošević Regime'. In *International Intervention in the Balkans since 1995*, edited by Peter Siani-Davies, 120–35. London and New York: Routledge, 2003.

Dragović-Soso, Jasna and Eric D. Gordy. 'Transitional Justice and Reconciliation in the Former Yugoslavia', in *New Perspectives on Yugoslavia*, edited by Dejan Djokić and James Ker-Lindsay 193–212. London: Routledge, 2010.

Dragović-Soso, Jasna. 'Apologising for Srebrenica: The Declaration of the Serbian Parliament, the European Union, and the Politics of Compromise'. *East European Politics* 28:3 (2012): 163–79.

Dragović-Soso, Jasna. 'The Parting of Ways: Public Reckoning with the Recent Past in Post-Milošević Serbia'. In *The Milošević Trial – An Autopsy*, edited by Tim Waters. New York: Oxford University Press, 2013.

Edmunds, Timothy. 'Intelligence Agencies and Democratisation: Continuity and Change in Serbia after Milošević'. *Europe-Asia Studies* 60:1 (2008): 25–48.

Edmunds, Timothy. 'Adapting to Democracy: Reflections on "Transition" in Serbia and the Western Balkans'. *Western Balkans Security Observer* 7–8 (2008): 4–9.

Elster, Jon. *Closing the Books: Transitional Justice in Historical Perspective.* New York and Cambridge: Cambridge University Press, 2004.

Falk, Richard. 'Accountability for War Crimes and the Legacy of Nuremberg', in *War Crimes and Collective Wrongdoing: A Reader*, edited by Aleksandar Jokić, 113–36. Oxford: Blackwell Publishing, 2001.

Fisher, Sharon. *Political Change in Post-Communist Slovakia and Croatia: from Nationalist to Europeanist.* New York: Palgrave Macmillan, 2006.

Fletcher, Laurel E., and Harvey Weinstein with Jamie Rowen. 'Context, Timing and the Dynamics of Transitional Justice: A Historical Perspective'. *Human Rights Quarterly* 31:1 (2009): 163–220.

Frei, Norbert. *Adenauer's Germany and the Nazi Past: The Politics of Amnesty and Integration.* New York: Columbia University Press, 2002.

Futamura, Madoka. *War Crimes Tribunals and Transitional Justice: the Tokyo Trial and the Nuremberg Legacy*. Abingdon: Routledge, 2008.

Goati, Vladimir. 'Partije Srbije od 1990 do 2002 u komparativnoj perspektivi' (Parties in Serbia from 1990 to 2002 in Comparative Perspective). In *Partijska scena Srbije posle 5 Oktobra 2000* (The Party Scene in Serbia after 5 October 2000), edited by Vladimir Goati, 9–45. Belgrade: Friedrich Ebert Stiftung and Institute of Social Sciences, 2002.

Goati, Vladimir. *Partijske borbe u Srbiji u postoktobarskom razdoblju* (Party Struggles in Serbia in the Post-October Period). Belgrade: Friedrich Ebert Stiftung and Institute of Social Sciences, 2006.

Goldstone, Richard J. and Rebecca J.Hamilton. 'Bosnia v. Serbia: Lessons from the Encounter of the International Court of Justice with the International Criminal Tribunal for the Former Yugoslavia'. *Leiden Journal of International Law* 21:1 (2008): 95–112.

Golob, Stephanie R. '"Forced to Be Free": Globalised Justice, Pacted Democracy, and the Pinochet Case'. *Democratisation* 9:2 (2002): 21–42.

Gonzales-Enriquez, Carmen. 'Decommunisation and Political Justice in Central and Eastern Europe', in *The Politics of Memory: Transitional Justice in Democratising Societies*, edited by Alexandra Barahona de Brito, Carmen Gonzales Enriquez, and Paloma Aguilar, 218–47. New York: Oxford University Press, 2001.

Gordy, Eric D. *The Culture of Power in Serbia: Nationalism and the Destruction of Alternatives.* Pennsylvania: Penn State Press, 1999.

Gordy, Eric D. 'Serbia's Bulldozer Revolution: Conditions and Prospects'. *Southeast European Politics* 1:2 (2000): 78–89.

Gordy, Eric D. 'Accounting for a Violent Past by Other than Legal Means'. *Southeast European and Black Sea Studies* 3:1 (2003): 1–24.

Gordy, Eric D. 'Rating the Sloba Show: Will Justice Be Served?' *Problems of Post-Communism* 50:3 (2003): 53–63.

Gordy, Eric D. 'Serbia after Djindjić: War Crimes, Organized Crime, and Trust in Institutions'. *Problems of Post-Communism* 51:3 (2004): 10–17.

Gordy, Eric D. 'Postwar Guilt and Responsibility in Serbia: The Effort to Confront It and the Effort to Avoid It', in *Serbia since 1989: Politics and Society under Milošević and After*, edited by Sabrina P. Ramet and Vjeran Pavlaković, 166–91. Seattle and London: University of Washington Press, 2005.

Gordy, Eric D. 'Confronting the Past in Serbia: Obstacles and Opportunities', in *Serbia Matters: Domestic Reforms and European Integration*, edited by Wolfgang Petritsch, Goran Svilanović and Eric Solioz, 137–41. Baden-Baden: Nomos, 2009.

Gordy, Eric D. 'Serbia's Kosovo Claim: Much Ado About…' *openDemocracy*, 2 October 2007. Accessed on www.opendemocracy.net on 20 May 2011.

Gordy, Eric D. 'Serbia Chooses a Future, Just'. *openDemocracy*, 5 February 2008. Accessed on www.opendemocracy.net on 20 May 2011.

Gordy, Eric D. *Guilt, Responsibility and Denial: The Past at Stake in Post-Milošević Serbia.* Philadelphia: University of Pennsylvania Press, 2013.

Hadžić, Miroslav. 'Izvorni Razlozi za Reformu' (The Genuine Reasons for Reform), in *Reforma vojske – Iskustva i izazovi* (Reform of the Army – Experiences and Challenges), edited by Miroslav Hadžić, 112–17. Belgrade: CCMR, 2003.

Hadžić, Miroslav. 'Dometi Reforme Sektora Bezbednosti u Srbiji' (The Scope of Reforms of the Security Sector in Serbia), in *Reforma sektora bezbednosti u Srbiji: dostignuća i perspective* (Reform of the Security Sector in Serbia: Achievements and Perspectives), edited by Miroslav Hadžić, 13–18. Belgrade: CCMR, 2007.

Haggard, Stephan and Robert R. Kaufman. 'The Political Economy of Democratic Transitions'. *Comparative Politics* 29:3 (1997): 263–83.

Hartmann, Florence. *Paix et châtiment* (Peace and Punishment). Paris: Flammarion, 2007.

Hartmann, Florence. 'Vital Genocide Documents Concealed'. Bosnian Institute, London, 2008.

Hayden, Robert M. 'Recounting the Dead. The Rediscovery and Redefinition of Wartime Massacres in Late- and Post-Communist Yugoslavia', in *Memory, History, and Opposition under State Socialism*, edited by Ruby S. Watson, (1994): 167–84 (Santa Fe: School of American Research Press, 1994).

Hayden, Robert M. 'Justice Presumed and Assistance Denied: The Yugoslav Tribunal as Obstruction to Economic Recovery'. *International Journal for the Semiotics of Law* 19:4 (2006): 389–408.

Hayden, Robert M. 'What's Reconciliation Got to do With It? The International Criminal Tribunal for the Former Yugoslavia (ICTY) as Antiwar Profiteer'. *Journal of Intervention and Statebuilding* 5:3 (2011): 313–30.

Hayner, Priscilla. *Unspeakable Truths: Confronting State Terror and Atrocity*. New York: Routledge, 2000.

Heer, Hannes et al., eds. *The Discursive Construction of History: Remembering the Wehrmacht's War of Annihilation*. Hampshire and New York: Palgrave Macmillan, 2008.

Herf, Jeffrey. 'The Emergence and Legacies of Divided Memory: Germany and the Holocaust since 1945', in *Memory and Power in Post-War Europe*, edited by Jan Werner Muller, 184–205. Cambridge: Cambridge University Press, 2002.

Hesse, Carla and Robert Post. *Human Rights in Political Transitions: Gettysburg to Bosnia*. New York: Zone Books, 1999.

Huntington, Samuel P. *The Third Wave: Democratisation in the Late Twentieth Century*. University of Oklahoma Press, 1991.

Humphrey, Michael. *The Politics of Atrocity and Reconciliation: From Terror to Trauma*. London: Routledge, 2002.

Huyse, Luc. 'Justice After Transition: On the Choices Successor Elites Make in Dealing with the Past'. *Law and Social Inquiry* 20:1 (1995): 52–78.

Ilić, Dejan. 'Jugoslovenska Komisija za Istinu i Pomirenje 2001-' (The Yugoslav Commission for Truth and Reconciliation, 2001- ?). *Reč* 73, no.19 (2005): 53–79.

Ilić, Vladimir. 'Tribunal u Hagu iz perspective Srbijanskog posrtaja pred globalizacijom' (The Hague Tribunal from the Perspective of Serbia's Staggering towards Globalisation). In *Haški Tribunal: Naš nesporazum sa svetom* (The Hague Tribunal: Our Disagreement with the World), edited by Milivoj Despot and Vladimir Ilić, 73–115. Belgrade: Helsinki Committee for Human Rights, 2001.

Jović, Dejan. *Yugoslavia: A State that Withered Away*. Indiana: Purdue University Press, 2009.

Jović, Dejan. 'Croatia after Tudjman: the ICTY and Issues of Transitional Justice'. *Chaillot Paper* 116 (2009): 13–28.

Judt, Tony. *Postwar: A History of Europe since 1945.* London: Heinemann, 2005.

Kaldor, Mary and Ivan Vejvoda. *Democratisation in Central and Eastern Europe.* London: Pinter, 1999.

Ker-Lindsay, James. *Kosovo: The Path to Contested Statehood in the Balkans.* New York: Palgrave Macmillan, 2009.

Ker-Lindsay, James. 'From Autonomy to Independence: The Evolution of International Thinking on Kosovo, 1998-2005'. *Journal of Balkan and Near Eastern Studies* 11:2 (2009): 141–56.

Kerr, Rachel. 'International Judicial Intervention: The International Criminal Tribunal for the Former Yugoslavia'. *International Relations* 15:2 (2000): 17–26.

Kerr, Rachel. *The International Criminal Tribunal for the Former Yugoslavia.* Oxford: Oxford University Press, 2004.

Kerr, Rachel. 'The Road from Dayton to Brussels? The International Criminal Tribunal for the Former Yugoslavia and the Politics of War Crimes in Bosnia'. *European Security* 14:3 (2005): 319–37.

Kerr, Rachel and Eirin Mobekk. *Peace and Justice: Seeking Accountability after War.* Cambridge: Polity Press, 2007.

Kesić, Obrad. 'An Airplane with Eighteen Pilots: Serbia after Milošević'. In *Serbia since 1989: Politics and Society under Milošević and After*, edited by Sabrina P. Ramet and Vjeran Pavlaković, 95–121. Seattle and London: University of Washington Press, 2005.

Klarin, Mirko. 'The Impact of the ICTY Trials on Public Opinion in the Former Yugoslavia'. *Journal of International Criminal Justice* 7:1 (2009): 89–96.

Krastev, Ivan. 'The Balkans: Democracy without Choices'. *Journal of Democracy* 13:3 (2002): 39–53.

Kritz, Neil J. *Transitional Justice: How Emerging Democracies Reckon with Former Regimes, Vol. I-IV.* Washington: United States Institute of Peace, 1995.

Krnjević-Mišković, Damjan. 'Serbia's Prudent Revolution'. *Journal of Democracy* 12:3 (2001): 96–110.

Lamont, Christopher K. *International Criminal Justice and the Politics of Compliance.* Farnham: Ashgate, 2010.

Lawson, George. *Negotiated Revolutions: The Czech Republic, South Africa and Chile.* Aldershot: Ashgate, 2005.

Lazić, Mladen. 'Serbia: The Adaptive Reconstruction of Elites'. In *Elites after State Socialism: Theories and Analysis*, edited by John Higley and Gyorgy Lengyel, 123–40. Lanham, MD: Rowman & Littlefield, 2000.

Lazić, Mladen. *Promene i Otpori* ('Changes and Resistance'). Belgrade: Filip Višnjić, 2005.

Lazić, Mladen. 'Nacrt za istraživanje savremenih društvenih promena u Srbiji' (Framework for the Study of Contemporary Social Changes in Serbia). In *Konsolidacija demokratskih ustanova u Srbiji: Godinu dana posle* (Consolidation of Democratic Institutions in Serbia: A Year Later), edited by Dušan Pavlović, 13–37. Belgrade: Službeni Glasnik, 2008.

Leebaw, Bronwyn A. 'The Irreconcilable Goals of Transitional Justice'. *Human Rights Quarterly* 30:1 (2008): 95–118.

Lindsey, Rose. 'Remembering Vukovar, Forgetting Vukovar: Constructing National Identity through the Memory of Catastrophe in Croatia', in *The Memory of Catastrophe*, edited by Peter Gray and Kendrick Oliver, 190–204. Manchester and New York: Manchester University Press, 2004.

Linz, Juan J. and Alfred C. Stepan. *Problems of Democratic Transition and Consolidation: Southern Europe, South America, and Post-Communist Europe.* Baltimore and London: The Johns Hopkins University Press, 1996.

Lipset, Seymour M. 'Some Social Requisites of Democracy: Economic Development and Political Legitimacy'. *American Political Science Review* 53 (1959): 69–105.

Logar, Svetlana and Srdjan Bogosavljević. 'Vidjenje istine u Srbiji' (The Perception of Truth in Serbia). *Reč* 62:8 (2001): 5–34.

Ludtke, Alf. '"Coming to Terms with the Past": Illusions of Remembering, Ways of Forgetting Nazism in West Germany'. *The Journal of Modern History* 65:3 (1993): 542–72.

Lukić, Reneo. 'From the Federal Republic of Yugoslavia to the Union of Serbia and Montenegro', in *Serbia since 1989: Politics and Society under Milošević and After*, edited by Sabrina P. Ramet and Vjeran Pavlaković, 55–94. Seattle and London: University of Washington Press, 2005.

Lutz, Ellen. 'Transitional Justice: Lessons Learned and the Road Ahead'. In *Transitional Justice in the Twenty-First Century: Beyond Truth versus Justice*, edited by Naomi Roht-Arriaza and Javier Mariezcurrena, 325–41. Cambridge: Cambridge University Press, 2006.

Macedo, Stephen, ed. *Universal Jurisdiction: National Courts and the Prosecution of Serious Crimes under International Law.* Philadelphia: University of Pennsylvania Press, 2004.

Malamud-Goti, Jaime. 'Transitional Governments in the Breach: Why Punish State Criminals?' In *Transitional Justice: How Emerging Democracies Reckon with Former Regimes, Vol. I*, edited by Neil J. Kritz 189–202. Washington: United States Institute of Peace, 1995.

Malamud-Goti, Jaime. *Game without an End: State Terror and the Politics of Justice.* Norman, London: University of Oklahoma Press, 1996.

Masson, Diane. *L'utilisation de la guerre dans la construction des systèmes politiques en Serbie et en Croatie, 1989–1995* (How War Was Used in the Construction of the Political Systems in Serbia and Croatia, 1989–1995). Paris : L'Harmattan, 2002.

McMahon, Patrice C. and David P. Forsythe. 'The ICTY's Impact on Serbia: Judicial Romanticism Meets Network Politics'. *Human Rights Quarterly* 30:2 (2008): 412–35.

McMahon, Patrice C. and Jennifer L. Miller. 'From Adjudication to Aftermath: Assessing the ICTY's Goals beyond Prosecution'. *Human Rights Review* 13:4 (2012): 421–42.

Mendeloff, David. 'Truth-Seeking, Truth-Telling, and Post-Conflict Peacebuilding: Curb the Enthusiasm?' *International Studies Review* 6:3 (2004): 355–80.

Meron, Theodor. 'The Case for War Crimes Trials in Yugoslavia'. *Foreign Affairs* 72:3 (1993): 122–35.

Milanović, Marko. 'State Responsibility for Genocide: A Follow-Up'. *The European Journal of International Law* 18:4 (2007): 669–94.

Minow, Martha L. *Between Vengeance and Forgiveness: Facing History after Genocide and Mass Violence*. Boston: Beacon Press, 1998.

Morrison, Kenneth. *Montenegro: A Modern History.* London and New York: I.B Tauris, 2009.

Munck, Gerardo L., and Carol S. Leff. 'Modes of Transition and Democratisation: South America and Eastern Europe in Comparative Perspective'. *Comparative Politics* 29:3 (1997): 343–62.

Nakarada, Radmila. *Raspad Jugoslavije: Problemi tumačenja, suočavanja i tranzicije* (The Fall of Yugoslavia: Problems of Interpretation, Reckoning and Transition). Belgrade: Službeni Glasnik, 2008.

Naumović, Slobodan. 'Otpor! et la "révolution électorale" en Serbie' (Otpor! and the 'Electoral Revolution' in Serbia). *Socio-anthropologie* 23/24 (2009): 41–73.

Neier, Aryeh. 'What Should Be Done about the Guilty?' In *Transitional Justice: How Emerging Democracies Reckon with Former Regimes, Vol. I*, edited by Neil J. Kritz, 172–83. Washington: United States Institute of Peace, 1995.

Neier, Aryeh. *War Crimes: Brutality, Genocide, Terror and the Struggle for Justice.* New York: Times Books, 1998.

Neier, Aryeh. 'Rethinking Truth, Justice and Guilt after Bosnia and Rwanda'. In *Human Rights in Political Transitions: Gettysburg to Bosnia*, edited by Carla Hesse and Robert Post, 39–52. New York: Zone Books, 1999.

Nettelfield, Lara J. *Courting Democracy in Bosnia and Herzegovina.* New York: Cambridge University Press, 2010.

Nino, Carlos S. 'The Duty to Punish Past Abuses of Human Rights Put into Context: The Case of Argentina'. In *Transitional Justice: How Emerging Democracies Reckon with Former Regimes, Vol. I*, edited by Neil J. Kritz, 417–36. Washington: United States Institute of Peace, 1995.

Nino, Carlos S. *Radical Evil on Trial.* New Heaven: Yale University Press, 1996.

Obradović-Wochnik, Jelena. 'Knowledge, Acknowledgment and Denial in Serbia's Responses to the Srebrenica Massacre'. *Journal of Contemporary European Studies* 17:1 (2009): 61–74.

Obradović-Wochnik, Jelena. *Ethnic Conflict and War Crimes in the Balkans*. London: IB Tauris, 2013.

O'Donnell, Guillermo, Phillip C. Schmitter, and Laurence Whitehead. *Transitions from Authoritarian Rule: Tentative Conclusions about Uncertain Democracies*. Baltimore and London: The Johns Hopkins University Press, 1986.

O'Donnell, Guillermo. 'Illusions about Consolidation'. *Journal of Democracy* 7:2 (1996): 34–51.

Offe, Claus. 'Capitalism by Democratic Design? Democratic Theory Facing the Triple Transition in Eastern Europe'. *Social Research* 58:4 (1991): 865–92.

Opotow, Susan. 'Reconciliation in Times of Impunity: Challenges for Social Justice'. *Social Justice Research* 14:2 (2001): 149–70.

Orentlicher, Diane F. 'Settling Accounts: The Duty to Prosecute Human Rights Violations of a Prior Regime'. In *Transitional Justice: How Emerging Democracies Reckon with Former Regimes, Vol. I*, edited by Neil J. Kritz, 375–416. Washington: United States Institute of Peace, 1995.

Orentlicher, Diane F. '"Settling Accounts" Revisited: Reconciling Global Norms with Local Agency'. *The International Journal for Transitional Justice* 1:1 (2007): 10–22.

Orentlicher, Diane F. 'Shrinking the Space for Denial: The Impact of the ICTY in Serbia'. Open Society Justice Initiative Report, May 2008.

Osiel, Mark. *Mass Atrocity, Collective Memory, and the Law*. New Brunswick, New Jersey: Transaction Publishers, 1997.

Ostojić, Mladen. 'Facing the Past While Disregarding the Present? Human Rights NGOs and Truth-Telling in Post-Milošević Serbia'. In *Civil Society and Transitions in the Western Balkans*, edited by Vesna Bojičić-Dželilović, James Ker-Lindsay and Denisa Kostovicova, 230–47. Basingstoke: Palgrave MacMillan, 2013.

Pavlaković, Vjeran. 'Serbia Transformed? Political Dynamics in the Milošević Era and After'. In *Serbia since 1989: Politics and Society under Milošević and After*, edited by Sabrina P. Ramet and Vjeran Pavlaković, 13–54. Seattle and London: University of Washington Press, 2005.

Pavlović, Dušan, ed. *Konsolidacija demokratskih ustanova u Srbiji: Godinu dana posle* (Consolidation of Democratic Institutions in Serbia: A Year Later). Belgrade: Službeni Glasnik, 2008.

Pavlović, Dušan, ed. *Razvoj demokratskih ustanova u Srbiji – Deset godina posle* (The Development of Democratic Institutions in Serbia – Ten Years After). Belgrade: Heinrich Böll Stiftung, 2010.

Perović, Latinka, Sonja Biserko and Seška Stanojlović, eds. *Tačka razlaza* (The Parting of the Ways). Belgrade: Helsinške sveske, 2003.

Pešić, Vesna. 'Rekonstrukcija petooktobarskih zbivanja na osnovu memoarske i stručne literature' (Reconstruction of 5 October Events on the Basis of

Memory and Expert Literature). In Dušan Pavlović *Razvoj Demokratskih Ustanova u Srbiji – Deset Godina Posle* (The Development of Democratic Institutions in Serbia – Ten Years After), edited by Dušan Pavlović, 25–40. Belgrade: Heinrich Böll Foundation, 2010.

Pešić, Vesna. *Divlje drustvo: kako smo stigli dovde* (Wild Society: How We Got Here). Belgrade: Peščanik, 2012.

Peskin, Victor A. *International Justice in Rwanda and the Balkans: Virtual Trials and the Struggle for State Cooperation.* New York: Cambridge University Press, 2008.

Peskin, Victor A. and Mieczyslaw P. Boduszynski. 'International Justice and Domestic Politics: Post-Tudjman Croatia and the International Criminal Tribunal for the Former Yugoslavia'. *Europe-Asia Studies* 55:7 (2003): 1117–42.

Peskin, Victor A. and Mieczyslaw P. Boduszynski. 'Balancing International Justice in the Balkans: Surrogate Enforcers, Uncertain Transitions and the Road to Europe'. *International Journal of Transitional Justice* 5:1 (2011): 1–23.

Petrović, Predrag. 'Nadzor službi bezbednosti na Zapadnom Balkanu: Slučaj Srbija' (The Oversight of Security Agencies in the Western Balkans: the Case of Serbia). *Belgrade Centre for Security Policy Working Paper*, 2012.

Popov, Nebojša, ed. *Srpska Strana Rata* (The Serbian Facet of the War). Belgrade: Republika, 1996.

Popović, Srdja. *Nezavršeni process* (The Uncompleted Trial) (Belgrade: Helsinki Committee for Human Rights in Serbia, 2007).

Przeworski, Adam. 'Some Problems in the Study of the Transition to Democracy'. In *Transitions from Authoritarian Rule: Comparative Perspectives*, edited by Guillermo O'Donnell, Philippe C. Schmitter and Laurence Whitehead, 47–63. Baltimore and London: The Johns Hopkins University Press, 1986.

Rajković, Nikolas M. 'The Limits of Consequentialism: ICTY Conditionality and (Non-)Compliance in Post-Milošević Serbia'. *Review of European and Russian Affairs* 4:1 (2008): 27–72.

Rajković, Nikolas M. *The Politics of International Law and Compliance*. London: Routledge, 2012.

Ramet, Sabrina P. 'The Denial Syndrome and Its Consequences: Serbian Political Culture since 2000'. *Communist and Post-Communist Studies* 40:1 (2007): 41–58.

Ramet, Sabrina P. and Vjeran Pavlaković, eds. *Serbia since 1989: Politics and Society under Milošević and After.* Seattle and London: University of Washington Press, 2005.

Rangelov, Iavor. 'International Law and Local Ideology in Serbia'. *Peace Review* 16:3 (2004): 331–7.

Roht-Arriaza, Naomi. 'State Responsibility to Investigate and Prosecute Grave Human Rights Violations in International Law'. *California Law Review* 78:2 (1990): 451–513.

Roht-Arriaza, Naomi. *The Pinochet Effect: Transnational Justice in the Age of Human Rights.* Philadelphia: University of Pennsylvania Press, 2005.

Roht-Arriaza, Naomi. 'The New Landscape of Transitional Justice'. In *Transitional Justice in the Twenty-First Century: Beyond Truth versus Justice*, edited by Naomi Roht-Arriaza and Javier Mariezcurrena, 1–16. Cambridge: Cambridge University Press, 2006.

Romano, Cesare P., Andrew Nollkaemper and Jann K. Kleffner, eds. *Internationalised Criminal Courts: Sierra Leone, East Timor, Kosovo and Cambodia.* Oxford: Oxford University Press, 2004.

Rotberg, Robert I., and Dennis Thompson. *Truth v. Justice: The Morality of Truth Commissions.* Princeton: Princeton University Press, 2000.

Rustow, Dwankart A. 'Transitions to Democracy: Towards a Dynamic Model'. *Comparative Politics* 2 (1970): 337–63.

Sartori, Giovanni. *Parties and Party Systems: A Framework for Analysis.* Colchester: ECPR Press, 2005.

Saxon, Dan. 'Exporting Justice: Perceptions of the ICTY among the Serbian, Croatian and Muslim Communities in the Former Yugoslavia'. *Journal of Human Rights* 4:4 (2005): 559–72.

Schedler, Andreas. 'What is Democratic Consolidation?' *Journal of Democracy* 9:2 (1998): 91–108.

Scheffer, David J. 'International Judicial Intervention'. *Foreign Policy* 102 (1996): 34–51.

Share, Donald. 'Transitions to Democracy and Transition through Transaction'. *Comparative Political Studies* 19:4 (1987): 525–48.

Sikkink, Kathryn and Ellen Lutz. 'The Justice Cascade: The Evolution and Impact of Foreign Human Rights Trials in Latin America'. *Chicago Journal of International Law* 2:1 (2001): 1–33.

Sikkink, Kathryn, and Carrie Booth Walling. 'The Impact of Human Rights Trials in Latin America'. *Journal of Peace Research* 44:4 (2007): 427–45.

Simpson, Gerry, ed. *War Crimes Law, Vol I-II.* Aldershot: Ashgate, 2004.

Simpson, Gerry. *Law, War and Crime: War Crimes Trials and the Reinvention of International Law.* Cambridge: Polity Press, 2007.

Snyder, Jack and Leslie Vinjamuri. 'Trials and Errors: Principles and Pragmatism in Strategies of International Justice'. *International Security* 28:3 (2003/04): 5–44.

Spasojević, Dušan. 'Dinamika političkih rascepa u Srbiji 2000–2010' (Dynamics of Political Cleavages in Serbia 2000–2010). In *Partije i izbori u Srbiji – 20 godina* (Parties and Elections in Serbia – 20 years), edited by Slaviša Orlović 105–18. Belgrade: Friedrich Ebert Stiftung, Faculty of Political Sciences of the University of Belgrade and Centre for Democracy, 2011.

Spoerri, Marlene and Annette Freyberg-Inan. 'From Prosecution to Persecution: Perceptions of the International Criminal Tribunal for the Former Yugoslavia (ICTY) in Serbian Domestic Politics'. *Journal of International Relations and Development* 11:4 (2008): 350–84.

Sriram, Chandra Lekha. *Confronting Past Human Rights Violations: Justice vs. Peace in Times of Transition.* New York: Frank Cass, 2004.

Sriram, Chandra Lekha. 'Transitional Justice and Peacebuilding'. In *Peace versus Justice? The Dilemma of Transitional Justice in Africa*, edited by Chandra Lekha Sriram and Suren Pillay, 1–17. Scottsville: University of KwaZulu-Natal Press, 2009.

Stepan, Alfred. 'Paths towards Redemocratisation: Theoretical and Comparative Considerations', in *Transitions from Authoritarian Rule: Comparative Perspectives, Vol.3*, edited by Guillermo O'Donnell, Phillip C. Schmitter, and Laurence Whitehead, 64–84. Baltimore and London: The Johns Hopkins University Press, 1986.

Stojanović, Sonja. 'Na pola puta – reforma policije u Srbiji 2000–2006' (Halfway Through – The Reform of the Police in Serbia 2000–2006), in *Reforma sektora bezbednosti u Srbiji: dostignuća i perspective* (The Reform of the Security Sector in Serbia: Achievements and Perspectives), edited by Miroslav Hadžić, 63–76. Belgrade: CCMR, 2007.

Stojiljković, Zoran. 'Partijska scena Srbije' (The Party Scene in Serbia), in *5 godina tranzicije u Srbiji* (5 Years of Transition in Serbia), edited by Srećko Mihajlović, 79–106. Belgrade: Friedrich Ebert Stiftung and Socijaldemokratski klub, 2005.

Subotić, Jelena. *Hijacked Justice: Dealing with the Past in the Balkans*. Ithaca: Cornell University Press, 2009.

Teitel, Ruti G. 'How Are the New Democracies of the Southern Cone Dealing with the Legacy of Past Human Rights Abuses?' In *Transitional Justice: How Emerging Democracies Reckon with Former Regimes, Vol. I*, edited by Neil J. Kritz, 146–53. Washington: United States Institute of Peace, 1995.

Teitel, Ruti G. *Transitional Justice*. New York: Oxford University Press, 2000.

Teitel, Ruti G. 'Transitional Justice Genealogy'. *Harvard Human Rights Journal* 16 (2003): 69–94.

Thomas, Robert. *Serbia under Milošević: Politics in the 1990s*. London: Hurst & Co, 1999.

Thompson, Mark R. and Philipp Kuntz. 'Stolen Elections: the Case of the Serbian October'. *Journal of Democracy* 15:4 (2004): 159–72.

Turner, Catherine. 'Delivering Lasting Peace, Democracy and Human Rights in Times of Transition: The Role of International Law'. *The International Journal of Transitional Justice* 2:2 (2008): 126–51.

Uvalić, Milica. *Serbia's Transition: Towards a Better Future*. Basingstoke: Palgrave MacMillan, 2010.

Vachudova, Milada Anna. 'Democratisation in Post-Communist Europe: Illiberal Regimes and the Leverage of the European Union', in *Democracy and Authoritarianism in the Post-Communist World*, edited by Valerie Bunce, Michael McFaul, and Kathryn Stoner-Weiss, 82–106. Cambridge University Press, 2009.

Varady, Tibor. 'Ambiguous Choices in the Trials of Milošević's Serbia', in *The Milošević Trial: An Autopsy*, edited by Timothy Waters. New York: Oxford University Press, 2013.

Vasić, Miloš. *Atentat na Zorana* (The Assassination of Zoran). Belgrade: Politika, B92, Vreme, Narodna Knjiga, 2005.

Vinjamuri, Leslie and Jack Snyder. 'Advocacy and Scholarship in the Study of International War Crimes Tribunals and Transitional Justice'. *Annual Review of Political Science* 7 (2004): 345–62.

Vujačić, Veljko. 'Re-examining the "Serbian Exceptionalism" Thesis', *Berkeley Program in Soviet and Post-Soviet Studies Working Paper Series*, spring 2004.

Weller, Marc. 'The Vienna Negotiations on the Final Status of Kosovo'. *International Affairs* 84:4 (2008): 659–81.

Whitehead, Laurence, ed. *The International Dimensions of Democratisation: Europe and the Americas.* Oxford University Press, 2001.

Wichmann, Nina. *Democratisation without Societal Participation? The EU as an External Actor in the Democratisation Processes of Serbia and Croatia.* Berlin: LIT, 2007.

Zakaria, Fareed. 'The Rise of Illiberal Democracy'. *Foreign Affairs* 76:6 (1997): 22–43.

Zalaquett, Jose. 'Confronting Human Rights Violations Committed by Former Governments: Principles Applicable and Political Constraints', in *Transitional Justice: How Emerging Democracies Reckon with Former Regimes, Vol. I*, edited by Neil J. Kritz, 3–31. Washington: United States Institute of Peace, 1995.

Zalaquett, Jose. 'Truth, Justice and Reconciliation: Lessons for the International Community', in *Comparative Peace Processes in Latin America*, edited by Cynthia J. Arnson, 341–62. Stanford: Stanford University Press, 1999.

Zverzhanovski, Ivan. 'Watching War Crimes: The Srebrenica Video and the Serbian Attitudes to the 1995 Srebrenica Massacre'. *Southeast European and Black Sea Studies* 7:3 (2007): 417–30.

Unpublished Papers And Conference Proceedings

Kranjc, Ana and Emilija Marinkov. 'Komisija za Istinu i Pomirenje' (Commission for Truth and Reconciliation). Student Papers Collection, Belgrade, 2008. Retrieved from http://www.most.org.yu/RADOVI/komisija.pdv on 20 August 2010.

Prelec, Marko. 'Justice, Truth and Peace at the Hague Bourse', paper presented at the conference 'The Milošević Trial: An Autopsy' at the Maurer School of Law, Indiana University, on 19 February 2010. Retrieved from www.law.indiana.edu on 22 April 2010.

Slapšak, Svetlana. 'Kulturna Poetika: Milošević – Srbija' (Cultural Poetics: Milošević – Serbia), paper presented at the round table on the trial of Milošević organised by the Humanitarian Law Centre on 18 December 2005 in Belgrade. Retrieved from www.hlc-rdc.org/Publikacije/857.sr.html on 13 May 2009.

Appendix

Results of Parliamentary Elections in Serbia 2000–2008

Table A.1 Votes and parliamentary seats received, December 2000 elections

Party	Number of Votes	Number of Seats
Democratic Opposition of Serbia (DOS)	2,402,387	176
Socialist Party of Serbia (SPS)	515,845	37
Serbian Radical Party (SRS)	322,333	23
Party of Serbian Unity (SSJ)	199,847	14

Source: Vreme.

Table A.2 Votes and parliamentary seats received, December 2003 elections

Party	Number of Votes	Number of Seats
Serbian Radical Party (SRS)	1,056,256	82
Democratic Party of Serbia (DSS)	678,031	53
Democratic Party (DS)	481,249	37
G-17 Plus	438,422	34
Serbian Renewal Party (SPO) – New Serbia (NS)	293,082	22
Socialist Party of Serbia (SPS)	291,341	22

Source: Electoral Commission of the Republic of Serbia.

Table A3 Votes and parliamentary seats received, January 2007 elections

Party	Number of Votes	Number of Seats
Serbian Radical Party (SRS)	1,153,453	81
Democratic Party (DS)	915,854	64
Democratic Party of Serbia (DSS) – New Serbia (NS)	667,615	47
G-17 Plus	275,041	19
Socialist Party of Serbia (SPS)	227,580	16
Liberal Democratic Party (LDP) – Civic Alliance of Serbia – Social-democratic Union – League of Social-democrats of Vojvodina	214,262	15
Union of Vojvodina's Hungarians (SVM)	52,510	3
Coalition 'List for Sandžak'	33,823	2
Union of Roma of Serbia	17,128	1
Coalition of Albanians of the Preševo Valley	16,973	1
The Roma Party	14,631	1

Source: Electoral Commission of the Republic of Serbia.

Table A.4 Votes and parliamentary seats received, May 2008 elections

Party	Number of Votes	Number of Seats
For a European Serbia (ZES)	1,590,200	102
Serbian Radical Party (SRS)	1,219,436	78
Democratic Party of Serbia (DSS) – New Serbia (NS)	480,987	30
Socialist Party of Serbia (SPS) – Party of United Pensioners (PUPS) – United Serbia (JS)	313,896	20
Liberal Democratic Party (LDP)	216,902	13
Hungarian Coalition	74,874	4
Bosniak List for a European Sandžak	38,148	2
Coalition of Albanians of the Preševo Valley	16,801	1

Source: Electoral Commission of the Republic of Serbia.

Index